"This book combines both theoretical knowledge and developmental components with practical and applied clinical applications. Readers will learn the theoretical and developmental principles necessary for working with adolescents and children and the importance of engaging the creative aspects of clinical work, which is foundational for affecting change in young clients. The authors do a masterful job of capturing the unique industry and artistry necessary for working with this population."

Shawn L. Spurgeon, PhD, *fellow of the American Counseling Association*

"This book was a pleasure to read! The authors have constructed a text that provides readers with strengths-based, experiential counseling activities that help promote change in youth. So few books have real-world applicability, but this text is practical, applied, and sure to assist mental health providers in supporting their young clients' change process. This book is essential for any mental health provider who works with young people and is searching for creative ways to invigorate their work."

Victoria Kress, PhD, *distinguished professor of counseling at the Youngstown State University*

"Through a social justice lens, the authors identify the realities of Western socialization as an oppressive underpinning to social structures that allow inequities and injustices to exist. By acknowledging a pathway of intentional personal and systemic behaviors that help to dismantle unjust practices, we are reminded that counselors and therapists are responsible for promoting social justice and for recognizing its direct impact on children, adolescents, and families."

Tiffany D. Stoner-Harris, PhD, *assistant professor of counseling and integrated programs at Adler University*

I0091882

Creativity in Counseling Children and Adolescents

Creativity in Counseling Children and Adolescents shows counselors and other mental health professionals how to use a wide variety of creative and experiential activities that emphasize strengths- and skills-focused work. The first section addresses the basic tenets of experiential learning, guiding readers through ways to build a creative and interactive environment for counseling. Later chapters lay out methods for choosing activities and finding the right match between diverse interests, skills, abilities, and cultural considerations. Once an activity is identified and implemented, the book shows counselors how to help children make meaning and capitalize on the benefits of the activity through processing and transferring skills.

Teresa Behrend Fletcher, PhD, LCPC, ACS (she/her), is a professor and program director of the Sport and Human Performance Program at Adler University in Chicago, Illinois.

Amanda C. DeDiego, PhD, LPC, NCC, BC-TMH (she/her), is an associate professor of counseling and a program coordinator at the University of Wyoming.

Creativity in Counseling Children and Adolescents

A Guide to Experiential Activities

Edited by
Teresa Behrend Fletcher and Amanda C. DeDiego

Routledge
Taylor & Francis Group

NEW YORK AND LONDON

Cover image: © Getty Images

First published 2024
by Routledge
605 Third Avenue, New York, NY 10158

and by Routledge
4 Park Square, Milton Park, Abingdon, Oxon, OX14 4RN

Routledge is an imprint of the Taylor & Francis Group, an informa business

Library of Congress Cataloging-in-Publication Data
Names: Fletcher, Teresa Behrend, editor. | DeDiego, Amanda C., editor.
Title: Creativity in counseling children and adolescents : a guide to experiential activities / edited by Teresa Behrend Fletcher, Amanda C. DeDiego.
Description: New York, NY : Routledge, 2023. |
Includes bibliographical references and index. |
Identifiers: LCCN 2023001463 (print) | LCCN 2023001464 (ebook) | ISBN 9781138291300 (hbk) | ISBN 9781138291317 (pbk) | ISBN 9781315213767 (ebk)
Subjects: MESH: Counseling | Child | Adolescent
Classification: LCC RC466 (print) | LCC RC466 (ebook) | NLM WS 105 |
DDC 362.1/04256—dc23/eng/20230522 LC record available at https://lccn.loc.gov/2023001463
LC ebook record available at https://lccn.loc.gov/2023001464

ISBN: 978-1-138-29130-0 (hbk)
ISBN: 978-1-138-29131-7 (pbk)
ISBN: 978-1-315-21376-7 (ebk)

DOI: 10.4324/9781315213767

Typeset in Baskerville
by codeMantra

Contents

Figures

Preface

This book is designed to be a resource for practicing counselors, counselor educators, and counseling students. This approach to creative and experiential counseling emphasizes strengths- and skills-focused work with children and adolescents. Early chapters of this text offer theoretical foundations for the approach, and discussion of addressing stress, trauma, and clinical issues for clients. Later chapters explore various avenues of creativity in experiential counseling work. For most chapters, in addition to content, practitioners will find example activities applicable to most counseling settings.

Current students and practitioners who have used creativity in their work with children and adolescents contributed these activities. These activities address a variety of creative modalities, counseling settings, skills, and goals. Students and practitioners also offer insights from their own use of these activities in their counseling work. The authors of this text would like to encourage readers to connect with contributors of activities to learn more about implementation and experiences in creative counseling work (see Appendix B).

Acknowledgments

Land Acknowledgments

It is important to understand the history that has brought us to reside on occupied land and our role within constructing history. The editors of this text acknowledge with respect that they live and work in communities occupying indigenous homeland.

Adler University: I live and work in the city of Chicago (the name Chicago is adopted from the Algonquin language) and acknowledge that my home and the campus of Adler University sit upon the ancestral homeland to the Anishinaabek, Niswi-mishkodewin (Council of the Three Fires): Ojibwe, Odawa, and the Potawatomi along with dozens of tribes who cultivated and molded the land to sustainably suit their needs since time immemorial. The city of Chicago acknowledges the land we occupy as Indigenous homelands and has great appreciation and gratitude to those whose territory we occupy. The land, shore, and waters of Lake Michigan were also a site of trade, travel, gathering, and healing for more than a dozen other Native tribes, including the Menominee, Michigamea, Miami, Kickapoo, Peoria, and Ho-Chunk nations. The history of the city of Chicago is intertwined with histories of native peoples. Relocation itself was a tragic undertaking for tribes. Those who survived the trip would face new hardships and this led to poverty, starvation, and severely difficult living circumstances that would continue to plague tribes into the present day.

University of Wyoming: "We collectively acknowledge that the University of Wyoming occupies the ancestral and traditional lands of the Cheyenne, Arapaho, Crow, and Shoshone Indigenous peoples along with other Native tribes who call the Great Basin and Rocky Mountain region home. We recognize, support, and advocate alongside Indigenous individuals and communities who live here now, and with those forcibly removed from their Homelands."

– Associated Students of University of Wyoming Senate Bill #2699

Personal Acknowledgments

Thank you to the spouses, families, pets, and friends who provide ongoing support in our work.

A great thanks to all of the graduate assistants, students, and practitioners who worked on this resource. Your work strengthens and supports your communities every day. We appreciate you.

This work was an effort supported a great deal in part by good music, strong coffee, chocolate, and frozen waffles.

Contributors

Madison Andrews is Clinical Coordinator for Volunteers of America in Minneapolis, Minnesota.

Tanner Biwer is a consultant at The Performance Pursuit in Williamsburg, Virginia.

Lay-nah Blue Morris-Howe is an Assistant Professor of Counseling at the University of Wyoming.

Hannah Conner is a clinician at Chase Wellness LLC in Chicago, Illinois.

Keith Davis is a Professor of Counseling at Radford University.

Amanda C. DeDiego is an Associate Professor of Counseling at the University of Wyoming.

Rebecca Edelman is an Assistant Professor of Counseling at Husson University.

Isabel C. Farrell is an Assistant Professor of Counseling at Wake Forest University.

Teresa B. Fletcher is a Professor, counselor educator, and faculty in sport and human performance at Adler University.

Ana K. Houseal is an Outreach Science Educator at the Science and Mathematics Teaching Center at the University of Wyoming.

Susan Hurley is a retired faculty member in counseling at the University of North Georgia.

R. Paul Maddox II is an Assistant Professor of Counseling at the University of Wyoming.

Monica Phelps-Pineda is a doctoral student in Counselor Education at the University of Missouri-Saint Louis.

Melanie Richburg is an Associate Professor in counseling at Grand Canyon University.

Melia A. Snyder is Education Director at Open Sky Wilderness Therapy in Durango, Colorado.

Leslie A. Stewart is an Associate Professor of Counseling at Idaho State University.

Felix Yu is a consultant at The Performance Pursuit in Williamsburg, Virginia.

Ricky Zambrowicz is a counselor as part of the student affairs staff at Toccoa Falls College.

Joshua Zettel is a career counselor at Queen's University in Ontario, Canada.

About the Editors

Teresa Behrend Fletcher, PhD, LCPC, ACS (she/her), is a professor and program director of the Sport and Human Performance program that includes dual degrees with clinical mental health counseling and clinical rehabilitation counseling at Adler University in Chicago, Illinois. Dr. Fletcher obtained her bachelor of business administration degree at Loyola University while playing division I volleyball. She obtained her master of arts in community counseling at Northeastern Illinois University and her PhD in counseling and counselor education (specializing in sport psychology) from the University of North Carolina at Greensboro in 2000. Dr. Fletcher has over 25 years of experience in working with both clinical and sport clients, athletes, teams, and sport organizations primarily at the youth and collegiate level. Dr. Fletcher is a USA Hockey level 4 certified coach and still participates in running, biking, and triathlon events for charity. She has been married to her partner, Mike, since 1997 and has two grown children, Noah and Isaac and multiple pets.

Amanda C. DeDiego, PhD, LPC, NCC, BC-TMH (she/her), is an associate professor of counseling and a program coordinator at the University of Wyoming. She has a PhD in counselor education from the University of Tennessee and has an MS in community counseling from the University of North Georgia. She has been a practicing counselor for ten years and embraces creativity in both her clinical work and teaching. She has also served as a board member for the Association for Creativity in Counseling. Her research agenda focuses on creative approaches to counselor development and mental health equity and access in underserved communities. Her goal is to effectively train counselors to address mental health needs in communities and act as advocates for mental health equity and access. Outside of her professional work, she loves the outdoors, a strong cup of coffee, and cuddling with her cat.

Introduction

The idea for this book started with a quest to find a textbook for a course for counseling students learning to work with children and adolescents. The topic of counseling with children and adolescents is often considered a specialty and allows more freedom and flexibility for an instructor. In the search for a text, we found that most books fell into one of two categories, either explaining development or focusing only on intervention. While developmental considerations are important with child and adolescent clients, most practitioners already gain content knowledge within a human growth and development course. Further, many of the developmental theories typically reflect Western and dominant culture assumptions. Also, interventions or activity-based books do not inform unique clinical skills or critical thinking to determine which intervention for what purpose at what time in a sequence of sessions and how to navigate skill development within those sessions.

Rather than trying to decide what we, the professors believe students need to know, we engaged with students to learn what they need and want in a course to feel proficient and confident in working with this population. The content was built around their perspectives and suggestions. Students wanted to learn how to identify what kids needed in a counseling session and what to do with them during the session. They wanted both content and process, so we built the class and now this book, as a resource. First, we grounded learning in the Cycle of Socialization (Harro, 2018) and the Cycle of Liberation (Harro, 2018). In other words, we wanted to focus on the intersecting identities of all children and adolescents to better understand that many of the rules, laws, and social norms were not developed by or for marginalized community members. We want to affirm that often, children are using behaviors to respond to unhealthy and oppressive systems and when we respond by teaching various ways to cope, we perpetuate systemic racism, sexism, ethnocentrism, ableism, and all the other-isms that exist (Chapter 1).

Following the experiences of counselor educators and offering continuing education for practicing counselors, it was clear that two areas of focus were very important: information that is both practical and culturally conscious. The goal is to provide students and practitioners with evidence-based foundational underpinnings as a framework (Chapter 2) to demonstrate the context for the work and the rest of the book. Because children and adolescents are a unique and vulnerable population, clinicians and educators need additional knowledge and clinical skills for both conceptualization and intervention (Chapter 3). To facilitate experiential learning, practitioners can benefit from models for processing experiential activities and meaning-making (Chapter 4). Finally, practitioners can operate from a positive psychology framework with the addition of a list of skills children and adolescents need for long-term health and well-being (Chapter 5) and work toward teaching, learning, and practicing these skills in a safe, nonjudgmental environment.

Meeting clients "where they are" can be a challenge and even more so for children and adolescents. In order to address this concept, we included chapters based on how clients are referred to counseling, which is often when they have experienced stress or trauma (Chapter 6) or have a disorder that complicates development and drives the need for additional and lifelong skill development (Chapter 7). One strategy to begin implementing activities is to find interests such as using literature or writing (Chapter 8), video or board games (Chapter 9), expressive arts (Chapter 10), or scientific thinking (Chapter 11) to build rapport and foster interest in skill building. Finally, working with additional resources to acquire and practice skills in group settings (Chapter 12), in community groups, teams, and organizations (Chapter 13), with animals (Chapter 14), or in nature (Chapter 15) can enhance long-term individual and relational health.

This book has been a culmination of lifelong learning and practice. We have included a variety of strengths and perspectives from academics, students, and practitioners in developing the content and activities in this book. Theory, research, and experience contributed to creating both content and process to empower children and adolescents for long-term health and well-being.

DOI: 10.4324/9781315213767-1

Chapter 1

A lens for social responsibility and advocacy

Melanie J. Richburg and Teresa Behrend Fletcher

> Now is the accepted time, not tomorrow, not some more convenient season. It is today that our best work can be done.
>
> — WEB Dubois

This book is centered on the following: (1) all children and adolescents have strengths and challenges; (2) when kids have challenges, they need skills to adapt to the world; and (3) children and adolescents need to be and feel loved and self-assured, engage in healthy relationships, and exist in supportive and empowering environments to flourish. Before we can get into this work and present the foundational underpinnings for skill development, we need to acknowledge the fact that society is not inclusive of all individuals or identities. It is far easier to teach someone skills to adapt to an unfair, oppressive, and exclusive system than it is to change a system to be equitable and inclusive of differences regarding race, culture, nationality, language, ethnicity, gender, sexuality, ability and disability, socioeconomic status, religion and spirituality, and age. When we conceptualize the child or adolescent as the problem, desired behaviors become the solution. Conversely, when we identify the system as the problem, the child becomes the symptom of a larger problem that also requires intervention. Therefore, we want to encourage and inspire socially responsible practice to better understand how vulnerable children and adolescents can face additional challenges based on intersectionality of identity(ies) while promoting advocacy *AND* systemic change in addition to skill development.

The origin of privilege is worthy of exploration as it contributes to the question, "Who decided that one group of people was better than another?" This is not a new question and one that is a plague on humanity as the right to rule over other human beings can be traced throughout world history. For the purposes of this chapter and the book, we are focusing on the United States, as the current culture was built on colonialism under Western Eurocentric values that continue to affirm and sustain patriarchy and capitalism. This land was already inhabited by a group of self-sufficient dwellers, and the explorers arrived and subjugated indigenous people with total disregard for their culture, imposed their own beliefs, values, and way of life, committed acts of genocide, and then built the infrastructure and system of government based on what served them best. As if that was not the worst thing that could happen, [the United States ruling class] then brought enslaved individuals to this country, committed inhumane acts of violence, and continued to discriminate, demoralize, and oppress any group that was not included in the "*original founding*" of the country. In essence, "We the People" does not actually mean "ALL" the people and what lies underneath is not everyone is created equally or treated equitably. In summary, this country was designed for Caucasian, Christian, heterosexual, binary, and male-identifying, able-bodied individuals with European heritage and enough money to manipulate, coerce, or pay for a way of life that suits them best. Everyone else is relegated to adapt and adjust to living in a world that was not designed by you or for you. The purpose of this chapter is to provide a perspective or a lens to inform working with children and adolescents with diverse and intersecting social backgrounds and identities. Further, the chapter will provide a basic understanding of the impacts of socialization to inform conceptualization, describe the process of liberation to inform strategies for advocacy and social justice, and promote skill building among children and adolescents for self-empowerment and long-term health and well-being.

Cycle of Socialization

Parents have visions, hopes, and dreams for their children (planned or unplanned) as they anticipate the journey of parenthood. Caregivers are tasked with working through the unknown while anticipating decisions, trials, and tribulations. Each child is unique and special with their own strengths, challenges, preferences (likes and dislikes),

DOI: 10.4324/9781315213767-2

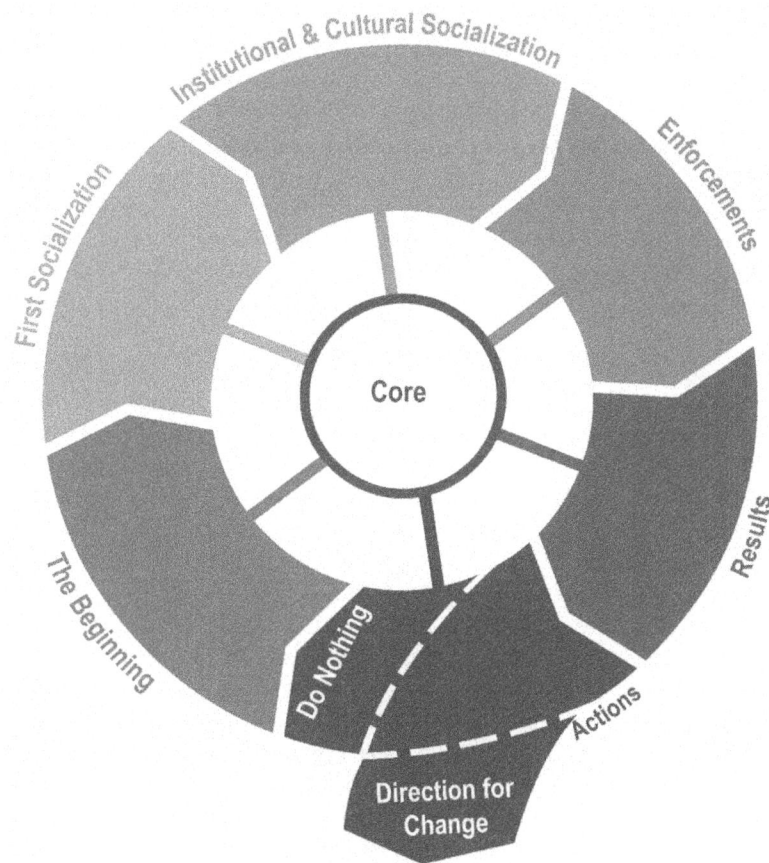

Figure 1.1 Cycle of Socialization.

personalities, and quirks. At the core of parenting is trying to navigate raising children to become healthy and conscientious human beings. This journey is complicated by a scary, unsafe world where deviation from identities within the hegemony, or dominant group, means additional barriers and challenges. In navigating the world, concepts of oppression and dominant culture narratives can be internalized by children and thus reinforced as adults. Unfortunately, parents can also perpetuate learned behaviors and oppressive systems out of *ignorance*, *insecurity*, *confusion*, *obliviousness*, and *fear*, which serve as the core of the Cycle of Socialization (see Figure 1.1). This framework serves to inform practitioners how children and adolescents are taught to make sense of the world by individuals, families, institutions, and culture as well as how oppression and discrimination are reinforced with devastating impacts on marginalized and underserved communities.

The beginning

Children are socialized before they are born. Norms are set by and for dominant groups based on history and tradition, assumptions, opportunities, power, and even myths. Oftentimes, we engage in these systems without even knowing or recognizing what we are doing or why as these norms and rules were already established. If an individual fits into the dominant group, they can experience more privilege and power, at times without insight (Harro, 2018a). We can demonstrate privilege by using the example of an individual walking several blocks to pick up items at the local grocery store. This simple task is riddled with privilege. An able-bodied individual may not have to think about the condition of the sidewalks or curb cuts such as someone who relies on a wheelchair. Many low socioeconomic neighborhoods are located in "food deserts" where affordable fresh fruits and vegetables are not available and options for shopping are not easily accessible. Walking down the street is more dangerous for a Black male, who is at risk for getting stopped or approached. Women may only feel comfortable shopping during the day or have to plan the timing of the trip to be mindful of safety. We are also assuming that the local grocery store carries items consistent with religious practices (i.e., kosher, halal) or offers a variety of options for those with food allergies and dietary restrictions.

Fortunately and unfortunately, children are not born accompanied by a complete manual or guide to parenting to assist in socialization in a world that falls short of valuing diversity, equity, and inclusion. Parents unconsciously use their own experiences as a foundation and repeat child-rearing practices based on *ignorance* or *obliviousness*. Parents can feel *insecure* about their ability to be a "good" parent and be easily *confused* when making decisions to balance both short- and long-term development. Further, *fear* can undermine good intentions when teaching children to navigate the world because no [healthy] parent wants to watch their child fail, be bullied, feel bad about themselves, or experience heartbreak, sadness, or grief. Parents are trying to do the best they can with the information and resources they have at any given point and time. However, when parents and caregivers operate out of ignorance, obliviousness, insecurity, confusion, and fear, they can unintentionally reinforce detrimental norms (Harro, 2018a).

First socialization

Parents and caregivers have the most influence on the socialization process and make decisions that shape identity and how children begin to see themselves in the world. Children and adolescents then internalize both subtle and not-so-subtle messages that begin to shape behavior, beliefs, and values both intrapersonally (how we think and feel about ourselves) and interpersonally (how we interact with others) (Harro, 2018a). These behaviors are then reinforced with reward or punishment, praise or criticism, as well as other methods of shaping behaviors.

Children are born into a pre-established identity shaped mostly by their parents and caregivers. For example, gender is one of the first identities to emerge even before birth. Through technological advances, parents can discover the sex of the baby(ies) early in pregnancy and use this information to prepare for the arrival as if caring for a newborn boy is vastly different than a baby girl. Babies need warmth, food, comfort, and love; they do not care if their onesie is pink or blue and yet importance is placed on how parents want their children to be perceived in the world, based on norms, beliefs, and values that were created by a patriarchal system. Further, gender is a social construct that ascribes qualities of masculine and feminine to people, which can change over time and vary between and among cultures (Gender Equity Resource Center, 2012). We, as a society, would be better humans if we adapted to gender as a continuum between masculinity and femininity that is present in one body, also known as *Two Spirited* and rooted in Native American culture (Sheppard & Mayo, 2013). Making assumptions about gender as binary or gender identification is the same as sex assigned at birth can perpetuate an oppressive system for those who do not fit into the dominant group.

In a culture that lends itself to being classed as a male-dominated/patriarchal society, the role of female can oftentimes be viewed as subservient, submissive, and compliant. This is evident in the messages sent to cisgender boys and girls. "Boys don't cry" is an example of the message, yet what may be internalized is far more damaging and can range from not being allowed to express emotion to not even being allowed to feel that emotion as it contributes to vulnerability and weakness and should be avoided at all costs. *Ignorant, oblivious*, or *confused* parents might send young girls more damaging messages regarding behavior and "knowing their place." For instance in sport, young [cisgender] girls might hear, "You run/throw/shoot like a girl," inferring that this is somehow inferior to their male counterparts. The best response to this particular statement puts this notion in perspective when Mia Hamm, a World Cup and Olympic champion soccer player, stated, "My coach said I run like a girl, and I said if he ran a little faster, he could too" (Mia Hamm in Staurowsky, 2016).

Children of color are socialized in two different communities with two sets of norms consisting of their own shared identity [race/ethnicity] and among the dominant culture, which again is White. From a historical perspective, children of color are taught to act and behave in a specific manner. Within their own community(ies), cultural norms can include a reinforced level of respect for one's elders and individuals of authority which include clergy, teachers, coaches, and adults, in general. Likewise, family norms are to play fair and follow the rules; not doing so is to dishonor or embarrass the family structure. When socialized outside of their communities, parents may be *confused* about how to best prepare their children or may socialize them to assimilate, acculturate, or mold specific behaviors due to imposed norms and out of *fear*. This shifting between the two communities can produce negative feelings and result in cognitive dissonance for the child. For example, in the Black community, parents may encourage their children to speak up for themselves and be assertive and then demonstrate *how* to act differently *when* they get approached by a police officer, which may be more compliant and submissive. The fear for their child's safety requires two different expectations and standards of behavior.

The intersection of identities can get complicated, even more so the more identities that do not align with the dominant culture (non-White, female, and non-binary, LGBTQIA+, non-Christian, disabled, lower socioeconomic, under the age of 18). The less these identities align with the dominant culture, the more conflicting and mixed these messages are related to socializing children to be happy, well-adjusted, and successful. For every message of what individuals can or cannot, should or should not do, there are many more stories of inspiration and resilience, necessitating the need to stop and think about the intentionality of socializing children differently (Table 1.1).

Table 1.1 Societal message versus reality

Societal Messages	Reality of Success Despite Societal Expectations
"Black people can't participate in activities" (e.g., swimming, hockey, tennis, golf, speed-skating)	− Cullen Jones (Olympic gold medal in freestyle swimming) − Simone Manuel (Olympic gold medal in freestyle swimming) − Shani Davis (Olympic gold medal in speed skating) − Erin Jackson (Olympic gold medal in speed skating) − Vonetta Flowers (Olympic gold medal in two-woman bobsled) − Arthur Ashe, Serena Williams, Venus Williams, Coco Gauff, Sloane Stephens (professional tennis) − Althea Gibson (Professional golf and tennis) − Lee Elder, Tiger Woods, Cheyenne Woods, and Mariah Stackhouse (Professional golf)
"Muslim girls can't play sports"	− Ibtihaj Muhammad (Olympic bronze medal in fencing) − Kaljo and Bilqis Abdul-Qaadir (NCAA Basketball) − Fatima Al Ali (UAE ice hockey)
"Marriage and adoption is only for opposite-sex couples"	− Obergefell v. Hodges ruling in 2015 [Marriage Equality Act]
"Women can't run a marathon"	− Kathrine Switzer (First woman to run the Boston Marathon) − Shalane Grace Flanagan (Winner of the New York City marathon) − Amy Cragg (Olympic marathon runner)
"Deaf/visually impaired people can't be creative or expressive" (e.g., play an instrument, sing, dance, act)	− Mandy Harvey (Musician who placed fourth on America's Got Talent) − Dame Evelynn Glennie (Hip-hop artist) − Shaheem Sanchez (Hip-hop artist) − Stevie Wonder (Musician) − Ray Charles (Musician) − Andrea Bocelli (Musician) − Marlee Matlin (Oscar winner) − Troy Kotsur (Oscar winner)
"Ballerinas can't be diverse in ethnicity and body type"	− Misty Copeland (Principal Dancer American Ballet Theater) − Alvin Ailey (American Dance Theater)
"Women can't compete with men in sports"	− Billie Jean King vs. Bobby Riggs (Battle of the Sexes tennis match) − United States Women's National Soccer Team
"People with disabilities can't function independently or be successful"	− Rick Hoyt (Boston University graduate, triathlete, author) − Stephen Hawking (Theoretical physicist) − Tammy Duckworth (US Senator – IL) − John Nash (Nobel Laureate in Economics)
"Children can't know they are transgender"	− Jazz Jennings (*I Am Jazz*) − Laverne Cox − MJ Rodriguez (*Pose*)
"Kids with disabilities can't play sports"	− Paralympics − Shaquem Griffin (Seattle Seahawks/Miami Dolphins) − Casey Martin (Golf)
"Individuals with Down Syndrome can't have ambitious goals" (e.g., act, get married, have careers, be entrepreneurs)	− TV Show Born This Way − Special Books (Special Kids.org) − Gareth and Deana Tobias (married 28 years) − 21 Pineapples Shirt Company − John's Crazy Socks
"Girls don't like/are not good at math and science"	− Marie Curie (Physicist and chemist) − Katherine Johnson (NASA mathematician) − Mae C. Jemison (First Black female astronaut) − Alice Ball (Chemist) − Sally Ride (First American female astronaut)

Institutional and cultural socialization

The communities that have the most impact on children outside of the family include education, places of worship (i.e., church, synagogue, temple, mosque, etc.), medical and mental health, business, social services, legal services, and the vast media. Conscious and unconscious messages are sent and reinforced by institutions and culture to embed standards of behavior, beliefs, and values, influenced by dominant identities. The more interactions with these systems, the more opportunities for unhealthy or mixed messages and, thus, cognitive dissonance. Businesses have refused to serve members of the LGBTQIA+ community (*Masterpiece Cakeshop, Ltd. v. Colorado Civil Rights Commission*, 2008). A child who receives public assistance is not encouraged to pursue a college education or a young Black child is advised that college may not be an option and steered toward a vocational track in high school. A young Orthodox Jewish girl is told she cannot pursue her passion of figure skating because of the costumes.

Some messages are more veiled. A little cisgender girl goes to church to only see males lead a congregation. In the education system, a child with a disability must be separated from able-bodied and/or able-minded children to learn or a visually impaired student has to sit on the sidelines during physical education because they "can't" play kickball. Parents can act out of ignorance, obliviousness, or fear when they try to stifle their child's gender identity or sexuality. Schools then affirm gender as binary by directing kids to specific restrooms and then pressure others to support gender-specific areas as opposed to gender-neutral facilities. The anti-trans and homophobic legislature at the local, state, and national levels (Hughes et al., 2021; Turban et al., 2021) further perpetuates this. Heterosexism can be reinforced by the curriculum, stories, and interactions between students and teachers with the use of non-inclusive language out of confusion or insecurity. For example, asking a young child if they have a boyfriend/girlfriend can affirm heterosexuality rather than support a more open concept of *Love Is Love*.

Some messages are rooted in systemic racism. In the legal system, Black, Indigenous, and People of Color (BIPOC) individuals experience inequity when interacting with law enforcement including increased police presence in neighborhoods with predominantly Black or Brown communities and higher likelihood of violence from officers (Rushing et al., 2022). Subsequently, there can be differences in response times for law enforcement to arrive in some poor, less affluent neighborhoods compared to White, upper class, and more affluent communities (Brunson, 2007) or an increased law enforcement presence in predominantly Black or Brown communities and a higher likelihood of violence when interacting with law enforcement (Rushing et al., 2022). There is a myth that people of color do not invest in self-care; however, there are long documented histories of discrimination, disparity, and obstacles to accessing basic healthcare for BIPOC individuals (O'Kane et al., 2021; Perzichilli, 2020; Wright, 2020). The medical field has a long history of racist ideology (*see Tuskegee Syphilis Studies*; Brandt, 1978). Biases and racism in the biomedical sciences result in fewer BIPOC biomedical researchers and a lack of diversity in biomedical research sampling (Clark & Hurd, 2020). The impact of systemic racism in the medical sciences was evidenced during the pandemic, and as a result, a lack of trust in the medical profession led to reluctance to get vaccinated and lower vaccination rates against COVID-19 in BIPOC communities (Quinn & Andrasik, 2021).

Curriculum can be biased in both content and through the process of teaching and the lack of history is even more harmful. Black history is American history, yet it is still considered whitewashed, or "portrayed in a way that increases the prominence, relevance, or impact of white people and minimizes or misrepresents that of non-white people" (Merriam-Webster, n.d.). White children and adolescents may see themselves as the heroes and never really understand the harm caused by power and privilege. Conversely, Black and Brown kids may not see themselves at all and then wonder how they can fit into the world or, worse, fall into the negative stereotypes as there may appear to be no other option (Reece, 2020; Wright et al., 2021). When kids fail to see themselves or only see a negative representation, they can begin to internalize they are "less than" or something is wrong with them. Everyone needs to know the history, including the good, the bad, and the ugly as a precursor to dismantling racism. In other words, "You have to teach people that racism is wrong and then they won't be racist" (Bryan, 2012, p. 611). One goal for diversity, equity, inclusion, and belonging is to promote an accurate narrative. Dr. Mae Jemison, the first African American cisgender female astronaut, once stated, "Never be limited by other people's limited imaginations. You can hear other people's wisdom, but you've got to re-evaluate the world for yourself" (Jemison, 2009).

Enforcements

All of these systems were established to benefit a specific population and are maintained and sustained by that same group, making systemic change difficult. Even when an individual is resilient and able to overcome obstacles, the status quo is enforced and reinforced at every step. Females are still making less than male colleagues and Black and Brown workers are making less than their White counterparts. Individuals are less likely to get interviews or be hired with names representing ethnicity or race other than European or White (Zschirnt & Ruedin, 2016). Same-sex couples still have difficulty adopting or receiving spousal benefits (Daum, 2020). Health insurance does not cover many of the costs associated with gender re-assignment surgery (Ngaage et al., 2019). Individuals in lower socioeconomic areas still struggle to obtain a livable wage, making renting an apartment, purchasing a vehicle, or saving for a down payment and owning a home more difficult or even hopeless. Fear of the consequences allows these systems to remain in place. For example, when a Black applicant confronts a company for failing to hire diverse candidates, the only way to challenge the decision is to file a lawsuit and proving discrimination upon hire is extremely arduous (Wiecek & Hamilton, 2014). When female faculty members challenged equal pay to male counterparts, they are often given the excuse that they should have negotiated more upon hire, but the negotiations were not allowed to take place with the male supervisor (Balmer v. HCA INC, 2005).

In the public domain, the scrutiny is swift and the criticisms are harsh even when inequity is clear and obvious. For example, Serena Williams questioned the judgment of a male official for code violations at the US Open in 2018. Understandably, Serena Williams contested the decision and penalty with swift criticism from some within the tennis community as well as the public. However, when comparing her behavior, reactions, and consequences to those of John McEnroe, a male tennis player known for his explosive temper and inappropriate behaviors, sexism and racism can be the only explanations for the difference in how these accomplished, talented, and successful athletes are perceived and treated. This comparison does not even come close to the constant and consistent acts of racism and sexism she has had to endure throughout her life as well as all individuals forced to live and work in oppressive systems. "The daily grind of being rendered invisible, or being attacked, whether physically or verbally, for being visible, wears a body down" (Rankin, 2015).

Hope is on the horizon as individuals and groups coalesce to dismantle and challenge the hegemony. For example, the United States Women's National Soccer Team reached a settlement after 6 years of fighting for an acknowledgment of discrimination, equal pay, and equitable working conditions (Das, 2022). Positive changes of the #MeToo movement have resulted in state laws, monetary compensation for survivors, and a push to solve systemic problems of sexual harassment, misconduct, and assault (North, 2019). These public battles have brought to the forefront the continuous need to challenge unfair, inequitable, and unjust systems and demand change.

Results and continuation

The impact of living in systems of oppression includes experiencing high levels of stress and low self-esteem or self-worth. A sense of frustration, hopelessness, and disempowerment can lead to acting out negative stereotypes that lead to dehumanizing and self-destructive behaviors. The targets of oppressive systems thereby reinforce and perpetuate the systems and contribute to maintaining the status quo (Harro, 2018a). As stated previously, when we teach children and adolescents skills to cope with faulty and discriminatory systems, we actually perpetuate systems of oppression and facilitate learned helplessness because we are acting out of *ignorance, insecurity, confusion, obliviousness*, and *fear*. Individuals or adults, especially those born with privilege or intersecting privileges, do not have to stop and question the status quo, mostly because the system is working for them, so why change or challenge something that is working, right?

Centering the most vulnerable in our community leads to understanding how individuals perform daily tasks such as taking a leisurely walk down the street (Manuel Ellis, Michael Brown), walking home from the store (Trayvon Martin, Elijah McClain), walking home from a neighbor's house (Gregory Gunn), or enjoying an afternoon jog (Ahmaud Arbery). Driving (Philando Castille, Daunte Wright) is not the same for everyone or following basic rules of the road such as using a turn signal (Sandra Bland). Children playing in a public park (Tamir Rice), riding a bicycle (Dijon Kizzee, Ronelle Foster), or standing in their grandmother's backyard (Stephon Clark) cannot be considered as dangerous as walking out of your garage with a cellphone (Andre Hill). Even relaxing at home (Michelle Cusseaux, Atatiana Jefferson, Janisha Fonville), sitting on the couch and eating ice cream (Botham Jean), going to sleep at night in your own bed (Breonna Taylor), or breathing (George Floyd) can be fatal. Individuals from marginalized and oppressed groups cannot be left to fight and demand equity alone, which is an infuriating and exhausting process. If WE are included in "We the People" then *WE* collectively need to push for change and engage more fiercely in advocacy, activism, and dismantling these systems as part of socially responsible practice in our work with children and adolescents.

TIPS FOR PRACTITIONERS:

1. Reflect honestly and consistently (ignorance, fear, and obliviousness) on core values and lean into difficult conversations about the experiences of others.
2. Be mindful of your own socialization and internalized messages related to your identity and intersecting identities that affirm oppression and discrimination (insecurity, confusion).
3. Embrace cultural humility, be vigilant in attending to implicit biases, and engage in the education of identities different than your own to move into freedom and liberation.

Cycle of Liberation

The thought of systemic change can be incredibly overwhelming because, let's be real, if it were easy, we already would have succeeded. Therefore, just as a framework for socialization helps us understand how we got to this place, another framework is needed to identify a process away from the current structures and toward a more equitable and inclusive system, which can be found in the Cycle of Liberation (see Figure 1.2; Harro, 2018b). This critical transformation is rooted in *self-love, self-esteem, balance, joy, support, security*, and a *spiritual base* which is necessary for the long and the never-ending crusade for systemic change.

Waking up and getting ready

Liberation typically begins with an event or an incident that sparks an intrapersonal change in a belief or an epiphany that provokes a reassessment of how the world works (Harro, 2018b). For example, when you find out your [gay] friend's partner is not eligible for health benefits because, despite the marriage equality act, the company/organization does not recognize gay marriage or claims it conflicts with company values. A White man gets handed two ballots walking into a polling place to vote while citizens of color are provided one ballot (D. Subasic,

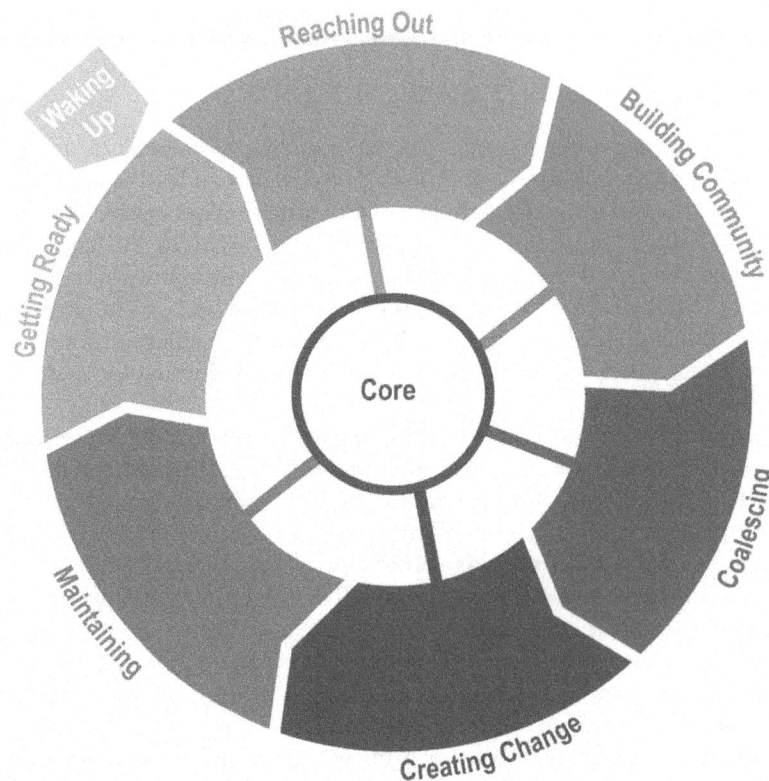

Figure 1.2 Cycle of Liberation.

personal communication, November 8, 2020). An election official prematurely determines there is not enough time for everyone to vote and turns away people already in line at a heavily Black precinct (R. Carter, personal communication, November 8, 2020). A Sikh adolescent chooses not to wear a dastaar (turban), a sign of adherence to faith, in public due to discrimination and getting bullied in school (Ahluwalia, 2019). Muslim women in countries like France face restrictions on what they can wear in public and female athletes wearing a hijab are prohibited from competing in sport (Meheut, 2022). These incidents occur on a regular basis to individuals not considered a part of the dominant culture. The call to action centers the experiences of these individuals and works toward inclusion and belonging so all identities are valued, accepted, and respected. With reverence to humanity, a larger collective group is needed to create systemic change.

Reaching out and building community

There are times when we need to expand our toolbox to include others as sources of support, guidance, knowledge, reinforcement, and confirmation of self. This allows us to build our community of helpers and adds to our repertoire of tools. When we extend ourselves to others, in ways that strengthen and support our existence, we become stronger and wiser in critical thinking and decision-making. Our sense of community is expanded, and we can analyze situations in a more balanced and informed manner. For children, this can include peers, trusted friends, teammates, school counselors, educators, coaches, troop leaders, and sensei, to name a few. For adults, parents, and caregivers, this can include clergy, trusted friends, colleagues, legal, medical, and mental health professionals. The key to building community is leaning in, reaching out, and engaging!

Students with outgoing personalities or advanced social skills may find it easy to engage, make friends, collaborate, or ask for help. For others, more effort may be required to build specific skills and find resources that reflect their age and ability. As an example, a basketball player with a failing grade can risk their own self-worth, academic standing, and position and status on the team. A player lacking basic skills may not consider resources, do nothing to improve their grade, lose eligibility, and suffer in isolation. Based on maturity level, critical thinking, and communication skills, an assertive and confident player might consult with their teacher, counselor, or coach for guidance in developing a plan to improve their grade and maintain active/eligibility status on the team. Additionally, they could find support through a tutor which could be initiated by their own efforts which reflects their ability to build a sense of community in the educational process. The ability to maintain active eligibility to reach out and build a community of helpers, thus playing the sport, can have a much more positive outcome both intrapersonally (sense of accomplishment, self-worth, confidence) and interpersonally (communicate needs, identify and solve problems) when we empower children and adolescents to build their own support system and sense of community.

Another example is the case of a Black student in the first year of attendance at a predominantly White school. When the make-up of the school (educators, staff, and students) is majority White, challenges can be multidimensional and persistent. The educational setting has the potential to perpetuate feelings of isolation, self-doubt, exclusion, and microaggressions (intentional or unintentional) where there is a lack of support for students who do not share a dominant identity. At an extreme, some parents and lawmakers are even attempting to influence curriculum and take out or censor (whitewash) content to fit the narrative of the dominant culture (Stitzlein, 2015). In this situation, the onus to reach out, engage, and support the Black student in the manner that is appropriate becomes the responsibility of the White community. This includes being respectful of the differences, communicating and collaborating with students to identify their needs, providing both high expectations and necessary support to meet those expectations, and not making assumptions based on the dominant culture. This fosters an inclusive environment and establishes a framework for incorporating diverse representation within the curriculum that reflects identities of all students. Further, many documented events are misrepresented or excluded based on the skewed narrative of the dominant culture. Generational beliefs, teachings, and traditions need to be scrutinized to identify the presence of deep-rooted oppression, discrimination, and acts of genocide.

As children and adolescents acquire and practice intrapersonal skills for empowerment, they also represent the most vulnerable group in need of advocacy and we would be remiss if we did not include the need for advocacy on behalf of children, adolescents, parents, caregivers, and communities where families live and work as an integral part of our work. All students should have the opportunity to learn about people with shared identities not always represented, let alone portrayed accurately, inclusively, or positively throughout much of history. Creating an inclusive curriculum for all students entails correcting inaccurate depictions of history that perpetuated a false narrative based on race, ethnicity, socioeconomic status, religion, gender, sexuality, and ability or disability. Unfortunately, one classroom or school will not be adequate in addressing the systemic change that is needed for society to become more inclusive and accepting of diversity in identity, thought, and belief.

Coalescing and creating change

Historically, the burden and responsibility for change has fallen on those most impacted by oppression and discrimination, which consists of the most vulnerable and powerless. Systemic change is impossible without the acknowledgment and support of the dominant culture. Joining with people with different and intersecting identities and sharing stories to develop empathy and mutual respect is part of the journey toward liberation. Systemic change requires collaboration in both understanding the need for change and developing inclusive infrastructure for more equitable spaces, rules, and laws. Those with privilege can leverage their power in spaces where others (marginalized and oppressed) do not have access. This process can include calling out injustices, renaming reality, refusing to collude, and being an ally to transform anger into action (Harro, 2018b). If the curriculum is not inclusive, actions can include meeting with a teacher, administrator, or attending a school board meeting. If a sport team is not willing to allow a transgender athlete to participate, advocate for inclusion to the league or governing body for change in policy or demand consequences for those who do not comply with inclusive policies or rules. Concomitantly, building relationships with like-minded individuals and joining organizations that share common beliefs or goals are action steps for addressing and supporting systemic change. Actively engaging with policy makers, representatives, or senators at the local, state, and national level to co-construct inclusive rules, policies, or laws can influence change in legislation. Fundraising, planning, lobbying, educating, and motivating others to act are an integral part of the Cycle of Liberation that also reinforces there is power in numbers (Harro, 2018b). As movements gain supporters and momentum, those currently in power may feel more pressure to hold onto their beliefs, privileges, and power. They may feel more emboldened to manipulate the system in their favor, creating more advantageous loopholes and suppressive laws that further perpetuate oppression. For example, voter suppression laws have been presented and passed in multiple states throughout history and most recently after the 2020 election. Diligence and persistence are needed to achieve and maintain inclusion within all systems.

Maintaining

The Cycle of Liberation is a salient framework for advocacy and social justice that informs activism and action steps on a systemic level. During the transition from childhood to adolescence, individuals are tasked with learning how these systems exist and influence behavior. Adolescents and young adults become less reliant on parents and teachers and are cognizant of the impacts of these systems (e.g., school, business, medical and mental health, legal/justice, social welfare) that set policy, control, and enforce societal norms and laws.

TIPS FOR PRACTITIONERS

1. Engage with those who have shared identities and work through experiences that perpetuate these systems.
2. Engage with those who have different identities and listen to their stories.
3. Join groups and support the work of organizations within these communities.
4. Be an ally and role model within your own groups and communities; be an activist and co-conspirator in re-writing the rules of society.

Advocacy and social justice

The justification for developing and implementing an action plan for advocacy and social justice has not been without challenges and criticism which includes keeping in existence misguided frames of reference. When the "evidence" (theory, research, experience) in evidence-based practice is flawed, professionals will need to re-examine ways of knowing, antecedents of conceptualization, and strategies for intervention. Theorists, researchers, practitioners, and educators can prioritize proposing and refining models through a social and cultural lens to fit the ever-changing needs of children and adolescents. This new modus operandi then needs to reflect the needs of parents who are caught in the middle of trying to navigate the conflicts between needs and the systems in which their children function. Finally, choosing skills that promote empowerment should be prioritized for long-term healthy development.

Providers of services to children and adolescents are encouraged to use evidence-based practice to inform conceptualization and intervention. Practitioners are encouraged to take a deeper dive into theory and understand the identity(ies) of the theorists, which means that historically, most theories were developed by and normed on the dominant group. Epistemological (theory of knowledge) oppression occurs when "one member of an epistemic community has more power in constructing the 'truth' or knowledge of a matter than another" (Sewel, 2016, p. 7). Practitioners then need to be aware of their own epistemological privileges when working with all children and adolescents to decrease and ameliorate further oppression of this already vulnerable group (Kay, 2019).

Research can follow a similar pattern of using theory to inform the practice, particularly as it relates to forming hypotheses rooted in systemic racism, patriarchy, White supremacy, and capitalism (especially if it involves a grant/funding source). Constructs are evolving to support the needs of students, parents, mental health professionals, and various practitioners to be more inclusive. For example, using they/them pronouns for individuals who identify as non-binary is more inclusive than gendered pronouns he/his or she/hers. Further, when everyone discloses pronouns, then we begin to normalize a non-binary system of gender as the status quo. The language and words we use to describe characteristics, behaviors, or actions require intentionality to promote positive development. The movement to work toward dismantling current systems also requires practitioners to be mindful of how language, theories, and research may not apply to certain populations or subgroups. As always, approach the use of theory and research with scrutiny, discretion, and vigilance.

The acknowledgment and recognition of the importance of social justice and advocacy, which can transform behaviors, cognitions, policies, practices, and systems, serves to provide equitable access to opportunities for oppressed, disenfranchised, and underserved students and their families. Parents from marginalized communities may have difficulty navigating the bureaucracy around services, consent for evaluations, placement, or available options and opportunities for students, particularly those with language and cultural barriers. For example, a child struggling with dyslexia can be labeled as inferior rather than different, which becomes a stigma and can be internalized to the detriment of their psychosocial development. These learning challenges often necessitate additional resources which can be costly and may not be provided unless requested or even demanded by the parent. Many parents may not be aware of learning disorders, the process required to determine or diagnose a [learning] disorder, or the resources required by law to be made available to support these students. Ultimately, the needs of students can be undermined by a flawed and faulty system that reinforces inequity and injustice within educational systems.

Marbley et al. (2011) affirmed the need to engage in multicultural social-justice work. Likewise, they support the application of the ACA advocacy competencies (Ratts & Hutchins, 2009). When working with students in a school setting, Locke and Bailey (2014; as cited in Studer, 2015) defined advocacy as "a compass to intentionally navigate the power structures, create bonds, teach self-advocacy skill, and use data to educate others as to how school counselors work to close achievement gap" (p. 366). Murray et al. (2010; as cited in Studer, 2015) asserted that advocacy, "as a tool for achieving social justice" (p. 366), is instrumental in assisting children and adolescents in developing skills that promote and support their ability to self-advocate. When doing so, they are serving as active participants to ensure access to opportunities that are not always accessible to them, due to disenfranchisement, underrepresentation, and biases that exist in society. Thus, these matters can be countered when students are given the skills and tools to self-advocate and have the support of others who advocate on their behalf.

TIPS FOR PRACTITIONERS

1. Conceptualize skill development with the Cycle of Liberation: core of self-love, self-esteem, balance, joy, support, security, and a spiritual base.
2. Design and implement activities focused on empowerment and intrapersonal strengths.
3. Create a safe space for the development of self-advocacy and practice interpersonal skills.
4. Name the injustices and differentiate between the temporary solution of developing coping skills within an environment that may not have been built for them AND engage in solution-focused skills for resilience, persistence, success, and happiness.

References

Ahluwalia, M. K., Nadrich, T., & Ahluwalia, I. S. (2019). Sikh youth coming of age: Reflections on the decision to tie a turban. *Counseling and Values, 64*, 20–34.

Brandt, A. M. (1978). Racism and research: The case of the Tuskegee Syphilis study. The *Hastings Report, 8*(6), 21–29. https://doi.org/10.2307/3561468

Brunson, R. K. (2007). Police don't like Black people": African-American young men's accumulated police experiences. *Criminology & Public Policy, 6*(1), 71.

Bryan, A. (2012). 'You've got to teach people that racism is wrong and then they won't be racist': Curricular representations and young people's understandings of 'race' and racism. *Journal of Curriculum Studies, 44*(5), 599–629.

Clark, U. S., & Hurd, Y. L. (2020). Addressing racism and disparities in the biomedical sciences. *Nature Human Behaviour, 4*(8), 774–777.

Das, A. (2022, May 18). U.S. Soccer and women's layers agree to settle equal pay lawsuit. *The New York Times*. https://www.nytimes.com/2022/02/22/sports/soccer/us-womens-soccer-equal-pay.html

Daum, C.W. (2020). Social Equity, Homonormativity, and Equality: An Intersectional Critique of the Administration of Marriage Equality and Opportunities for LGBTQ Social Justice. *Administrative Theory & Praxis, 42*, 115 - 132.

Gender Equity Resource Center (2012). *LGBT resources: Definition of terms.* http://geneq.berkeley.edu/lgbt_resources_definition_of.terms

Harro, B. (2018a). The cycle of socialization. In M. Adams, W. J. Blumenfeld, D. C. J. Catalano, K. DeJong, H. W. Hackman, L. E. Hopkins, B. J. Love, M. L. Peters, D. Shlasko, & X. Z'uniga (Eds.), *Readings for Diversity and Social Justice* (4th ed., pp. 27–34). Routledge.

Harro, B. (2018b). The cycle of liberation. In M. Adams, W. J. Blumenfeld, D. C. J. Catalano, K. DeJong, H. W. Hackman, L. E. Hopkins, B. J. Love, M. L. Peters, D. Shlasko, & X. Z'uniga (Eds.), *Readings for Diversity and Social Justice* (4th ed., pp. 27–34). Routledge.

Hughes, L. D., Kidd, K. M., Gamarel, K. E., Operario, D., & Dowshen, N. (2021). "These laws will be devastating": Provider perspectives on legislation banning gender-affirming care for transgender adolescents. *Journal of Adolescent Health, 69*(6), 976–982.

Jemison, M. (2009, November 4-7). Find where the wind goes [Keynote Address]. Annual Biomedical Research Conference for Minority Students, Phoenix, AZ, United States.

Kay, D. (2019). On the participation of children with medical conditions in risk assessment: A case for development of self-advocacy. *Educational Psychology in Practice, 35*(4), 357–367.

Marbley, A. F., Malott, K. M., Flaherty, A., &Frederick, H. (2011). Three issues, three approaches, three calls to action: Multicultural social justice in the schools. *Journal for Social Action in Counseling and Psychology, 3*, 59–73.

Masterpiece Cakeshop, Ltd. v. Colorado Civil Rights Commission, 584 U.S. 370 (2018). https://supreme.justia.com/cases/federal/us/584/16-111/

Meheut, C. (2022, April 18). The female soccer players challenging France's Hijab ban. *The New York Times*. https://www.nytimes.com/2022/04/18/sports/soccer/france-hijab-ban-soccer.html

Merriam-Webster (n.d.) Whitewash. *Merriam-Webster.com dictionary*. Retrieved May 28, 2022, from https://www.merriam-webster.com/dictionary/whitewash

Ngaage, L. M., Cantab, M. A.O., M.B., B.Chir.; Knighton, Brooks J. B.S., McGlone, Katie L. B.S., Benzel, Caroline A. B.S., Rada, Erin M. M.D., Bluebond-Langner, Rachel M.D., Rasko, Yvonne M. M.D. (October 2019). Health Insurance Coverage of Gender-Affirming Top Surgery in the United States. *Plastic and Reconstructive Surgery 144*(4), 824–833. https://doi.org/10.1097/PRS.0000000000006012

North, A. (2019). 7 positive changes that have come from the #MeToo movement: The impact of the movement goes far beyond powerful men losing their jobs. *Vox*. https://www.vox.com/identities/2019/10/4/20852639/me-too-movement-sexual-harassment-law-2019

Perzichilli, T. (2020). The historical roots of racial disparities in the mental health system. *Counseling Today*. https://ct.counseling.org/2020/05/the-historical-roots-of-racial-disparities-in-the-mental-health-system/

Quinn, S. C., & Andrasik, M. P. (2021). Addressing vaccine hesitancy in BIPOC communities—toward trustworthiness, partnership, and reciprocity. *New England Journal of Medicine, 385*(2), 97–100.

Rankin, C. (2015). *The meaning of Serena Williams: On tennis and black excellence.* https://www.nytimes.com/2015/08/30/magazine/the-meaning-of-serena-williams.html

Ratts, M. J., & Hutchins, A. M. (2009). ACA advocacy competencies: Social justice advocacy at the client/student level. *Journal of Counseling and Development, 87*(3), 269–275.

Reece, R. L. (2020). Whitewashing slavery: Legacy of slavery and white social outcomes. *Social Problems, 67*(2), 304–323. https://doi.org/10.1093/socpro/spz016

Rushing, M. D., Montoya-Barthelemy, A. G., Abrar, F. A., Medina, E. M., Popoola-Samuel, H. A., & McKinney, Z. J. (2022). Law enforcement violence in the Black community: A catalyst for clinician engagement in social justice. *American Journal of Preventive Medicine, 62*(1), 122–127.

Sewel, A. (2016). A theoretical application of epistemological oppression to the psychological assessment of special education needs: Concerns and practical implications for anti-oppressive practice. *Educational Psychology in Practice, 32*(1), 1–12.

Sheppard, M., & Mayo, J. B. (2013). The social construction of gender and sexuality: Learning from two spirit traditions. *The Social Studies, 104*, 259–270.

Staurowsky, E. J. (2016). *Women and sport: From liberation to celebration.* Human Kinetics.

Stitzlein, S. M. (2015). Improving public schools through the dissent of parents: opting out of tests, demanding alternative curricula, invoking parent trigger laws, and withdrawing entirely. *Educational Studies, 51*(1), 57–71.

Studer, J. R. (2015). *The essential school counselor in a changing society.* Sage.

Turban, J. L., Kraschel, K. L., & Cohen, I. G. (2021). Legislation to criminalize gender-affirming medical care for transgender youth. *JAMA, 325*(22), 2251–2252.

United States Census Bureau (2020). *2020 census illuminates racial and ethnic composition of the country.* https://www.census.gov/library/stories/2021/08/improved-race-ethnicity-measures-reveal-united-states-population-much-more-multiracial.html

Wiececk, W. M., & Hamilton, J. L. (2014). Beyond the Civil Rights Act of 1964: Confronting structural racism in the workplace. *Louisiana Law Review, 74.*

Wright, K. C., Carr, K. A., & Akin, B. A. (2021). The whitewashing of social work history: How dismantling racism in social work education begins with an equitable history of the profession. *Advances in Social Work, 21*(2/3), 274–297.

Wright, J. L., Jarvis, J. N., Pachter, L. M., & Walker-Harding, L. R. (2020). "Racism as a public health issue" APS racism series: At the intersection of equity, science, and social justice. *Pediatric Research, 88*(5), 696–698.

Zschirnt, E. & Ruedin, D. (2016). Ethnic discrimination in hiring decisions: A meta-analysis of correspondence tests 1990–2015. *Journal of Ethnic and Migration Studies, 42*(7), 1115–1134, https://doi.org/10.1080/1369183X.2015.1133279

Chapter 2

Experiential Learning Theory and theoretical framework

Amanda C. DeDiego and Teresa Behrend Fletcher

Give a man a fish and you feed him for a day; Teach a man to fish and you feed him for a lifetime.

(Maimonides)

Students often ask what is the more powerful influence on human behavior in the battle of Nature and Nurture. My response is always the same, it is not nature vs. nurture as an either/or answer, but the recognition, validation, and acceptance of what nature provides while supplementing skill development for long-term health and well-being through a nurturing environment. It is the combination and interaction between nature and nurture that contributes to subjective experiences and respective worldviews. A child who has qualities that are considered strengths that are valued or "nurtured" will be more likely to feel worthy and see the world as hopeful. Conversely, when only flaws or weaknesses are exposed, children may be more likely to develop shame that contributes to a more pessimistic worldview. In this sense, we will discuss the role of counseling to include the development of skills to resolve the many conflicts between nature and nurture. In this way, we hope to teach our child and adolescent client how to fish by developing social and coping skills to manage life stressors.

Experiential activities in counseling

Beyond use with traditional counseling theories, specialties including Expressive Arts Therapy (Chapter 10), animal-assisted therapy (Chapter 14), and outdoor or adventure-based therapy (Chapter 15) evolved from aspects of Experiential Learning Theory. It is important to differentiate experiential activities in this text from play therapy, which has a different theoretical foundation and requires additional training, certification, and supervision considerations. Play therapy has a theoretical framework that can incorporate various counseling theories, with a focus on the therapeutic relationship and play (Schaefer & Peabody, 2016). Play therapy provides a co-created learning experience based on the relationship between therapist and client (Axline, 1979). This interaction allows insight as to the perceptions of the child. In essence, the therapist helps to connect behavior to emotions in the moment. Play therapy is a process occurring over multiple sessions in a designated playroom (Landreth, 2012) with toys that allow the child autonomy to explore and choose the activity and which toy or game is used in the session (Axline, 1979). Overall, the therapist has a more reflective and less directive role in the therapy experience. The therapist sets limits on behavior in the playroom, but generally, less restriction is set regarding the specific objects or structure of play. The play therapy modality of counseling incorporates specific skills and dispositions for counselors beyond that typically received in counseling training (Ray, 2011). The Association for Play Therapy offers resources, training, and certification for play therapists. As such, the play therapy approach is valuable in counseling work with children, but differs from experiential activities, which offer a tool for counselors of all specialties without additional certification or training.

Counseling children and adolescents

Children and adolescents differ from adults in how they perceive, interpret, and view their environment (Piaget, 2002) and thus require clinicians to consider their developmental differences in counseling. Children have natural resilience to overcome trauma and cope with stress (Murphy & Moriarty, 1976). As we navigate life stressors over time, individuals develop daily habits contributing to overall health and wellness. However, methods of coping with stress can affect a child's self-image positively or negatively. Similarly, especially for adolescents, emotion plays a major role in wellness and decision-making. Emotion, or affect, drives behavior, often based on reaction to the consequences of decisions (Schneider & Caffray, 2012). For adolescents, change in affect influences behavior. Adolescents lack skills in emotional regulation, and so stress or intense emotional states can be very disruptive.

DOI: 10.4324/9781315213767-3

For example, adolescents may be more impulsive after a breakup or may decide to drink alcohol at a party after a fight with a friend. Emotions and urges, such as sexual desire, may engage in risky behavior, which has the capacity to influence long-term health, for example, in teens who contract a sexually transmitted infection or become pregnant (Schneider & Caffray, 2012). Younger adolescents are prone to risky decision-making, more so within a peer group (Gardner & Steinberg, 2005). Additionally, youth tend to focus more on the potential benefit of risk-taking than potential consequences.

Regardless of school or clinical setting, counselors working with children and adolescents must consider development in their approach to counseling (Prout & Fedewa, 2015). For example, a counselor must consider how to discuss counseling goals and modalities with children and adolescents (Cook-Cottone et al., 2015). A developmental approach to counseling can help counselors to unlock understanding of a child's world, allowing connection through empathy (Davies, 2011). In activity, children lose self-consciousness as their focus shifts from awareness of themselves to awareness of engaging in the experience (Hecker et al., 2010). To externalize processing and accommodate developmental level, experiential activities are useful tools in counseling with children and adolescents (Gladding, 2016).

Children and adolescents represent an underserved population with great need for mental health support (Prout & Fedewa, 2015). Counselors must approach work with children and adolescents differently than one might approach work with adults (Cook-Cottone et al., 2015). Counselors cannot assume children and adolescents interpret the world as small adults, and thus must incorporate consideration of development into counseling with children and adolescents. For example, youth who have experienced trauma may not progress developmentally as a typical child (Murphy & Moriarty, 1976). Development is not as simple as identified biological age, but is a complicated process including considerations of cultural and societal influences (Kohlberg, 1983). Culture influences affect, wellness, and development for children (Wiley & Rappaport, 2000). In working with children, healthcare professionals cannot ignore environmental factors, and should consider how to explore cultural, environmental, and societal factors with children in a developmentally appropriate way.

Mental health professionals learn a variety of theories that serve to inform best practices to develop accurate conceptualizations of client issues and effective treatment strategies that respect individual differences. For the purposes of this book, Positive Psychology is used to provide a framework for the content of counseling sessions for children and adolescents while Experiential Learning Theory is used to describe the process of how children and adolescents learn new skills. Our goal is to provide counseling professionals the ability to understand how to work with children and adolescents and adapt the content of the counseling session to identify and utilize the unique strengths, interests, and resources of clients and develop creative interventions for learning skills experientially to meet their evolving needs.

Positive Psychology

Positive Psychology sets the tone for re-framing the purpose of counseling, particularly with children and adolescents, by promoting health and well-being rather than utilizing a disease model for repairing damage (Seligman & Csikszentmihalyi, 2000). In other words, we should spend just as much time identifying and nurturing individual strengths, developing healthy relationships, and creating productive environments to produce and promote positive subjective experiences as we do making diagnoses and trying to "fix" what is wrong with our clients (Fletcher & Hurley, 2016; Park & Peterson, 2008). Therefore, Positive Psychology is a good fit for directing Experiential Learning Theory to develop healthy intrapersonal, interpersonal, and coping or solution-focused skills that are consistent with living a successful and happy life (Fletcher & Hurley, 2016).

Character traits (nature), or those aspects of personality that contribute to youth development, provide the starting point for practitioners to identify signature strengths that children and adolescents either possess with validation and positive reinforcement, need to develop further, or acquire and incorporate into daily living. These positive traits can work to combat or prevent negative outcomes (e.g., Botvin et al., 1995; Park, 2004) as well as promote healthy functioning (e.g., Colby & Damon 1992; Seligman, 2011). Examples of positive traits can include but are not limited to hope, kindness, social intelligence, self-control (Park & Peterson, 2006), showing tolerance, valuing diversity, and the ability to delay gratification (Scales et al., 2000).

The identification of strengths and skills that children and adolescents already possess can be helpful during the first session to initiate conversation and build rapport. These "signature strengths" can further be used to acquire and develop those additional characteristics or skills that will be helpful moving forward (Seligman, 2011; Seligman & Csikszentmihalyi, 2000). These strengths are divided into intrapersonal, interpersonal, and coping/ solution-focused skills (Fletcher & Hurley, 2016; Park & Peterson, 2008). For example, the ability to get out of our comfort zone and try something new is an intrapersonal skill that can be taught, learned, practiced, and repeated throughout the lifespan. The ability to communicate and express emotions are interpersonal skills that contribute to healthy relationships, while developing persistence, resilience, or perseverance are necessary coping skills when navigating challenges. Acquiring solution-focused skills such as problem-solving or being assertive can contribute to positive and productive environments necessary for long-term psychological well-being and happiness.

Developing positive character traits or intrapersonal and interpersonal skills can be helpful in identifying traits in others to form healthy relationships. When individuals can recognize positive traits in others, they can then become more discerning when choosing friendships, intimate partnerships, and the time spent engaging with others. Additionally, these intra- and interpersonal skills contribute to the development of healthy coping or solution-focused skills essential to lifelong happiness and success (Fletcher & Hurley, 2016). As such, the best way to learn or practice skills is by actively engaging in activities that promote skill development, which is best explained using Experiential Learning Theory, or ELT.

Experiential Learning Theory

Experiential learning can be defined as "learning by doing combined with reflection" (Gass, 1993, p. 4) and serves as the foundation for our work. Founded in the field of education, the concept of experiential learning is not considered a "product" of learning but rather the "process of learning" which is more active and requires that the learner be responsible for learning and the teacher, or in this case the counselor, be responsible to the learner (Kolb, 2015). Introducing experiential activities to the learning process within counseling offers a dynamic growth experience and adaptive skills that become more easily accessed in the future than typical talk therapy, which may be more appropriate for adult populations.

Experiential Learning Theory, developed by Kolb, provides a foundation for the use and processing of activities in a myriad of contexts, including counseling (Murrell & Claxton, 1987). Experiential Learning Theory offers counselors a framework to engage children and adolescents in the therapy process (Pereira, 2014) and incorporates the application of complex concepts into dynamic experiences from which the client derives new meaning through reflection (Bergsteiner et al., 2010). The experiential learning process helps provide structure to the use of activities in any stage of the counseling process and presents opportunities for connecting with a client within various theoretical orientations. Counselors can use activities to build rapport, process difficulties the client may not be comfortable discussing directly, teach skills supporting counseling goals, offer homework to help clients practice skills between sessions, or reinforce lessons learned in counseling before termination (Murrell & Claxton, 1987). Additionally, activities can be useful in helping a child or adolescent client communicate counseling work with caregivers. Teaching family members to dialogue with clients about counseling work can help build relationships. For example, teaching caregivers to ask "What kind of things did you do in counseling today?" may create more dialogue than asking "What did you and your counselor talk about today?"

Developmentally, children's brains have plasticity, meaning they mature and form over time (Davies, 2011). In early developmental years, children's brains are reactive to their environment and during this time, facilitation of development occurs through interactive activities, social exchanges, and other stimulation. So a child might learn more from playing a math game with classmates than if a student completed a workbook on their own. These interactions positively or negatively influence neural development, with such interactions facilitating optimal development and/or creating long-term challenges for youth. Thus, Experiential Learning Theory focuses on the process of "meaning making" through experiences (i.e., behaviors have consequences), rather than static outcomes (i.e., behavior change). "Meaning making" is the process of a child interacting with the environment and reflecting to gain understanding (Kolb & Kolb, 2005).

Using experiential activities in counseling with child and adolescent clients offers a means for counselors to work with the natural developmental process of children, rather than using modalities and measures of growth more appropriate for adult brains. Traditional talk therapy with counselors can be difficult for adolescent clients, as developmentally the ability to be self-aware and verbalize thoughts and emotions may be lacking (Coyle et al., 2009). Practitioners must seek new, innovative ways to connect with adolescent clients. Focusing on the process and incorporating Experiential Learning Theory to facilitate growth provides positive experiences and interactions to support optimal development. Using static outcomes, such as measuring frequency of a behavior, to represent growth is incongruent with the neural developmental process of children and adolescents and can be misleading and frustrating. For example, public schools use standardized testing to represent comprehension, but these outcomes do not necessarily capture the unique growth process of each student or the process of learning. As school systems attempt to capture student learning through standardized testing, the experiences in the classroom become a means to a positive outcome on the test. Further, students develop understanding that their worth is based on a test score. Shifting focus to an experiential learning process, students can derive their own meaning from classroom experiences. This fosters student development of self-worth based on meaning making.

Foundations of Experiential Learning Theory

Experiential learning was first introduced within the field of education where Dewey (1926; 1940) developed the concept of pragmatism, founded upon a need for connecting classroom learning with real-world contexts. An advocate for progressive education, he postulated that education must be adaptive to support growth in practical knowledge and the developmental changes of children over time (Dewey, 1938). This adaptive and practical approach to developmental growth used experience as the catalyst for learning. Through experiences, children could develop meaning and understanding of consequences. Describing his pragmatic philosophy of education, Dewey (1964) stated two principles should guide education and personal growth: participation in meaningful experiences and perception of consequences. Dewey advocated that teachers should help create real-life scenarios in the classroom so students could interact with real-world decisions and issues. This progressive education also shifted the role of the teacher from authoritarian to guide, invested in accommodating students' needs and allowing student ownership over the learning environment (Dewey, 1964).

Continuing the focus of learning through experience, Lewin (1948) explored individual growth through life experiences in psychology by suggesting individuals develop a unique sense of reality based on perceptions of experiences. This process of acculturation within social norms guides the development of values, which in turn influence how one makes decisions. In an educational context, according to Lewin, this process requires the facilitation of meaning making based on experience in order for children to learn and grow. This systemic consideration of behaviorism created the basis for field theory, an educational approach focused on deep processing to discover the basis of behavior (Lewin, 1951). Field theory purports that cognitive growth is best fostered through interaction with the environment, so a child would learn more from interacting with an environment than by reading a book.

Lewin also developed the concept of life spaces. This combination of personal history and social context explains a complex human experience, which is different for each individual. As each person has a unique life space, a teacher should facilitate deep meaning making which changes cognitive structures and challenges personal beliefs and values. Changing these cognitive structures, which is an intrapersonal skill, is critical for forming future motivations for decision-making.

A prominent behaviorist and psychologist, Piaget (1973) created developmental learning theory, which proposed learning as a series of experiences facilitating understanding of complex concepts. Within this theory, in order for children to grow into adaptive and productive members of society, learning must be a process of experimentation and meaning making. Incorporating his developmental stages, Piaget (1978) also described learning as a lifelong process occurring throughout the lifespan explored later in this chapter. These early theorists outlined the importance of practical experience and developmental consideration for growth in children. In challenging the concept of educating children as small adults, early behaviorists created important dialogue that inspired Kolb's development of Experiential Learning Theory. Kolb (2015) shared the value of individuality for students established by Dewey, considered Lewin's life spaces and the various roles educators play in development, and acknowledged the developmental nature of learning occurring throughout the lifespan. Thus, with considerations of theoretical influences, including Dewey (1926; 1938), Lewin (1948; 1951), and Piaget (1973; 1983), Kolb (2015) developed Experiential Learning Theory to guide educators in facilitating meaningful learning experiences in the classroom.

Kolb et al. (2001) describe learning as a dynamic process occurring in a cyclical nature. Thus, the core tenet of Experiential Learning Theory conceptualizes learning and growth as a process occurring over time, not a static outcome. For example, in the case of public education, teachers may focus on facilitating the learning of developmental benchmark skills throughout the year as opposed to measuring learning with only one standardized test taken at the end of the school year. The teacher in tracking growth throughout the school year would then spend time interacting with students and building learning opportunities in the classroom to address progressive developmental gains, instead of using one test to determine how well a student learned. Focusing on a learning process instead of a single outcome gives flexibility for a teacher or counselor to adjust for the individual learning of each child. Focusing on activities, this interaction between individual and environment through experience represents a dynamic and holistic process, which facilitates personal growth (Kolb, 2015; Kolb et al., 2001).

Experiential Learning Cycle

Experiential Learning Theory is progressive and dynamic while individuals navigate a cyclical developmental process when creating meaning from experience (Kolb & Kolb, 2005, 2009). Aligning with the natural development of children, meaning making and change happen naturally for children through interaction with environment. While several models of the experiential learning process exist (e.g., Dewey, 1938; Kolb, 2015), general consensus is a four-phase model. According to Kolb's model the phases include the following: concrete experience, reflective observation, abstract conceptualization, and active experimentation (see Figure 2.1; Kolb et al., 2001). The model presented by Nadler and Luckner (1992) is similar, with stages identified as follows: experiencing, reflecting, generalizing, and applying.

The cycle begins with a concrete experience, described as an interaction with a facilitated experience (Kolb & Kolb, 2005). Fishing, at a most simplified level, requires basic equipment (pole, bait, body of water containing fish) and allows for reflection to also be uncomplicated, which can be beneficial when learning a skill for the first time. The experience of fishing together creates an opportunity for metaphors and skills useful in life outside of counseling. In the concrete experience, or experiencing phase, the counselor would show the client how to use the fishing equipment. The counselor might discuss different baits with the client and then take the client fishing, helping the client experience fishing with the support of their expertise. Following this interaction, the learner must reflect on the experience to determine meaning through reflective observation (Kolb et al., 2014). Reflection can be prompted by questions such as, "What was your least/most favorite thing about fishing?" or "What was the hardest/easiest part of fishing?" Engaging clients in the reflection process in a positive way can guide children and adolescents on how to reflect when engaging in a new experience. The reflection also helps the client search for meaning from and conceptualize observations about the fishing experience.

Armed with the outcome of the reflection, clients can then apply new meaning and implications to her own understanding of the content for abstract conceptualization (Kolb & Kolb, 2005) or generalizing (Nadler & Luckner, 1992). In this process, the client having reflected on the experience would think about the fishing trip to gain an understanding of the skills and lessons learned. The client may consider how best to catch certain types of fish using bait, or how they might need to use patience in order to be successful in catching a fish. In this process, the counselor can also consider information gained through the experience. When we focus on both the likes and dislikes or most/least favorite, we now have a framework to move forward to other phases. Clinicians will want to continue to validate the reflection and positively reinforce the joy found through the experience. So if the client likes being in the fresh air, sitting in silence without having to interact, or the feeling of anticipation when reeling in a fish, we want to continue to be mindful of incorporating these into future activities. Similarly, if kids were uncomfortable sitting on the wet ground or frustrated at the lack of activity, addressing these for future trips can validate their feelings and thoughts in that moment and reflection serves as the content for the active experimentation phase (Kolb et al., 2001).

In the active experimentation, or applying phase, the client then try applying skills and lessons for a future fishing experience. In making plans for the next fishing trip, the counselor and client can discuss options for improvement such as bringing chairs so they don't have to sit on the wet ground and whether to try a different bait, go fishing at a different time, or try a different location. The client may also gain the confidence to try the fishing process without the help of the counselor, or may have gained a curiosity to experiment with strategies gained through reflecting and generalizing. Some of the skills introduced include but are not limited to learning a new skill (fishing), reflecting on feelings about the new activity, identifying how to make the new experience better, and engaging in solution-focused discussion to continue behaviors that are working and change what is unpleasant or unfulfilling. By navigating this cycle, experience-based learning evolves from the application of

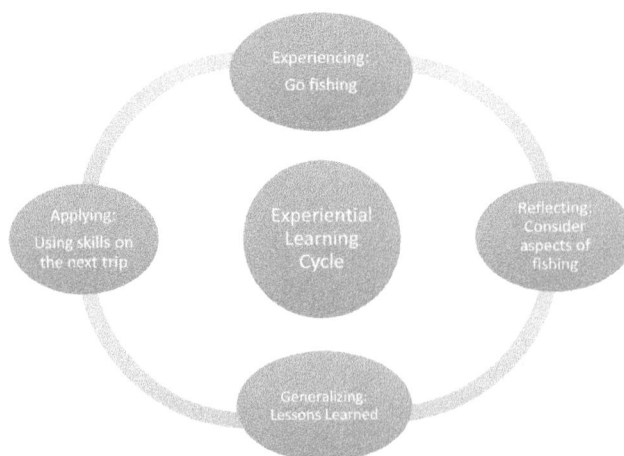

Figure 2.1 The Experiential Learning Cycle as applied to the activity of fishing.

abstract concepts within real-world contexts, yielding new understanding through the development of meaning. Kolb (2015) described this cycle as occurring repeatedly through development to facilitate learning through experience.

Integration of counseling theory

While Experiential Learning Theory provides a general framework for work with clients, additional theories serve to provide further structure and enhance the counseling experience and may include Positive Psychology, constructivist, narrative, and solution-focused therapies. Both Positive Psychology and Experiential Learning Theory provide a general framework for the content as well as the process of skill development with the child and adolescent population. Both Positive Psychology and Experiential Learning Theory emphasize the value of the individual experience (Kolb, 2015; Seligman & Csikszentmihalyi, 2000). Positive Psychology as a strengths-based approach encourages individuals to seek happiness by engaging in experiences (Seligman, 2011). Experiential Learning Theory emphasizes the need to consider the individual needs of the learner so the environment can support those unique needs (Kolb, 2015). Both approaches focus on the individual process of meaning-making through engaging in experiences to facilitate lifelong learning. Various theories can be applied to facilitate this process of experience and development, including constructivist, narrative, and solution-focused counseling.

Constructivist counseling

Constructivism is a metatheory supporting a holistic approach to counseling (McAuliffe & Eriksen, 1999). This postmodern approach considers clients to be active creators of their life experiences, which includes the counseling relationship. Knowing and learning are created collaboratively, not consumed objectively. Counselors using a constructivist approach to counseling would increase collaboration with a client, inviting them to be an active participant in shaping the therapeutic experience as reality and meaning are constructed concepts. Growth is a dynamic process, an exchange between the counselor and the client (Payne, 2006). This approach acknowledges the lack of an "ideal" counseling approach, instead exercising empathy to explore the client's perspective (McAuliffe & Eriksen, 1999). Constructivism, in allowing for other perspectives, also allows for diverse cultural views (Wiggins, 2012). Metaphor and experience can be powerful connections across cultures. Constructivism considers the importance of environment and experience, describing learning as "doing" and "being" rather than consuming static information (Payne, 2006). As such, the counselor would also consider systemic influences on the client, not assuming the client is alone accountable for his suffering (McAuliffe & Eriksen, 1999). The counselor takes time to explore family, environment, social influences, and how these factors shape the client's meaning-making process. Incorporating development, counselors may also use a constructivist developmental approach to counseling.

Incorporating consideration of development and a collaborative approach to counseling is empowering for child and adolescent clients (Crespi & Generali, 1995). With children and adolescents, the concept of social constructionism considers the influence of others in the development of meaning and sense of self (Russo et al., 2006). Counselors can use creative activities and experience with young clients to facilitate a constructivist approach to counseling. A constructivist approach including considerations of development and social learning incorporates stages of development, according to Piaget (1983). Externalizing processing through activity creates a developmentally appropriate way to help clients co-construct the counseling process and make meaning from counseling.

Narrative counseling

Narrative therapy allows the client to share experiences through story (Hecker, Lettenberger et al., 2010; Veronese et al., 2010). Narrative counseling focuses on storying and the voice of the client (White & Epston, 1990). In counseling, clients share their story in therapy, externalize the issues to be addressed, and then re-story, creating a new narrative, having addressed the issue. The narrative therapy process includes alternative stories constructed around cultural identity. Clients may share stories verbally, or they may share story through other mediums such as expressive arts (Hecker et al., 2010). This approach is especially useful with child and adolescent clients. Narrative therapy with children promotes the development of social and emotional skills (Beaudoin et al., 2016). Narrative therapy guides children to externalize issues and author a new story for the future. Through this empowerment process, children gain self-awareness, emotional regulation, empathy, social awareness, and decision-making skills. Narrative focuses on client experience, conceptualizing client issues as experiences, which influence behavior.

Sharing stories through art or activity allows the child to externalize the experiences, emphasizing the problem as independent from the person (Hecker et al., 2010). The therapist would explore how the issues were influencing decision-making or other behaviors negatively (Beaudoin et al., 2016). This process allows clients to gain perspective, be empowered to take responsibility for their own actions, and develop identity through problem-solving skills in the future. This process is useful with children and adults. Externalizing may be different with children, as they experience emotion intensely, and may lack developmental language skills to describe complex, abstract concepts. Through the therapy process, the client becomes empowered to re-write their story (Hecker et al., 2010). This approach is especially effective with clients presenting with trauma-related issues, considering the focus on empowerment and externalizing issues.

Counselors can use narrative with children to build rapport and help children better understand problems (Eppler et al., 2009). Counselors may also use narrative stories to convey complex interpersonal concepts to children in an accessible way (Burns, 2005). Counselors may tell stories about characters using skills to overcome challenges, or relate to others. As such, counselors may strategically choose stories to share with clients to illustrate skills or issues, then discuss them through metaphor. Metaphors can be experiential. Experiential metaphors may include activities such as acting out a story or may include meaning making through experience. For example, a counselor may take a child on a walk, and then talk about how the journey related to the client's own story. Other examples of techniques used with children include oral or written stories, the creation of characters representing the client to externalize the issue, the use of children's books to illustrate the client's issues through metaphor, or using movie clips to embody the student's experiences (Eppler et al., 2009). Movies in therapy can be especially useful, discussing the movie character who navigates issues, and then applying those skills with the client through metaphor (Turns & Macey, 2016).

Solution-focused counseling

The focus of solution-focused brief therapy is using the tools the client brings to the session to meet the client's needs (de Shazer et al., 1986). This approach is strengths-based, accounting for the natural resilience of children (Taylor, 2009). As such, solution-focused counseling is especially useful with clients in acute care or struggling with trauma (Rice et al., 2014; Tyson & Baffour, 2004). This approach emphasizes the client's own ability to solve problems (Tyson & Baffour, 2004). Focus is on goal setting and work toward goals in counseling.

Counselors work to identify client strengths (i.e., Positive Psychology) and how strengths can be used to promote wellness as opposed to focusing on an issue or on symptoms (Taylor, 2009). Counselors use compliments, the relationship between behavior and outcomes, and identifying exceptions, which indicate strengths. Through stages of therapy, the counselor first helps the client describe the presenting problem. Then, they work to develop goals. A common tool in SFT is the miracle question, asking the client to describe what life might be like without the current problem. The counselors then highlight the strengths of the client and bridge the strengths highlighted in session to issues beyond the counseling relationship.

Counselors may use creative means to facilitate this process. For example, the client may create a sand tray demonstrating their current issue, then another showing life without the current issue. Creative experiences, using things like art or music, can express problems or goals (Tyson & Baffour, 2004). It is important for the counselor to be strengths-based in the use of activities, as the focus is not on the quality of art produced or the music choice of the client. Solution-focused therapy is used with children and adolescent clients as the focus is on problem-solving instead of pathology (Taylor, 2009). Adolescents feeling self-conscious and private may not engage in talk therapy openly (Coyle et al., 2009). Solution-focused therapy with children and adolescents includes the use of developmentally appropriate language and the inclusion of activities to externalize problems (Taylor, 2009). The use of activities or another medium, especially those using technology, may provide a more conducive environment for interpersonal growth (Coyle et al., 2009).

Applying theory with the individual

Counseling theory is necessary to establish a foundation and systematic process for creating a dynamic and effective practice with child and adolescent clients and their families. Positive Psychology is helpful in creating a mindset and approach when considering long-term health and development. Experiential Learning Theory best describes how skills are best taught, learned, and practiced as a complement to Seligman and Csiksczentmihalyi (2000). However, individual differences, family systems, culture, and societal pressures also contribute to what skills need to be learned as well as the priority and sequencing of skill development. These developmental theories, which are presented in Chapter 3, contribute to a better understanding of how to manage the complex intersectionality of life skill development for the child and adolescent population.

References

Axline, V. M. (1979). Play therapy procedures and results. In C. Schaefer (Ed.), *The Therapeutic Use of Child's Play* (pp. 209–218). Jason Aronson, Inc.

Beaudoin, M. N., Moersch, M., & Evare, B. S. (2016). The effectiveness of narrative therapy with children's social and emotional skill development: An empirical study of 813 problem-solving stories. *Journal of Systemic Therapies, 35*(3), 42–59.

Bergsteiner, H., Avery, G. C., & Neumann, R. (2010). Kolb's experiential learning model: Critique from a modeling perspective. *Studies in Continuing Education, 32*(1), 29–46.

Botvin, G. J., Baker, E., Dusenbury, L., Botvin, E. M., & Diaz, T. (1995). Long-term follow-up results of a randomized drug abuse prevention trial in a white middle-class population. *The Journal of the American Medical Association, 273*(14), 1106–1112.

Burns, G. W. (2005). *101 healing stories for kids and teens.* Wiley.

Colby, A., & Damon, W. (1992). *Some do care: Contemporary lives of moral commitment.* The Free Press.

Cook-Cottone, C. P., Kane, L. S., & Anderson, L. M. (2015). *The elements of counseling children and adolescents.* Springer Publishing Company.

Coyle, D., Doherty, G., & Sharry, J. (2009). An evaluation of a solution focused computer game in adolescent interventions. *Clinical Child Psychology and Psychiatry, 14*(3), 345–360.

Crespi, T. & Generali, M. (1995). Constructivist developmental theory and therapy: Implications for counseling adolescents. *Adolescence, 30*(119), 735.

Davies, D. (2011). *Child development: A practitioner's guide* (3rd ed.). The Guilford Press.

de Shazer, S., Berg, I. K., Lipchik, E., Nunnally, E., Molnar, A., Gingerich, W., & Weiner-Davis, M. (1986). Brief therapy: Focused solution development. *Family Process, 25*(2), 207–221.

Dewey, J. (1926). My pedagogic creed. *The Journal of Education, 104*(21), 542.

Dewey, J. (1938). *Experience & education.* Touchstone.

Dewey, J. (1940). *Education today.* G. P. Putnam's Sons.

Dewey, J. (1964). Individuality and experience. In R. D. Archambault (Ed.), *On education: Selected writings* (pp. 149–156). Random House.

Eppler, C., Olsen, J. A., & Hidano, L. (2009). Using stories in elementary school counseling: Brief, narrative techniques. *Professional School Counseling, 12*(5), 387–391.

Fletcher, T. B., & Hurley, S. (2016). Positive psychology in counseling: Integrating sport as a framework for performance enhancement. In J. K. Edwards, A. Young, & H. J. Nikels (Eds.), *Handbook of Strengths-Based Clinical Practices: Finding Common Factors* (pp. 207–226). Routledge.

Gardner, M., & Steinberg, L. (2005). Peer influence on risk taking, risk preference, and risky decision making in adolescence and adulthood: An experimental study. *Developmental Psychology, 41*(4), 625–635.

Gass, M. A. (1993). *Adventure therapy: Therapeutic applications of adventure programming.* The Association for Experiential Education.

Gladding, S. T. (2016). *The creative arts in counseling* (5th ed.). American Counseling Association.

Hecker, L., Lettenberger, C., Nedela, M., & Soloski, K. L. (2010). The body tells the story: Using art to facilitate children's narratives. *Journal of Creativity in Mental History, 5*(2), 192–203.

Kohlberg, L. (1983). The development of children's orientations toward a moral order. In W. Damon (Ed.), *Social and Personality Development: Essays on the Growth of the Child* (pp. 388–407). W. W. Norton & Company.

Kolb, A. Y., & Kolb, D. A. (2005). Learning styles and learning spaces: Enhancing experiential learning in higher education. *Academy of Management Learning & Education, 4*(2), 193–212.

Kolb, A. Y., & Kolb, D. A. (2009). The learning way: Meta-cognitive aspects of experiential learning. *Simulation & Gaming, 40*(3), 297–327.

Kolb, A. Y., Kolb, D. A., Passarelli, A., & Sharma, G. (2014). On becoming and experiential educator: The educator role profile. *Simulation & Gaming, 45*(2), 204–234.

Kolb, D. (2015). *Experiential learning: Experience as the source of learning and development* (2nd ed.). Pearson Education Ltd.

Kolb, D., Boyatzis, R., & Mainemelis, C. (2001). Experiential learning theory: Previous research and new directions. In R. J. Sternberg & L. F. Zhang (Eds.), *Perspectives on Thinking, Learning, and Cognitive Styles* (pp. 193–210). Lawrence Erlbaum Associates.

Landreth, G. L. (2012). *Play therapy: The art of the relationship* (3rd ed.). Routledge.

Lewin, K. (1948). Conduct, knowledge, and acceptance of new values. In G. W. Lewin & G. W. Allport (Eds.), *Resolving social conflicts: Selected papers on group dynamics* (pp. 48–55). Harper & Row.

Lewin, K. (1951). *Field theory in social science: Selected theoretical papers.* Harper & Brothers.

Maimonides, M. (n.d.). *The Guide of the Perplexed.* Trans. Shlomo Pines. University of Chicago Press.

McAuliffe, G. J., & Eriksen, K. (1999). Toward a constructivist and developmental identity for the counseling profession: The context-phase-stage-style model. *Journal of Counseling & Development, 77*, 267–280.

Murphy, L. B., & Moriarty, A. E. (1976). *Vulnerability, coping, and growth from infancy to adolescence.* Yale University Press.

Murrell, P. H., & Claxton, C. S. (1987). Experiential learning theory as a guide for effective teaching. *Counselor Education and Supervision, 27*(1), 4–14.

Nadler, R. S., & Luckner, J. L. (1992). *Processing the adventure experience.* Kendall/Hunt.

Park, N. (2004). The role of subjective well-being in positive youth development. *The ANNALS of the American Academy of Political and Social Science, 591*(1), 25–39.

Park, N., & Peterson, C. (2006). Moral competence and character strengths among adolescents: The development and validation of the values in action inventory of strengths for youth. *Journal of Adolescence, 29*(6), 891–909.

Park, N., & Peterson, C. (2008). Positive psychology and character strengths: Application to strengths-based school counseling. *Professional School Counseling, 12*(2), 85–92.

Payne, P. G. (2006). Environmental education and curriculum theory. *The Journal of Environmental Education, 37*(2), 25–35.

Pereira, J. K. (2014). Can we play too? Experiential techniques for family therapists to actively include children in sessions. *The Family Journal, 22*(4), 390–396.

Piaget, J. (1973). *To understand is to invent: The future of education.* Grossman Publishers.

Piaget, J. (1978). *Success and understanding.* Harvard University Press.

Piaget, J. (1983). *The child's conception of the world.* Rowman & Allanheld.

Piaget, J. (1999). *Judgment and reasoning in the child.* Routledge.

Prout, H. T., & Fedewa, A. L. (2015). Counseling and psychotherapy with children and adolescents: Historical, developmental, integrative, and effectiveness perspectives. In H. T. Prout & A. L. Fedewa (Eds.), *Counseling and Psychotherapy with Children and Adolescents: Theory and Practice for School and Clinical Settings* (pp. 1–24). Wiley.

Ray, D. C. (2011). *Advanced play therapy: Essential conditions, knowledge, and skills for child practice.* Routledge.

Rice, K., Girvin, H., & Primak, S. (2014). Engaging adolescent youth in foster care through photography. *Child Care in Practice, 20*(1), 37–47.

Russo, M. F., Vernam, J., & Wolbert, A. (2006). Sandplay and storytelling: Social constructivism and cognitive development in child counseling. *The Arts in Psychotherapy, 33*, 229–237.

Scales, P. C., Benson, P. L., Leffert, N., & Blyth, D. A. (2000). Contribution of developmental assets to the prediction of thriving among adolescents. *Applied Developmental Science, 4*(1), 27–46.

Schaefer, C. E., & Peabody, M. A. (2016). Glossary of play therapy terms. *Play Therapy, 11*(2), 20–24.

Schneider, S. L., & Caffray, C. M. (2012). Affective motivators and experience in adolescents' development of health-related behavior patterns. In V. F. Reyna, S. B. Chapman, M. R. Dougherty, & J. Confrey (Eds.), *The Adolescent Brain: Learning Reasoning, and Decision Making* (pp. 291–335). American Psychological Association.

Seligman, M. E. P. (2011). *Learned optimism: How to change your mind and your life.* Vintage Books.

Seligman, M. E. P., & Csikszentmihalyi, M. (2000). Positive psychology: An introduction. *American Psychologist, 55*(1), 5–14.

Taylor, E. R. (2009). Sandtray and solution-focused therapy. *International Journal of Play Therapy, 18*(1), 56–68.

Turns, B., & Macey, P. (2016). Cinema narrative therapy: Utilizing family films to externalize children's 'problems'. *Journal of Family Therapy, 37*, 590–606.

Tyson, E. H., & Baffour, T. D. (2004). Arts-based strengths: A solution-focused intervention with adolescents in an acute-care psychiatric setting. *The Arts in Psychotherapy, 31*, 213–227.

Veronese, G., Castiglioni, M., & Said, M. (2010). The use of narrative-experiential instruments in contexts of military violence: The case of palestinian children in the west bank. *Counselling Psychology Quarterly, 23*(4), 411–423.

White, M., & Epston, D. (1990). *Narrative means to therapeutic ends.* W. W. Norton & Company.

Wiggins, B. E. (2012). Toward a model for intercultural communication in simulations. *Simulation & Gaming, 43*(4), 550–572.

Wiley, A., & Rappaport, J. (2000). Empowerment, wellness, and the politics of development. In D. Cicchetti, J. Rappaport, I. Sandler, & R. P. Weissberg (Eds.), *The Promotion of Wellness in Children and Adolescents* (pp. 59–99). CWLA Press.

Chapter 3

Successful counseling

Teresa Behrend Fletcher and Melanie J. Richburg

Excellence is an art won by training and habituation. We do not act rightly because we have virtue or excellence, but we rather have those because we acted rightly. We are what we repeatedly do. Excellence, then, is not an act, but a habit.

(Aristotle)

There is no single way for counselors or psychotherapists to succeed in a profession that works differently for everyone. There is no one theory, model, framework, or approach that works for every client which allows clinicians to develop their own process and style that is unique to their strengths and abilities. If the client is performing better and/or resolving issues impeding healthy functioning, we may consider their counseling experience a success. Effective clinicians working from a systematic framework, or habit, will contribute to positive change for clients, particularly in the long term. In writing a book about best practices for counseling children and adolescents, it became imperative that we examine both the clinical skills and process of being successful in our work that can be adapted by a diverse group of mental health professionals and client populations. It makes sense, then, to integrate Successful Intelligence into the counseling process when forming and establishing proficiency within that systematic framework. As such, Successful Intelligence (Sternberg, 1997; Sternberg & Kaufman, 1998) is used as a framework to inform the process by which we develop proficiency in our profession. To build a successful counseling practice lends itself to developing a *culture of excellence*.

Successful Intelligence can be defined as the ability to achieve one's goals in life, given one's sociocultural context; by capitalizing on strengths and correcting or compensating for weaknesses; in order to adapt to, shape, and select environments; and through a combination of analytical, creative, and practical abilities (Sternberg, 1997; 2005). Successful counseling will then be described through the framework of analytical intelligence, creative intelligence, and practical intelligence to promote the concept of excellence in counseling as a habit when working with children and adolescents.

The process of counseling essentially lies in problem-solving methodology. Clients come to counseling with "presenting problems" and clinicians then work to promote change to alleviate negative or unpleasant symptoms and improve functioning for a more satisfying life experience (Table 3.1).

Analytical intelligence

Parents, as a primary source of information regarding the presenting problem, may not be accurate or complete in their knowledge, understanding, and interpretation of events. Similarly, children and adolescents may not have the capacity to define or accurately and comprehensively communicate their struggles. In fact, a typical referral includes behavior(s) that are problematic, inferring that a behavioral intervention will alleviate negative

Table 3.1 Six-step problem-solving model applied to the counseling process and the corresponding intelligence

Six-Step Problem-Solving Model	Counseling Process	Successful Intelligence
Recognition	Presenting problem/assessment	Analytical
Definition	Assessment/diagnosis/conceptualization	Analytical/creative
Formulating strategy	Conceptualization/hypothesis	Creative
Representing information	Conceptualization/treatment planning	Creative/practical
Allocating resources	Treatment strategies and implementation	Practical
Monitoring and evaluation	Treatment/evaluation	Practical/analytical

DOI: 10.4324/9781315213767-4

symptoms…problem solved. However, mental health professionals understand that the root cause of these behaviors is complex and multidimensional and requires a vast amount of knowledge and skill to accurately differentiate symptom from problem, contributing factor from cause, and the evolution of how a situation can go from bad to worse when left untreated or unresolved.

The information-gathering process includes a formal intake process as well as an application of knowledge and an understanding of child development or the ability to process information to analyze, evaluate, judge, or compare and contrast, which is also known as analytical intelligence (Sternberg, 2005). Developmental models, theories, and frameworks serve to inform and provide context for expectations regarding behavior and identify potential conflicts. A summary of some of these models is included in the table to emphasize the multidimensionality of development during childhood and adolescence (see Appendix A). Developmental limitations and conflicts, life circumstances during childhood and adolescence, and adaptive abilities will be described as a means to develop clinical conceptualization skills and enhance analytical intelligence.

Child and adolescent development

We identify developmental norms as a way to provide context for expectations and establish milestones. Many children do not develop all parts of themselves at the same rate, and consequently, they do not develop at the same pace as their peers. External and environmental stressors can further complicate healthy development when kids have more challenges in life than they have skills to manage and cope. When this happens consistently and over a long period of time, development can get substantially delayed. If we look at the concept of normal distribution as an example of context, 68% of children will typically fall within the average or normal range, leaving 16% developmentally ahead or 16% developmentally behind at any given time (Figure 3.1).

Developmental limitations and conflicts

All children will (and should) experience some form of adversity but they will vary in how they perceive, process, and approach a challenge. For example, the identification of a problem may depend on their analytical skills or cognitive ability. Their ability to acknowledge their strengths and use those to their advantage may depend on their sense of self-worth or psychological development. Their ability to engage in communicating with peers and adults may depend on their personality or social development. Their ability to understand how others may perceive them may depend on their environment or physical, sexual, or cultural development. Their ability to manage emotions (intrapersonal skill), engage with others (interpersonal skills), adjust to challenges (coping skills) and implement solutions may depend on an intermingled set of factors interacting together within a particular time and space.

Developmental analysis can consist of acknowledging the concept of nature vs. nurture as described in Chapter 2. Children are born with genetic predispositions (i.e., physical attributes, personality) and then function in environments where they learn to use what they have OR develop strategies to adapt to situations to meet their needs. For example, schoolchildren of average intelligence may accept average grades OR adapt study habits, get tutoring, or change to a different learning environment to exceed educational goals. Cognitive ability (nature) does not

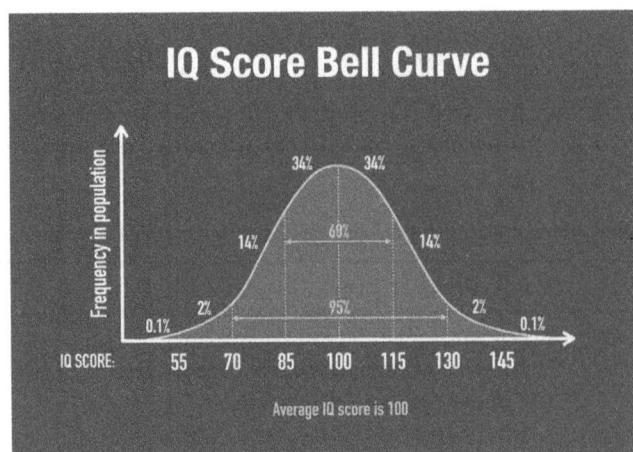

Figure 3.1 Developmentally typical intelligence distribution.

necessarily determine success as much as how they learn to utilize (nurture) their gifts (Sternberg, 1997). Children who meet developmental expectations learn to become aware of strengths and limitations (intrapersonal skills), find a way to relate to peers (interpersonal skills), and manage life circumstances (coping/solution-focused skills) with a healthy balance of challenge, failure, and success. Conversely, these well-adjusted kids aren't the ones who come to counseling. Developmental challenges are presented below to demonstrate analytical intelligence, or conceptualization skills, as they pertain to understanding both symptoms and associated skill development utilizing the Positive Psychology (Seligman & Csikszentmihalyi, 2000) framework presented in Chapter 2.

Developmental delays or shortcomings

Children who experience developmental delays or limitations without skills or an environment conducive to skill development are more typical counseling clients. A child who presents in counseling lagging behind peers may be at risk for developing a multitude of problems. For example, a child or adolescent with a learning disability will need to find strategies or activities to build confidence (intrapersonally) or risk internalizing feelings of inadequacy. An introverted adolescent who is home-school will need to be involved in activities with peers outside of the home to develop social skills (interpersonal) or risk feelings of loneliness and isolation. Physically challenged or disabled children and adolescents will need an inclusive environment (solution-focused) or risk isolating themselves (coping) from able-bodied children.

Developmentally advanced

Children and adolescents ahead of peers in developmental areas can also experience challenges. Adolescents, particularly those who mature physically and reach puberty earlier than their peers, may appear older and encounter incongruous interactions (i.e., sexual advances, responsibilities) based on appearance and do not have the skills to respond appropriately (interpersonally) or act on inappropriate expectations (coping). Gifted children can experience a lack of challenge in the classroom (intrapersonal), learn not to communicate boredom (interpersonal), particularly when "rewarded" with more work when finishing early, or lose motivation to learn (intrapersonal), thus failing to complete assignments and engage in school (coping).

Exceeding developmental milestones in one area may contribute to a lack of progress in another, or compensating and overcompensating over time can lead to fatigue or deficits. Those children and adolescents who show advanced kinesthetic (i.e., athletic) ability may experience so much success early and receive attention and positive reinforcement for performance that they can experience stress and burnout (intrapersonal), become fearful of consequences and not express thoughts or feelings (interpersonal), and engage even more in training and competition (coping), resulting in injury or unhealthy behaviors. These children may also be discouraged from engaging in activities outside their expertise where they can learn to experience inadequacy and accept failure (coping). These children may appear successful; however, experiencing success in one area may lead to stereotypes that they are proficient in many areas and should be happy while subjective experiences or any struggles, problems, or negative feelings are invalidated and subsequently suppressed (coping).

Perception of abilities and strengths

Environmental factors can influence how children and adolescents perceive their strengths, particularly when inconsistent with interests. Children can internalize feelings of inferiority or be treated as a disappointment by peers, teachers, coaches, leaders, and even their parents. A tall person who is not athletic or isn't interested in playing basketball may be perceived as a "waste of height." An intellectually gifted adolescent who enjoys woodworking and isn't interested in pursuing a college degree may be treated as a failure. A child who shows a natural talent for music but does not enjoy practicing or performing may be subjected to constant pressure to pursue any and all musical endeavors. It becomes imperative for counselors to be mindful of the notion that just because children or adolescents have an exceptional ability does not mean they acknowledge it as a strength.

Within normal limits falls short

It is worth mentioning that even children and adolescents who fall "within normal limits" of development can also experience difficulty and pressure to excel. In a world with "tiger moms" and "sport dads" or helicopter parents, children and adolescents are encouraged more and more to specialize in an activity and devote at least 10,000 hours as quickly as possible to achieve more and more at younger ages (Gladwell, 2008). This pressure to exceed developmental milestones can be beneficial to learning certain life skills such as setting and pursuing goals, self-discipline, or persistence. However, as development is interrelated, overdevelopment in one area can lead to underdevelopment in others.

Children may not develop an openness to taking opportunities to pursue a range of interests (intrapersonal), interact with peers of varying interests and abilities (interpersonal), or learn to enjoy activities without having the pressure to excel (coping). For example, a ten-year-old who receives an offer for a collegiate football scholarship may be perceived as successful, entitled, or privileged. However, in reality, children are encouraged to over-train, resulting in over-use and career-ending injuries at higher rates than ever before. Kids are discouraged from participating in other age-appropriate activities and can experience intense pressure with long-term consequences. Overall healthy development is a balance that is accomplished over a long period of time while counselors may need to advocate for the balance of long-term health and happiness (delayed gratification) with short-term accomplishments (instant gratification).

Some children may need to learn adaptive skills ahead of the developmental curve to manage life situations or family circumstances which may include military deployment of a parent, illness, grief, divorce, abuse, family transitions, or other hardships. Children and adolescents also experience developmental challenges as a result of systemic or societal influences which show a lack of respect, understanding, or acceptance of individual differences. These children are at risk for being discriminated based on religion or spirituality, sexuality, race, ethnicity or national origin, gender identity, ability (or disability), language, and culture. Children may need to develop self-awareness of emotions and thoughts surrounding traumatic events or tragic circumstances (intrapersonal) and express feelings or communicate needs to caregivers (interpersonal). They may need to become more assertive (coping) to remain safe while taking on more responsibility, forcing them to mature faster than their respective peers (solution-focused). Mental health professionals can be supportive in providing a safe environment to learn and practice skills while validating subjective experiences. Further, activism for this at-risk population is needed to influence systemic change as well as empower those who are limited in their ability to advocate for themselves.

School or educational settings

Many children referred for counseling services have difficulty in school. When academic success is defined by high grades and test scores, children who do not fit into that limited framework of intelligence can find meaning and value outside of those narrow confines. Kids can always benefit from exploring and developing strengths outside of school, engaging with peers who share similar interests, and working toward fun, fulfillment, or mastery in other areas of life. The incompatibility between learner and environment has necessitated exploration into education reform, such as the theory of multiple intelligences developed by Gardner (1983; 1993), where intelligence is reframed to be more than cognitive ability to include genetic inheritance, training, and socialization of cultural values (Gardner, 1993). Reframing the concept of being "smart" to include linguistic, logical/mathematical, spatial, musical, bodily kinesthetic, intrapersonal, and interpersonal intelligences can help in reducing stigmas related to cognitive limitations that contribute to psychological problems for children and stigmatized adults. Further changes to learning environment can be explored (i.e., online programs, private schools, public/specialized school, or home-schooling) as a means to meet educational requirements.

When schools or programs are not accessible or are not compatible with the needs of a diverse learning population, or when resources for success in schools are limited, children and adolescents may have to develop advanced skills in other areas to be validated and find meaning. However, these decisions on choosing an educational environment need not come at the cost of other developmental needs to falsely promote adequacy (poor performance is the teacher's fault), avoid conflict (the first resort when experiencing bullying), or change schools every time there is a problem (coping). Oftentimes in these situations, children fail to develop healthy intra- and interpersonal skills, which creates a deficit in the ability to solve problems or cope with a prolonged detrimental situation, which necessitates a referral for counseling. Seemingly simple or developmentally appropriate tasks can be overwhelming for children and adolescents who are struggling and life can quickly become all about survival rather than growth.

The ability to obtain these life skills given developmental considerations has a lasting impact on how kids perceive themselves, interact with others, manage adversity, or even implement change and pursue new endeavors. As development during childhood and adolescence changes drastically, so does the need to expand intra- and interpersonal skills, and coping or solution-focused skills to manage perceptions, differences, and needs. Development is multidimensional and interrelated, or contains a complex interaction of factors that contribute to healthy functioning. These developmental theories assist mental health professionals in assessing strengths and identifying challenges and needs to promote accurate and comprehensive conceptualization skills, or analytical intelligence. Thus, the next challenge is to personalize therapeutic interventions to engage with children and adolescents through the development of creative intelligence.

Creative intelligence

The concept of using creativity in counseling is not necessarily new and innovative as evidenced by articles (e.g., Carson, 1999; Sternberg & Lubart, 1996) and books (i.e., Csikszentmihalyi, 2013; Gladding, 2016), as well as organizations such as the *Association for Creativity in Counseling* division of the American Counseling Association. When mental health professionals use creativity in their interactions and interventions, they co-construct emotional experiences for their clients thus contributing to positive change by making therapy engaging, fun, memorable, and an overall good experience (Duffey et al., 2009). Promoting creativity requires a definition specific to the counseling profession as well as the traits and skills counselors can develop. The creative process can facilitate how to be "live" in the moment, run with an idea, and reach a "flow" state (Csikszentmihalyi, 1997).

Creativity tends to be defined differently based on the discipline and the result or "product," which is measured against the norms of that domain or its own rules, approaches, or outcomes (Reid & Petocz, 2004). Artistic creativity reflects expression of inner needs, perceptions, and motivations while scientific and technological creativity deals with novel solutions for existing problems. A hybrid creativity exhibits both personality and expression with novel problem-solving (MacKinnon, 2017). In counseling, the product tends to be related to an experience that gives a client insight OR a different way for clinicians to interact or conduct the counseling session to build rapport, establish therapeutic norms, and promote client change. Creativity has no barriers with regard to gender, age, ability, culture, or ethnicity and promotes new and unique ways to have a positive impact on client well-being and how clinicians can be more engaging and effective in their work with individuals, couples, and families (Carson & Becker, 2004). Further, creativity lends itself to identifying client strengths and co-constructing meaningful interventions within sessions to take advantage of moment-to-moment experiences (Carson & Becker, 2004).

Creative traits and skills

Csikszentmihalyi (2013) differentiates creative individuals from others by describing them as complex, or containing contradictory poles that involve the ability to move from one extreme to the other as an occasion or situation requires. This adaptability is useful when generating ideas within counseling and also in the finesse or delivery of the intervention. For example, caring confrontations can be soft and gentle or assertive and humorous. I once worked with a client who was a big fan of Star Wars. While I believe we both quickly became frustrated with a lack of progress, rather than being gentle and accepting a lack of effort to engage in different behaviors with multiple and creative excuses, I did my best Yoda impression: "Do or do not. There is no try." Csikszentmihalyi (2013) has identified ten opposing traits present in individuals and integrated within the counseling field (see Table 3.2).

Mental health professionals can work to expand on traits to become more creative clinicians even when the aforementioned traits are not naturally present. Hecker and Kottler (2002) conceptualized that creativity, although not emphasized in clinical training, is a skill that can be taught, learned, and improved over time. Training counselors to expand on their natural tendencies and traits and engage in the creative process then becomes the central focus of this chapter and book as well as a necessity to becoming a successful counselor or clinician.

Given that creativity can be discipline-specific, reviewing the creative process can also be open for interpretation. The creative process has been explored as a process in therapy with different stages of intervention, including four critical steps (Carson & Becker, 2004), five steps (Csikszentmihalyi, 1997), or six steps (Witmer, 1985; see Table 3.3).

All aforementioned processes include the first two steps of preparation and incubation. Preparation can be considered the time when information is acquired or even becoming immersed in a problem. As such, this could also be consistent with the development of analytical intelligence. Knowledge can be collected over time, as is the case with various theories, frameworks, models, and approaches to counseling, along with the historical and contextual information provided by the client during the intake and/or assessment process. Incubation is the process of leaving the problem to shift focus to other things, which allows the brain to take a break from working on a problem or solution. This period of shifting focus to something unrelated is important; however, theorists are not exactly sure why. One explanation allows the unimportant details of a problem to leave our active memory, thus allowing us to focus on more important aspects of a problem and view it from a different perspective. Further, as time passes, we are open to new stimuli which alter our perception (Sternberg, 1997).

Table 3.2 Opposing traits present in individuals

Traits of Creative Individuals (Csikszentmihalyi, 2013)	Cultivating the Dichotomous Interaction in Counseling
Creative individuals have physical energy, but take time for quiet and rest.	Physical activity and passion create energy while quiet reflection and rest help balance and rejuvenate. Be active, then be quiet.
Creative individuals tend to be smart, but also naïve.	Engage in new challenges and learning new things to stay humble and hungry for knowledge. The new-ness of approaching a challenge helps relate to client learning new skills.
Creative individuals combine playfulness with discipline or responsibility and irresponsibility.	The counseling session needs to include the combination of fun and enjoyment (i.e., games, activities) along with the discipline (i.e., skill development).
Creative individuals alternate between realism and optimism or even fantasy.	Clinicians understand that children operate within limits relative to their environment, yet promote the generation of fantasy and optimism that their reality or at least their perception of it can change with imagination.
Creative individuals express both extroversion and introversion, at the same time.	The creative process is a delicate balance between solitary self-reflection and interacting with peers and others to develop and evolve ideas.
Creative individuals are both humble and proud at the same time.	The balance between success and what it takes to achieve it while also understanding that the client struggling tomorrow doesn't really care how brilliant you were yesterday.
Creative individuals escape rigid gender role stereotyping	Work toward balance with all clients—aggressive and nurturing, sensitive and rigid, assertive and submissive developing strengths associated with all genders.
Creative individuals tend to be rebellious and independent.	Learn the parameters in which to function, but work toward pushing limits to challenge both yourself and your clients.
Creative individuals are passionate and objective about their work.	Become part of your work, yet be able to detach from it to develop objectivity.
Creativity requires openness and sensitivity and therefore they are exposed to suffering and pain as well as enjoyment and elation.	We learn more from our failures than our successes, so it is imperative to reflect on what doesn't work in our practice and use that as motivation to figure out what will work.

Table 3.3 Commonalities among all models

Creative Problem-Solving Carson and Becker (2004)	The Creative Process Csikszentmihalyi (1997)	Process of Creativity Witmer (1985)
Preparation	Preparation	Preparation
Incubation	Incubation	Incubation
Inspiration	Insight	Ideation
Verification	Evaluation	Illumination
	Elaboration	Evaluation
		Verification/production

Although the incubation period can last as little as a few minutes or hours to as long as months or years, ideation and illumination or insight typically follow. During this period, both divergent and convergent thinking contribute to evolving an insight or idea to fruition. This stage requires most of the work in order to evaluate whether or not the creative endeavor will be successful and how to evaluate the outcome. In counseling, it is important to remember that even when creative interventions don't appear to be successful, the information gained as a result of trying something new is valuable. Cycling through the process again is necessary as new information can then trigger incubation to create a more cyclical process rather than a linear one (Csikszentmihalyi, 1997).

Creativity in the counseling profession involves the person (traits) as well as the process and culminates in the product, which can be considered the change within the client or the relationship (Carson & Becker, 2004). Ironically, a creative person following the creative process can still have an unsuccessful outcome. For example, I once had a 7 year-old boy who expressed fears of snakes and requested to make a "snake trap" so that he wouldn't be afraid anymore (Fletcher, 2000). As I consider myself a fairly creative person, I constructed a very technical, yet metaphorical "snake trap" so that he might be able to sleep better, confront his fears, and hopefully reduce bed-wetting incidents. As a graduate student, I was commended for my creative intervention and was even proud of my ingenuity. The immediate results were promising after introducing the trap along with specific instructions, but they were short-lived. The panic that followed this perceived failure resulted in conceptualizing multiple fears (rather than one specific fear – snakes) that created a more comprehensive intervention to re-structure the role of the parent to be more protective, thus alleviating my client being fearful (Fletcher, 2000).

I clearly remember that moment of feeling discouraged when I was informed that my client had regressed. I took a moment to feel the disappointment, both within myself and for my client. However, the important lesson was to reframe the failure as a new, important piece of information in my conceptualization and treatment strategies. The creativity of the intervention was not as important as the practical implementation of both the snake trap and the continuing effort to work toward the product or goal of counseling. Creative interventions need to ultimately result in positive change, which can be achieved through pragmatism, or practical intelligence.

Practical intelligence

When we think of individuals as being "smart," we often consider an academic description associated with grades, degrees, or success within a formal education setting. Contrary to academic knowledge, the acquisition of tacit knowledge, or action-oriented knowledge, appears to be more important to real-world endeavors. Tacit knowledge is about doing rather than knowing how to do something, particularly in how to reach goals and achieve them, and it is typically acquired with little help from others (Sternberg, 1997). "It is the knowledge that reflects the practical ability to learn from experience [learn by doing] and to apply that knowledge in pursuit of personally valued goals" (Sternberg, 1997, p. 104). Tacit knowledge also influences practical intelligence, which is described as common sense or as a social intelligence with the ability to select, shape, and adapt to everyday environments (Sternberg, 2000).

Tacit knowledge, a main tenet of practical intelligence, has more to do with intuition or instinct and can be difficult to teach, learn, or express in a concrete or logical manner. Envision Michael Jordan on a basketball court and ask him how he does what he does. Most likely, he won't be able to provide a thorough explanation of his thoughts or actions as he simply performed. In the sport world, we call this "court sense" or describe an athlete as having a good "soccer brain" or a high "hockey IQ." Perceptual-cognitive skills, or the ability to "read and react" is required within the counseling profession, thereby making practical intelligence necessary to successful counseling.

I remember one of my first assignments in a developmental course during my master's program, which necessitated an interview with an adolescent. I met with my interviewee on the basketball court and played a game of H-O-R-S-E, where we took turns trying to make baskets from various locations around the court. Every once in a while, I made a comment or asked a question, but nothing too scripted or rigid...just enough to cover the assignment. In the meantime, we had some fun and what I considered a good conversation. I checked in with his caregivers to thank them for their time, unknowing at the time that they were unaware of his struggles, thoughts, and emotions that he readily shared with me on the court. I went home and wrote the paper, not really thinking anything of it other than completing an assignment. I didn't realize until later that I was unconventional in my interview compared to my classmates. When I got my paper back, my professor asked to speak with me...in true form, my first reaction was to think I did the assignment wrong by not sitting down in an office for a more formal interview. Contrary to my fear, he asked, "How did you know to play basketball?" Ummmm....I didn't really think about why, I just did it. I attributed my interview choice to common sense. What else would you do to get information from a kid? Apparently, I was the only one who took this approach, which yielded a much more in-depth and meaningful description of the client and my experience, thus exceeding expectations. I think back over 20 years ago and the memory of my professor questioning how I knew to grab the basketball, and I still can't describe it other than to now attribute it to practical intelligence.

Practical intelligence can be divided into two different skill sets that include practical problem-solving and practical intellectual skills. Each can be differentiated from academic situations where problems are presented in a more linear fashion, are well-defined, and typically characterized with one correct answer or method of obtaining the right answer. Conversely, a practical problem tends to exist in real life or be related to everyday experiences with no clear definition, being characterized by multiple solutions and various consequences with a possible best option available rather than a correct or right answer (Sternberg, 2000). The ability to utilize intellect to identify and implement the best solution to these practical problems is considered practical intellectual skills. Further, higher-level constructs associated with practical intelligence include wisdom and intuition (Sternberg, 2000).

Intuition operationalized can be described as what leads individuals to action with reasoning that is difficult to explain or knowing without being able to provide a logical explanation of how we know (Goldberg, 1983; Vaughan, 1979). Counselors use intuition when developing and implementing treatment strategies to determine *how* to best engage with clients, build rapport, use humor, introduce concepts, challenge schemas, deliver feedback, initiate skill development, or sequence sessions to meet goals. Wisdom seems to increase over the lifespan and includes knowledge, process, judicial thinking style, personality, motivation, and environmental context (Sternberg, 2000). For the purposes of counseling, wisdom can influence *how* we conduct ourselves as professionals and apply the knowledge and experience that is acquired over time. Wise counselors use intuition and employ *finesse* in our delivery of directives based on a myriad of experiences accumulated over time. Practical intelligence in counseling then is the ability to make a plan, read and react, then cope and adjust in a moment-to-moment, high-stress environment...and do it consistently well.

Counseling includes a series of failures, successes, and opportunities to learn and improve the quality of work as well as the efficiency in how we deliver services. The acquisition of knowledge and information regarding understanding human behavior and promoting change is ongoing. The ability to reflect on experiences and learn from counseling experiences creates insight and these lessons learned present an opportunity to enhance our intelligence for successful counseling. Some counseling professionals may argue that successful counseling is based on a continuous, lifelong process of accumulating knowledge for analytical intelligence, collecting ideas and interventions for creative intelligence, and actively counseling with reflection for practical intelligence. Mental health professionals become proficient in their craft by following the same model as their clients by improving both intra- and interpersonal skills, as well as coping and solution-focused skills. Counselors are in a constant state of monitoring their own well-being (intrapersonal), utilizing their resources to check-in and consult (interpersonally), and engaging in self-care strategies (coping) and continuing education (solution-focused) for long-term health and success in both personal and professional development. It takes effort and energy to promote change, so finding positive energy in the work can influence our success and longevity.

One of the most common traits associated with creativity is divergent thinking which is characterized by originality along with flexibility in producing many possible new ideas or solutions or redefining the problem to generate the flow of ideas (Gomez, 2007). So, mental health professionals who only subscribe to a specific theoretical orientation may be missing out on creativity as this is more along the lines of convergent thinking, or the understanding that there is one solution. The results of creativity enrich the culture and improve the quality of life for our clients as well as ourselves as clinicians. Creativity makes our job more interesting and productive as we have the flexibility to adapt strengths of our clients to our own strengths and co-construct a meaningful experience, consistently over time and can begin with a basic understanding of our own individual learning styles.

Individual learning styles

The Experiential Learning Cycle as part of Experiential Learning Theory provides a four-stage model to guide individuals with different learning styles in gaining meaning from experiences (Kolb, 2015; Kolb et al., 2001, 2014). Based on learning style, an individual will develop meaning through the resolution of creative tension and through navigating the Experiential Learning Cycle. Considering the developmental and individualized conceptualization of growth within Experiential Learning Theory, it would be incongruent to assume all individuals make meaning through an identical process (Kolb et al., 2014). Based on each individual's unique learning process, learning styles describe the ideal learning process which corresponds with phases of the Experiential Learning Cycle (Kolb & Kolb, 2005). According to Kolb and Kolb (2005), the basic learning styles are convergent, divergent, assimilation, and accommodative (see Table 3.4).

Table 3.4 Four basic experiential learning styles described within Experiential Learning Theory (Kolb, 2015; Kolb & Kolb, 2005)

Learning Style	Learner Strengths	Dominant Learning Abilities	Examples of Activities
Convergent (doing and thinking)	Problem-solving, decision-making, practical application of content	Generalizing, applying	Role-playing or using puppets to act out different scenarios
Accommodative (doing and feeling)	Action-oriented, open to new experiences, takes risks	Experiencing, applying	Science experiments testing different theories to get a desired outcome
Divergent (feeling and watching)	Imaginative, connection to meaning and values, brainstorming	Experiencing, reflecting	Creating through art or sand trays to represent experiences through metaphor
Assimilation (watching and thinking)	Inductive reasoning, theoretical thinking, generating explanation from experience	Generalizing, reflecting	Use of puzzles or board games to talk about problem-solving

Kolb (2015) described convergent styles as students who excel in the generalizing and applying phases of experiential learning. Convergent learners are thinkers and doers and naturally excel in problem-solving and practical application of content. These individuals prefer to consider the possibilities, but find a single solution. This client may become frustrated with the lack of a clear solution to problems. They naturally grow through opportunities to experiment, trying out new ideas in a practical way to find solutions to problems. An activity useful with a convergent client would be acting out different scenarios, allowing the client to manipulate different variables to try out different strategies for problem-solving. For example, a counselor may use puppets or toys to have the client act out different possibilities.

Accommodative learners excel in experiencing and applying. These individuals are naturally action-oriented and reactive, are doers and feelers, and prefer hands-on activities using an experiential and practical approach to counseling. This client will ask for instructions and advice from the counselor, preferring the analysis of others to their own. However, these clients are naturally intuitive and can create meaning through adaptation to the environment and experimentation. They also excel in collaborative group experiences. As this client enjoys taking risks and trying new things, the counselor may bring science experiments to the counseling session, allowing the client to play with different possibilities in a supported environment.

Divergent learners excel in experiencing and reflecting phases of experiential learning. These clients excel at feeling and watching. These imaginative individuals have a natural propensity for connecting experience with meaning and values. Thus, unlike convergent learners, divergent learners consider multiple possibilities and perspectives. These clients also tend to be more sensitive to emotions and reactions of others. They are naturally interested in the creative process, where counselors may use metaphor through art or sand trays to explore the client's perspective.

Similar to convergent learners, assimilative individuals prefer to focus on facts, ideas, and abstract concepts and may be naturally drawn to the generalizing and reflecting phases of the learning cycle. Assimilative clients may not easily describe emotions and tend to value ideas more than relationships with others. These children may also insist upon clear explanations for each aspect of counseling, needing to understand why the counselor uses certain activities. For example, these individuals may prefer structured activities with logical rules such as board games or puzzles. A problem-solving approach through metaphor using such activities allows the client to use logic and reasoning.

Learning styles contribute to identifying client strengths, which serves as a starting point for the counseling process. Further, integrating a variety of learning styles, regardless of preference, can advance skill development in areas that present deficits for a more well-rounded treatment strategy. In fact, children can benefit from new experiences that provide a variety of challenges to promote adaptability and confidence. In other words, they learn they don't have to be good at everything, thus embracing both strengths and challenges while consistently engaging in the skill-building process to contribute to a healthy and positive sense of self even in the most stressful situations. The ability of the counselor to initiate teachable moments through experiential activities is the basis for *meaning making*.

References

Aristotle (n.d.). *Poetics*. Trans. Hackett Publishing Company.

Carson, D. K. (1999). The importance of creativity in family therapy: A preliminary consideration. *Family Journal, 7*(4), 326–334.

Carson, D. K., & Becker, K. W. (2004). When lightning strikes: Reexamining creativity in psychotherapy. *Journal of Counseling & Development, 82*, 111–115.

Csikszentmihalyi, M. (1997). Happiness and creativity. *The Futurist, 31*(5), 8–12.

Csikszentmihalyi, M. (2013). *Creativity: The psychology of discovery*. Harper Perennial.

Duffey, T., Haberstroh, S., & Trepal, H. (2009). A grounded theory of relational competencies and creativity in counseling: Beginning the dialogue. *Journal of Creativity in Mental Health, 4*(2), 89–112.

Fletcher, T. B. (2000). Primary nocturnal enuresis: A structural and strategic family systems approach. *Journal of Mental Health Counseling, 22*(1), 32–44.

Gardner, H. (1983). *Frames of mind: The theory of multiple intelligences*. Basic Books.

Gardner, H. (1993). *Multiple intelligences: The theory in practice*. Basic Books.

Gladding, S. T. (2016). *The creative arts in counseling* (5th ed.). American Counseling Association.

Gladwell, M. (2008). *Outliers: The story of success*. Little Brown and Company.

Goldberg, P. (1983). *The intuitive edge*. Tarcher.

Gomez, J. G. (2007). What do we know about creativity? *Journal of Effective Teaching, 7*(1), 31–43.

Hecker, L. L., & Kottler, J. A. (2002). Growing creative therapists. *Journal of Clinical Activities, Assignments, & Handouts in Psychotherapy Practice, 2*(2), 1–3.

Kolb, A. Y., & Kolb, D. A. (2005). Learning styles and learning spaces: Enhancing experiential learning in higher education. *Academy of Management Learning & Education, 4*(2), 193–212.

Kolb, A. Y., Kolb, D. A., Passarelli, A., & Sharma, G. (2014). On becoming and experiential educator: The educator role profile. *Simulation & Gaming, 45*(2), 204–234.

Kolb, D. (2015). *Experiential learning: Experience as the source of learning and development* (2nd ed.). Pearson Education Ltd.

Kolb, D., Boyatzis, R., & Mainemelis, C. (2001). Experiential learning theory: Previous research and new directions. In R. J. Sternberg & L. F. Zhang (Eds.), *Perspectives on Thinking, Learning, and Cognitive Styles* (pp. 193–210). Lawrence Erlbaum Associates.

MacKinnon, D. W. (2017). IPAR's contribution to the conceptualization and study of creativity. In D. W. Mackinnon (Ed.), *Perspectives in Creativity* (pp. 60–89). Routledge.

Reid, A., & Petocz, P. (2004). Learning domains and the process of creativity. *The Australian Educational Researcher, 31*(2), 45–62.

Seligman, M. E. P., & Csikszentmihalyi, M. (2000). Positive psychology: An introduction. *American Psychologist, 55*(1), 5–14.

Sternberg, R. J. (1997). *Successful intelligence: How practical and creative intelligence determine success in life.* Pume.

Sternberg, R. J. (2000). *Handbook of intelligence.* Cambridge University Press.

Sternberg, R. J. (2005). The theory of successful intelligence. *Journal of Psychology, 39*(2), 189–202.

Sternberg, R. J., & Kaufman, J. C. (1998). Human abilities. *Annual Review of Psychology, 49,* 479–502.

Sternberg, R. J., & Lubart, T. I. (1996). Investing in creativity. *Arts in Psychotherapy, 31,* 677–688.

Vaughan, F. E. (1979). *Awakening intuition.* Anchor Press/Doubleday.

Witmer, J. M. (1985). *Pathways to personal growth. Developing a sense of worth and competence: A holistic education approach.* Accelerated Development, Inc.

Chapter 4

Trust the process

Teresa Behrend Fletcher

> If you make listening and observation your occupation you will gain much more than you can by talk.
> (Robert Baden-Powell)

Success in counseling begins with reinforcing the notion that mental health professionals can implement experiential activities within a systematic framework that augments the counseling process. Typically, clinicians receive client information through an intake process that includes a description of the presenting problem, consisting of problematic behaviors, stressful or traumatic life circumstances, and/or clinical diagnoses. This book is structured similarly so that activities are intentionally chosen as applicable to the presenting problem while also being designed to gain interest, engage with clients, and build rapport. When a child or adolescent is referred to counseling, clinicians can begin to conceptualize strengths and interests in the form of skills and deficits as challenges to begin sequencing and planning sessions for long-term skill development.

Accurate and comprehensive clinical conceptualization skills contribute to building a successful treatment plan. When incorporating experiential activities with children and adolescents, this process is best informed by a combination of theoretical constructs derived from strategic family therapy, adventure therapy, and adventure-based counseling. Conceptualization is based on identifying a sequence of events and extrapolating behavioral patterns that inform treatment planning and goals. Activities are then strategically and intentionally chosen in succession (Glass & Shoffner, 2001) and implemented with a level of challenge to promote growth and success (Gass, 1993). Counselor skills are derived from adventure-based counseling to generate opportunities for teachable moments and stimulate insight organically within the counseling session and transfer skills to enhance meaning-making in real life (Fletcher & Hinkle, 2002).

Strategic creativity

Children behave and respond to external stimuli as a means of getting their needs met, which requires clinical skills to interpret behavior enhanced by analytical intelligence. During the initial stages of the counseling process, clinicians formulate an understanding of how difficulties manifest as a sequence of events. The sequence is often repeated to form patterns of functioning whereby counselors can develop a working hypothesis (Haley, 1987) and incorporate interventions designed to test and confirm or gather information to postulate a new hypothesis. While developing an understanding of how events unfold, clinicians begin to accumulate a list of skills that need to be learned, developed, enhanced, or utilized more effectively for clients to be successful. Further, these skills are learned in a distinct order or hierarchy, beginning with intrapersonal skills which contribute to interpersonal skills and influence coping and solution-focused skills (see Table 4.1).

Any third-grade teacher may perceive one child taking another's pencil as common and therefore a random or innocuous event. Due to limitations of the adult (teacher or parent) and environment (school or home), a child's perception of events may be minimized or misunderstood. Discerning the sequence of events is a challenge for clinicians as this type of information may not be observed, distinguished, or reported as the source of the presenting problem. However, clinicians use their own skills of deducing, inferring, and generalizing to identify the sequence or pattern of behaviors rather than tracking the initial source (Haley, 1987). Based on dysfunctional patterns, a hypothesis is generated, tested within the counseling process, and when corroborated, it serves as a basis for skill development. The skills can then be placed in a hierarchical order to create a series of interventions where intrapersonal skills contribute to healthy interpersonal and coping/solution-focused skills to culminate in positive subjective experiences.

DOI: 10.4324/9781315213767-5

Table 4.1 Example of skills development

Event	Patterns	Skills
Two children are working on a project in class and one (whom we'll call a shark) takes the other's pencil (whom we'll call a minnow). The minnow tells the teacher who then tells the minnow to stop talking and complete work. Shark laughs.	Violation of boundaries occurs; adult reinforces negative behaviors	Self-worth, expression of thoughts and feelings, overcoming adversity
The minnow is an introverted child and begins to disengage.	Stops participating when others violate boundaries or rules	Empower, establish boundaries, confidence, assertiveness
The shark then antagonizes the minnow by continuing to take minnow's belongings, making derogatory comments, and is joined by classmates.	Internalizes feelings of helplessness	Seek adult consultation, persistence until situation is changed; identify strengths to problem-solve
Minnow begins to feel weak and ostracized by all classmates and shuts down completely.	Internalizes shame and stops engaging altogether to avoid negative interactions	Resilience, internal locus of control
Parents notice minnow not completing homework and provide natural consequences/punishment, thereby confirming feelings of worthlessness and validating inadequacy.	Lack of understanding of parents presents validation of inadequacy	Communication, problem-solving
Hypothesis: The minnow is swimming along. The shark sees the minnow as a target and capitalizes on easy prey. The minnow can't compete with the shark and tries to stay hidden to avoid all sharks hoping they will eventually move onto another minnow.	Hypothesis: boundary violation (validated by the teacher and later parents) created an opportunity for bullying, and a lack of skills created continuous exploitation of client challenges/weaknesses.	Solution: the minnow needs to feel and act like a whale so the shark will think twice before attacking. Sequence: develop activities to build self-worth, confidence, and feel empowerment to establish boundaries; communicate and express thoughts and feelings; persist in solving problems until the environment is safe.

Generally, professional counselors determine the course of counseling by delineating between the content (what we do) and the process (how we do it) to ensure best practices for success. When it comes to utilizing experiential activities, giving directions or providing directives is fundamental. Directives or tasks with parameters allow an activity to serve as a mechanism to guide clients through a session. Clinicians use observation and inquiry to modify the directives of an activity, develop and substantiate hypotheses, challenge dysfunctional patterns, and assist clients in transferring skills from one setting to another (Erickson et al., 1989; Haley, 1987).

First, directives serve to disrupt unhealthy patterns of behavior and empower clients with options and alternative choices. Ending a session with a directive (i.e., homework) is beneficial for clients to be engaged in the therapeutic process between sessions and holds clients (and potentially parents) accountable to report outcomes that serve to inform future directives. How a client responds to a directive (completes the task with success, forgets, tries and fails, or fails to try) is information the therapist would not have without assigning a task (Erickson et al., 1989; Haley, 1987). Mental health professionals can then explore the difference between ability and willingness to adapt and change. The inability to complete the task exposes additional skills that need to be developed. For example, a failed directive to confront a bully might lead to directives designed to empower a client to develop confidence that may need to precede assertiveness training and confrontation skills. Further, failure to try or complete a task may reveal an unwillingness to change, thereby exposing additional fears or barriers that would not have been explored otherwise.

Executing a directive can best be described as a combination of creative and practical intelligence to include finesse to achieve a favorable response. Clinicians must consider how to implement a directive to optimize the chances of accepting a challenge and successfully completing a task. A counselor's ability to read and react to both verbal and non-verbal cues is essential to developing proficiency in delivering directives, which can be straightforward or more indirect and can include a range of detail and specificity or allow for a more organic or spontaneous experience (Haley, 1987). Clinicians can develop and accumulate a range of techniques to introduce activities as well as invite children and adolescents to be active participants (see Table 4.2).

Table 4.2 Techniques for implementing directives

Technique	Examples of Implementation
Collaboration child/adolescent	"I have an idea, but I'm going to need your assistance because I'm not sure how this will work. Are you up for helping me figure it out?"
Collusion child/adolescent	"I think we need to set up a plan so that there is no other option but for you to get what you want. The trick is you'll have to make some changes and be willing to compromise, so what would you be willing to do initially to make that happen?"
Thinking out loud child/adolescent	"I wonder...what would happen if...?"
Columbo adolescent	"I'm confused...how is it that you're going to lose weight without changing your eating or exercising habits?"
Share the struggle adolescent	"I'm struggling...I have some thoughts that you need to hear, but I'm concerned that I won't be able to say it right. What is the best way to tell you what I'm thinking?"
Client as expert adolescent	"You're the expert on you...what can you do differently to change your situation or what are you willing to do first?"
Caring confrontation adolescent	"I'm concerned about you...I would like to see you be happy and successful. I get the feeling we need to figure out how we can work together. I have some ideas but I don't think they'll work without your help."
Disservice adolescent	"If I don't challenge you, I would be doing you a disservice because my job is to make sure you have all the skills you need to be successful. In order to do my job, you'll also have to do some things differently, so are you willing to try something new?"
The build-up child/adolescent	"I have an idea, but I'm not sure you can do it or that you're ready for it. How much of a challenge can you manage today?"
Metaphor child/adolescent	"Counseling is like building a bridge, so we'll need materials, tools, and instructions for how to put it together. You have all the materials that are called strengths and I have the tools and instructions. If you can bring all your strengths, I'll teach you how to use the tools so we can work together and our bridge will be strong and solid."

The success or failure of a directive is difficult to predict, yet attention to detail can be helpful to eliminate common problems. Asking the client to restate the task will assist in making sure the directive is understood and provide an opportunity to clarify any confusion. Prompting clients to commit to a time as well as how they might go about completing a task allows them to think about potential barriers as well as model solution-focused skills. Finally, asking the client to think of possible distractions that might interfere with the directive diminishes the ability to provide legitimate excuses and helps identify the difference between the inability to perform a task and unwillingness. Directives require clients to engage in different or alternative behaviors to break patterns, which include an appropriate level of challenge and the courage to take a risk and try something new that is best described with concepts from adventure therapy.

Challenge by choice

Children and adolescents will differ in both ability and willingness to engage in the change process. The Circles of Comfort include the comfort, stretch, and panic zones that depict how individuals perceive events and maneuver through life by their willingness to initiate, accept, adapt to, or avoid challenges (Outward Bound, 2007; Vygotsky, 1978). The comfort zone consists of what is familiar or comfortable such as a home, school, neighborhood, or family and friends (Vygotsky, 1978). When children and adolescents are denied challenging opportunities, they will not learn new skills and grow from their experiences, which reinforces learned helplessness (Seligman & Csikszentmihalyi, 2000). The stretch zone acknowledges the discomfort of a new experience or environment while still exhibiting a willingness to move forward with a change, which is ideal for growth (Vygotsky, 1978). Finding the stretch zone, or implementing a state of disequilibrium, is the goal of introducing experiential activities as it allows children and adolescents to be challenged in a way that is conducive to developing skills for success (Fletcher & Hinkle, 2002; Gass, 1993). When the challenge produces debilitating fears that cause individuals to disengage or shut down, they experience the panic zone and very little growth can occur (Vygotsky, 1978). When operating in the panic zone over a long period of time due to stress and trauma, children tend to focus on survival skills and are at risk for developing unhealthy coping skills while learning the world is not a safe place.

When considering zones of functioning, the book *Who Moved My Cheese? for Kids: An Amazing Way to Change and Win!* is an excellent way to assess the pattern of perceiving new experiences and the stage of change (Johnson, 2002).

In the book, the characters Sniff, Scurry, Hem, and Haw are presented with the challenge of finding "new cheese," which serves as a metaphor for change. As their names might suggest Sniff and Scurry engage in a new adventure with optimism and vigor while Hem and Haw are more resistant to leaving what is familiar in search of the unknown. These characters also provide a framework to describe the circles of comfort used by Outward Bound (2007) to determine the level of challenge and risk to consider when implementing experiential activities. Sniff and Scurry can be described as having a larger comfort zone where change is accepted as part of their everyday experience. They pay attention to their surroundings and are proactive in their search for new cheese. These characters can serve as an example of how to reframe challenges as opportunities.

Hem and Haw perceive change with fear while uncertainty surpasses their ability to adapt and solve a seemingly simple problem. These clients can appear defiant or oppositional; however, resistance can be evidence of operating in the panic zone and requires a different approach and/or additional skills. When challenges incite panic, exploration of barriers, fears, or obstacles can assist clinicians to adjust their hypotheses, identify additional skills to be developed, and modify the sequence of activities and interventions to operate within the stretch zone. It is also important to note that everyone needs to maintain a comfort zone, or a place to take a break from life's challenges to rest, recover, and gather strength for the next task, encounter, or obstacle (Outward Bound, 2007).

Encouraging children and adolescents to perceive difficult circumstances as opportunities to learn, grow, and embrace change is a positive way to reframe a situation and develop solution-focused skills. Adventure education employs the philosophy of Challenge by Choice to empower children and adolescents to become active learners and to choose their own level of challenge while counselors provide support and encouragement to accept challenges within the stretch zone to promote intra- and interpersonal growth and change (Carlson & Cook, 2007; Gass, 1993). The concept of challenge by choice contributes to a respectful and safe environment where children and adolescents can thrive while engaging in fun yet therapeutic activities. These experiential activities are chosen for specific purposes to stimulate participation, inspire hope, and acquire necessary life skills, which can be accomplished by processing.

Processing skills

Counselors or facilitators use the experience to direct learning and skill development to empower clients in reaching their therapeutic objectives (Gass, 1993). The success or therapeutic quality of using an activity will rely on the ability of the clinician to effectively process, which is a series of facilitation skills that employ techniques that supplement purposefully designed experiential activities for optimal learning and skill development (Luckner & Nadler, 1997). When clinicians prepare for sessions, they choose activities for a specific purpose and provide directives to reinforce intentionality (i.e., macro-processing); facilitate change during an activity (i.e., micro-processing); reflect, describe, analyze, or discuss the experience after it is completed (i.e., debrief); and reinforce change through integration into other aspects of life (i.e., transfer of knowledge; Fletcher & Hinkle, 2002; Fletcher & Meyer, 2009; Gass, 1993).

Macro-processing

The term "macro-processing" can be defined as a structured facilitation process that provides intentionality in both choosing and making meaning of activities (Fletcher & Hinkle, 2002) and includes basic instructions to the participants as well as the incorporation of expected outcomes. Activities are informed by client self-report (i.e., intakes, assessments, strengths/interests of clients) or observations by clinicians. Further, dynamics that present in real time provide opportunities for insight, growth, and additional, unintended benefits. There is a delicate balance between structure and ambiguity when preparing for experiential activities. Overly structured activities can allow the counselor's agenda to supersede client needs and disrupt the freedom and flexibility of clients while missing opportunities for teachable moments, insight, and processing. Conversely, when there isn't enough instruction, clients can get lost in obscurity, stop participating, try to focus more on what the counselor may want rather than what is happening internally, or nothing is gained from participation.

The following six facilitation styles can be used to identify the structure and develop directives: no loading, front loading, back loading; front and back loading, metaphor, and paradox (Fletcher & Hinkle, 2002; Gass 1993; see Table 4.3).

Table 4.3 Macro-processing facilitation styles

Facilitation Style	Description
No loading	Limited instructions to allow participation in the activity to speak for itself; clients create their own meaning
Front loading	Discussion and meaning are established prior to the activity
Back loading	Meaning is learned through reflection once the activity has taken place
Front and back loading	Proactive and intentional discussion before and after the experience to create a more powerful experience
Metaphor	A statement about one experience resembles another; metaphoric emphasis is used to transfer skills learned in counseling to real life
Paradox	Directives are established for clients to resist the counselor in order to change (Haley, 1987)

Table 4.4 Paradoxical interventions

Paradoxical Interventions	Examples of Directives
Double bind	Respond in anger and yell every time a parent tells you to do something (resistance will allow a different response OR they are compliant and demonstrate the ability to follow directions while yelling without being angry, which is humorous). The double bind presents both options as an opportunity to change something about their interactions.
Prescribing the symptom	All communication over the next week must be yelled in an angry tone; parents must not respond unless requests are yelled.
Symptom displacement	When one parent communicates a request, get mad and yell at the other parent and vice versa. Consider this paradox when triangulation occurs.
Proactive reframing	You may believe that your parents are incapable of hearing you. I wonder if your parents are hard of hearing and that's why you need to yell to get their attention. This week, try whispering and see if they change how they respond to you.

Mental health professionals can choose facilitation styles that link each activity with a specific purpose that contributes to a sequence of interventions aligned with intended outcomes and therapeutic goals. During a first session, counselors may want to engage in activities where no loading (e.g., an icebreaker) is used to build rapport and establish trust. Front loading or back loading can be helpful to engage clients, establish boundaries, or observe behaviors that contribute to case conceptualization and developing a hypothesis.

As clients and clinicians become more engaged in the counseling process, front and back loading may become more prevalent for skill development. Metaphors are valuable for providing a mechanism for clients to externalize painful, unpleasant emotions while still being open to learning new skills and changing dysfunctional patterns. For example, a bucket overflowing with water can be a metaphor for carrying an overabundance of stress. Strategies to remove liquid can be metaphoric for stress management skills so the bucket can be transported (through life) without making a mess. The contents of the bucket can be solid (i.e., rocks, sticks, bowling ball, etc.) or thick (i.e., mud, sludge, sand, etc.) to be consistent with the type of stress (i.e., rocks are synonymous with bullies, sludge with sexual abuse, etc.) without talking directly about difficult topics. Similarly, a paradox can be useful with resistant clients in changing the direction of therapy and breaking rigid or dysfunctional patterns necessary to proceed with learning new skills.

A paradoxical intervention is more advanced and requires the mental health professional to take a calculated risk in giving directives (Gass, 1993; Haley, 1987; Madanes, 1980). Consider the following situation with an adolescent client who responds in anger and yells when asked to complete a household task (see Table 4.4).

Within the counseling setting, experiential activities can be used to identify skill deficits and dysfunctional patterns. When interacting with clients, observations can serve as information to design directives which can be altered or manipulated anytime during the session. Clinicians can increase or decrease the challenge, modify the directive to stimulate change, or introduce a new skill. The goal for mental health practitioners is to accumulate a variety of activities while becoming proficient at choosing the right activity for the right purpose with the right client at the right time and in the right way for optimal skill development. Mirroring the skill development of clients, the best way (for clinicians) to learn is by doing, followed by reflection.

Micro-processing

Activities promote challenges whereby clients can come to an impasse and hesitate to proceed or become "stuck" instead of attending to what is happening in that moment. In doing so, clients benefit from that "here and now" experience by addressing events in real time. This counseling skill is called micro-processing as clinicians can bring attention to what is happening in the moment to offer support, call attention to an observation, elicit insight, or positively reinforce skill development. Experiential activities provide an opportunity to participate and have a direct experience with their senses, which can be accessed and become a powerful tool for skill development (Zinker, 1978). These emotionally meaningful experiences serve as "teachable moments" and assist clients in becoming more self-aware of thoughts and feelings (intrapersonal) while interacting with the counselor or in the group or family (interpersonal) to learn more effective ways of managing life events and engaging in problem-solving (coping/solution-focused). Once activities are chosen and facilitation style is established, clinicians move from the "make a plan" phase of counseling to "read and react" which is live, in the moment and best informed by Gestalt therapy (Perls et al., 1951; Zinker, 1978).

Field theory

Gestalt therapy is grounded in field theory, which is based on the notion that individuals must be seen in their milieu or context to fully understand how they interact with their respective environments (Parlett & Lee, 2005). Realistically, observing behaviors in the home or school of each child or adolescent client is not often a viable option for clinicians. Therefore, experiential activities can be used to simulate how children and adolescents interact with their environment by stimulating their senses and observing how they cooperate with the counselor, organize information, and respond to challenges.

Many children tend to be energetic, particularly if their school environments do not promote enough physical activity during the day. Therefore, providing kinesthetic opportunities to move their bodies and activate their physical senses – visual images, sounds and words, taste, touch, and smell – will allow them to interact with their environment in a variety of ways. Sensation is the foundation for mindfulness and is often used to promote self-awareness as well as perception. Additionally, incorporating multiple senses at once will allow for children with disabilities to be equally engaged in the counseling process as clinicians can equip their offices with a variety of materials to stimulate all the senses (i.e., art supplies, games, musical instruments, toys, and other random household supplies). When children and adolescents are overly sensitive to external stimuli or lack skills to cope with discomfort, they can become desensitized and unconsciously block awareness as a defense mechanism. They can appear to lack focus or become distracted particularly when challenged, whereby clinicians can begin to promote awareness through observation and phenomenological inquiry.

Phenomenological inquiry

Shifts in mood or changes in facial expressions, tone of voice, or non-verbal communication can be observed during participation in experiential activities. Tearful eyes, clinched jaws, fluctuating volume, and crossed arms are all worthy of exploration as they signal that something might be happening within the session, which is an opportunity for clinicians to implement levels of processing based on the work of Luckner and Nadler (1997). This begins with phenomenological inquiry, or paying attention to what is occurring in the now to better understand a client's lived experience (Kordes & Klauser, 2016; Moustakas, 1994), and includes observations of both non-verbal and verbal communication. Some of these observations can be anticipated due to the nature of the activity; however, most will be spontaneous (see Table 4.5).

Micro-processing is imperative to the success or effectiveness of using experiential activities, and clinicians are encouraged to create and capture as many of these moments as possible. Best practices include informed consent and abiding by ethical codes of conduct, which apply to experiential activities within the counseling session as well as when considering external resources. Mental health professionals are equally encouraged to appreciate individual differences and incorporate multicultural competencies as best practices when considering experiential activities and collaborating with clients, parents, guardians, and caregivers when with diverse populations. A cooperative and inclusive environment is the basis for establishing mutual respect and trust while allowing clients to negotiate the change process for optimal development through the meaning they create from their cumulative experiences.

Table 4.5 Levels of phenomenological inquiry

Level	Topic of Focus	Questions/Prompts
I	Awareness	– What are you feeling in your body? Can you locate any sensations throughout your body? – Are you aware of your (body language)? – Right now I am experiencing you as (angry, defensive, passive, etc.). – How do you imagine that others react to you when you...? – What was your goal when you...? – How can we help you raise your awareness about this pattern?
II	Responsibility	– Did you notice that you were controlling, interrupting, withdrawing, etc.? – Can you accept that controlling, interrupting, withdrawing, etc. might be a pattern of yours? – How does your style of responding work for you at school/home? – Can you recall a time when you responded in a different way? – Who will be the first person to notice if you change this behavior?
III	Choice	– Are you willing to try something different today? – What would be the risk of responding differently? – What's preventing you from doing something different? – How will you sabotage your attempt to get a different response? – How can I support you in taking a risk?
IV	Stay the same or experiment	– What was the hardest part about doing...? – What did you learn about yourself? – How would you like others to respond to your changes? – Who is most surprised about your experiment? – What else do you think you might be capable of?
V	Choice	– What happens when you take a risk? – What does it take for a successful change? – What happens when people don't recognize your change and treat you the same? – How do you want to receive feedback so you can learn from what others are trying to tell you? – What kind of mechanism or trick do you think you can use to keep going in a positive direction?
VI	Stay the same or transfer new learning to home/school	– What are the blockers that will keep you from being successful? – What are the positive forces that you need to keep close to you and how can we enhance them? – How will you know you've made a good decision? – What will you do if/when you get stuck? – Did you notice any patterns in the way you make decisions, solve problems, etc.?
	Personal renewal/ closure	– How could you lessen the burden you carry? – Are there things you can do to feel stronger and more capable? – What adventures would you like to go on? – What can we do to make school/life/home more enjoyable? – How can we improve your relationships with parents? – How could you initiate more meaningful relationships with your friends? – What have you learned about yourself? – What are you most proud of having been through...? – What skill would you like to get better at and how can you go about practicing? – How will you remove other obstacles?

Meaning-making through debrief and transfer

The concept of meaning-making is easily described by examples, but it becomes more complicated when referring to a concrete definition as well as the process by which individuals learn to make sense of the world. Meaning comprises "what," including word references and an understanding of the world (Lewis, 1975; Peterson, 2013) or significance to life events (Kray et al., 2010), and "why" something happens to us specifically (Park, 2010) or the reason anything happens at all (Peterson, 2013). Meaning is created based on information that is filtered and absorbed and allows us to understand or make sense of our experiences (Park, 2010) and provides a guide for action (Peterson, 2013). Meaning-making includes a cognitive (epistemological), intrapersonal, and interpersonal component and people actively construct perspectives by interpreting experiences Kegan (1982; 2018). Over time, children and adolescents organize their experiences to develop expectations, or meaning frameworks (schemata) (Proulx & Inzlicht, 2012). When appropriate, healthy, and consistent meaning frameworks are established and reinforced, children and adolescent clients can acquire skills that align with their overall healthy development.

When expectations are not met or are inconsistent, a violation of the meaning framework, or cognitive dissonance, occurs and follows a certain pattern. First, there is a contradiction of expectations, followed by an aversive arousal response. This physiological reaction can be detected by observing changes in both verbal and nonverbal communication as discussed previously through phenomenological inquiry. In an attempt to cope with the discomfort that accompanies such a violation, clients will then respond to compensate for incongruence between what has been their experience and what they are currently experiencing in order to make sense of what is happening in that particular space and time. These compensatory behaviors include assimilation, accommodation, affirmation, abstraction, and assembly (Proulx & Inzlicht, 2012; see Table 4.6).

Allowing children and adolescents to experience disequilibrium, cognitive dissonance, discomfort, or a meaning violation is consistent with the maneuvering through the stretch zone. Within the stretch zone, children will attempt to make sense of new information, allowing the clinician the opportunity to guide them through the process of meaning-making to enhance their evolving worldview in a healthy, positive, and productive manner. Meaning-making is both a skill and a process that plays out live in each session and throughout the counseling experience and is emphasized during the debrief to reinforce what is learned. Children and adolescents who feel empowered and confident are more likely to form healthy relationships and find solutions to difficult problems, and have the persistence to keep moving forward regardless of the obstacles. Through adversity, they learn the value of delayed gratification and persistence and develop an optimistic worldview. These positive subjective experiences influence meaning-making so they are more likely to keep moving through the positive psychology framework (Seligman & Csikszentmihalyi, 2000).

The ability to make meaning from an experiential activity relies on the ability to "process" what happens before, during, and after the experience to enhance an intentional learning outcome, such as develop insight, communicate more effectively, or learn solution-focused problem-solving skills. Experiential activities that involve problematic behaviors and reframe skills as strengths are presented in Chapter 5. For example, when children are referred to counseling due to destructive behaviors known as non-suicidal self-injury, the self-inflicted harm can be reframed as a mechanism or skill that is used to control painful emotions or as a mechanism to escape feeling numb or empty (Hollander, 2008). The ability to express thoughts and emotions is a strength; however, these child and adolescent clients will need to learn alternatives for self-expression as well as a variety of healthy coping/solution-focused skills. These presenting problems can be identified as a child's attempt to develop a necessary skill and reframed as the need to learn different, more effective, or healthy skills.

Many children experience stress and trauma without the skills to manage their life circumstances, which is addressed in Chapter 6. For example, bullying is one issue where both bully and target may struggle with a lack of self-worth and confidence combined with limited social skills and the inability to cope with an unsafe environment. Oftentimes, these kids may refrain from asking for help for fear of retribution from peers or have experienced a lack of support. Many adults may be unable or unwilling to differentiate bullying from "kids just being kids," oftentimes leaving clients feeling helpless and hopeless that they can find a place to grow, learn, and succeed in life. These kids often need a combination of skills to feel empowered (intrapersonal) and become assertive in expressing their thoughts, feelings, and needs (interpersonal). These clients will benefit from a variety of ways to manage the adversity that accompanies learning to tolerate and get along with others (cope) until the school environment can become safe (solution-focused) to learn and be successful.

Table 4.6 Compensatory behaviors

Compensatory Behaviors (The Five As)	Definitions
Assimilation	Indirectly or directly addressing the meaning violation by masking; reinterpretation of the event to fit or *assimilate* into an existing cognitive schema, perception, or understanding that is familiar and may be mostly unconscious.
Accommodation	Indirectly or directly addressing the meaning violation by resolving; alter the meaning framework, or schema, to *accommodate* the new experience which is mostly a conscious effort.
Affirmation	Look for meaning elsewhere within an existing worldview; reject inconsistency as individuals are committed to a belief and return to the familiar as a means to *affirm* or validate experiences, values, and beliefs.
Abstraction	Looking for meaning elsewhere within the external environment, taking fragments or *abstracting* information (possibly out of context) to fit familiar patterns.
Assembly	New meaning is *assembled* from existing meaning frameworks or creating a new way to make sense of experiences.

Some children and adolescents present in counseling with a diagnosis that contributes to difficulty functioning at home as well as at school (see Chapter 7). For example, a child with attention-deficit/hyperactive disorder (ADHD) will need additional skills to manage their symptoms to accomplish tasks and develop confidence (intrapersonal) as well as engage and get along with peers (interpersonal). These clients will benefit from developing a variety of mechanisms to stay on task (coping) in an environment that is conducive to learning and being successful (solution-focused). Based on the presenting problem, clinicians can begin to develop experiential activities designed to meet the individual needs of clients as part of the counseling process.

As counselors begin to build rapport and engage with child and adolescent clients, common practice includes exploring various interests, extracurricular activities, and strengths (see Chapters 8–15). Board games, books, or favored school subjects tend to be a good beginning to building rapport and engaging clients in the therapeutic process. Further, mental health professionals can incorporate community resources in environments where they can practice and strengthen skills outside of the counseling experience. For example, some children may benefit from participating in organized physical activities like karate or soccer. Karate is an excellent opportunity to develop self-discipline and gain confidence to feel empowered. Soccer is a sport where kids learn how to be part of a team and develop social skills. Other children may find value and a sense of belonging among organizations such as churches, scouting, participating in expressive or performing arts, or spending time with animals. Regardless, counselors can supplement their counseling practice to promote skill development while fostering client interests (see Chapters 8–15).

As clinicians gain experience working with children and adolescents, they become more proficient in adapting a systematic process of meeting the goals for short-term relief and long-term psychological well-being. As members of a larger community tasked with the care of both children and their families, mental health professionals are in a unique position to gain an intimate knowledge of the systems in which these clients live and function.

References

Carlson, K. P., & Cook, M. (2007). Challenge by choice: Adventure-based counseling for seriously ill adolescents. *Child and Adolescent Psychiatric Clinics of North America, 16*(4), 909–919.

Erickson, M. F., Egeland, B., & Pianta, R. (1989). The effects of maltreatment on the development of young children. In D. Cicchetti & V. Carlson (Eds.), *Child Maltreatment: Theory and Research on the Causes and Consequences of Child Abuse and Neglect* (pp. 647–684). Cambridge University Press.

Fletcher, T. B., & Hinkle, J. S. (2002). Adventure based counseling: An innovation in counseling. *Journal of Counseling & Development, 80,* 277–285.

Fletcher, T. B., & Meyer, B. B. (2009). Cohesion and trauma: An examination of a collegiate women's volleyball team. *The Journal of Humanistic Counseling, Education, and Development, 48*(2), 173–194.

Gass, M. A. (1993). *Adventure therapy: Therapeutic applications of adventure programming.* Kendall/Hunt.

Glass, J. S., & Shoffner, M. F. (2001). Adventure-based counseling in schools. *Professional School Counseling, 5*(1), 42–48.

Haley, S. M. (1987). Sequence of development of postural reactions by infants with down syndrome. *Developmental Medicine and Child Neurology, 29*(5), 674–679.

Hollander, M. (2008). *Helping teens who cut.* Guilford Press.

Johnson, S. (2002). *Who moved my cheese? For Kids: An a-mazing way to change and win!.* Putnam Publishing Group.

Kegan, R. (1982). *The evolving self.* Harvard University Press.

Kegan, R. (2018). What "form" transforms?: A constructive-developmental approach to transformative learning. In K. Illeris (Ed.), *Contemporary Theories of Learning* (pp. 29–45). Routledge.

Kordes, U., & Klauser, F. (2016). Second-person in-depth phenomenological inquiry as an approach for studying enaction of beliefs. *Interdisciplinary Description of Complex Systems 14*(4), 369–377.

Kray, L. J., George, L. G., Liljenquist, K. A., Galinsky, A. D., Tetlock, P. E., & Roese, N. J. (2010). From what might have been to what must have been: Counterfactual thinking creates meaning. *Journal of Personality and Social Psychology, 98*(1), 106–118.

Lewis, M. (1975). *The meaning of fear.* Educational Testing Service.

Luckner, J. L., & Nadler, R. S. (1997). *Processing the experience: Strategies to enhance and generalize learning* (2nd ed.). Kendall/Hunt.

Madanes, C. (1980). Protection, paradox, and pretending. *Family Process, 19*(1), 73–85.

Moustakas, C. (1994). *Phenomenological research methods.* Sage.

Outward Bound (2007). *Leadership the outward bound way: Becoming a better leader in the workplace, in the wilderness and in your community.* The Mountaineers Books.

Park, C. L. (2010). Making sense of the meaning literature: An integrative review of meaning making and its effects on adjustment to stressful life events. *Psychological Bulletin, 136*(2), 257–301.

Parlett, M., & Lee, R. G. (2005). Contemporary gestalt therapy: Field theory. In A. Woldt & S. Toman (Eds.), *Gestalt Therapy: History, Theory, and Practice* (pp. 41–64). Sage.

Perls, F., Hefferline, R., & Goodman, R. (1951). *Gestalt therapy: Excitement and growth in the human personality*. Dell.

Peterson, J. B. (2013). Three forms of meaning and the management of complexity. In K. D. Markman, T. Proulx, & M. J. Lindberg (Eds.), *The Psychology of Meaning* (pp. 17–48). American Psychological Association.

Proulx, T., & Inzlicht, M. (2012). The five "A's of meaning maintenance: Finding meaning in the theories of sense-making. *Psychological Inquiry, 23*, 317–335.

Seligman, M. E. P., & Csikszentmihalyi, M. (2000). Positive psychology: An introduction. *American Psychologist, 55*(1), 5–14.

Vygotsky, L. S. (1978). Socio-cultural theory. *Mind in Society, 6*, 52–58.

Zinker, J. (1978). *Creative process in gestalt therapy*. Brunner/Mazel.

Chapter 5

Strengths and skills

Teresa Behrend Fletcher, Hannah Conner, and Madison Andrews

Children and adolescents are in a constant and perpetual state of growing, learning, and improving skills to manage and thrive in a variety of environments (Bandura, 1997). Although parenting and childcare books are in abundance, individualized manuals do not accompany infants after birth to inform parents of what skills need to be developed when and in what order for long-term health and happiness relative to the needs of each individual child. When children are born, parents and caregivers are challenged with how best to nurture each child with a basic understanding of common needs and milestones while adapting to real-life challenges and circumstances. To complicate matters, parents often develop preconceived notions of how children should be raised based on past experiences, which may or may not be accurate for development. Mental health professionals, parents, and other professionals can benefit from a model that is inclusive with respect to culture, gender, race, ethnicity, ability, religion, spirituality, sexual orientation, height, weight, body type, shoe size, and all other aspects that make each and every child unique.

Historically, children progress in their development until challenging behaviors surface and evolve into a crisis or pathology that is detrimental to both the child and the environment in which they function (Roth & Brooks-Gunn, 2003). This "deficit perspective" or the absence of problematic behaviors has led researchers to determine what youth should avoid (i.e., violence, drugs, unprotected sex), rather than the characteristics and skills to promote healthy functioning as a deterrent or prevention of mental illness (Bowers et al., 2010). As such, in an attempt to move away from a pathology-based practice, a more inclusive model is crucial, as youth who appear to be problem-free are not necessarily prepared for the future (Pitman et al., 2001). The challenge for practitioners is to identify a comprehensive set of "life skills" and dispositions associated with optimal development and formulate a systematic way of providing opportunities to learn, practice, and even master these skills in a variety of settings.

Positive Youth Development

The World Health Organization (WHO) defines life skills as, a psychosocial competence or

> A person's ability to deal effectively with the demands and challenges of everyday life. It is a person's ability to maintain a state of mental well-being and to demonstrate this in adaptive and positive behavior while interacting with others, his/her culture and environment.
>
> (World Health Organization, 1997, p. 1)

The WHO (1997) further identified ten core competencies associated with life skills that include decision-making, problem-solving, creative thinking, critical thinking, effective communication, interpersonal relationship skills, self-awareness, empathy, coping with emotions, and coping with stress. Although this is a great start to identifying a fundamental set of skills, in practice these often need to be broken down into smaller skills learned in progression, adapted over time, and transferred to multiple areas of their lives. For example, the ability to express and communicate emotions is a skill that is often difficult until children develop a vocabulary of emotions and the self-awareness to know what they are feeling in the moment in which they are feeling it. Further, when to express these emotions and to whom often becomes a challenge in meeting needs and thriving within a complex and ever-changing world. In an attempt to develop and organize a comprehensive catalog of skills, models of positive development serve to inform mental health practitioners.

After an extensive review of the literature, Tolan et al. (2016) identified four frameworks that have independently attempted to progress the field of positive development and include Social Competence (SC; Waters & Sroufe, 1983), Social Emotional Learning (SEL; Elias et al., 1997), Positive Psychology (PPsy; Seligman & Csikszentmihalyi, 2000), and Positive Youth Development (PYD; Lerner et al., 2002). Further, these four frameworks fall

DOI: 10.4324/9781315213767-6

into two categories of conceptualization: (1) individual characteristics and dispositions or (2) skills and practices. (For further comparison see Tolan et al., 2016.) For the purposes of this chapter, we attempted to utilize the concept and framework of Positive Youth Development (PYD), identified and defined the skills associated with positive development within all four frameworks, and presented them based on the model of Positive Psychology presented in Chapter 2.

Positive Youth Development is a strength-based approach (given the plasticity and potential for growth during childhood and adolescence) for optimal development when aligned with positive resources (Lerner, 2004; Roth & Brooks-Gunn, 2003). The PYD framework consists of the five Cs of Competence, Confidence, Connection, Character, and Caring (Lerner et al., 2002). In expanding on this framework, practitioners may find additional life skills identified in the literature and grounded in evidence-based practice that contribute to both positive functioning and long-term psychological well-being. These skills are defined relative to intrapersonal, interpersonal, coping, and solution-focused skills and presented with supplemental frameworks for acquisition and transfer models.

Intrapersonal and interpersonal skills

Intrapersonal means "within the self" and therefore includes skills revolving around self-awareness. The notion of this ability as an "intelligence" was introduced by Howard Gardner in redefining and expanding the concept of general intelligence (IQ) with the theory of Multiple Intelligences (Gardner, 1983; 2011). Intrapersonal intelligence is the ability to have a deep understanding of one's strengths and weaknesses, thoughts, imagination, interests, and innermost feelings and to manage and use them effectively (Gardner, 1999). These skills serve as a foundation for all other skills as they directly influence how individuals perceive and interact with the world. As children and adolescents develop a positive sense of self at earlier ages, they tend to be more successful at navigating life stress as they get older, when challenges can be more intense and complicated. Intrapersonal skills allow children to identify strengths, differentiate between likes and dislikes, and develop beliefs, morals, and values that contribute to well-being.

Children and adolescents can learn to identify and utilize their strengths and interests to generate confidence and competence and accept their weaknesses as challenges with an understanding that failures can be expected and overcome. Insight can improve the ability to identify triggers and patterns that can lead to impulse control and decision-making. Learning a vocabulary of feeling words that includes a safe space to feel and accurately identify emotions is necessary to learning how to communicate, express, manage, and cope with a variety of situations and circumstances. Learning to reflect and generate insights can be integral to push the boundaries of the stretch zone and initiate changes that lead to autonomy and healthy differentiation of self in later stages of life (Outward Bound, 2007). Further, once individuals can be secure in establishing a positive identity, they can learn to recognize qualities in others that influence interactions and friendships and establish healthy relationships.

Interpersonal skills, also known as relationship or social skills, allow individuals to connect with others effectively. Interpersonal intelligence enables children and adolescents to have empathy, understand others' intentions, feelings, motivations, wishes, desires, and ideals, and interact in a positive and productive manner (Gardner, 1999). Children and adolescents need to learn how to establish healthy boundaries and relationships in order to fulfill the need for connection and belonging. These skills contribute to identifying positive qualities in others, such as trustworthiness, honesty, and compassion, and to paying attention to what others say and the manners in which they communicate. These social skills also include the ability to pick up on non-verbal or social cues from others that include facial expressions and body language. Quite often, individuals labeled as "socially awkward" will not have the ability to make eye contact or will lack social norms that govern encounters which leaves them at risk for teasing, bullying, or being ostracized by peers.

Healthy and positive interpersonal skills that are both genuine and empathic allow individuals to connect with others and form relationships in unfamiliar environments and in uncomfortable situations such as starting a new school or trying out for a new team. The ability to initiate and engage in conversation as an outsider contributes to confidence when taking on new challenges or opportunities. Children who are introverted and naturally shy may need encouragement to reach out and connect with others as friendships are crucial to healthy development throughout the lifespan. When parents or caregivers (i.e., helicopter parents) step in to facilitate these interactions, they deny children the ability to develop these skills and form relationships on their own. Mental health professionals are encouraged to be mindful to include with both parents and children in skill development.

The development of social skills is more important now than at any other time in recent history as unprecedented levels of conflict based on race, ethnicity, nationality, and religion are contributing to unrest and violence (Cameron & Turner, 2016). Social skills and the promotion of cross-group interactions (i.e., more diverse classroom settings, activities) can promote positive outcomes for children, leading to inclusive friendships (Bagci et al., 2014). However, for minority children in diverse settings, poor psychological adjustment, well-being, and academic success can be negative consequences of a diverse classroom (Brown et al., 2013). Therefore, mental health professionals are encouraged to be mindful of culturally competent practices and promote acceptance of differences for all children while they are learning and practicing interpersonal skills.

Skill development is an ongoing process and can involve a combination of smaller skills combined over time to form more complex skills. For example, autonomy is a necessary skill that becomes more important as adolescents prepare to leave home and pursue their own interests, educational training, and careers. Autonomy can be described by including independent thinking or problem-solving as well as the practical abilities to plan meals, cook, clean, manage a bank account, pay bills, maintain transportation, or secure employment. In an attempt to begin the process of identifying intra- and interpersonal skills necessary for psychological well-being and success, a review of evidence-based literature is presented in Table 5.1. These skills are far from conclusive and should be taken as a beginning to an ongoing skill identification and development process.

Table 5.1 Positive intrapersonal and interpersonal skills

Skills	Definition	Evidence-Based Research Resource(s)
Positive sense of self	The possession of self-awareness, agency, and high self-esteem	Guerra & Bradshaw, 2008
Self-control	The ability to regulate and manage affect and behavior (i.e., self-regulation, impulse control)	Guerra & Bradshaw, 2008
Self-awareness and emotion recognition	Comprehension of one's own emotions, evaluation of one's strengths, self-efficacy, and confidence	Elias et al., 1997; Mayer & Salovey, 1997
Self-management	Skills and abilities, including motivation, goal setting, impulse control, and stress management	Pitman et al., 2001
Competence	The ability to do something successfully or efficiently in specific academic, occupational, social arenas	Lerner et al., 2002
Confidence	Having a positive internal self-worth and self-efficacy and one's global self-regard	Bowers et al., 2010; Lerner et al., 2002
Self-efficacy	An expectation that one's behavior will be effective	Bandura, 1997
Social awareness	Abilities and skills related to empathy, perspective-taking, and respect for others	Pitman et al., 2001
Prosocial relationships	Abilities and skills related to empathy, perspective-taking, and respect for others as well as cooperation and collaboration, providing and seeking assistance from others and effective communication	Pitman et al., 2001
Connection	Positive and strong relationships with peers, family, schools, and community	Bowers et al., 2010; Lerner et al., 2002
Caring/compassion	Caring, sympathy and empathy [for self] and others	Bowers et al., 2010; Galla, 2016; Lerner et al., 2002
Optimism	Positivity in the way of thinking about causes relative to permanence, pervasiveness, and personalization in explaining events, both bad and good; a general tendency to expect positive outcomes	Gillham & Reivich, 2004; Seligman, 1995
PARMA	The ability to develop positive emotions; engagement; relationship connectedness; meaning or sense of engagement with something larger than self; accomplishment or satisfaction	Seligman, 2011
Character	An individual's respect for societal and cultural rules	Lerner et al., 2002
Initiative or goal-setting/attainment	The capacity for devoting effort over time toward achieving a goal, including developing plans, organizing time, contingency thinking, and problem-solving	Heath, 1998; Larson, 2000
Self-expression or communication	The ability to identify and express emotion, thoughts, and needs effectively	Goleman, 1995; Mayer & Salovey, 1997
Assertiveness	The ability to initiate and maintain socially supportive relationships and hence enjoy better emotional well-being; the ability to appropriately and constructively express emotions and feelings	Doyle & Biaggio, 1981; Eskin, 2003

Coping and solution-focused skills

Childhood and adolescence are periods of tremendous growth and also a time to prepare individuals to be independent from their caregivers. Children and adolescents must tolerate situations where they tend to have very little control over their environments. As such, they must learn positive coping skills to navigate challenges and rely on adults and caregivers to guide their skill development or risk unhealthy or maladaptive coping as a means to survive. Coping is described as the behavioral and cognitive efforts individuals use when managing stressful situations and can include both adaptive and maladaptive strategies (Lazarus & Folkman, 1984). Some of these challenges can be expected such as transitioning between grades and schools while others may be erratic or unpredictable such as experiencing abuse, the loss of a parent, or social unrest. Healthy coping is critical to tolerating stress and adapting to change, which is inevitable during childhood and adolescence.

Stressors can be explored to include type, intensity, and controllability to promote flexibility and adaptability for the best outcomes (Pincus & Friedman, 2004). Children can develop three different coping strategies that include primary and secondary control engagement or disengagement. Primary control is the ability to identify and change their own reaction to a situation through emotion regulation or problem-solving. Secondary control is the ability to adapt by cognition (positive self-talk or thinking), changing focus, or distraction, and disengagement is exactly how it sounds, withdrawing or removing oneself from the source of stress (Compas et al., 2001). Responsible parents and both professional (i.e., counselors, teachers, clergy, pediatricians, etc.) and non-professional adults (i.e., family members, coaches, scout leaders, etc.) serve as role models for healthy coping, which is imperative to long-term well-being (Glasser, 1965; 1984). Some strategies can be considered equally adaptive/maladaptive and healthy/unhealthy depending on the situation. For example, when a child is bullied, he/she/they can withdraw and find other activities or sources of support to distract from negative interactions. However, if the child withdraws and bullying continues and progresses, withdrawal becomes maladaptive in solving the problem. When children and adolescents do not have support in learning healthy and adaptive coping, they become at risk for self-blame, feeling unworthy or unloved, substance abuse, and a myriad of other negative consequences. In these situations, a solution-focused approach is needed, such as seeking support, engaging in conflict resolution, or using humor to alleviate what has evolved into a negative environment.

The ability to understand the concept of locus of control as internal or external is helpful in determining the difference between coping and solving problems. For example, coping with a challenging teacher is better than changing classrooms or schools every time there is a dispute. Conversely, staying in a classroom that is unsafe or counterproductive to psychological well-being can be devastating. Solution-focused strategies can be helpful in promoting healthy development so children and adolescents can become proficient in engaging in the change process and understanding the direct impact of consequences that serve to inform future decisions. Generating ideas and options in a creative and practical manner can be explored within the counseling session and breaking skills down into smaller increments is recommended. Similar to intra- and interpersonal skills, Table 5.2 is presented to highlight coping and solution-focused skills related to evidence-based practice and well-being.

Table 5.2 Positive coping and solution-focused skills

Skills	Definition	Evidence-Based Research
Problem-solving	Attempts to figure out how to solve problems or prevent from happening	Zimmer-Gembeck & Skinner, 2011
Information or help-seeking	Recognizing a problem and going to another person (either formally or informally) as a resource for coping	Rickwood et al., 2005; Zimmer-Gembeck & Skinner, 2011
Support or comfort seeking	Turning to others for emotional support or consolation	Zimmer-Gembeck & Skinner, 2011
Self-reliance	Attempts to regulate one's emotions by bolstering confidence and optimism	Zimmer-Gembeck & Skinner, 2011
Accommodation	Attempts to remind oneself why a challenge is important and worth the effort	Zimmer-Gembeck & Skinner, 2011
Negotiation	The ability to engage dialogue to compromise	Zimmer-Gembeck & Skinner, 2011

Skills	Definition	Evidence-Based Research
Resilience	Ability and resource to cope with stress and adapt to a stressful environment flexibly and resourcefully	Connor & Davidson, 2003
Humor	An important strategy for reconciling embarrassments, alleviating interpersonal conflicts and breaking through difficulties; a comprehensive and multidimensional construct comprised of a number of modestly related factors, including but not limited to a cognitive ability, an aesthetic response, a habitual behavior, and emotion-related temperament trait, an attitude, and a coping strategy or defense mechanism	Martin, 2007; Martin et al., 2003
GRIT	The combination of abilities that include self-discipline, persistence, and passion to pursue endeavors	Seligman, 2011
Conflict resolution	The ability to engage in positive problem-solving by understanding others' points of view and work out compromise	Kurdek, 1994
Decision-making	The process of choosing between different alternatives while in the midst of pursuing a goal; the ability to: (1) identify a problem; (2) generate alternatives; (3) consider possible consequences; (4) collect information to improve one's ability to evaluate alternatives; (5) evaluate advantages and disadvantages of alternatives; (6) identify an appropriate alternative; and (7) employ decision, make plans, and evaluate consequences	Janis & Mann, 1977; Miller & Byrnes, 2001
Internal locus of control	The ability to focus on what is within your control (i.e., thoughts, feelings, actions) and let go of what cannot be controlled (i.e., actions of others)	Glasser, 1984

Strengths and limitations

This strengths-based approach is a shift away from pathology as the contributing factor to treatment where labels and stigmas can be internalized and personalized. The identification and development of skills is a generalized process where everyone can learn to recognize their strengths and challenges and engage in the process of improving skills regardless of individual differences. A child or adolescent does not have to demonstrate pathology in order to receive assistance and those who experience tremendous hardship or difficulties can benefit from learning more skills that will contribute to success later in life. Skills can be taught and learned with respect to cultural differences in a variety of settings where every situation is an opportunity.

The generalizability of skill development can also be daunting as there is no concrete map for what skill needs to be developed when, by whom, how, and in what order. The development of skills necessary to thrive in life is endless and ongoing. Mental health professionals can get overwhelmed with developmental considerations while trying to assess for strengths and weaknesses while attempting to engage with clients who may appear to be resistant or unmotivated to change. Frustration can be exacerbated when children have far more deficits than they have skills to survive their predicaments, where progress is slow and gaining momentum in life seems an ongoing, uphill battle. Nevertheless, mental health professionals can become relentless in knowing that children and adolescents will always need to be able to use the skills learned in the therapeutic environment, which highlights the concept of meaning-making as well as the transferability of skills ever more important.

Meaning-making

Children and adolescent can engage in the therapeutic process and acquire new skills in a supportive, nurturing, and safe environment. However, these clients will only experience benefits and life-long psychological well-being when these skills are rehearsed and then transferred to other environments or areas of life. Transfer of learning can be defined as the application of knowledge gained in one setting or for one purpose to another setting/purpose (Gagne et al., 1993). The transfer process includes three elements consisting of the individual learner, the learning context, and the transfer context (Baldwin & Ford, 1988; Burke & Hutchins, 2007; Pierce et al., 2017). As such, the child or adolescent client can be considered the learner, the counseling/therapeutic environment can be the learning context, and school, home, neighborhood, workplace, socio-cultural environment, etc. would be the transfer context. The transfer process has been examined mostly in education and business and may be limited in that the content of the transfer appears to be more knowledge-based rather than a transfer of skills. More recently, life skills transfer has been examined in the youth sport literature, which may be more appropriate when considering a transfer model (i.e., skills-based transfer) (see Pierce et al., 2017).

Mental health professionals can engage with the client to collaborate through the transfer process by breaking down skills into smaller increments in a concrete and practical manner to assist in a successful transfer process. Clinicians can also assist in identifying any barriers to the transfer of skills and then reflect once attempts to utilize those skills in another setting have occurred. Engaging with other professionals, parents or facilitating the transfer process outside of the therapeutic setting needs to be strategic as clients may need additional support but still need to experience discomfort and challenge at a level they can manage.

References

Bagci, S. C., Kumashiro, M., Smith, P. K., Blumberg, H., & Rutland, A. (2014). Cross-ethnic friendships: Are they really rare? Evidence from secondary schools around London. *International Journal of Intercultural Relations, 33*(6), 125–136.

Baldwin, T. T., & Ford, J. K. (1988). Transfer of training: A review and directions for future research. *Personnel Psychology, 41*(1), 63–105.

Bandura, A. (1997). *Self-efficacy: The exercise of control.* Freeman.

Bowers, E., P., Li, Y., Kiely, M. K., Brittian, A., Lerner, J. V., & Lerner, R. M. (2010). The Five Cs model of positive youth development: A longitudinal analysis of confirmatory factor structure and measurement invariance. *Journal of Youth and Adolescence, 39*(7), 720–735.

Brown, R., Baysu, G., Cameron, L., Nigbur, D., Rutland, A., Watters, C., Hossain, R., LeTouze, D., & Landeau, A. (2013). Acculturation attitudes and social adjustment in British South Asian children: A longitudinal study. *Personality and Social Psychology Bulletin, 39*(2), 1656–1667.

Burke, L. A., & Hutchins, H. M. (2007). Training transfer: An integrative literature review. *Human Resource Development Review, 6*, 263–296.

Cameron, L., & Turner, R. N. (2016). Confidence in contact: A new perspective on promoting cross-group friendship among children and adolscents. *Social Issues and Policy Review, 10*(1), 212–246.

Compas, B. E., Connor-Smith, J., Saltzman, H., Thomsen, A. H., & Wadsworth, M. E. (2001). Coping with stress during childhood and adolescence: Problems, progress and potential in theory and research. *Psychological Bulletin, 127*, 87–127.

Connor, K. M., & Davidson, J. R. (2003). Development of a new resilience scale: The Connor-Davidson Resilience Scale (CDRISC). *Depression and Anxiety, 18*(2), 76–82.

Doyle, M. A., & Biaggio, M. K. (1981). Expression of anger as a function of assertiveness and sex. *Journal of Clinical Psychology, 37*(1), 154–157.

Elias, M. J., Zins, J. E., Weissberg, R. P., Frey, K. S., Greenberg, M. T., Haynes, N. M., Kessler, R., Schwab-Stone, M. E., & Shiver, T. P. (1997). *Promoting social and emotion learning: Guidelines for educators.* Association for Supervision and Curriculum Development.

Eskin, M. (2003). Self-reported assertiveness in Swedish and Turkish adolescents: A cross-cultural comparison. *Scandinavian Journal of Psychology, 44*, 7–12.

Gagne, E. D., Yekovich, C., & Yekovich, F. (1993). *The cognitive psychology of school learning* (2nd ed.). HarperCollins.

Galla, B. M. (2016). Within-person changes in mindfulness and self-compassion predict enhanced emotional well-being in healthy but stressed adolescents. *Journal of Adolescence, 49*, 204–217.

Gardner, H. (1983). *Frames of mind: The theory of multiple intelligences.* Basic Books.

Gardner, H. (1999). *Intelligence reframed.* Basic Books.

Gardner, H. (2011). *Frames of mind: The theory of multiple intelligences* (3rd ed.). Basic Books.

Gillham, J., & Reivich, K. (2004). Cultivating optimism in childhood and adolescence. *The Annals of the American Academy, 591*, 146–163.

Glasser, W. (1965). *Reality therapy: A new approach to psychiatry.* Harper & Row.

Glasser, W. (1984). *Control theory: A new explanation of how we control our lives.* Harper & Row.

Goleman, D. (1995). *Emotional intelligence: Why it can matter more than IQ.* Bantam.

Guerra, N. G., & Bradshaw, C. P. (2008). Linking the prevention of problem behaviors and positive youth development: Core competencies for positive youth development and risk prevention. In N. G. Guerra & C. P. Bradshaw (Eds.), *New Directions for Child and Adolescent Development* (pp. 1–17). Jossey-Bass.

Heath, S. (1998). Working through language. In S. M. Hoyle & C. T. Adjer (Eds.), *Kids Talk: Strategic Language Use in Later Childhood* (pp. 217–240). Oxford University Press.

Janis, I. L., & Mann, L. (1977). *Decision-making: A psychological analysis of conflict, choice and commitment.* Free Press.

Kurdek, L. A. (1994). Conflict resolution styles in gay, lesbian, heterosexual nonparent, and heterosexual parent couples. *Journal of Marriage and the Family, 56*, 705–722.

Larson, R. (2000). Toward a psychology of positive youth development. *American Psychologist, 55*, 170–183.

Lazarus, R. S., & Folkman, S. (1984). *Stress, appraisal and coping.* Springer.

Lerner, R. M. (2004). *Liberty: Thriving and civic engagement among American youth.* Sage.

Lerner, R. M., Brentano, C., Dowling, E. M., & Anderson, P. M. (2002). Positive youth development: Thriving as the basis of personhood and civil society. *New Directions for Youth Development, 2002*(95), 11–34.

Martin, R. A. (2007). *The psychology of humor: An integrative approach.* Elsevier Academic Press.

Martin, R. A., Puhlik-Doris, P., Larsen, W., Gray, J., & Weir, K. (2003). Individual differences in uses of humor and their relation to psychological well-being; Development of the humor styles questionnaire. *Journal of Research in Personality, 37*, 48–75.

Mayer, J. D., & Salovey, P. (1997). Emotional intelligence. In P. Salovey & D. J. Sluyter (Eds.), *Emotional Development and Emotional Intelligence: Educational Implications* (pp.528–549). Basic Books.

Miller, C. C., & Byrnes, J. P. (2001). Adolescents' decision-making in social situations: A self-regulation perspective. *Journal of Applied Developmental Psychology, 22*, 237–256.

Outward Bound (2007). *Leadership the outward bound way: Becoming a better leader in the workplace, in the wilderness and in your community.* The Mountaineers Books.

Pierce, S., Gould, D., & Camire, M (2017). Definition and model of life skills transfer. *International Review of Sport and Exercise Psychology, 10*(1), 186–211.

Pincus, D., & Friedman, A. (2004). Improving children's coping with everyday stress: Transporting treatment interventions to the school setting. *Clinical Child and Family Psychology Review, 7*(4), 223–240.

Pitman, K. J., Irby, M., Tolman, J., Yohalem, N., & Ferber, T. (2001). *Preventing problems, promoting development, encouraging engagement: Competing priorities or inseparable goals?* The Forum for Youth Investment, Impact Strategies, Inc.

Rickwood, D., Deane, F. P., Wilson, C. J., & Ciarrocki, J. (2005). Young people's help-seeking for mental health problems. *Advances in Mental Health, 4*, 218–251.

Roth, J. L., & Brooks-Gunn, J. (2003). What exactly is a youth development program? Answers from research and practice. *Applied Developmental Science, 7*, 94–111.

Seligman, M. E. P. (1995). *The optimistic child.* Houghton Mifflin Company.

Seligman, M. E. P. (2011). *Flourish: A visionary new understanding of happiness and well-being.* Atria.

Seligman, M. E. P., & Csikszentmihalyi, M. (2000). Positive psychology: An introduction. *American Psychologist, 55*(1), 5–14.

Tolan, P., Ross, K., Arkin, N., Godine, N., & Clark, E. (2016). Toward an integrated approach to positive development: Implications for intervention. *Applied Developmental Science, 20*(3), 214–236.

Waters, E., & Sroufe, L. A. (1983). Social competence as a developmental construct. *Developmental Review, 3*(1), 79–97.

World Health Organization (1997). *Life skills education for children and adolescents in schools: Introduction and guidelines to facilitate the development and implementation of life skills programmes.* Author.

Zimmer-Gembeck, M. J., & Skinner, E. A. (2011). The development of coping across childhood and adolescence: An integrative review and critique of research. *International Journal of Behavioural Development, 35*(1), 1–17.

Activity 5.1: The Bucket

Teresa B. Fletcher

Theme/Goals of Activity	Identify Sources of Stress/Anger
Population/Age	7+
Intrapersonal Skills	Self-awareness, emotional regulation
Interpersonal Skills	Communication
Coping/Solution-Focused Skills	Managing stress, problem-solving
Materials	Paper with a bucket and markers, crayons, or colored pencils

Description of the Activity:

Either draw a bucket or download a bucket picture on a piece of paper. The client can draw, color, or use words to represent bucket stress/anger in the bucket. The bucket is a metaphor or metaphoric container for themselves and their ability to handle a limited amount of stress/anger. The quality and quantity of stress/anger should be included in the bucket.

Macro-Processing:

Backloading and metaphor:

Once the clients have drawn their stress/anger on the bucket, each source of stress/anger can be explored relative to the total stresses/anger. Some stressors/sources of anger will be easily identified or more tangible. Other stresses may increase and decrease relative to various situations and can be more malleable or fluid, such as water or oil, and can be combined. For example, dirt and water can become muddy or murky. The contents can be solid and represent concrete examples of stress that can be placed, moved, or removed more readily and consistently. Liquids are more fluid and require a different strategy to remove and can also include different consistencies such as mud, sludge, and oil/syrup, requiring more thought and different strategies to remove or reduce the stress/anger.

Micro-Processing:

"[This] seems to be the biggest source/contributor of stress/anger." (self-awareness, communication)
"Which stresses can you control/cannot control?" (internal locus of control)
"What happens if someone comes along and drops a small rock in your bucket?"
"What happens if someone comes along and drops a bigger rock in your bucket?"
"What happens if someone comes along and drops a bowling ball in your bucket?"
"What are the contents of the bucket [solid, liquid] and how easily can your bucket be reduced?"
"How might you remove items from your bucket (solid and/or liquid)?" (problem-solving)
"What if you had a spigot at the bottom to drain your bucket?" (coping)
"What if the spigot is the only mechanism to relieve stress/anger and there is sludge blocking it?" (solution-focused problem-solving)
"How might you remove a bowling ball lodged or stuck in the bucket?"

Debrief and Transfer:

The bucket serves as a metaphor for a container for stress/anger in that everyone has limits to what they can carry. The type of weight, quantity, and length of time you have to carry the bucket, the more awkwardness and fatigue you will experience. When a client has experienced abuse or trauma, the contents can be changed to reflect emotions and lack of skills to remove the contents of the bucket to a healthy level of functioning.

Tips or Lessons Learned for Counselors:

The bucket can be easily used with paper and markers; however, it can be adapted to include an actual bucket with contents and fluids (outside is recommended). One of my clients had a tremendous amount of anger and was getting punished for outbursts and having difficulty with peer relationships. We filled half of the bucket with water and used hockey pucks as triggers that generally contributed to his overall anger. As pucks were dropped in the bucket, water spilled. The more pucks in the bucket, the higher the water level and consequently the easier the water splashed out onto the sidewalk. We then added unpredictable instances and which then caused the bucket to overflow. I then instructed the client to put the water that had spilled back into the bucket. The process of putting the water back was metaphoric for trying to apologize for taking his anger out on someone else (i.e., his family, peers).

In order to change others' perception of the client, he needed to remove some of the pucks from the bucket and then be mindful of the water level to make sure that whatever was in the bucket was manageable. We then discussed strategies to remove some of the pucks as well as remove some of the water in a manner that didn't cause a mess. Each session the bucket served as a metaphor to communicate stress and coping as well as solution-focused strategies.

About the Author: Teresa Fletcher, PhD, LCPC, ACS, is a Counselor Educator and Professor in the Counseling/Sport & Human Performance program at Adler University in Chicago, IL.

Activity 5.2: Strength Bubbles

Keith Davis

Theme/Goals of Activity	Identification of Strengths to Facilitate Change and Visually Represent Growth in Therapy
Population/Age	7–17
Intrapersonal Skills	Identify strengths and assets
	Building strengths/using strengths to promote growth
	Boosting self-esteem and confidence
Interpersonal Skills	N/A
Coping/Solution-Focused Skills	N/A
Materials	General art supplies and paper

Description of the Activity:

This activity can be completed in individual or group therapy sessions. In each session, the counselor invites the client(s) to draw, write, color, paint, or decorate a strength on a circle of paper (the bubble). If possible, give the client(s) a choice in the medium used to depict the strength. For younger children, the counselor may need to define strengths by explaining that a strength is "something that is part of us that makes us able to deal with hard times." If the client continues to struggle with identifying a strength, the counselor may also participate by demonstrating a client strength on a separate bubble (see micro-processing). The counselor collects the "bubbles" in an envelope and keeps the envelope in a secured and locked place (possibly a chart if available). When the therapy process is complete, the counselor and client(s) create the mobile, stringing together the different strengths of the client(s). The finished product is a tangible demonstration of the strengths and assets the client has and has developed over time (see macro-processing).

Macro-Processing:

No loading:

Give clients minimal instructions to identify a strength and demonstrate the strength on the circle. "Today, we are going to come up with one strength that has helped you up to now. You can use any of these materials to show that strength on this circle."

Front and back loading:

Front: Each week clients will be able to identify a strength they have used. The strengths will be collected and used to help make changes.

Back: The end of the final session will consist of using all the strengths to build a mobile that the client can then take home as a reminder of strengths, how to use them, and progress made in counseling. Each strength can be identified as an obstacle that was overcome by the client as evidence of success.

Metaphors:

First, pictures on each bubble can be metaphoric. For example, bridges (metaphor), sunshine (metaphor), rainbows (metaphor), trees (metaphor), and mountains (metaphor) were common. Each metaphor signifies something unique to each client, so it is important to allow the client to share the meaning behind the metaphor.

Second, the entire activity is a metaphorical intervention: the visual display of strengths (both quality and quantity) identified and/or built will be demonstrated in the final product. The mobile represents the foundation from which the client moves forward into a desired life.

Micro-Processing:

Observations: During the activity, a client may struggle with identifying a strength, and the counselor may need to give some examples of strengths he or she has witnessed in the client. In these cases, the client may need to process the difficulty in coming up with a strength. Encouraging the client to feel proud of his or her strengths can also promote client growth and change (identify strengths and assets).

- The counselor may want to suggest areas of strengths, such as "something you are" (e.g., "I am creative"). (identify strengths)
- "something you are working on" (e.g., "I am working on not letting my anger get the best of me, even though it is hard"). (building strengths)
- "something you did" (e.g., "I stood up for myself for the first time in school"). (using strengths to promote growth)

Observations: Over time, children may not be aware of progress or remember how they have used their strengths, making it easy to lose what is learned and accumulated in counseling. While constructing the mobile, client strengths can be revisited. (boosting self-esteem and confidence)

- "Look at all of these strengths floating her on this mobile showing us how strong and capable you are!" (boost self-esteem and confidence)
- "I remember how hard it was to talk about (abuse), but looking at this bubble, I remember the power you felt when you broke your silence." (using strengths to promote growth)
- "You've got this! Look at all of the skills, strengths, and habits you have to be successful/capable to withstand stress and have the life you wish to have!" (boost self-esteem and confidence)

Debrief and Transfer:

This activity contains many transferrable benefits to clients. A client begins to understand what comprises a strength, and learns how to identify this in him/herself. Further, when a client is able to identify a strength, the counselor can use this moment to enhance self-esteem, e.g., "I saw you were having a hard time coming up with something, but were able to figure it out." The client then is able to refer to these strengths to foster a sense of competence and resiliency. Further, this activity can be used to demonstrate to a client how many skills he or she has and can rely on in times of stress. It may also be used to modify how clients view strengths. For example, sometimes strength is showing up for therapy when you had a really rough day, and sometimes strength is making big changes in your life. Both are worthy of recognition.

Tips or Lessons Learned for Counselors:

This is an activity that allows the counselor to help the client identify core strengths, but also assesses how well the client can self-identify internal positive qualities. Some clients may need more encouragement to identify these strengths. For example, a client who has been told he is bad and worthless may need to process this first before proceeding to the activity.

When confronting resistant clients with this activity, the authors recommend that counselors allow them some space, but continue inviting them to join in this activity. The counselor may also complete a bubble for the client, but attempt to refocus the responsibility back to the client by asking "this is what I am seeing. Do you see this too?" or "Wow, you just described a major strength. How should I show this on the bubble?" This same idea was applied in a group setting when, after receiving bubbles from the rest of the group, one resistant client began participating in the group activity.

The actual bubble-making is best done at the beginning or end of each session. The authors preferred using it at the end of the session to summarize growth, and to identify a strength the client can reflect on during the time between sessions. However, it could also be used at the beginning of a session with an allotted time for designing the bubble.

About the Author: Keith M. Davis, PhD, NCC, is a Professor at Radford University. Dr. Davis teaches courses in both school and clinical mental health counseling and has more than 20 years of experience teaching, working as an elementary and high school counselor, a family intervention specialist, and an EAP therapist.

Activity 5.3: Cultural Identity Exploration

Lay-nah Blue Morris-Howe

Theme/Goals of Activity	Cultural identity exploration, validation, empowerment
Population/Age	10 and above
Intrapersonal Skills	Ability to identify aspects of personal identity (with facilitation), such as personal/family language, traditions, food, music, art, interests, religious/spiritual practices (other examples below)
Interpersonal Skills	Communication with counselor and expression through activity of self-reflection
Coping/Solution-Focused Skills	Acknowledgment of aspects of identity that represent culture, reinforcement of personal identity, pride for personal identities
Materials	Paper and desired writing materials (markers, crayons, colored pencils, paint), digital art may also be used where developmentally appropriate, magazines for images to be cut out

Description of the Activity:

This activity is used to help youth explore what makes them who they are in regard to their cultural identity. It helps them identify tangible examples of things that they feel represent their identity, such as music (a particular song, genre, or artist), type of food or specific dish, language, form of art (i.e., beadwork, pottery), a sport, style of clothing, geographic place, family traditions, religious/spiritual practices, or other significant symbols or images.

Art supplies are provided for the child to choose from, and the clinician describes the way the child will move through the activity by choosing to draw themselves and/or their house, and around the drawing of themselves and/or their house, they will add drawings or cutout images that represent these different aspects of their cultural identity. The clinician will facilitate this by asking prompting questions from their knowledge of the client,

• "What things can you think of that make you who you are? Such as your language? Or is there a family favorite food that is a good representation of your heritage?" "Can you think of music that might be a good representation of your identity?"

The clinician moves through different prompting questions only after the child has completed a supplementary drawing around their original picture of themselves or their house, then moves slowly from one question to the next. This activity could span over a full counseling session or even into multiple sessions, honoring the child's pace. The clinician allows the child to determine when they have completed the activity and would prompt reflection by asking:

- "Do you think you have included everything about yourself (and your family) that represents your heritage and your culture? Have you included everything that is important to YOU?"

Macro-Processing:

No loading:

"This is an activity to explore your personal identity and heritage in a creative and fun way using some art supplies."

Front and back loading:

Front:

"It can be helpful for us to take the time to think about all the things that make us who we are and are important to us. These might be some things that really connect us to some family and friends, or maybe even some of those things that make us feel unique or different."

Back:

The clinician allows the child to reflect on their finished product and "present" it to them. The clinician elicits introspective thoughts—possible questions are:

- "How was it for you to think about all these aspects of your heritage? What was it like to share it with me? How do you feel about your culture and your identity now that you've completed this activity?" "Do you think you would share this with anyone else? How might you do that?"

Micro-Processing:

Clinician observes and tracks the child's artwork,

- "You are putting a lot of detail into the design on that shirt." "You really worked hard to include as many pieces of your heritage as you could." "Wow, the colors are so vibrant there."

When the child does not respond to a specific prompt:

- "You may not have something significant that you want to include here, and that's okay. You get to choose what's important to share in this activity."

Debrief and Transfer:

Some clients will share about how their interests differ from other family members, which elicits great communication about how we have unique identities as individuals and can still be part of a greater collective, or for some youth, it is validating for them to see some similarities and some differences between themselves and family members as they start to share their drawings. This creates an opportunity to build communication skills with others about their heritage and culture as well. The clinician validates the child's identity and shares appreciation and gratitude for the child communicating/sharing with them throughout the activity, aiding in confidence building and empowering the child to share about their cultural identity.

Tips or Lessons Learned for Counselors:

Clinicians should be sensitive to the inclusion of a house drawing for children who may be displaced from their home due to divorce/move/foster care. In these cases, clinicians should assess if only a drawing of self is appropriate for the child, or if including a house may be beneficial. Similarly, the association and connection to family members should be considered carefully by the clinician.

The paper for the "self" drawing should be large; a poster board works well, or three to five full sheets of paper stacked in letter orientation high, taped together in the back work as well.

About the Author: Dr. Lay-nah Blue Morris-Howe is an Assistant Professor at the University of Wyoming. She is also a licensed professional counselor with 15 years of experience who works with youth, families, couples, individuals, and groups from a multiculturally informed humanistic approach.

Activity 5.4: Lost in RIASEC Island

Rachael C. Marshall

Theme/Goals of Activity	This group activity, using the Holland Codes, aids children and adolescents to explore their interests (*traits*): gain awareness of their work interests, imagine an environment that fits well with their interest, work in groups to create work environments
Population/Age	12–19
Intrapersonal Skills	Self-worth, showing initiative, and finding meaning in the Holland Codes
Interpersonal Skills	Cooperativeness with others and awareness of own impact on others as they explore/create the island with the Holland Codes
Coping/Solution-Focused Skills	Decision-making and career decision-making skills
Materials	Large enough room for the group to move around, five tables to represent the islands, instructions and descriptions of each of the five islands—either on PowerPoints or handouts (see Figure 5.1)

Description of the Activity:

Begin with the introduction to the prompt:

- "Imagine you are flying in an airplane alone, having taken off for a day's pleasure excursion.
- After flying for some time, you find yourself approaching six remote islands.
- Suddenly, your plane develops engine trouble, and you realize you are going to have to make a forced landing on one of the islands.
- You realize that you will be on the island for a long time since ships make only infrequent visits.
- You also know that transportation between these six islands is nonexistent.
- Where you land, determines what kind of people you will be staying with for a long while. You will need to choose your landing spot with care.
- Look at the aerial view of the islands.
- From the information available, you know that highly civilized and advanced people populate each island.
- They have moved to these locations to associate with other compatible people and to enjoy the balmy climate.
- The people on each island have the characteristics described by each theme.
- Which group of people would you prefer as companions for a significant amount of time?"
- You have 3 min to decide and go to your island.

After they choose an island, discuss Holland Codes and theory. After the clients choose their island as a group, they will work to answer these questions:

REALISTIC- 1
Conservative
Common-sense orientation
Personal freedom
Honesty
Thrift
Nature

ARTISTIC- 2
Beauty
Self-expression
Imagination
Creativity
Liberal

ENTERPRISING- 3
Success
Status
Chain-of-command
Responsibility
Loyalty
Risk-taking

INVESTIGATIVE- 4
Accuracy
Inventiveness
Achievement
Independence

SOCIAL- 5
Service to others
Fairness
Justice
Understanding
Empathy

CONVENTIONAL- 6
Conservative
Persistence
Honesty
Thrift
Accuracy
Chain-of-command

ISLANDS:

Figure 5.1 Island characteristics.

"On your island discuss….(30 min)

– What do you see on the island?
– What do you do each day?
– How do people do work on this island?
– What are your island's strengths? Areas of growth?
– What community would you build?"

After discussions, each island will answer these questions as a small presentation to the other islands. I sometimes ask them to create a sales pitch for their island so they can use the questions to present.

Macro-Processing:

Front and back loading:

Front: While each island is talking introduce the questions for discussion and the presentation.
Back: Discuss how these islands relate to the Holland codes, their connection to career development, and the fact that they will find connections to their islands. Open discussion to what other islands they would choose and what types of jobs align with those islands. The use of O*net is very helpful with this project.

Micro-Processing:

Observations in choosing islands: Some are more comfortable making a decision, others need some time, normalize the difficulty of choosing one, and let them know they can go with their first impulse or instinct there are no wrong answers.

- "It can be challenging choosing one island, remember it is temporary?"
- "Which island helped you feel the most interested for a long time and not a short time?" (problem-solving)

Observations in group discussions: Walk to each island to listen to their discussion, see what questions come up. Notice how the groups work together. You will notice the different islands work differently together; these comments can help them process the discussion questions.

- "For the social island, I noticed no one individual is the leader, you are all working together as a team—how can this impact the community's ability to build on the island?"
- "For the Enterprising island, I noticed you chose a leader for your group—how does this relate to how you do work on the island?" (linking and self-awareness)

Observations in island presentations: As each group presents you will see difference; process and exploring these difference will help children engage in self-awareness and find other Holland code connections. (generate insight and self-awareness)

- What did we notice about how each group presented their island?
- Remember our Holland code usually has three interest codes—what other two islands would you visit?

Debrief and Transfer:

For this group activity, it can cause competition between islands. We find Enterprising to be a more competitive island in their presentation. It can be helpful to outline that each island has strengths and areas of growth. Both Exploring this competition as a connection to the Holland interest code (self-awareness) and work environments (career development) can help outline specific elements of the island's interests. Then asking what other islands interest them will help facilitate discuss across islands, bringing the group together again.

Use O*net to explore different interests and specific jobs associated. Notice which specific jobs speak to the group members.

Tips or Lessons Learned for Counselors:

Always consider individuals that represent neurodiversity or have a disability that may ask for a heads up when a room is shifting or there are more movements involved than a usual session. Consider the physical space and the room each child needs to move around. For example, an adolescent on the autism spectrum asked that they have an update before class on when things will change so they can be prepared and fully immerse in the experience.

Another tip is to be well versed in Holland code themes and O*net. Take some time to play with the O*net website and learn what you can find there through interest searches.

About the Author: Dr. Rachael C. Marshall is an Assistant Professor and Fieldwork Coordinator at California State University, Sacramento in Counselor Education in the Career Counseling Specialization. Her career counseling work focused on trauma, grief, and advocacy with first-generation college students, immigrants, international students, and LGBTQ+ clients.

Chapter 6

Stress and trauma

Lay-nah Blue Morris-Howe and Ricky Zambrowicz

Stress is a daily part of the human experience and can be considered essential for growth when challenges can be contained within the "stretch zone" and facilitated with positive support (Outward Bound, 2007; Vygotsky, 1978). However, when stress represents significantly disruptive experiences, known as Adverse Childhood Experiences (ACEs), development can be impacted, resulting in trauma (Felitti et al., 1998). As childhood and adolescence can represent a period of storm and stress, children and adolescents are often referred to counseling after experiencing stressors or traumas that influence the developmental process. In response to stress, adolescents may learn skills to adapt to future stressful events or may experience dysregulation, leading to mental health issues (Stroud et al., 2009). Systemic factors, such as community demographics and district funding, create barriers to accessing resources for children, families, and schools (Bronfenbrenner, 1994). Thus, inequity exists in the types of stressors youth experience and the resources available to support them developmentally as they adapt to trauma and stress. Cultural identity can also significantly influence how youth experience and cope with various life and systemic stressors.

While children who experience significant traumatic events are more likely to develop subclinical and clinical posttraumatic stress disorder (PTSD), even low-magnitude stressors with increased frequency can still have a lasting impact on youth development (Copeland et al., 2010). Hence, it is vital for counselors to help children and adolescents to develop skills necessary to identify stress (intrapersonal skills), communicate their thoughts and feelings with caregivers (interpersonal skills), and develop appropriate strategies to manage and limit the impact of stress in their lives (coping/solution-focused skills).

Stress and trauma impact student achievement and emotional regulation over time (Fraser et al., 2021). Children experience exaggerated amygdala function increasing with the magnitude of stress response and slower recovery from stressful events over time (Choudhury et al., 2008; LaRue & Herrman, 2008). As stress continues, the hippocampus and cerebral cortex are negatively affected, and one's memory, learning, and ability to complete complex cognitive tasks declines (Arnsten, 2009; LaRue & Herrman, 2008; Lupien et al., 2009). As children and adolescents' prefrontal cortex is not yet adept at handling the limbic system's stress response, they need assistance in developing stress management and reduction skills. If children and adolescents do not receive assistance in reducing their stress levels, they are at risk for structural changes in their prefrontal cortex's development and adult mental illness (Arnsten, 2009; Lupien et al., 2009). LaRue and Herrman (2008) examined adolescent perspectives of the stressors they face, and identified several key sources of stress, including school, family and home life, systemic factors, and other stressors.

School stressors

School stressors include, but are not limited to exams, homework, grades, learning disabilities, conflicts with other students and teachers, bullying, possessing a dislike of school, fears of success and failure, seeking acceptance from others, intersectional identity development (see Appendix A), and anxieties regarding their future (Pascoe et al., 2019; Pratt et al., 2019). Beyond academic stressors, peer relationships and disruption in identity development can challenge concepts of self-worth through comparison of self to others (e.g., social media perceptions; Woods & Scott, 2016). School stress can be attributed to a variety of factors, including social and academic challenges (Sotardi, 2017). While perhaps not a daily stressor for all youth, one of quite significance is youth suicide. The death of a peer or friend by suicide can be perceived as a traumatic event, and a youth's one suicidal ideation is often also quite distressing. Bullying is a common form of Adverse Childhood Experiences (ACEs; Felitti et al., 1998), with one in five high school students experiencing bullying at some point in their academic career either physically or electronically (Centers for Disease Control and Prevention, 2021).

DOI: 10.4324/9781315213767-7

Academic achievement

Homework and grades are staples of the American educational system, while bullying affects one fifth of all students. Currently school stressors can also include various issues due to the COVID-19 pandemic (see Implications and Future Directions). After nearly 2 years of pandemic restrictions and alternative learning, grief, anxiety, and depression are rampant in school-age children, resulting in increased outbursts and maladaptive behavior in younger children, and bullying and violence in older students (see Implications and Future Directions). The PEW Research Center (2021) found that 59% of parents with lower incomes reported that their children struggled with adequate technology and internet access to complete schoolwork. In addition to these "new normal" issues, research has already established that children who grow up in lower socioeconomic standards and marginalized communities tend to be behind in several subjects. These factors influence education gaps between groups of children.

Adults and counselors can be helpful to identify the impact of stress for youth and their families. Students reporting more support and structure over their lives tend to experience less stress in school (Ainslie et al., 1996). Intrinsic motivation positively correlates with diminished stress, while students extrinsically motivated tend to experience elevated stress, possibly due to extrinsically motivated students internalizing external stressors (Flink et al., 1992). Additionally, enhancing self-efficacy, intrinsic motivation, and social and relational skills supports the developmental process for students (Hoffman, 2009).

Bullying

Multiple studies demonstrate the negative effects of bullying on psychological and physical health (Maji et al., 2016; see Table 6.1). Students who experience bullying are more likely to miss school, feel lonely and depressed, perform poorly in school, have lower self-esteem, and experience suicidal ideation (Hepburn et al., 2012; Nansel et al., 2001). Research into bullied students frequently finds maladaptive coping strategies, including catastrophization, self-blame, blaming others, rumination, resignation, aggression, passive avoidance, and internalizing problems (Maji et al., 2016). Youth from marginalized populations are often at an increased risk of experiencing bullying due to their identities. Identity-based bullying can be perpetrated by both peers and adults within a school setting (Benner & Graham, 2013; Graham, 2021). Students from stigmatized and devalued social identities related to their religion, gender, immigrant status, race/ethnicity, mental and physical disabilities, and sexual orientation are often targets of identity-based bullying (Galán et al., 2021).

Research suggests proactive aggressors tend toward generalized hostility and antisocial behavior due to internalized resentment and anger over unmet needs for security (McAdams & Schmidt, 2007). Heydenberk et al. (2006) analyzed a bully prevention program which taught children and adolescents affective vocabulary, social and emotional literacy, and conflict resolution skills; through this program, students were empowered by learning how to better recognize their own perspective – including cognitive and emotional aspects – and how to effectively communicate and resolve. Many schools are focusing their curriculum and relationship building with students around Social-Emotional Learning (SEL). SEL is a methodology of helping students become aware of their emotions and focuses attention on empathy toward self and others (Hoffman, 2009). The hope of SEL is to foster increased achievement and practices with emphasis on ideals of caring, community, and diversity.

Family and home stressors

Stress and trauma impact intrapersonal and interpersonal skill development. Vast negative impacts, including withdrawal from peer relationships and self-blame and self-injurious behavior, can overtake a child. Family and

Table 6.1 Types of bullying representing Adverse Childhood Experiences (ACEs; Centers for Disease Control and Prevention, 2021)

Types of Bullying	Description
Physical bullying	Physical altercations including hitting, kicking, shoving, tripping, spitting on someone
Verbal bullying	Microaggressions, name-calling, slurs, teasing told to someone
Relational/social bullying	Excluding from social groups, spreading rumors with peers, embarrassing someone in public
Damage of property	Stealing or breaking personal property
Cyberbullying	Use of cell phones, computers, social media to share negative or false information about someone

home environment stressors are often reported as a significant source of stress in children and adolescent lives (Moos, 2002). Some of these stressors include family values conflicts, cultural identity and family dynamics, parental divorce or re-partnering, death of a family member or friend, or changes in family status (Moos, 2002).

Divorce

Fagan (2013) refers to children and adolescents as the "quiet sufferers" of divorce. Children of divorce experience more social, psychological, and educational distress (Angarne-Lindberg et al., 2009; Fagan, 2013). Deficits in relational and social skills are frequently cited as a primary issue stemming from divorce (Angarne-Lindberg et al., 2009). Whitten and Burt (2015) argue for utilizing creative expressive techniques within a group therapy format for children of divorce. Some of the methods and techniques they include are listening to songs about divorce, creating a genogram, having children role play negative communication patterns that occur within the parent-child relationship with each other, watching a short film, using meditation and relaxation techniques, and ultimately writing a poem summarizing their experience within the group. These activities intend to normalize children's intra- and interpersonal experiences of divorce, develop a new sense of self outside of the family unit, enhance social connectedness, and counteract low self-esteem via empowering children to develop healthier relationships with themselves and others (Whitten & Burt, 2015). Important to consider is the cultural background of children, particularly the collectivistic or individualistic emphasis of that background prior to engagement in activities, and how those may impact children, as these aspects of culture may have a strong influence on how the divorce is perceived (Toth & Kemmelmeier, 2009).

Children in foster care

According to the Children's Bureau (2021), trends in foster care placements have been consistent for the last 10 years. Placement settings for children in foster care include relative placements, nonrelative placements, institutions, trial homes, group homes, and supervised independent living. Beyond these placement settings, foster care agencies oversee placements in pre-adoptive homes and track runaway rates. The goal of the foster care model is reunification with parents with focus on establishing safe environments for youth. According to the most recent statistics, the average stay in the foster care system was 15.5 months. Due to the developmental time frame and experience of complex trauma in relation to primary attachment figures, children in foster care typically lack a sense of safety and security (Fraser et al., 2013; Hodgdon et al., 2013). Children who are placed with families outside their cultural identity experience the added stress of negotiating a hybrid cultural space, whereas those who are placed in kinship homes maintain a stronger sense of self and connectedness (Waniganayake et al., 2019).

Exposure to violence and substance use

Due to its prevalence and negative consequences, the US Department of Justice claims exposure to violence is a national epidemic. Witnessing, or experiencing, violence represents a detrimental impact to emotional and physical health (Finkelhor et al., 2014). Zimmerman and Posick (2016) argue the impact of violence is significant for youth, whether violence is experienced directly or witnessed. Exposure to violence alters neurobiological development, including a heightened arousal and stress response, increased muscle tone and sleep disturbance, abnormalities in cardiovascular regulation, and even delays in pubertal development (Lepore & Kliewer, 2013; Perkins & Graham-Bermann, 2012). Infants and toddlers often experience behavioral and emotional regression, such as developing sleeping issues, mood lability, somatic complaints, distress while being alone, and/or retrogressing in toilet and language skills (Zeanah & Scheeringa, 1997). Children's and adolescent's social development may be stunted due to a lack of safety (Dodge et al., 1997). Consequently, in addition to altering one's neurobiological development, exposure to violence is correlated with internalizing problems, negative coping strategies, self-directed violent behavior, and interpersonal violence (Lepore & Kliewer, 2013; Perkins & Graham-Bermann, 2012; Zimmerman & Posick, 2016).

The family system is the primary source of attachment and socialization in current society (Lander et al., 2013, Howsare, & Byrne, 2013). According to the Substance Abuse and Mental Health Services Administration (SAMHSA), an estimated one in eight children (8.7 million) aged 17 or younger live in households with at least one parent who has a substance use disorder (Lipari & Van Horn, 2017). A parent struggling with substance use or recovering from substance use is unable to foster healthy attachment. In some situations, the child may take on the responsibilities of the parent. This phenomenon is called the "reversal of dependence needs." The parent's needs are placed before the child's, which can lead to an inability to set healthy boundaries, a lack of self-awareness, and an over-awareness of others' needs (Zucker et al., 2009).

Figure 6.1 Maslow's hierarchy of needs.

Trauma-informed care

Some children experience stress and trauma from a myriad of external sources, including chronic illness, accidents, threats or experience of abuse, relocation of the family, oppression, discrimination, war, and other sources. Maslow and Lewis (1987) discuss that a lack of basic needs and safety in the environment stifles the capacity for individuals to develop psychologically (see Figure 6.1).

It is important to understand that a distinction exists between common daily stressors and traumatic experiences. Although events that are typically stressful for youth can be quite significant for some, these do not have the same psychological impact as traumatic experiences. When life experiences become disruptive in the developmental process, Adverse Childhood Experiences (ACEs) represent trauma for youth that have lasting effects throughout the lifespan (Felitti et al., 1998).

Grief and loss

Grief and loss are a painful part of childhood and adolescence through both bereavement and other losses. The concept of grief is socially regulated, and thus certain types of loss can be disenfranchised, or not considered socially acceptable (Doka, 2008; Robson & Walter, 2013). Further, complex grief and bereavement can become labeled as a clinical disorder despite the reality that loss is a uniquely personal and cultural experience (Klass & Chow, 2011). Grief and loss can disrupt social and academic relationships, causing the youth to grieve what was considered previously stable or familiar. Grief experiences can include the loss of friendships, locations due to moving, connections with caregivers or mentor adults, and concepts of identity. Further, bereavement can include loss due to deaths of family members, friends, pets, or others in the community. These transitions can lead to difficulties in adjustment and possibly depression or anxiety symptoms. Especially for younger children, truthful conversations about loss and outlets to express grief through creative activities can help support the developmental and healing processes (Griffith, 2003). Grief, loss, and trauma can intersect, and similar to one another, the way in which they are experienced is unique to each individual and is influenced by values, beliefs, culture, cognitive development, and many additional factors. The new revision of the DSM-5-TR (American Psychiatric Association, 2022) introduces the diagnosis of "Prolonged Grief Disorder" with criteria for children and adolescents. This diagnostic option represents persistent symptoms of grief at least 6 months after a death. While the grief process is unique to each individual and strongly tied to cultural context, this diagnosis accounts for symptoms interfering with daily functioning and in excess of what is considered typical for the individual context.

Trauma

The current edition of the *Diagnostic and Statistical Manual of Mental Disorders, 5th edition, text revision* [DSM-5-TR] (American Psychiatric Association, 2022) has revised the definition of events that qualify as "traumatic" (i.e., those that can lead to trauma-specific diagnoses such as PTSD) to include those that the child directly experiences, witnesses, or learns about that involve actual or threatened death, serious injury, or sexual violence (American Psychiatric Association, 2022). Complex trauma represents multiple or prolonged exposure to trauma within

Table 6.2 Key principles of trauma-informed approach (SAMHSA)

Types of Bullying	Description
Safety	Physical and psychological safety needs of children and adults are ensured.
Trustworthiness and transparency	Trust is built and maintained between clients, family members, staff, and others through transparent organizational operations.
Peer support	Peer support is key in the promotion of recovery and healing by establishing hope and safety, enhancing collaboration, and building trust.
Collaboration and mutuality	Importance is placed on partnering and the leveling of power differences between clients and organizational staff.
Empowerment, voice, and choice	Shared decision-making, choice, and goal setting to determine a plan of action to heal and move forward. Staff need to feel safe in their work and are empowered to do their work well, with support.
Cultural, historical, and gender issues	Actively moves past cultural stereotypes and biases, provides access to gender-responsive services, acknowledges traditional cultural healing, addresses historical trauma, and addresses cultural needs of clients.

the caregiving environment, beginning early in development (Spinazzola et al., 2005). The effects of trauma can vary among children based on aspects such as developmental understanding, parental reaction to trauma, age, and a unique and personal focus upon the traumatic experience or event. In severe cases of trauma, such as domestic violence or sexual exploitation, children can become "trauma bonded" (Cohen et al., 2017). This is when an emotional attachment (trauma bond) develops out of a repeated cycle of abuse. Oftentimes children who experience trauma will struggle with interpersonal relationships and avoid healthy peer interactions.

Treatment of complex trauma requires a multifaceted approach due to the dysregulation of multiple domains impacting development and functioning (Substance Abuse and Mental Health Services Administration, 2014). When working with youth who have experienced trauma, it is critical that counselors employ a trauma-informed approach (SAMHSA, 2014) which employs key principles that aim to avoid re-traumatization of clients and staff and promote healing and recovery (see Table 6.2). An evidence-based treatment appropriate for traumatized youth aged 3–18 is Trauma-Focused Cognitive Behavioral Therapy (TF-CBT). Motivational interviewing techniques can also be used for youth who deny their trauma history or the negative effects. These treatment approaches, when used in appropriate phases, have strong positive outcomes in the reduction of symptoms associated with PTSD and complex trauma and an increase in adaptive coping behaviors (Cohen et al., 2017).

Meaning-making

Youth have incredible potential for resilience and thriving (Lupien et al., 2009). When children and adolescents face and overcome traumatic events, the sense of intrinsic strength and posttraumatic growth process is powerful (Tedeschi & Calhoun, 1996). Schools, communities, and society can be connected to assist with creating protective factors and address barriers to accessing support for children and adolescents (Bronfenbrenner, 1994). Counselors can help by evaluating protective factors and resources for youth. Protective factors including self-regulation, family support, school support, and peer support can help foster resilience and create a safety net of support for youth (Yule et al., 2019). Counselors can also aid children and families to have more direct and honest, yet developmentally appropriate communication (Griffith, 2003). This assists youth in dealing with covert and overt emotions related to their traumatic experiences. Counselors can address trauma with creative activities through the provision of individual therapy, family therapy, and group therapy in a variety of inpatient, outpatient, in-home, and community-based settings. Finding a sense of intrinsic meaning (Hoffman, 2009) through the therapeutic process can help youth to make meaning and grow from stressful and traumatic events.

References

Ainslie, R. C., Shafer, A., & Reynolds, J. (1996). Mediators of adolescents' stress in a college preparatory environment. *Adolescence, 31*(124), 913–925.

American Psychiatric Association (2022). *Diagnostic and statistical manual of mental disorders* (5th ed., text rev). Author.

Ängarne-Lindberg, T., Wadsby, M., & Berterö, C. (2009). Young adults with childhood experience of divorce: Disappointment and contentment. *Journal of Divorce & Remarriage, 50*(3), 172–184.

Arnsten, A. F. T. (2009). Stress signalling pathways that impair prefrontal cortex structure and function. *Nature Reviews Neuroscience, 10,* 410–422.

Benner, A. D., & Graham, S. (2013). The antecedents and consequences of racial/ethnic discrimination during adolescence: Does the source of discrimination matter? *Developmental Psychology, 49*(8), 1602–1613.

Bronfenbrenner, U. (1994). Ecological models of human development. *Readings on the Development of Children, 2*(1), 37–43.

Centers for Disease Control and Prevention (2021, September). *Preventing bullying.* https://www.cdc.gov/violenceprevention/youthviolence/bullyingresearch/fastfact.html

Children's Bureau (2021, March). *Foster care statistics 2019.* https://www.childwelfare.gov/pubpdfs/foster.pdf

Choudhury, S., Charman, T., & Blakemore, S. J. (2008). Development of the teenage brain. *Mind, Brain, and Education, 2*(3), 142–147.

Cohen, J. A., Mannarino, A. P., & Kinnish, K. (2017). Trauma-focused cognitive behavioral therapy for commercially sexually exploited youth. *Journal of Child & Adolescent Trauma, 10*(2), 175–185.

Copeland, W. E., Keeler, G., Angold, A., & Costello, E. J. (2010). Posttraumatic stress without trauma with children. *The American Journal of Psychiatry, 167*(9), 1059–1065.

Dodge, K. A., Lochman, J. E., Harnish, J. D., Bates, J. E., & Pettit, G. S. (1997). Reactive and proactive aggression in school children and psychiatrically impaired chronically assaultive youth. *Journal of Abnormal Psychology, 106*(1), 37.

Doka, K. J. (2008). Disenfranchised grief in historical and cultural perspective. In M. S. Stroebe, R. O. Hansson, H. Schut, & W. Stroebe (Eds.), *Handbook of Bereavement Research and Practice: Advances in Theory and Intervention* (pp. 223–240). American Psychological Association.

Fagan, J. (2013). Effects of divorce and cohabitation dissolution on preschoolers' literacy. *Journal of Family Issues, 34,* 460–483.

Felitti, V. J., Anda, R. F., Nordenberg, D., Williamson, D. F., Spitz, A. M., Edwards, V., Koss, M., & Marks, J. S. (1998). Relationship of childhood abuse and household dysfunction to many of the leading causes of death in adults: The adverse childhood experiences (ACE) Study. *American Journal of Preventive Medicine, 14*(4), 245–258.

Finkelhor, D., Shattuck, A., Turner, H. A., & Hamby, S. L. (2014). The lifetime prevalence of child sexual abuse and sexual assault assessed in late adolescence. *Journal of Adolescent Health, 55*(3), 329–333.

Flink, C., Boggiano, A. K., Main, D. S., Barrett, M., & Katz, P. (1992). Children's achievement-related behaviors: The role of extrinsic and intrinsic motivational orientations. In A. K. Boggiano & T. S. Pittman (Eds.), *Achievement and Motivation: A Social-Developmental Perspective* (pp. 189–214). Cambridge University Press.

Fraser, A. M., Bryce, C. I., Alexander, B. L., & Fabes, R. A. (2021). Hope levels across adolescence and the transition to high school: Associations with school stress and achievement. *Journal of Adolescence, 91,* 48–58.

Fraser, J. G., Lloyd, S., Murphy, R., Crowson, M., Zolotor, A. J., Coker-Schwimmer, E., & Viswanathan, M. (2013). A comparative effectiveness review of parenting and trauma-focused interventions for children exposed to maltreatment. *Journal of Developmental & Behavioral Pediatrics, 34*(5), 353–368.

Galán, C. A., Stokes, L. R., Szoko, N., Abebe, K. Z., & Culyba, A. J. (2021). Exploration of experiences and perpetration of identity-based bullying among adolescents by race/ethnicity and other marginalized identities. *JAMA Network Open, 4*(7), e2116364.

Graham, S. (2021). Exploration of identity-based bullying by race/ethnicity and other work with young adults from divorced families. *Journal for Specialists in Group Work, 25*(1), 50–66.

Griffith, T. (2003). Assisting with the "big hurts, little tears" of the youngest grievers: Working with three-, four-, and five-year-olds who have experienced loss and grief because of death. *Illness, Crisis & Loss, 11,* 217–225.

Hepburn, L., Azrael, D., Molnar, B., & Miller, M. (2012). Bullying and suicidal behaviors among urban high school youth. *Journal of Adolescent Health, 51*(1), 93–95.

Heydenberk, R. A., Heydenberk, W. R., & Tzenova, V. (2006). Conflict resolution and bully prevention: Skills for school success. *Conflict Resolution Quarterly, 24*(1), 55–70.

Hodgdon, H. B., Kinniburgh, K., Gabowitz, D., Blaustein, M. E., & Spinazzola, J. (2013). Development and implementation of trauma-informed programming in youth residential treatment centers using the ARC framework. *Journal of Family Violence, 28*(7), 679–692.

Hoffman, D. M. (2009). Reflecting on social emotional learning: A critical perspective on trends in the United States. *Review of Educational Research, 79*(2), 533–556.

Klass, D., & Chow, A. Y. M. (2011). Culture and ethnicity in experiencing, policing, and handling grief. In R. A. Neimeyer, D. L. Harris, H. R. Winokuer, & G. F. Thornton (Eds.), *Grief and Bereavement in Contemporary Society: Bridging Research and Practice* (pp. 341–353). Routledge.

Lander, L., Howsare, J., & Byrne, M. (2013). The impact of substance use disorders on family and children: From theory to practice. *Social Work in Public Health, 28*(0), 194–205.

LaRue, D. E., & Herrman, J. W. (2008). Adolescent stress through the eyes of high-risk teens. *Pediatric Nursing, 34*(5), 375–380.

Lepore, S. J., & Kliewer, W. (2013). Violence exposure, sleep disturbance, and poor academic performance in middle school. *Journal of Abnormal Child Psychology, 41*(8), 1179–1189.

Lipari, R. N., & Van Horn, S. L. (2017). *Children living with parents who have a substance use disorder.* Center for Behavioral Health Statistics and Quality, Substance Abuse and Mental Health Services Administration.

Lupien, S. J., McEwen, B. S., Gunnar, M. R., & Heim, C. (2009). Effects of stress throughout the lifespan on the brain, behaviour and cognition. *Nature Reviews Science, 10,* 434–445.

Maji, S., Bhattacharya, S., & Ghosh, D. (2016). Cognitive coping and psychological problems among bullied and non-bullied adolescents. *Journal of Psychosocial Research, 11*(2), 387–396.

Maslow, A., & Lewis, K. J. (1987). Maslow's hierarchy of needs. *Salenger Incorporated, 14*(17), 987–990.

McAdams III, C. R., & Schmidt, C. D. (2007). How to help a bully: Recommendations for counseling the proactive aggressor. *Professional School Counseling, 11*(2), 2156759X0701100207.

Moos, R. H. (2002). 2001 Invited address: The mystery of human context and coping: An unraveling of clues. *American Journal of Community Psychology, 30*(1), 67–88.

Nansel, T. R., Overpeck, M., Pilla, R. S., Ruan, W. J., Simons-Morton, B., & Scheidt, P. (2001). Bullying behaviors among US youth: Prevalence and association with psychosocial adjustment. *Jama, 285*(16), 2094–2100.

Outward Bound (2007). *Leadership the outward bound way: Becoming a better leader in the workplace, in the wilderness and in your community.* The Mountaineers Books.

Pascoe, M. C., Hetrick, S. E., & Parker, A. G. (2019). The impact of stress on students in secondary school and higher education. *International Journal of Adolescence and Youth, 25*(1), 104–112.

Perkins, S., & Graham-Bermann, S. (2012). Violence exposure and the development of school-related functioning: Mental health, neurocognition, and learning. *Aggression and Violent Behavior, 17*(1), 89–98.

Pew Research Center (2021, October). *What we know about online learning and the homework gap amid the pandemic.* https://www.pewresearch.org/fact-tank/2021/10/01/what-we-know-about-online-learning-and-the-homework-gap-amid-the-pandemic/

Pratt, M. E., Swanson, J., van Huisstede, L., & Gaias, L. M. (2019). Cumulative family stressors and kindergarten adjustment: The exacerbating role of teacher-child conflict. *Merrill-Palmer Quarterly, 65*(1), 28–53.

Robson, P., & Walter, T. (2013). Hierarchies of loss: A critique of disenfranchised grief. *OMEGA-Journal of Death and Dying, 66*(2), 97–119.

Sotardi, V. A. (2017). Exploring school stress in middle childhood: Interpretations, experiences, and coping. *Pastoral Care in Education, 35*(1), 13–27.

Spinazzola, J., Ford, J., Zucker, M., van der Kolk, B., Silva, S., Smith, S., & Blaustein, M. (2005). National survey of complex trauma exposure, outcome and intervention for children and adolescents. *Psychiatric Annals, 35*(5), 433–439.

Stroud, L. R., Foster, E., Papandonatos, G. D., Handwerger, K., Granger, D. A., Kivlighan, K. T., & Niaura, R. (2009). Stress response and the adolescent transition: Performance versus peer rejection stressors. *Development and Psychopathology, 21*, 47–68.

Substance Abuse and Mental Health Services Administration (2014). *SAMHSA's concept of trauma and guidance for a trauma-informed approach.* HHS Publication No. (SMA) 14–4884. Rockville, MD: Substance Abuse and Mental Health Services Administration.

Tedeschi, R. G., & Calhoun, L. G. (1996). The posttraumatic growth inventory: Measuring the positive legacy of trauma. *Journal of Traumatic Stress, 9*, 455–471.

Toth, K., & Kemmelmeier, M. (2009). Divorce attitudes around the world: Distinguishing the impact of culture on evaluations and attitude structure. *Cross-Cultural Research, 43*(3), 280–297.

Vygotsky, L. S. (1978). Socio-cultural theory. *Mind in Society, 6*, 52–58.

Waniganayake, M., Hadley, F., Johnson, M., Mortimer, P., McMahon, T., & Karatasas, K. (2019). Maintaining culture and supporting cultural identity in foster care placements. *Australasian Journal of Early Childhood, 44*(4), 365–377. https://doi.org/10.1177/1836939119870908

Whitten, K. M., & Burt, I. (2015). Utilizing creative expressive techniques and group counseling to improve adolescents of divorce social-relational capabilities. *Journal of Creativity in Mental Health, 10*(3), 363–375.

Woods, H. C., & Scott, H., (2016). #Sleepyteens: Social media use in adolescence is associated with poor sleep quality, anxiety, depression and low self-esteem. *Journal of Adolescence, 51*, 41–49.

Yule, K., Houston, J., & Grych, J. (2019). Resilience in children exposed to violence: A meta-analysis of protective factors across ecological contexts. *Clinical Child and Family Psychology Review, 22*(3), 406–431.

Zeanah, C. H., & Scheeringa, M. S. (1997). The experience and effects of violence in infancy. In J. D. Osofsky (Ed.), *Children In a Violent Society* (pp. 97–123). The Guilford Press.

Zimmerman, G. M., & Posick, C. (2016). Risk factors for and behavioral consequences of direct versus indirect exposure to violence. *American Journal of Public Health, 106*(1), 178–188.

Zucker, R. A., Donovan, J. E., Masten, A. S., Mattson, M. E., & Moss, H. B. (2009). Developmental processes and mechanisms: Ages 0–10. *Alcohol Research & Health, 2*(1), 16–29.

Activity 6.1: Letter Writing and Cultivating Voice in Grief

Tina L. Nirk

Theme/Goals of Activity	Letter writing/cultivating voice; letter writing is an opportunity to be heard especially when life circumstances like emotional cut-off, death, isolation, or marginalization prevent the child from meaningfully expressing themselves
Population/Age	7+
Intrapersonal Skills	Acknowledging and conveying needs, positions, and vulnerabilities
Interpersonal Skills	Imaginal conversation when communication is blocked by circumstance or relational rupture
Coping/Solution-Focused Skills	Identifying thoughts, feelings, and behaviors in a relational context that helps the author's perspective matter
Materials	Writing utensils and paper and/or a word processor

Description of the Activity:

Letter writing is an opportunity to be heard especially when life circumstances like emotional cut-off, death, isolation, or marginalization prevent the child from meaningfully expressing themselves. Teaching children that their inner selves matter prepares them to be adults who also honor their voice. The concise, intentional, and thoughtful practice of letter writing is a safe space to explore emotional complexity and vulnerability. A counselor who proposes the experiential activity of letter writing to a verbal child should be aware that this is an intrapersonal and interpersonal way of examining thoughts related to a relationship.

Puppets or a painting easel might be the perfect modality for some children to express their intrapersonal and interpersonal selves. However, for children who are verbal processors, evidenced by a tendency to convey what was said or not said in their relationships, a letter provides them the right canvas to craft a conversation that is supported in counseling, from start to finish. Initially, the counselor should support the practice by asking questions and encouraging the child's letter to unfold in their own voice, as well as secondarily teaching the child to reflect on the experience of letter writing and the impact the letter could have on others. Lastly, brainstorming plans to use and enhance this skill in future scenarios is an important way to set a child up for turning to this skill again as they grow older.

Macro-Processing:

No loading:

Present the opportunity to write a letter to a person, pet, former/future self, difficult experience, or group of people. For example, Goodbye letters to family members who have left or died offer continued bonds and space to explore unresolved questions, and letters to a future self can aid in seeing beyond current difficulties to a resilient future self who resolves problems.

Front and back loading:

Front: While brainstorming together about the recipient of the letter, share that often it is easier and safer to express one's thoughts and feelings in a letter than in person. Emphasize that the letter writer is total in control of what is shared and whether the letter is ever read by anyone.

Back: Allow the child to reflect on what it was like to write the letter. Frame the reflection by offering a prompt about how letter writers can learn meaningful, brave, surprising, painful or even cathartic aspects of themselves.

Micro-Processing:

First ask questions about the behavior involved in the letter-writing process. For example, "When I suggested writing a letter, what went through your mind and how did you feel about doing it? What made you decide to write this letter?"

Next, provide here-and-now feedback about how the child approached the letter to facilitate relational self-awareness. For example, "You wrote that letter with a lot of serious concentration and seem to now be relaxed and lighter. What did you notice about yourself? When have you felt that way before? What helped you express yourself so genuinely in your letter?"

Finally, encourage the child to consider other perspectives as well as needs that might be explored further. For example, "What do you think your mother would have written back to you if she were alive to read your letter? How might your future-self feel after reading your letter? Or, have you ever been disappointed by someone's response to you expressing yourself? What would an encouraging response to your letter sound like?"

Debrief and Transfer:

Extend any metaphors the child created to transfer the practice of letter writing to future problems. For example, "You opened up the treasure chest of your heart in that letter. Now and again when hard things happen, the treasure chest gets locked without a key. A letter written in a safe space can help it open again so the jewels inside can shine." Also, reminding the child that they can create any letter they need. For example, the child of non-English speaking parents can slip a note in her school lunch box that wishes her a good day at school in English from the perspective of her parents.

Tips or Lessons Learned for Counselors:

Letters provide intentional dialogue, voice, and catharsis when a conversation is not possible. Letters also serve as a theater-of-the-mind with letter writers picturing their intended audience in perceptive detail to the extent that sometimes it is not even necessary to share the letter. Often children are left out of serious conversations and the format of a letter is a permissible expression of a child's viewpoint. Handwritten letters can be especially artistic since handwriting and signatures convey even more authentic personhood than typed letters.

In my practice, letters to people who have died seem to be profoundly helpful in processing grief related to death. Encouraging children to write individuals or pets who have passed away has seemed to provide them with the much-needed, safe experience of mourning. It also seems that supporting adults who read these letters begin to better understand the perspective of the child; trying to guess how the child is processing loss is often off base. The focus on the task and product of the letter has been helpful in easing the understandable pain that can otherwise stymie creative expression.

About the Author: Tina L. Nirk, PhD, LPC, has been a licensed counselor for the past 20 years. She uses letter writing in qualitative research, in personal growth, and in her work with oncology patients.

Activity 6.2: The Real Me

Rachel Ratliff

Theme/Goals of Activity	Authentic self-expression
Population/Age	12+
Intrapersonal Skills	Self-worth, confidence, or finding meaning
Interpersonal Skills	Giving and receiving feedback, sensitivity to individual and cultural differences, empathy
Coping/Solution-Focused Skills	Self-awareness, self-esteem, self-worth, confidence
Materials	Foil sheets, various colored paper, ribbon, pipe cleaners, fabric scraps, glue, and/or tape

Description of the Activity:

Children and adolescents, either consciously or unconsciously, have some intentionality around how they present themselves to the world. This presentation can be in line with the cultural influences of their family, friends, school, and/or community. It can also be opposite of these influences, or if a child or adolescent is more in tune with their inner world their presentation can reflect that. Depending on the age of the child or adolescent, and their unique situation, this reflection can be a comfortable or uncomfortable one for them. This activity is a way for children and adolescents to explore how they present themselves to the world and then do some reflecting on whether this is how they truly want to represent themselves to others.

Participants in the activity will be asked to make a foil person that represents themselves. Once the foil person is made, the participant is asked to decorate the foil person in a way that represents who they are. After processing their foil person and discussing the choices they made and why, the participants will be asked to again decorate their foil person in a way that represents how they wish they could present themselves to the world. Once this is completed, the participants and counselor will process this new version of themselves and could also discuss what keeps the participant from presenting this way in their lives.

This activity can be an important activity for many children and adolescents, and especially for students who are exploring their gender and/or sexuality.

How to make a foil person:

- You will need three foil sheets, roll each sheet into long tubes.
- The first tube will be made into the legs/feet. Fold the tube in half and bend each end to make the feet.
- The second tube will be added to the legs/feet and make the torso/head. Fold the bottom third of the tube around the middle of the legs/feet to secure together, then fold the top third into a circle for the head.
- The third tube wrap around the torso once or twice to create the arms.

Macro-Processing:

No loading

Present the opportunity to create a foil person that represents themselves. Show the participants the variety of materials they can utilize for the project and walk participants through making the base of their foil person with the foil sheets.

Front and back loading:

Front: Brainstorm various attributes that participants could highlight with their foil person; some examples include activities they participate in, recreating their favorite outfit, making accessories that match favorite items that they own, etc. Emphasize the allotted amount of time that participants will have when creating their first foil person to help those engaged in the activity keep track of their time while working; this can be especially helpful for the participants who work slowly.

Back: After first foil person prompt each participant to share their foil person and explore the choices that they made when deciding what aspects of themselves to share through their foil person. After redoing their foil person to represent the way they wish they could represent themselves, prompt each participant to share their foil person again and explore the similarities and differences between the two. Discuss aspects of their lives that may be keeping them from being able to show this part of themselves in their daily life.

Micro-Processing:

Observations: At the beginning of the activity have a discussion about who you are and the various ways that each person reveals aspects of themselves in their daily lives. You could possibly, depending on the age of your participants, show pictures of various people and discuss what we know about each person based on the photos. An example might be someone wearing their favorite team's colors or jersey.

After the first foil person you can comment on participants' demeanor and various behaviors while they were building. You might notice that it took a while for a participant to get started, or that a participant rushed or went very slowly. You can also discuss with participants what they chose to highlight with their foil person and, depending on how well you know the participant, point out aspects of them that they didn't highlight with their foil person.

After recreating their foil person, have a discussion about the new foil person and discuss various similarities and differences between the two. Discuss any life circumstances that prevent the participants from feeling like they can present in the way they want in their everyday life. Explore various ways that participants can include some aspect of their second foil person as they move forward from the activity.

Debrief and Transfer:

After completing this activity, follow up with more conversations about ways participants are being and/ or feeling more like themselves. This can include dressing in ways that they enjoy more or feeling like they can be more honest about aspects of themselves they had kept hidden before. Follow-up sessions can also include discussions that normalize keeping some aspects of yourself private, especially if feeling unclear about feelings.

Tips or Lessons Learned for Counselors:

Depending on how long your time with participants is, this activity may need to be completed over a few sessions. This is especially true for participants who have difficulty making decisions or work slowly. There may also be a lot of differences between the first foil person and the second, especially if a participant is exploring their gender or sexuality. Ensure that the space in which the activity is taking place, especially if in a group setting, has established norms and safety for each participant.

About the Author: Rachel Ratliff earned her master's degree from the University of Wyoming in Community Mental Health Counseling and is currently a doctoral student in the Counselor Education and Supervision program at the University of Wyoming. Rachel spent over a decade in education before returning to school to become a counselor. She currently works on the Behavioral Health Services unit at Ivinson Memorial Hospital and as a Mental Health Examiner for Albany County in Wyoming.

Activity 6.3: The Unfair Game

Tanya N. Brown

Theme/Goals of Activity	Anger management
Population/Age	8–14
Intrapersonal Skills	Fairness
Interpersonal Skills	Managing frustrations/ODD
Coping/Solution-Focused Skills	Anger management
Materials	Deck of cards, bag of candy (each piece individually wrapped) – about five pieces per person, copies of the rules

Description of the Activity:

Start by gathering the individuals into a circle and by giving everyone five pieces of candy. Let the individuals know that they will be able to keep whatever candy they have at the end of the game (and candy may not be eaten until the end of the game). Have the rules handy for individuals to see throughout the game. You the leader must participate in the game.

You can set a time limit or end the activity when a few people are eliminated or when the pot is filled with a bunch of candy. At the end of the time limit, select the person with the best sportsmanship (this person will be you the leader, since this is an unfair game), so you select yourself and take all the candy left in the middle.

Rules of the Game: When it is your turn, select a card from the deck. If you draw a card and get:

- Heart: you must give a piece of candy to the person on your right
- Club: you must give a piece of candy to the person on your left
- Diamond: you must put a piece of candy in the pot
- Spade: you get two pieces of candy from the pot (or from the person of your choice if the pot is empty).

If anyone loses all their candy, they are then eliminated from the game.

If eliminated, the person must continue to sit in the circle but can return to the game if someone gives them a piece of candy during the course of the game (no candy may be given to the eliminated person out of the goodness of their heart but instead must be determined by the cards or dice).

The leader decides who displayed the best sportsmanship (leader) during the game, and this person (leader) gets to keep all the candy left in the pot at the end of the game.

After an allotted time, the person who has the most candy wins, and everyone may keep any candy they have acquired.

Before the activity starts, take all but a couple of the spades out of the deck of cards and mix the few spades left toward the top of the deck. If possible, have two identical decks of cards and replace the spades with cards from a different suit from the spare deck. The idea is to make sure that this game is truly unfair, just as life can be unfair.

Macro-Processing:

No loading:

Don't let the individuals know that the game is called "The Unfair Game" (until the end). Give it another name, for example, "The Candy Game" or "The Card Game" (or something that will not give away what the game is really about).

Micro-Processing:

Observations: During the activity, it is important to liken the experience to life being unfair for some (if not all) and that life can be unfair for some more than others. It is also useful to talk about the emotions (especially anger) that arise as things get more unfair as the game progresses.

Questions:

1. Was this game unfair? Why or why not?
2. How do you feel right now?
3. Do you ever feel like your life is unfair? If so, when and how do you handle it when things seem unfair?
4. Do you think it would help you in your own life to change how you act when life seems unfair? If so, how?
5. How did you feel when the game was in your favor?
6. How did you feel when the game was not in your favor?
7. Do you ever feel like your life is like this game? Are you usually winning or losing?
8. Do you ever get angry when things seem to be unfair?
9. How do you release your anger that you feel when things are unfair?
10. Is there a better way to handle an unfair situation?

Debrief and Transfer:

Follow up at the end of the game with a more concrete discussion (those that feel like the game was more unfair to them will have a lot to say). The discussion usually focuses on why the game was unfair or not unfair, how they felt. Then try to link the game to real life and how they feel or experience unfairness and how they handle it and how they can handle it. Also try to talk about how it would help them in their own life to consider reactions when life seems unfair.

Tips or Lessons Learned for Counselors:

I have done this game several times as this was a staple for our different therapeutic groups which consisted of mainly kids/adolescents diagnosed with ODD and ADHD. So as a result, there were usually high emotions (mostly anger) that came out of playing the game. This is good as it allowed us an opening to have an open discussion about it and then offer some anger management strategies and coping skills techniques, etc.

One thing that sometimes happens too is that one or two kids (who end up with lots of candy) almost always at the end show a caring side and will often times offer those left with no candy some of their candy. This too will often lead to a follow-up conversation about sharing and giving to those to whom life has been unfair and how we can share and help them when in a position to do so.

About the Author: Tanya N. Brown is currently a PhD graduate student at the University of Wyoming in the Counselor Education and Supervision program. She holds an MA in Professional Counseling from Liberty University and graduated magna cum laude from PACE University with a BS in Psychology. Tanya has over 15 years of experience working in the Mental Health field, working in multiple settings (group homes and K-12 school systems).

Activity 6.4: Coloring Your Feelings

Gissel Molina

Theme/Goals of Activity	Expressing feelings in the body, healthy expression of grief and loss
Population/Age	4–8
Intrapersonal Skills	Expressing how youth are feeling to others so they can better understand or help
Interpersonal Skills	Understanding how youth feel and how feelings are affecting the body
Coping/Solution-Focused Skills	This activity helps the child name their feelings and give them room to be/feel them
Materials	Blank piece of paper and any coloring tool the child wishes to use

Description of the Activity:

The child is asked to draw an outline of their body. It can be as big or as small as they want. Then using a color-coded key, the child picks the colors that correspond with their emotions (Figure 6.2). The child then "draws" the emotion wherever they feel it in their body. For example, let's say the color blue stands for sadness and the child colors their stomach area in blue because they feel the sadness in their belly.

* Adapted from The Color-Your-Life Technique (O'Connor, 1983) and Color Your Feelings Activity

Macro-Processing:

Front and back loading:

Front: Present the instructions for drawing the person. The child can get the crayons that correspond with the color key to create their drawing. Create clear connections to recent loss.

Back: The child can make up their own color key they do not have to use the one given. The child can describe the character they are coloring. The counselor can create connections to recent loss as the child explains the drawing.

Micro-Processing:

Observations: The clinician can observe what colors the child picks and how their emotions change with each color. They can observe where the child places each color in the figure. They can also observe how much of each color is used and if the child mixes any colors together. Use reflecting skills to track the child's choices as they create the person.

Debrief and Transfer:

This activity provides a way to teach the client about feelings and to help them learn how to express their feelings. It is also a way to help normalize things for the client. For example, the counselor could say "I also feel nervousness in my stomach when I get anxious."

Tips or Lessons Learned for Counselors:

When doing this activity with the client I sat quietly and let her color. Depending on the client and their age I may use some tracking skills, for example, you are using the green crayon, or you feel really jealous. With my client I noticed that when she did this, she got really quiet afterward and did not want to explain her drawing much. I got the feeling that she felt uncomfortable and maybe wanted me to feel the way she was feeling, so we sat in silence until she was ready to start talking again.

About the Author: Gissel Molina is a master's student at the University of Wyoming. She is originally from Los Angeles, California but moved to Wyoming when she was 11 years old. She is passionate about becoming a counselor and helping her community.

Color the places you feel your feelings…
Blue – sad
Afraid – black
Guilty – gray
Mad – red
Jealous – green
Nervous – purple
Happy – orange

Figure 6.2 Color your feelings template.

Chapter 7

Treating DSM-5 diagnoses

Isabel C. Farrell

This book is promoting a model based on identifying strengths of child and adolescent clients and positive development. However, children are often referred for counseling services when their concerning or disruptive behavior at home, school, or in the community warrants an assessment, or when they have received a diagnosis from another mental health professional or physician. The diagnostic system includes the current edition of the *Diagnostic and Statistical Manual of Mental Disorders, 5th edition, text revision* [DSM-5-TR] (2022), along with *International Classification of Diseases* [ICD-11], which is more commonly used outside the United States (World Health Organization [WHO], 1994, 2022). This system of assessment is utilized by mental health professionals to categorize, study, and treat mental illness. Therefore, we would be remiss if we failed to acknowledge that one out of six children in the United States is diagnosed with a mental, behavioral, or developmental disorder (Center for Disease Control and Prevention [CDC], 2021). Of children age 6–17, 16.5% will experience a mental health disorder (National Alliance on Mental Illness [NAMI], 2021). Due to the prevalence of mental, behavioral, or developmental disorders among children and adolescents, counselors often need to direct counseling focus or treatment plans based on the child or adolescent's diagnosis (e.g., Jongsma & Peterson, 2014a; 2014b).

According to the National Survey of Children's Health (CDC, 2021), in the United States, the most common diagnoses among children and adolescents from ages two to 17 include Attention-Deficit Disorder/Attention-Deficit/Hyperactivity Disorder (ADD/ADHD), Oppositional Defiant Disorder (ODD)/Conduct Disorder (CD), anxiety, depression, and Autism Spectrum Disorder (ASD). According to the National Alliance on Mental Illness (2021), there is an average delay of 11 years between onset symptoms and diagnosis and intervention. Left without treatment, 80% of chronic mental disorders will continue through adulthood (Merikangas et al., 2010).

Children and adolescents with a mental disorder often internalize negative feelings and can be stigmatized and/or ostracized in their various environments, making even simple, everyday tasks strenuous and daunting. Additionally, they must manage symptoms related to the diagnosis(es) and medication with related side effects. As mentioned in Chapter 2, a diagnosis can inhibit the capacity to develop age-appropriate skills at the same rate as their peers. These disorders can also impede participation in extracurricular activities where they can learn and practice skills and develop or enhance strengths. In general, children and adolescents face added adversity with school-related and vocational skills (i.e., writing, reading, etc.) and they endure more challenges when attempting to engage in self-care (intrapersonal) and relational or prosocial skills (interpersonal). This population then becomes vulnerable for developing maladaptive coping skills; thus, over 70% of adolescents involved with the juvenile justice system meet the criteria for at least one mental health diagnosis (NAMI, 2021).

Counseling children and adolescents with DSM-5 diagnoses

Each diagnosis comes with unique challenges; thus, the goal of counseling is to identify the strengths and interests of each client in addition to skill deficits to gain insight and manage problematic behaviors (intrapersonal), learn how to make friends and gain a support system (interpersonal), and utilize resources to adapt to a variety of environments (coping/solution focused). This chapter is limited to the most prevalent diagnoses (Attention-Deficit/Hyperactivity Disorder, Oppositional Defiant/Conduct Disorders, Generalized Anxiety Disorder, depression, and Autism Spectrum Disorder) with the understanding that activities can be adapted for other disorders based on similar concepts.

Attention-Deficit/Hyperactivity Disorder

Children and adolescents with Attention-Deficit/Hyperactivity Disorder (ADHD) have difficulty regulating focus, concentration, and impulse control. Inadequate attentional skills can hinder learning, often leading to low

DOI: 10.4324/9781315213767-8

academic performance (CDC, 2021), frequent truancy and suspensions, as well as high rates of high school drop-outs (Ziereis & Jansen, 2016). The lack of self-control correlates with increased aggression and hinders prosocial behavior and peer relationships (Eisenberg et al., 2006), causing isolation and decreased self-confidence (Van der Oord et al., 2005). Children and adolescents are challenged with learning how to complete tasks, stay organized, and control impulses so they may become more successful in maintaining friendships and adapting to or choosing environments more suited to their strengths. Additionally, the struggle to learn, study, and complete homework may be exacerbated in subjects that are least interesting or most difficult to students.

Oppositional Defiant Disorder and Conduct Disorder

These disorders include behaviors that exhibit poor impulse control in addition to disruptive or harmful behaviors. Intrapersonal deficiencies include attention, cognitive flexibility, inhibition, and making associations between behaviors and consequences due to reduced sensitivity to rewards and punishments (Matthys et al., 2012). Children and adolescents with these diagnoses also lack interpersonal skills contributing to poor grades, frequent delinquency, and limited or unhealthy peer relationships (Baker, 2008). For example, girls with ODD present higher risk of early pregnancy and intimate partner violence (Baker, 2008). Children and adolescents with ODD and Conduct Disorder lack decision-making and problem-solving skills (Matthys et al., 2012) and are often placed in classes with other children with emotional, conduct, or psychiatric disorders (Greene et al., 2002) or in high level in-patient programs (Cederna-Meko et al., 2014). Children and adolescent clients diagnosed with Conduct Disorder exhibit more antisocial behaviors such as physical fighting, aggression, and engaging in criminal activity while exhibiting maladaptive coping and solution-focused strategies (Mannuzza et al., 2004).

Anxiety and depressive disorders

Anxiety disorders can include generalized anxiety, phobias, separation anxiety as well as posttraumatic stress, panic, and obsessive-compulsive disorders (Thompson et al., 2013). Symptoms compromise intrapersonal skill development, causing deficits in self-esteem and self-efficacy, and can also contribute to somatic symptoms (i.e., stomachaches, headaches, nausea). Anxiety can impact memory and concentration (Ma, 1999), leading to poor school attendance and performance. Avoidant behavior can develop as a means to reduce anxiety, leading to self-isolation, limited peer relations, and social interactions, thereby impeding interpersonal skill development and increasing the co-occurrence of other disorders (i.e., depression). Avoidance also becomes a maladaptive coping skill (Ollendick & Pincus, 2008) that leads to poor emotional well-being and a lack of healthy coping/solution-focused skills (Rapee et al., 2009).

Children and adolescents with depression often lack the intrapersonal skills of self-esteem (Vogel, 2012) and emotion regulation which leads to overwhelm with negative cognitions. They tend to have little participation in the classroom (Huberty, 2012; Schulte-Körne, 2016) and poor academic achievement (Huberty, 2012; Mufson et al., 2004; Schulte-Körne, 2016). Due to their struggles with emotional regulation, children and adolescents with depression have inhibited social interactions and social skills (Segrin, 2000; Vogel, 2012) and strained peer and familial relationships (interpersonal), which further exacerbates their isolation, withdrawal, and inability to develop coping/solution-focused skills (Huberty, 2012).

Autism Spectrum Disorder

Autism Spectrum Disorder (ASD) contributes to difficulty in academic settings and hinders learning, concentration (Estes et al., 2011), and the development of self-sufficiency (Jasmin et al., 2009). ASD consists of deficits in communication and socio-emotional reciprocity, or the ability to read and react to social cues. These symptoms lead to social isolation, social anxiety, and lack of interpersonal skills (Gerber et al., 2011). Children and adolescents with ASD are often in special education classrooms, have low rates of high school graduation, and limited higher education opportunities. Struggles in academic achievement combined with limited prosocial behavior present challenges for future occupational opportunities and the application of coping/solution-focused skills.

Addressing DSM-5 diagnoses

Based on the criteria and nature of each disorder and individual differences of each client, clinicians can develop a systematic process of identifying skills needed to promote healthy functioning despite the challenges associated with these or other disorders. For example, children who are diagnosed with depression may need to become skilled at positive self-talk or incorporating affirmations (intrapersonal) into daily tasks to increase their self-esteem or self-worth. Adolescents with autism can learn to establish eye contact and engage in casual conversation for social skill development (interpersonal). Clients who have been diagnosed with ADHD may benefit from playing a sport such as soccer as a healthy way to cope with extra "energy" (coping/solution-focused) prior to working on homework.

The counseling process can facilitate skill development at a manageable pace that supports individual learning styles or strengths. Clinicians can enhance skill development in counseling by providing a supportive nonjudgmental environment to educate, facilitate acquisition, and create opportunities to rehearse or practice skills (Martens, 1987) as mentioned in Chapter 3. Further, clinicians can utilize evidence-based activities and interventions to initiate the experiential learning process.

Intrapersonal skills

Intrapersonal skills involve introspection that allows the identification of feelings, behaviors, and actions and can help children and adolescents with certain diagnoses address self-efficacy and self-esteem. Children and adolescents can learn to identify and regulate emotions or control impulses that lead to other social and academic problems. At the foundation of intrapersonal skills is mindfulness, or the nonjudgmental attention to experiences in the present moment (Kabet-Zinn, 1990). Mindfulness meditation has been associated with reducing symptoms of clinical disorders, including anxiety (Roemer et al., 2008) and depression (Teasdale et al., 2000). In fact, Holzel et al. (2011) suggest mindfulness meditation can include components of attention regulation, body awareness, emotion regulation (i.e., reappraisal, exposure, extinction, reconsolidation), and change in perspective about the self. Although most evidence-based research has been conducted with adult populations, outcome studies suggest mindfulness meditation has a positive impact on brain gray matter density or changes in neural structure (Holzel et al., 2011). This research is promising for children and adolescents given the malleability of their developing brains in learning mindfulness techniques and the potential positive impact on further skill development.

Mindfulness activities can include yoga, breathing exercises, progressive muscle relaxation, and mandalas. Being mindful can be considered an intrapersonal skill of awareness of thoughts and feelings and acceptance without judgment (Geisler et al., 2018). For children and adolescents, this awareness can help regulate emotions, empower a sense of self-control, as well as increase attention and decrease impulsivity (Cassone, 2015). Yoga assists in being mindful and can also be used for physical exercise. Physical activity has been associated with reduction of a variety of mental health symptoms, including impulse control and attention skills (Gapin et al., 2011). Gapin et al. (2011) and Chang et al. (2012) found that daily moderate exercise decreased symptoms of impulsivity, aggression, and increased self-regulation in adolescents diagnosed with ADHD.

Other examples of experiential activities for intrapersonal skill development include the use of creative or expressive arts activities for children diagnosed with ODD or depression as an emotional regulation and identification tool. For example, having clients draw a picture using colors that represent their current emotions, or using playdough to construct a sculpture that shows their current concerns. Averett et al. (2015) studied the effects of a local community arts-based program working with at-risk youth. The art included drawing, metal work, and painting. The authors found that participants of the program gained the intrapersonal skills of confidence and self-regulation.

Interpersonal skills

Interpersonal skills involve relational and social abilities that increase empathy, connection, and prosocial behavior. These skills can help children and adolescents with a diagnosis that affects their social skills and peer interaction learn how to make and maintain peer and familial relationships. Examples of interpersonal skills include communication and listening skills, empathy, giving and receiving feedback, and cooperation. Some activities can attend to both intra- and interpersonal skills. For example, Averett et al. (2015) also found that a community arts-based program increased interpersonal skills of communication and relationship building.

Several experiential programs address interpersonal skills related to DSM diagnoses. Young et al. (2012) proposed interpersonal psychotherapy-adolescent skills training (IPT-AST) to reduce anxiety and depression. The group-based program uses psychoeducation and skill-building activities like role-plays and games to educate clients about depression and anxiety and examine the relationship between feelings and interpersonal interactions (Young et al., 2012). Cunningham et al. (2017) implemented a three-day camp using the Resourceful Adolescent Program (RAP-A) to teach resilience. During the camp, participants engaged in workshops, campfires, and diverse sport-related activities. The authors found that the camp increased the participants' interpersonal functioning by increasing self-efficacy and social skills (Cunningham et al., 2017).

Beyond more structured experiential approaches, the use of activities within a typical therapeutic setting can also address symptoms or stigma related to DSM diagnoses. Guivarch et al. (2017) proposed the use of various board games with children and adolescents with various diagnoses such as ADHD, ODD, and ASD to improve empathy and prosocial skills such as taking turns, sharing, and communication. Board games also teach how to socialize in group settings if the board games required more than two people (see Chapter 8). Experiential games that require physical activity are also used to treat children and adolescent with various diagnoses and teach interpersonal skills (Forgan & Jones, 2002; Gates et al., 2017). Other examples of experiential activities that teach interpersonal skills can include a name game that teaches communication and assertiveness skills to a client with anxiety. Games that require clients to learn how to read facial expressions can help children diagnosed with ASD learn empathy, nonverbal cues, and other prosocial skills.

Gates et al. (2017) and Forgan and Jones (2002) used an outdoor adventure program as an intervention for children with ASD and learning disabilities. During this program, children had to complete several physical activities that required them to communicate and collaborate with each other. The authors found that children who participated improved their communication skills, were more likely to seek social interaction, and increased their prosocial skills. Outdoor physically engaging activities, like sports, can teach children with ASD, ODD, and ADHD impulse control and social skills often lacking due to their diagnoses. Outdoor physically engaging games can also stimulate children and adolescents with anxiety and depression toward socialization, reengaging with peers, and coping with symptoms. Some examples of outdoor physical engaging games include group sports (i.e., basketball, soccer, etc.), rope courses, and tug-of-war.

Coping and solution-focused skills

Coping skills are aimed to assist with emotional regulation and de-escalation. The majority of diagnoses directly affect the child or adolescent's ability to cope with adversity. In addition, a lack of healthy coping role models is often an added barrier for developing adaptive skills. Teaching coping skills can assist clients in coping with diagnoses like depression and anxiety. Coping skills can also prevent truancy due to symptoms like explosive behaviors. Webster-Stratton et al. (2001) showed children diagnosed with ODD ten brief videotaped vignettes of children modeling coping skills while facing stressful circumstances. The authors found that children who engaged in these activities showed decreased aggression and increased prosocial behaviors. Coping skills can be shown through video, modeled in person, or played as a game like charades.

Swank (2013) and DeDiego et al. (2017) proposed the use of a ropes course for children and adolescents coping with grief and loss. Swank (2013) found that rope courses increase coping, communication, and support. DeDiego et al. (2017) explored camp programming that incorporated experiential activities including adventure-based counseling for grieving youth. Similarly, Erichter et al. (2016) proposed yoga training for children and adolescents with anxiety. The authors found that yoga training decreased avoidant behaviors and increased healthy coping strategies in children. By engaging in physical activity, children with emotional regulation skill deficits are able to be more in tune with their bodies, identify emotions as they arise, and receive social support for peers engaging in the same activity. Focusing on specific symptoms or behaviors can offer a solution-focused approach to addressing DSM-5 diagnoses. A solution-focused approach that includes modeling or practicing skills to address specific issues is ideal for short-term, inpatient settings or in schools.

Counselors can use a wide range of experiential activities to teach interpersonal, intrapersonal, and coping skills. The goal of the activities is aimed at decreasing symptoms that impede functioning and increase age-appropriate developmental skills.

Strengths and limitations

Children who lack the necessary interpersonal, intrapersonal, and coping life skills to function in the real world due to their mental illness will need unique supports from counselors. Experiential learning can play out through peer interactions in environments such as a classroom, camp, or playground. Experiential activities in therapy can help externalize symptoms and diagnoses for children who may feel alienated from neuro-typical peers (Gapin et al., 2011). Experiential activities can also engage parents or guardians in the therapeutic process with activities they can practice at home to reinforce skills. For school settings, using experiential activities to build skills and manage symptoms can offer trackable data to show changes in functioning over time (Forgan & Jones, 2002). These data can be useful in support of Individualized Education Programs (IEPs) or behavior contracts.

Teaching interpersonal, intrapersonal, and coping skills through experiential activities has limitations. Counselors need to determine the clients' level of comfort and developmental abilities before introducing certain kinds of experiential activities. While the developmental level of clients is always a consideration in using experiential interventions, clinicians need to consider how symptoms or diagnoses influence the developmental process of a client. Certain activities can be intimidating for clients as they may be physically or intellectually outside of their capabilities. In the cases of more severe mental illness or symptoms, the use of experiential activities alone may not be sufficient for treatment. In these cases, an experiential approach can be a helpful adjunct to other methods of treatment including specialized interventions or medication. Thus, additional treatment strategies may be implemented in combination with experiential activities.

Meaning-making

Various interventions have been created to diminish the impact of these disorders on the clients' day-to-day functioning as well as their lives moving forward. Some of these interventions include, but are not limited to, school-based, individual-/family-based, exercise- and physical activity-based, digital platforms, interpersonal problem-solving skills training, interpersonal psychotherapy-adolescent skills training, social skills training, and behavioral interventions (Bonete et al., 2021; Das et al., 2016; Sukhodolsky & Butter, 2007; Sukhodolsky et al., 2016; Young et al., 2012). Some skill development interventions include experiential activities. Counselors, however, need to be intentional about the purpose and goal of the skill development activities and match the clients' capabilities. Introducing activities that are beyond the clients' development or functioning can exacerbate symptoms and further stigmatize the client and the helping relationship.

Children and adolescents with mental health diagnoses have a variety of skill deficits due to symptoms, developmental difficulties, and limited functioning. Skill deficits affect their social, academic, and family life and restrict their ability to cope. Experiential activities directed toward learning intrapersonal, interpersonal, and coping/solution-focused skills can help clients limit symptoms' effect and resume personal functioning. Examples of treatment goals include teaching how to communicate with others (interpersonal) for children with autism, relaxation and breathing techniques for children (coping/solution-focused) with ADHD, or teaching children with depression mindfulness in order to identify and verbalize feelings (interpersonal).

References

American Psychiatric Association (2022). *Diagnostic and statistical manual of mental disorders* (5th ed., text revision). Author.

Averett, P., Crowe, A., & Hall, C. (2015). The youth public arts program: Interpersonal and intrapersonal outcomes for at-risk youth. *Journal of Creativity in Mental Health, 10*(3), 306–323.

Baker, K. (2008). Conduct disorders in children and adolescents. *Pediatrics and Child Health, 19*, 73–78.

Bonete, S., Osuna, Á., Molinero, C., & García-Font, I. (2021). Magnitive: Effectiveness and feasibility of a cognitive training program through magic tricks for children with attention deficit and hyperactivity disorder. A second clinical trial in community settings. *Frontiers in Psychology, 12*, 1–12.

Cassone, A. (2015). Mindfulness training as an adjunct to evidence-based treatment for ADHD within families. *Journal of Attention Disorders, 19*(2), 147–157.

Cederna-Meko, C., Koch, S. M., & Wall, J. R. (2014). Youth with oppositional defiant disorder at entry into home-based treatment, foster care, and residential treatment. *Journal of Child and Family Studies, 23*(5), 895–906.

Centers for Disease Control and Prevention (2021). *Data and statistics on children's mental health.* https://www.cdc.gov/childrensmentalhealth/data.html

Chang, Y. K., Liu, S., Yu, H.-H., & Lee, Y. H. (2012). Effect of acute exercise on executive function in children with attention deficit hyperactivity disorder. *Archives of Clinical Neuropsychology, 27*(2), 225–237.

Cunningham, L. C., Shochet, I. M., Smith, C. L., & Wurfl, A. (2017). A qualitative evaluation of an innovative resilience-building camp for young carers. *Child & Family Social Work, 22*(2), 700–710.

Das, J. K., Salam, R. A., Lassi, Z. S., Khan, M. N., Mahmood, W., Patel, V., & Bhutta, Z. A. (2016). Interventions for adolescent mental health: An overview of systematic reviews. *Journal of Adolescent Health, 59*(4), S49–S60.

DeDiego, A. C., Wheat, L. S., & Fletcher, T. B. (2017). Overcoming obstacles: Exploring the use of adventure based counseling in youth grief camps. *Journal of Creativity in Mental Health, 12*(2), 230–241.

Eisenberg, N., Fabes, R. A., & Spinrad, T. L. (2006). Prosocial development. In W. Damon & R. M. Lerner (Eds.), *Social, Emotional, and Personality Development* (N. Eisenberg, vol. ed.) *Handbook of Child Psychology* (6th ed., Vol. 3, pp. 646–718). Wiley.

Erichter, S., Etietjens, M., Eziereis, S., Equerfurth, S., & Ejansen, P. (2016). Yoga training in junior primary school-aged children has an impact on physical self-perceptions and problem-related behavior. *Frontiers in Psychology, 7*(203), 1–34.

Estes, A., Rivera, V., Bryan, M., Cali, P., & Dawson, G. (2011). Discrepancies between academic achievement and intellectual ability in higher-functioning school-aged children with autism spectrum disorder. *Journal of Autism and Developmental Disorders, 41*(8), 1044–1052.

Forgan, J. W., & Jones, C. D. (2002). How experiential adventure activities can improve students social skills. *Teaching Exceptional Children, 34*(3), 52–58.

Gapin, J. I., Labban, J. D., & Etnier, J. L. (2011). The effects of physical activity on attention deficit hyperactivity disorder symptoms: The evidence. *Preventive Medicine, 52*, S70–S74.

Gates, J. A., Kang, E., & Lerner, M. D. (2017). Efficacy of group social skills interventions for youth with autism spectrum disorder: A systematic review and meta-analysis. *Clinical Psychology Review, 52*, 164–181.

Geisler, F. C. M., Bechtoldt, M. N., Oberländer, N., & Schacht-Jablonowsky, M. (2018). The benefits of a mindfulness exercise in a performance situation. *Psychological Reports, 121*(5), 853–876.

Gerber, F., Bessero, S., Robbiani, B., Courvoisier, D. S., Baud, M. A., Traoré, M. C., Blanco, M., Giroud, G., & Galli Carminati, G. (2011). Comparing residential programmes for adults with autism spectrum disorders and intellectual disability: Outcomes of challenging behaviour and quality of life. *Journal of Intellectual Disability Research, 55*(9), 918–932.

Greene, R. W., Biederman, J., Zerwas, S., Monuteaux, M. C., Goring, J. C., & Faraone, S. V. (2002). Psychiatric comorbidity, family dysfunction, and social impairment in referred youth with oppositional defiant disorder. *American Journal of Psychiatry, 159*, 1214–1224.

Guivarch, J., Murdymootoo, V., Elissalde, S. N., Salle-Collemiche, X., Tardieu, S., Jouve, E., & Poinso, F. (2017). Impact of an implicit social skills training group in children with autism spectrum disorder without intellectual disability: A before-and-after study. *PLoS ONE, 12*(7), 1–18.

Holzel, B. K., Carmody, J., Vangel, M., Congleton, C., Yerramsetti, S. M., Gard, T., & Lazar, S. W. (2011). Mindfulness practice leads to increases in regional brain gray matter density. *Psychiatry Research: Neuroimaging, 191*, 36–43.

Holzel, B. K., Lazar, S. W., Gard, T., Schuman-Olivier, Z., Vago, D. R., & Ott, U. (2011). How does mindfulness meditation work? Proposing mechanisms of action from a conceptual and neural perspective, *Perspetives on Psychological Science, 6*(6), 537–559.

Huberty, T. J. (2012). *Anxiety and depression in children and adolescents: Assessment, intervention, and prevention.* Springer Science & Business Media.

Jasmin, E., Couture, M., McKinley, P., Reid, G., Fombonne, E., & Gisel, E. (2009). Sensori-motor and daily living skills of preschool children with autism spectrum disorders. *Journal of Autism and Developmental Disorders, 39*(2), 231–241.

Jongsma, A. E., & Peterson, L. M. (2014a). *The child psychotherapy treatment planner: Includes DSM-5 updates.* Wiley.

Jongsma, A. E., & Peterson, L. M. (2014b). *The adolescent psychotherapy treatment planner: Includes DSM-5 updates.* Wiley.

Kabet-Zinn, J. (1990). *Full catastrophe living.* Delta Publishing.

Ma, X. (1999). A meta-analysis of the relationship between anxiety toward mathematics and achievement in mathematics. *Journal for Research in Mathematics Education, 30*(5), 520–540.

Mannuzza, S., Klein, R. G., Abikoff, H., & Moulton, J. L. (2004). Significance of childhood conduct problems to later development of conduct disorder among children with ADHD: A prospective follow-up study. *Journal of Abnormal Child Psychology, 32*(5), 565–573.

Martens, R. (1987). *Coaches guide to sport psychology: A publication for the American coaching effectiveness program: Level 2 sport science curriculum.* Human Kinetics Books.

Matthys, W., Vanderschruen, L. J., Schutter, D. J., & Lochman, J. E. (2012). Impaired nerurocognitive functions affect social learning processes in oppositional defiant disorder and conduct disorder: Implications for interventions. *Clinical Child and Family Psychology Review, 15*(3), 234–246.

Merikangas, K. R., He, J., Burstein, M., Swanson, S. A., Avenevoli, S., Cui, L., Benjet, C., Georgiades, K., & Swendsen, J. (2010). Lifetime prevalence of mental disorders in us adolescents: Results from the national comorbidity study-adolescent supplement (NCS-A). *Journal of the American Academy of Child and Adolescent Psychiatry, 49*(10), 980–989.

Mufson, L., Dorta, K. P., Wickramaratne, P., Nomura, Y., Olfson, M., & Weissman, M. M. (2004). A randomized effectiveness trial of interpersonal psychotherapy for depressed adolescents. *Archives of General Psychiatry, 61*, 577–584.

National Alliance on Mental Illness (2021). *Mental health by the numbers.* https://www.nami.org/mhstats

Ollendick, T. H., & Pincus, D. B. (2008). Panic disorder in adolescents. In R. Steele & M. Roberts (Eds.), *Handbook of Evidence-Based Therapies for Children and Adolescents* (pp. 83–102). Springer.

Rapee, R. M., Schniering, C. A., & Hudson, J. L. (2009). Anxiety disorders during childhood and adolescence: Origins and treatment. *Annual Review of Clinical Psychology, 1*, 311–341.

Roemer, L., Orsillo, S. M., & Salters-Pedneault, K. (2008). Efficacy of an acceptance-based behavior therapy for generalized anxiety disorder: Evaluation in a randomized controlled trial. *Journal of Consulting and Clinical Psychology, 76*(6), 1083.

Schulte-Körne, G. (2016). Mental health problems in a school setting in children and adolescents. *Deutsches Ärzteblatt International, 113*(11), 183–190.

Segrin, C. (2000). Social skills deficits associated with depression. *Clinical Psychology Review, 20*(3), 379–403.

Sukhodolsky, D. G., & Butter, E. M. (2007). Social skills training for children with intellectual disabilities. In J. W. Jacobson, J. A. Mulick, & J. Rojahn (Eds.), *Handbook of Intellectual and Developmental Disabilities* (pp. 601–618). Springer.

Sukhodolsky, D. G., Smith, S. D., McCauley, S. A., Ibrahim, K., & Piasecka, J. B. (2016). Behavioral interventions for anger, irritability, and aggression in children and adolescents. *Journal of Child and Adolescent Psychopharmacology, 26*(1), 58–64.

Swank, J. (2013). Obstacles of grief: The experiences of children processing grief on the ropes course. *Journal of Creativity in Mental Health, 8*(3), 235–248.

Teasdale, J. D., Williams, J. M., Soulsby, J. M., Segal, Z. V., Ridgeway, V. A., & Lau, M. A. (2000). Prevention of relapse/recurrence in major depression by mindfulness-based cognitive therapy. *Journal of Consulting and Clinical Psychology, 68*, 615–623.

Thompson, E. H.., Robertson, P., Curtis, R., & Frick, M. H. (2013). Students with anxiety: Implications for professional school counselors. *Professional School Counseling, 16*(4), 222–234.

Van der Oord, S., Van der Meulen, E. M., Prins, P. J. M., Oosterlaan, J., Buitelaar, J. K., & Emmelkamp, P. M. G. (2005). A psychometric evaluation of the social skills rating system in children with attention deficit hyperactivity disorder. *Behavioral Research and Therapy, 43*, 733–746.

Vogel, W. (2012). Depression in children and adolescents: Depression is a relatively common presentation and needs to be recognized in children and adolescents. *Journal of Continuing Professional Development, 30*(4), 114–117.

Webster-Stratton, C., Reid, J., & Hammond, M. (2001). Social skills and problem-solving training for children with early-onset conduct problems: Who benefits? *Journal of Child Psychology And Psychiatry, 42*(7), 943–952.

World Health Organization (1994). *International classification of diseases, 10th Revision* (ICD-10). Author.

World Health Organization (2022). *International classification of diseases, 11th Revision* (ICD-11). Author.

Young, J. F., Makover, H. B., Cohen, J. R., Mufson, L., Gallop, R. J., & Benas, J. S. (2012). Interpersonal psychotherapy-adolescent skills training: Anxiety outcomes and impact of comorbidity. *Journal of Clinical Child & Adolescent Psychology, 41*(5), 640–653.

Ziereis, S., & Jansen, P. (2016). Correlation of motor abilities and executive functions in children with ADHD. *Applied Neuropsychology: Child, 5*(2), 138–148.

Activity 7.1: Externalizing the Disorder

Amanda C. DeDiego

Theme/Goals of Activity	Understand mental health diagnoses and externalize symptoms/ disorder to address mental health stigma
Population/Age	5+
Intrapersonal Skills	Self-awareness, monitoring of symptoms, resilience
Interpersonal Skills	Ability to communicate about own wellness, communicating with parents and professionals about mental health
Coping/Solution-Focused Skills	Externalizing mental illness to help address self-worth and stigma
Materials	Options include art supplies, pottery, sculpting

Description of the Activity:

This activity is appropriate for a range of ages. The focus is to externalize a mental health diagnosis to see a diagnostic label as one *part* of a person, not the *whole* person. Following a DSM-5-TR diagnosis, the therapist will work with the client to determine a name for the illness (e.g., Stanley, Patricia, Anger Monster). The client guides this process and finds the name that feels right. Going forward, when discussing the disorder, the therapist and client will refer to the illness by the client-assigned name. For example, when anger symptoms are very present on a certain day, the client can say "Stanley paid me a visit today" or "Stanley picked a fight with my friend." The client can create a visual representation of the illness, drawing a picture or creating a sculpture of "Stanley." This is also useful in assessment, as the therapist can ask how many days Stanley paid a visit in the last week, or how loud Stanley was in the last week. This is a developmentally appropriate way to discuss DSM-5-TR symptomology.

Macro-Processing:

No loading:

Ask the client if we were to name the illness, what would it be named? What would it look like? Then proceed to create the visual representation.

Front and back loading:

Front: Provide psychoeducation about the DSM-5-TR diagnosis that is being assigned. Then introduce a different way to think and talk about the diagnosis.
Back: After creating the name and visual of the disorder, explain how the character relates to the symptoms of the DSM-5-TR and provide instructions about how the character will be used to track symptoms.

Metaphors:

The character serves as a metaphor for the illness, and the symptoms/prevalence of the illness are externalized to the metaphor of the character.

Micro-Processing:

Observation: The client may be experiencing symptoms in session, so the therapist may ask if the character has shown up today during the counseling process. Similarly, if the client is sharing about behavioral issues in school that week, you may inquire if the character went to school with them that day.

Observation: Symptoms seem to be improving or worsening, so use the character to track symptoms. For example, asking "Has Stanley been hanging around a lot lately?" or observing "Stanley hasn't been around as much lately."

Comments/questions: (include skill identified)

Using the character as part of symptom tracking

- "How many times did Stanley show up this week?"
- "Are there different things that make Stanley show up or make him louder?"
- "What kinds of things help you to put Stanley in time out when he shows up?"

Debrief and Transfer:

This is a really useful activity use with caregivers and teachers. After creating the character to represent the DSM-5-TR disorder, bringing in caregivers and having the client explain the character to the parents is really helpful. The caregivers can use the externalizing language to discuss the disorder and symptoms outside of session. Caregivers can also use this character to track symptoms and report back to therapists, primary care physicians, school counselors, etc. Sharing this character with teachers and school counselors can help all supports be together in how they are discussing DSM-5-TR diagnoses with the client.

Tips or Lessons Learned for Counselors:

This activity is so useful across the lifespan. There is so much stigma associated with diagnostic labels. This externalizing tool really helps to emphasize that the illness is not the whole person. It also helps externalize the symptoms of the disorder, so a child can consider that anger outbursts or behavioral problems that result from mental illness do not make them a "bad kid" but are just symptoms. In adapting to adolescents, they may still enjoy sculpting the character but just creating a name and listing the symptoms that the character embodies creates a helpful way to discuss symptoms and externalize illness.

About the Author: Amanda C. DeDiego, PhD, NCC, is an Associate Professor of Counseling. Her research in counselor development includes counseling pedagogy and creative interventions useful in coursework and supervision.

Activity 7.2: Expressive and Reflective Scheduling

Andrew Southerland

Theme/Goals of Activity	Expressive and creative arts
Population/Age	6+
Intrapersonal Skills	Identifying emotions, mindfulness, optimism, motivation
Interpersonal Skills	Communication, expressing emotions appropriately and effectively
Coping/Solution-Focused Skills	Problem-solving, decision-making, and initiating change
Materials	Markers/pencils/crayons, paper, additional craft materials as desired

Description of the Activity:

During this activity, the client will be invited to write out and/or draw their schedule for the week using markers, pencils, or crayons on a blank piece of paper (Figure 7.1). Clinicians will provide little directions beyond the invitation to allow for a more expressive space. During the activity, the clinician should attend to and reflect the client's body language, tone, behaviors, expressed emotions, and method of construction. Following the completion of the activity, the clinician transitions the focus from the activity into a time of reflection. Then the client is invited to share their observations and reactions to the schedule that they have expressed. Additionally, during this time, the clinician may offer wonderings or things they noticed while witnessing the activity and observing the final product.

Macro-Processing:

No loading:

Present the child or adolescent the opportunity to write and/or draw their schedule for the week.

Front and back loading:

Front: While materials are being gathered, invite the client to write and/or draw their schedule in any way that they would like.

  Back: Invite the client to point out their own observations of their constructed schedule, along with naming how they felt while they were engaged in the activity.

Micro-Processing:

Observations while collecting materials: Notice and reflect the materials the client selects for their schedule. At the same time, attune and reflect any emotions or behaviors that are expressed during the selection process (i.e., "you are unsure which materials you want to use" or "you knew exactly what you wanted to use"), as this can help assist the therapeutic relationship and build self-awareness within the client.

During schedule construction: Attune and reflect any behaviors, choices, or emotions that you notice. Pay close attention to how the child writes or draws the different daily tasks, as well as how they organize their schedule. For example, maybe the child uses a lot of force and aggression in writing "SCHOOL" in large lettering or maybe Tuesday appears to be overwhelmed with many unorganized tasks written in various sizes. By not only attending to what the child writes or draws but also how they go about it, we are able to better connect with the emotions associated with their daily experiences.

Upon completion of schedule construction: Invite the child to name what it was like for them to write and/or draw their schedule. Then encourage the child to observe their schedule and reflect on what they notice or how they feel looking at it. While this step may be more challenging for younger clients, it is crucial to allow space for them to begin to recognize and name what they have expressed and what they are experiencing. For example, a child may say "Mondays look terrible" or "Saturdays look like the most fun." Next, take a moment to reflect on what you notice about their schedule, as this can offer the opportunity for connection and the development of self-awareness. For example, you might say, "I notice that Tuesday looks like there is a lot going on" or "I notice that SCHOOL looks big and scary" or "I notice that the first half of the week looks far busier than the second half."

Debrief and Transfer:

Following the construction and reflection of their schedule for the week, it is important to spend time processing the activity in an effort to transfer and apply skills to navigate weekly tasks that might be stressful, unpleasant, or chaotic. For example, you may choose to discuss coping skills, such as positive self-talk, mindfulness-based practices, or identifying enjoyable tasks to look forward to during the week. In addition, there may be opportunities to promote client autonomy by identifying times in the week the client can choose what tasks to complete or maybe even rearrange the order of events.

Tips or Lessons Learned for Counselors:

It is helpful to adapt this activity based on client development and abilities. For example, some clients may not be able to write out their events of the week. As a result, you can adapt this activity to be done either verbally or through the use of drawings or pictures. Furthermore, it is also helpful to draw out metaphors from the schedule to discuss expressed emotions and coping strategies. For example, if a client draws "homework" on Thursday as if it were a monster, you can use the metaphor by saying, "You have to face a monster on Thursday. I wonder what you might need to face a monster." Maybe the client responds with "a sword

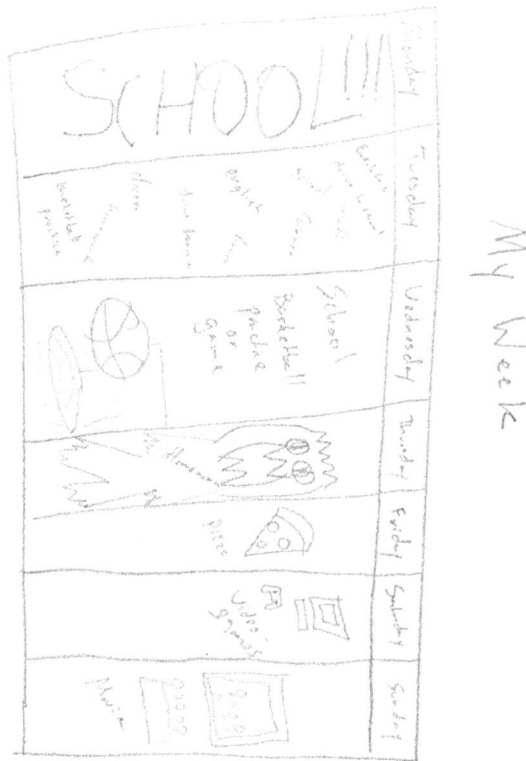

Figure 7.1 **Example of weekly schedule.**

and shield," which becomes a rich metaphor for discussing practical strategies and resources available to them that might act as a source of strength and protection. Finally, if the activity is found to be beneficial, you can also encourage the client's parents to go through this activity with their child every week. Doing so does not only allow for continued expression and reflection but also provides the client an opportunity to prepare for what lies ahead, which can ultimately promote time management skills.

About the Author: Andrew Southerland, PhD, LPC, NCC, is a counselor educator and community mental health counselor based in Laramie, Wyoming. Andrew has over 5 years of clinical experience supporting clients across the lifespan and has effective utilized Expressive and Reflective Scheduling with children, adolescents, and college students.

Activity 7.3: "Inside Out"

Patrice Parkinson

Theme/Goals of Activity	Teaching emotion regulation to help foster emotional awareness, empathy, and compassion (for children and adolescents) in their daily lives, develop insight about dreams, long-term memory, and the unconscious, provide a visual representation of the interplay between emotions, thoughts, and behavior, improve communication, understand emotions and how they interact with each other (having more than one emotion at the same time), identify and learn about core concepts of the self, and enhance relationships by exploring the meaning behind behavior and deepening understanding
Population/Age	7+

Intrapersonal Skills	Increase self-awareness, develop introspection and reflective practice, and increase awareness of how emotions work together on the inside to influence behavior
Interpersonal Skills	Increase effective communication of emotions, increase assertiveness, verbalize feelings and deepen empathy for others, lessen avoidance of uncomfortable situations involving intense feelings, increase trust in intimate or close relationships
Coping/Solution-Focused Skills	Emotion-focused coping (confront emotions – sadness can help honor a loss), social support, meaning making, core experiences, and concepts that form our worldview can be reconstructed to help with resilience.
Materials	Digital device (television, mobile phone, tablet, laptop, or computer), access to the movie *Inside Out*

Description of the Activity:

Watch the film *Inside Out* that uses characters to represent the core emotions of joy, sadness, fear, disgust, and anger (surprise was left out). This is a great tool to talk about what each emotion looks like and feels like. The client will write down or draw how Anger, Sadness, Fear, Disgust, and Joy would feel about an event, for example the death of a loved one or divorce. The activity helps the client recognize they are angry their loved one has left and sad about the loss. The client describes current experiences of difficulty explaining emotions at school, home, etc. The activity has been used with an adolescent to explore the feelings they had when considering terminating a romantic relationship.

Inside Out focuses particularly on experiencing difficult transitions such as moving to a new place or home, making new friends, enrolling in a new school, and adjusting to parents' new schedules. Emphasis is placed on the significance of sadness and how it can foster connection with other people. All emotions aid us. These feelings can change over time. In addition, childhood memories significantly impact us, and during adolescence, our emotions change.

The activity is useful for exploring grief and loss, life transitions, emotional intelligence challenges, understanding memories, those feeling ignored or abandoned, anger management, and coping strategies.

Macro-Processing:

No loading:

Watch the film *Inside Out.*

Front and back loading:

Back: Allow the individual to describe the characters and their understanding from different scenes in the film. For example, when the globes change to the colors of yellow (joy) and blue (sadness).

Metaphors: Use metaphors to aid in meaning making. Examples from the film – expanding the Master console, train of thought, running away when you are angry, etc.

Micro-Processing:

Observations: Some children find it difficult to express what they are feeling or explain the feelings they are having.

- What feeling are you having right now? (after talking about the film)
- What did you like?
- What stood out to you?
- Could you relate to Riley?
- What are our different emotions?
- What is the purpose of each emotion?
- How do we express emotions we are feeling?
- How can we recognize the emotion someone else is feeling? (body language, actions, words)

You can task children, adolescents, and caregivers/loved ones to imagine what the five characters are feeling in another person's head. This increases empathy and deepens connection.

Debrief and Transfer:

The client talked about feeling angry and unheard. After watching *Inside Out*, the client talked about feeling sad, angry, and happy at the same time when their loved one died (emotion-focused skills). The client was able to communicate the different feelings to mother. The activity is used as a foundation for transition into different ways of viewing the world and how others feel. Follow-up includes communication with peers and understanding emotions during difficult times.

Tips or Lessons Learned for Counselors:

Socio-economic status and not having access to the movie, seeing the film as too childlike, disability, culture, age, and a lack of interest in films may be barriers. The family, for example, may not value technology or films or the lessons portrayed by the media. A visual impairment or color blindness may impede the full experience. It may be difficult to shift from understanding emotions as monochrome to versatile and working together. Our memories might include trauma. This activity is not for everyone.

About the Author: Patrice Parkinson, MA, NCC, PPC, is a doctoral student in the Counselor Education and Supervision program at the University of Wyoming. Parkinson earned her MA in Clinical Mental Health Counseling from Liberty University and a BS in Psychology from the University of the West Indies.

Activity 7.4: Melter Beads

Jennifer Bays

Theme/Goals of Activity	Increase in duration of attention, increase in frustration tolerance
Population/Age	7+
Intrapersonal Skills	Promotes persistence, increases ability to overcome distractions
Interpersonal Skills	Improves self-confidence
Coping/Solution-Focused Skills	Emotional regulation
Materials	Perler beads, peg boards, ironing paper, iron, template (if desired)

Description of the Activity:

This activity involves using perler beads to create patterns or designs. Templates can be used, or client can create their own pattern or design. Beads are place on the peg board in the desired pattern. Once the desired pattern or design is complete the ironing paper is placed on top and the iron is used to fuse the beads together. Perler beads are small and easily disturbed. This activity requires concentration and frustration tolerance.

Macro-Processing:

Front and back loading:

Back: If the client is able to finish the project, process how it felt to be focused long enough to do so and how that could carry over into school and home. Client could also explore struggles they experienced working on the project and how they were able to complete the project.

Micro-Processing:

Observations: The first time a child does this activity, they may not be able to complete it due to attentional difficulties or low frustration tolerance.

When a child does complete the project bring awareness by:

- "You really had to focus for a long time to finish this project, what was that like for you?"
- "How can you take this experience and apply it to things at home and school?"
- "This project seemed to cause you a lot of frustration, how did you work through the frustration you were feeling?"
- "Are there other times you can use those same skills?"

Debrief and Transfer:

The client struggled to complete a perler bead design in a previous session and wanted to try again. In the second attempt to complete a perler bead design, they were able to finish.

- "You were able to remain focused and finish your project. How does that feel? I wonder what it would be like if you tried to be this focused at school/home?"

Checking in each session on how many times the client was able to focus during a lesson at school or while at home encourages them to continue working and will let you know if additional strategies are needed.

Tips or Lessons Learned for Counselors:

This activity may need to be attempted several times before the client will be able to remain focused enough to complete the project. That is okay, any progress is progress.

About the Author: Jennifer Bays, MS, LPC, graduated with her masters in counseling and is currently pursuing her doctorate in Counselor Education and Supervision. She works with all ages and primarily with children.

Chapter 8

Parables, storytelling, literature, and books

R. Paul Maddox II and Rebecca Edelman

Children are born telling stories. Whether it be through play or verbal expression, stories are a part of who they are and what they do (Pehrsson, 2006). Reading stories can assist children to develop an awareness and understanding of their own attitudes and feelings while engaging in an exploration of the world in which they live (DeVries et al., 2017). When the reading of stories or parables is combined with processing or discussion as a therapeutic intervention it is known as bibliotherapy (DeVries et al., 2017). Hynes and Hynes-Berry (1994) asserted that bibliotherapy uses "…literature to bring about a therapeutic interaction between a participant and facilitator" (p.10), while Pehrsson and McMillen (2007) described bibliotherapy as "the use of books and other media to facilitate both normal development and clinically significant problems" (p. 1). In keeping these definitions in mind, there are various applications to using parables, storytelling, books, and other media within clinical and school settings with children and adolescents to aid in interpersonal and intrapersonal communications, processing and normalizing trauma, and facilitating emotional healing and growth (Chitra & Noor, 2019; Hahlweg et al., 2008; Heath et al., 2005; Hynes & Hynes-Berry 1994; Mumbauer & Kelchner, 2017; Pehrsson, 2006).

Counseling children and adolescents with bibliotherapy

Parables, storytelling, books, and literature have a long history of being utilized to help teach people how to effectively face various issues by encouraging them to connect with characters and situations and engage in self-evaluation based upon the experiences communicated through stories (De Vries et al., 2017; Jackson, 2006; Schneck, 1945). Three primary categories of bibliotherapy have been identified in the literature. These are clinical bibliotherapy, developmental bibliotherapy, and client-developed bibliotherapy (De Vries et al., 2017; Gavigan et al., 2010). Clinical bibliotherapy represents a technique in which directed reading is utilized by professional mental health counselors/therapists in a clinical setting to help facilitate processing and insight for individuals with emotional or behavioral issues (De Vries et al., 2017; Gavigan et al., 2010; Pehrsson & McMillen, 2005; Pehrsson & McMillen, 2007). By contrast, developmental bibliotherapy focuses on personal well-being and is most often utilized by school counselors, teachers, and social workers in school or community settings that serve children. Developmental bibliotherapy as an intervention can assist children in facing challenges in their lives by providing characters and examples with which children can identify (Gavigan et al., 2010; Mendel et al., 2016). Finally, client-developed bibliotherapy refers to an intervention utilizing a form of journaling that addresses a concern that may be shared between the writer and characters within a story (De Vries et al., 2017; McCulliss, 2012).

Interpersonal and intrapersonal skills

The use of children's books within the context of psychotherapy in a clinical setting with children and families can be helpful in a variety of ways. Books can help provide children and their caregivers with developmentally appropriate language for psychoeducation related to mental health and wellness. The use of stories and books can also be an effective medium for counselors in a clinical setting who are interacting and engaging with child and adolescent clients about difficult topics (Mendel et al., 2016). Bibliotherapy represents a collaborative interaction between a counselor and a client. It is important to keep in mind that in the implementation of bibliotherapy the interactions between the counselor and the client are more important than the content of the media itself (Mendel et al., 2016). Bibliotherapy offers clients and counselors a medium through which they communicate with one another in an engaging, meaningful, and safe way.

In clinical mental health counseling settings, bibliotherapy can be a tool for clients of all ages and their families. Bibliotherapy provides a space for psychoeducation, teaches parental competencies, and holds strong efficacy

DOI: 10.4324/9781315213767-9

rates and connections with specific diagnoses, including anxiety, depression, and other mental health diagnoses (Hahlweg, 2008). Often used in conjunction with Cognitive Behavioral Therapy (CBT), bibliotherapy can assist children in changing their thinking processes regarding their personal situations and can also be a tool to help them modify their behaviors (DeVries et al., 2017; Heath et al., 2005). This can occur when the child connects with aspects of a character from a story and, by doing so, begins to have greater understanding and awareness regarding their own life situations and emotions (DeVries et al., 2017; Heath et al., 2005). Additionally, research has indicated that bibliotherapy can be a resource in building self-esteem, particularly when working with girls and young women. Studies indicate that individuals with higher self-esteem are more likely to succeed, communicate more effectively, transition more smoothly, and think critically (Salimi et al., 2014). Such skills may then be transferred by the client to their own life helping foster personal development and wellness. Numerous research studies have indicated that the use of bibliotherapy can have positive therapeutic outcomes for children who have experienced trauma. For example, the use of bibliotherapy in clinical mental health settings has been shown to have therapeutic positive outcomes for children facing a wide range of situations such as abuse and neglect (Betzalel & Shechtman, 2010; DeVries et al., 2017; Pardeck 1990), aggression (Shechtman, 1999), surgeries, medical issues, or hospitalizations (DeVries et al., 2017; Duncan, 2010; Goddard, 2011; Koppenhaver et al., 2001), and natural disasters (Stewart & Ames, 2014).

Coping and solution-focused skills

With the wide range of issues that can be addressed using bibliotherapy, its use is not limited to clinical mental health settings. Bibliotherapy can be implemented in other treatment settings as well to support coping strategies for diagnoses and life events as well as solution-focused interventions in clinical and school settings. For example, it offers an excellent outlet for school counselors to aid students and faculty in improving prosocial behaviors for students in school settings through group lessons or individual counseling services (Chitra & Noor, 2019; Cook et al., 2006; Mumbauer & Kelchner, 2017).

Elementary school

Many school counselors in elementary schools regularly find themselves in the teaching rotation or visiting classrooms to teach and work with students through the presentation of classroom lessons. When working with groups in elementary schools, bibliotherapy offers an opportunity to provide students a metaphorical opportunity to express their knowledge, fears, concerns, ideas, and experiences (Akgun & Benli, 2019; Cook et al., 2006; Mumbauer & Kelchner, 2017; Pehrsson, 2006). In an elementary school, bibliotherapy can offer an opportunity to connect students across grade levels to a similar theme or lesson each week. For example, as a part of their school counseling curriculum, school counselors can create a theme for each week. Using these themes, they can find grade-appropriate literature that can act as a storytelling tool to teach a lesson around the theme.

The story could be used to connect the class using conversations and on a larger scale the school through a universal theme of multiple stories. Group work with elementary students also provides a great space for integrating and utilizing parables and moral stories with students. Through learning together with stories and parables, the students can explore life lessons in a context that reaches their imaginations and language developmentally. An example would be the use of bibliotherapy to teach about bullying prevention school wide. Using books like *Stand up for Yourself and Your Friends: Dealing with Bullies & Bossiness and Finding a Better Way* by Patti Kelley Criswell and Angela Martini (2016) or *Confessions of a Former Bully* by Trudy Ludwig (2016), school counselors can create a lesson around safety, advocacy, and understanding that would impact the school climate and culture immensely.

When working with elementary school-aged children individually, bibliotherapy using parables, storytelling, and books can provide children with opportunities to experience and understand better the experiences in their lives or of classmates. These types of interventions can provide a strong outlet for young students to learn about and connect to differences in their peers or process their own traumas. An example in individual counseling might be if a child's parents are divorcing. Stories often allow a child to see a different side of the experience and have an opportunity to process and understand differently what is happening in their families. Through using books like *It's Not Your Fault, KoKo Bear* by Vicki Lansky (1998), *A Smart Girl's Guide to Her Parents' Divorce: How to Land on Your Feet When Your World Turns Upside Down* by Nancy Holyoke (2009), or *Dinosaurs Divorce: A Guide for Changing Homes* by Laurie Kransy Brown and Marc Brown (1986), counselors are able to process and work with children whose parents may be divorcing or separating. Stories such as these allow the child's imagination to grasp language they developmentally can understand and to which they can relate.

Secondary school

Bibliotherapy can also be utilized in secondary school settings to help facilitate healthy social and emotional development among students (McCulliss & Chamberlain, 2013). In a group setting bibliotherapy can be used to process and understand grief and loss, build a better understanding of mental health concerns, foster a deeper understanding of themselves, and aid in developing a variety of life skills. In groups with high school students, stories have the ability to connect various students to a place of understanding and growth. Bibliotherapy groups can also aid students better understanding their mental health and connecting to other students who are experiencing similar life events to themselves. By having a bibliotherapy group, school counselors can normalize different events, themes, and concerns that are impacting students and the school culture. Through reading and having a guided group discussion with a story, students can be more equipped to handle life's road bumps in various facets of their lives. High school bibliotherapy groups can span a variety of topics and have had high efficacy rates for students with anxiety, abuse, bullying, aggression, anxiety, grief and loss, parent relations, illness, self-image, living through a natural disaster, and various other hurdles high school students may face (McCulliss & Chamberlain, 2013). This tool can be used in a group setting to support at-risk students. Through creating an engaging, respectful, challenging, caring environment, bibliotherapy groups allow students to interact and collaborate with other students, counselors, and teachers to build a stronger, more productive working relationship (Schreur, 2006). Reading about characters and processing as a small group allows students an opportunity to realize they are not alone, and others have faced experiences similar to their circumstances.

Fiction has an ability to weave a world with a golden thread outside of daily life. Bibliotherapy with individual high schoolers can allow for an opportunity to explore that world and themselves more holistically. Through exploring poetry, fiction, and non-fiction stories high school students are given an opportunity to develop, grow, and have a different understanding and regard for their experiences and the experiences of others. Whether a student is struggling with athletics, mental health, academics, or exploring their gender identity and sexuality, bibliotherapy provides a place to explore and gain understanding and knowledge. Stories like *Bottled Up* by Jaye Murray (2004), *This Book Is Gay* by Juno Dawson (2015), or *Bullied* by Jeff Erno (2011) create a world for students to relate, understand, and look beyond just their perspective and experiences.

These interventions aid in multiple life transitions, including the transition to college or the workforce for students (Becker et al., 2008; & Salimi et al., 2014). Research supports that bibliotherapy utilized during periods of transition (sometimes referred bibliolinking) can aid in the establishment and growth of relationships in transitional phases for adolescents (Becker et al., 2008; & Salimi et al., 2014). Through these transitions, stories, experiences, and self-expression, bibliotherapy can allow high schoolers an opportunity to connect with their counselor about the deeper meanings of what is being shared through the literature.

Strengths and limitations

One of the primary strengths of bibliotherapy is its versatility for application within diverse practice settings. Whether in a clinical mental health or school setting, bibliotherapy can be used and adapted to fit the specific needs of clients in a wide range of settings (DeVries et al., 2017). Another strength related to bibliotherapy is that it can be implemented at relatively low financial cost. Books, in multiple languages, applicable for use in bibliotherapy are often available through public libraries, allowing it to be a useful treatment intervention for children and families of diverse social and cultural backgrounds (Mendel et al., 2016).

While there are strengths to utilizing bibliotherapy, there are limitations as well. One limitation of bibliotherapy is that it may not be an appropriate fit for clients who experience reading challenges and comprehension difficulties such as low literacy and language barriers (Mendel et al., 2016). Along with this, many counselors who would like to use bibliotherapy may not have a sufficient understanding of what is available in children's literature that is appropriate to the child's developmental level and the situation that the child is facing in life (Akgun & Benli, 2019). Another limitation to bibliotherapy as an intervention is that it is not necessarily a stand-alone treatment or approach (DeVries et al., 2017). It needs to be combined with other treatment interventions or approaches, and because of this it may not align well with all treatment interventions, approaches, or theories.

Bibliotherapy can be a useful intervention for working with children and adolescents experiencing a variety of situations and symptoms (DeVries et al., 2017). Through the process of bibliotherapy, children can gain greater understanding of the circumstances they are facing in life and increase their awareness of their own thoughts, feelings, and behaviors. This can help children express themselves more freely, increase their coping skills, and face difficult situations (Akgun & Benli, 2019). It can be utilized both in school and clinical mental health counseling settings (Akgun & Benli, 2019; Chitra & Noor, 2019; Cook et al., 2006; DeVries et al., 2017; Mendel et al.,

2016; Mumbauer & Kelchner, 2017). There are many positive uses and outcomes that have been identified in the literature for bibliotherapy. However, it is important that counselors understand the process of bibliotherapy and its limitations before attempting to utilize it when working with clients.

Meaning-making

Bibliotherapy can provide opportunities for students to connect and feel understood through the expression of storytelling they themselves often use. Research into therapy using stories supports that it has a positive impact on classroom behaviors (Schreur, 2006). As a tool in school counseling, storytelling through parables and literature allows students an opportunity to think critically as they read and transition into thinking with them. When incorporating bibliotherapy into the therapeutic process, it is vital for counselors to keep in mind a few parameters for meaningfully selecting materials. The stories, books, or media chosen should be read/reviewed by the counselor prior to recommending or providing them to clients. It is also imperative that the materials chosen are credible and appropriate to the client's needs and developmental level. Materials should be inclusive and respective of the client's culture (Pehrsson & McMillen, 2007).

Material selection

There are several stages within the process for implementing bibliotherapy that are important to keep in mind. Whether describing the use of developmental bibliotherapy, clinical bibliotherapy, or client-developed bibliotherapy, many advocates for bibliotherapy describe the process of the client's experiences in bibliotherapy as occurring in three primary stages: (a) Identification, (b) Catharsis, and (c) Insight (Catalano, 2008; Mendel et al., 2016). In the identification stage, the child begins to see aspects of themselves and their own lives in the characters and situations presented in the story. Building upon this identification, the Catharsis stage involves the child becoming more emotionally connected to parts of the story and engaging in a process of seeing and experiencing characters' feelings. Within the confines of a safe therapeutic environment, this stage can result in a release of emotional tension for the client. Upon the release of emotional tension, the Insight stage can occur which involves the child gaining greater awareness and new understanding of their own feelings and life situations so that they may be able to approach them in healthier ways.

Taking a slightly different perspective of the bibliotherapy process, DeVries et al. (2017) describe the therapeutic stages in terms of (a) assessment, (b) planning/selection, and (c) implementation/sharing. As a part of the assessment stage, the counselor is evaluating the developmental and readiness level of the child relevant to the therapeutic work in which they are engaging. The information gathered in this stage is vital for the next stage of planning/selecting. During the planning/selecting stage, the counselor needs to choose appropriate and relevant topics, stories, books, prompts, and activities for the child in bibliotherapy. When selecting stories to use in bibliotherapy, counselors need to pick stories that will align with the child's own experiences and have some personal connection for the child. As a part of this, it is important that any story that is selected be representative of the child's culture, language, specific situation, and familial beliefs (DeVries et al., 2017; Goddard, 2011; Heath et al., 2005).

For the implementation/sharing phase, the selected stories will be shared among the counselor and child. This involves engaging with the child through the implementation of pre-reading, guided reading, and closure activities. As a part of pre-reading, the counselor will do things such as review the book's cover with the child and discuss with the child the overall topic that the story(ies) in the book address. During this discussion, the counselor might outline with the child some of what may happen during the course of the story and allow the child to share some of their own related experiences. Following these pre-reading activities, the counselor and child will engage in the guided reading phase. During guided reading, the counselor will read the story and direct questions or prompts to the child, encouraging connections with characters from the story. The counselor will allow the child time to reflect upon the story and provide space for them to digest what they are experiencing through the story (DeVries et al., 2017; Heath et al., 2005). Finally, the counselor will transition to the closure phase of the intervention. For the closure phase, the counselor is mindful of the child's reactions as they facilitate opportunities for the child to explore and process the emotions they may be experiencing that are difficult to express.

With the prevalent use of developmental bibliotherapy in schools and the utilization of clinical and client-developed bibliotherapy in clinical counseling settings, it is important that counselors be knowledgeable regarding the diverse applications of bibliotherapy within treatment settings (Catalano, 2008; DeVries et al., 2017; Mendel et al., 2016). There are a number of activities that can be utilized in the facilitation of the therapeutic process when implementing bibliotherapy. Activities such as creative writing, role playing, journaling, drawing pictures, making/using puppets, re-telling/re-writing parts of the story, or developing a timeline of events from the story are all examples of things that can help children process what has happened in the story and make meaningful connections to their own experiences in life (DeVries et al., 2017; Heath et al., 2005). When deciding how to incorporate bibliotherapy into the therapeutic process, counselors need to ensure that its application and the activities chosen are congruent with the overall theory or treatment approach being utilized (Pehrsson & McMillen, 2007).

References

Akgün, E., & Karaman Benli, G. (2019). Bibliotherapy with preschool children: A case study. *Psikiyatride Güncel Yaklaşimlar, 11*(1), 100–111.

Becker, K. M., Pehrsson, D. E., & McMillen, P. S. (2008) Bibliolinking: An adaptation of bibliotherapy for university students in transition. *Journal of Poetry Therapy, 21*(4), 231–235.

Betzalel, N., & Shechtman, Z. (2010). Bibliotherapy treatment for children with adjustment difficulties: A comparison of affective and cognitive bibliotherapy. *Journal of Creativity in Mental Health, 5*(4), 426–439.

Brown, L. K., & Brown, M. T. (1986). *Dinosaurs divorce: A guide for changing families*. Little, Brown and Company Books for Young Readers.

Catalano, A. (2008). Making a place for bibliotherapy on the shelves of a curriculum materials center: The case for helping pre-service teachers use developmental bibliotherapy in the classroom. *Education Libraries: Childrens Resources 31*(1), 17–22.

Chitra, C. I., & Noor, M. (2019). Development of guidance and counseling's model services with bibliotherapy techniques to improve prosocial behavior for student of primary school. *Journal of Physics: Conference Series, 1179*, 1–7.

Cook, K. E., Earles-Vollrath, T., & Ganz, J. B. (2006). Bibliotherapy. *Intervention in School and Clinic, 42*(2), 91–100.

Criswell, P. K., & Martini, A. (2016). *Stand up for yourself & your friends: Dealing with bullies & bossiness and finding a better way*. American Girl Publishing

Dawson, J. (2015). *This book is gay*. Sourcebooks Fire.

DeVries, D. D., Brennan, Z., Lankin, M., Morse, R., Rix, B., & Beck, T. (2017). Healing with books: A literature review of bibliotherapy used with children and youth who have experienced trauma. *Therapeutic Recreation Journal, 51*(1), 48–74.

Duncan, M. K. W. (2010). Creating bibliotherapeutic libraries for pediatric patients and their families: Potential contributions of a cognitive theory of traumatic stress. *Journal of Pediatric Nursing, 25*(1), 25–27.

Erno, J. (2011) *Bullied*. Dreamspinner Press, LLC

Gavigan, K., Kurtts, S., & Mimms, M. (2010). Bibliotherapy as an intervention approach for children and adolescents with emotional disabilities. In C. L. Norton (Ed.), *Innovative Interventions in Child and Adolescent Mental Health* (pp.124–140). Taylor & Francis Group.

Goddard, A. T. (2011). Children's books for use in bibliotherapy. *Journal of Pediatric Health Care, 25*(1), 57–61.

Hahlweg, K., Heinrichs, N., Kuschel, A., & Feldmann, M. (2008). Therapist-assisted, self-administered bibliotherapy to enhance parental competence: Short- and long-term effects. *Behavior Modification, 32*(5), 659–681.

Heath, M. A., Sheen, D., Leavy, D., Young, E., & Money, K. (2005). Bibliotherapy: A resource to facilitate emotional healing and growth. *School Psychology International, 26*(5), 563–580.

Holyoke, N. (2009). *A smart girl's guide to her parents' divorce: How to land on your feet when your world turns upside down*. American Girl Publishing.

Hynes, A. M., & Hynes-Berry, M. (1994). *Biblio/Poetry therapy, The interactive process: A handbook*. North Star Press of St. Cloud Inc

Jackson, M. N. M. (2006). *Bibliotherapy revisited: Issues in classroom management. Developing teachers' awareness and techniques to help children cope effectively with stressful situations*. M-m-mauleg Publishing.

Koppenhaver, D. A., Erickson, K. A., Harris, B., McLellan, J., Skotko, B. G., & Newton, R. A. (2001). Storybook-based communication intervention for girls with rett syndrome and their mothers. *Disability and Rehabilitation, 23*(3–4), 149–159.

Lansky, V. (1998). *It's not your fault, Koko bear*. Book Peddlers.

Ludwig, T. (2016). *Confessions of a former bully*. Dragonfly Books.

McCulliss, D. (2012). Bibliotherapy: Historical and research perspectives. *Journal of Poetry Therapy, 25*(1), 23–38.

McCulliss, D., & Chamberlain, D. (2013). Bibliotherapy for youth and adolescents - School-based application and research. *Journal of Poetry Therapy, 26*(1), 13–40.

Mendel, M. R., Harris, J., & Carson, N. (2016). Bringing bibliotherapy for children to clinical practice. *Journal of the American Academy of Child & Adolescent Psychiatry, 7*(55), 535–537.

Mumbauer, J., & Kelchner, V. (2017). Promoting mental health literacy through bibliotherapy in school-based settings. *Professional School Counseling, 21*(1), 1096–2409.

Murray, J. (2004). *Bottled up, A novel*. ABC-Clio.

Pardeck, J. T. (1990). Children's literature and child abuse. *Family Therapy, 69*(1), 83–88.

Pehrsson, D. E. (2006). Benefits of utilizing bibliotherapy within play therapy. *International Journal of Play Therapy, 15*(1), 6–10.

Pehrsson, D., & McMillen, P. S. (2005). A bibliotherapy evaluation tool: Grounding counselors in the therapeutic use of literature. *The Arts in Psychotherapy, 32*(1), 47–59.

Pehrsson, D., & McMillen, P. S. (2007). Bibliotherapy: Overview and implications for counselors. *Professional Counseling Digest, 2,* 1–2.

Salimi, S., Zare-Farashbandi, F., Papi, A., Samouei, R., & Hassanzadeh, A. (2014). The effect of group bibliotherapy on the self-esteem of female students living in dormitory. *Journal of Education and Health Promotion, 3,* 89–95.

Schneck, J. M. (1945). Bibliotherapy and hospital library activities for neuropsychiatric patients. *Psychiatry, 8*(2), 207.

Schreur, G. (2006). Using bibliotherapy with suspended students. *Reclaiming Children and Youth, 15*(2), 106–111.

Shechtman, Z. (1999). Bibliotherapy: An indirect approach to treatment of childhood aggression. *Child Psychiatry and Human Development, 30*(1), 39–53.

Stewart, P. E., & Ames, G. P. (2014). Using culturally affirming, thematically appropriate bibliotherapy to cope with trauma. *Journal of Child & Adolescent Trauma, 7*(4), 227–236.

Witek, J., & Roussey, C. (2014). *In my heart: A book of feelings.* Abrams Appleseed.

Activity 8.1: Alexander and the Terrible, Horrible, No Good, Very Bad Day

R. Paul Maddox II

Theme/Goals of Activity	Identification and validation of feelings, increase self-awareness, explore potential coping skills and solutions, determine a healthy, helpful course of action
Population/Age	5–10
Intrapersonal Skills	Identifying and distinguishing between thoughts and emotions, thought stopping, managing emotions, optimism
Interpersonal Skills	Expressing emotions appropriately and effectively, giving and receiving feedback, awareness of one's own impact on others
Coping/Solution-Focused Skills	Feelings identification, reframing negative thoughts to make them positive, recognizing and acknowledging what things are within our control and what things are not with our control as individuals
Materials	Book: *Alexander and the Terrible, Horrible, No Good, Very Bad Day* by Judith Viorst and Ray Cruz (1972). Various creative art supplies and mediums such as paper, crayons, markers, colored pencils, paints, stickers, glue, scissors, etc. *Note:* There are a number of links online of the book being read aloud.

Description of the Activity:

1. Read aloud with the child the book *Alexander and the Terrible, Horrible, No Good, Very Bad Day* by Judith Viorst and Ray Cruz (1972). As you are reading the book, take time to highlight the illustrations and discuss how Alexander may be feeling as the story progresses.
2. Discuss with the child the various problems that the character Alexander faces and how he may feel in each situation that he experiences in the story.
3. Explore with child ways in which they identify with Alexander or any of the other characters in the story.
4. Invite the child to create an artistic depiction (such as drawing a picture) of what one of the characters from the story may be feeling and some healthy ways that the character could possibly cope with the various situations presented in the book.
5. Process and reflect with the child client ways in which they sometime feel similar to the character in their artistic depiction and how they may be able to apply some of the coping skills represented in their artwork to their own life.

*Adapted from Thrive Therapy Houston, PLLC.

Macro-Processing:

No loading:

Present the opportunity for the child to create an artistic depiction of a character from the story.

Front and back loading:

Front: While the book is being read have the child identify what character(s) they connect with the most.
Back: Allow the child to describe the character(s) and what they might be doing in the artwork.

Micro-Processing:

Observations while reading the book aloud: Some children are more aware of how thoughts can influence the feelings that they experience than others. Also, some may experience discomfort with some of the situations that Alexander experiences in the story.

Comments/Questions:

Use verbal and non-verbal cues to address comfort or discomfort as you read the story aloud.

- "Do you like the story? What do you like/dislike about it?" "What is the best/worst thing about the story?"
- "How are the situations in the story similar to thing that you have experienced in your own life?"

Observations making art: What to look for…

- "What does the _____ [something in the drawing they are creating] represent?
- "What do you think they [the character in the drawing] are feeling?"
- "What can they [the character they are drawing] do when they feel that way?

Debrief &and Transfer:

Experiential activities include teachable moments (within the session) as well as provide an opportunity to identify skills and how to use it outside the session. Follow-ups between sessions can also be included.

Example:

While creating an artistic depiction of one of the characters from the story, a child experiences difficulty finding a specific color they wanted to use when creating their picture. They identified the problem (can't find the color they want) and was prompted to express their feelings regarding the problem in the moment (communicate) and ask the counselor if they could help find it, identify another color that would be similar, or use another art medium (problem-solving). Highlight the process of identifying the problem, then generalizing (i.e., you had a challenge, you felt _____, you told me about it, then you figured out how to address it). "So, next time you have a problem, you can recognize your feelings, tell someone, then you can figure out how to best address the situation." The activity then gets transferred to other problems/solution actions. Follow-up includes any problems at school/home, communication, and if any solutions generated. If so, opportunity for positive reinforcement and if not, opportunities to practice solutions.

Tips or Lessons Learned for Counselors:

Fear of being judged for their artistic abilities, certain disabilities, or a lack of interest in the story can be barriers to using this activity. In this case, it is helpful to have additional options/alternatives for the book and a wide range of artistic supplies representing various creative mediums available. The child is then still able to see that there are other books with similar themes and many kinds of materials that can be used to express themselves in the artistic process.

About the Author: Robert Paul Maddox II, PhD, LPC (MO & WY), NCC, is a counselor educator at the University of Wyoming at Casper. His academic credentials include a PhD in Counselor Education and Supervision, an EdS in Counseling Education, and an MA in Community Counseling. Additionally, he is a Licensed Professional Counselor (LPC) and a National Certified Counselor (NCC) with experience as a school counselor and a mental health counselor.

Activity 8.2: Graphic Novels and Songs

R. Paul Maddox II

Theme/Goals of Activity	Increase self-awareness, explore potential coping skills
Population/Age	13+
Intrapersonal Skills	Identifying feelings and emotions, managing emotions, optimism
Interpersonal Skills	Expressing emotions appropriately and effectively, giving and receiving feedback
Coping/Solution-Focused Skills	Feelings identification, exploring healthy options for expressing one's self, identifying strengths and supports in one's life
Materials	A graphic novel related to client's presenting issue. For example for a child whose parent or family member is fighting cancer a potential book could be *Mom's Cancer* by Brian Fies (2006), computer with internet access and speakers, notebook, writing utensils, copies of lyrics (if using a song)

Description of the Activity:

Client will choose and share a song that explores topics similar to the graphic novel.

Before the activity:

1. Have the client read the graphic novel outside of session (this may take some clients several days or weeks to do depending upon their reading abilities and schedules).
2. Consider the important ideas and situations conveyed through the graphic novel.
3. Have the client choose a song which conveys or addresses similar ideas or feelings to what is expressed in various parts of the graphic novel.

During the activity:

1. During the activity, the counselor and client will listen to a song together and look over a copy of the lyrics as they listen (if the song has lyrics).
2. Invite the client to jot down notes of ideas that stand out as meaningful and feelings that they are experiencing in the moment as they listen to the song.
3. Process and reflect with the client ways in which the feelings that they have while listening to the song may be similar or different to what they imagine one or more of the characters in the graphic novels may feel.

Explore how they may be able to apply some of the coping skills when they experience in their own life situations and feelings similar to what is conveyed in the graphic novel.

*Activity adapted from the activity *Video or Song Connection* outlined in McPherson-Leitz (2018).

Macro-Processing:

No loading:

Present the opportunity for the child to choose a song that conveys ideas and feelings similar to what is presented in the graphic novel.

Front and back loading:

Front: While the book is being read have the child identify what character(s) they connect with the most.
Back: Allow the child to describe the character(s) and what they might be doing in the artwork.

Micro-Processing:

While listening during session to the song that the child has chosen, be mindful to be open to what they are sharing regardless of style or genre. Also, some may experience discomfort during session with some of the situations that are presented in the story and/or song.

Comments/questions:
Use verbal and non-verbal cues to address comfort or discomfort as you listen to the song and process the story.
–   "Do you like the story [or song]? What do you like/dislike about it?" "What is the best/worst thing about the story [or song]?"
–   "What parts of the song speak to you the most?" "How do you feel right now listening to the song?"
–   "How are the situations in the story or the song similar to things that you have experienced in your own life?"

Observations making art: What to look for…
–   "What does the _____ [something in the song] represent to you?"

- "What do you think they [the character in the story and/or song] are feeling?"
- "What can they [the character from the story or song] do when they feel that way?"

Debrief and Transfer:

Potential questions to debrief and transfer:

- What song(s) do you find yourself listening to most often? What feelings do you experience when listening to them?
- How does music help you cope with certain feelings?
- What situations from the story would you have responded to differently than the characters? How would you respond? What connections do you see in your own life experiences?
- What strengths do you see in yourself that you can build upon when you face similar situations in the future?
- What supports might you draw upon when you experience such situations?

Tips or Lessons Learned for Counselors:

Fear of being judged for musical tastes, certain disabilities, or lack of interest in the story can be barriers to using this activity. In this case, it may be helpful to have additional options/alternatives for the graphic novel and a possible list of songs consisting of a wide range of recordings representing various genres and styles available from which the client can choose if needed.

About the Author: Robert Paul Maddox II, PhD, LPC (MO & WY), NCC, is a counselor educator at the University of Wyoming at Casper. His academic credentials include a PhD in Counselor Education and Supervision, an EdS in Counseling Education, and an MA in Community Counseling. Additionally, he is a Licensed Professional Counselor (LPC) and a National Certified Counselor (NCC) with experience as a school counselor and a mental health counselor.

Activity 8.3: Spaghetti in a Hot Dog Bun

R. Paul Maddox II

Theme/Goals of Activity:	Identification and validation of feelings, increase self-awareness, explore potential coping skills and solutions, determine a healthy, helpful course of action
Population/Age:	5–12
Intrapersonal Skills:	Identifying and distinguishing between thoughts and emotions, recognizing positive self-talk and healthy ways to communicate personal thoughts and feelings, thought stopping, managing emotions, optimism
Interpersonal Skills:	Expressing emotions appropriately and effectively, giving and receiving feedback, awareness of one's own impact on others
Coping/Solution-Focused Skills:	Feelings identification, reframing negative thoughts to make them positive, recognizing and acknowledging what things are within our control and what things are not within our control as individuals, problem-solving
Materials:	The book *Spaghetti in a Hot Dog Bun: Having the Courage to Be Who You Are* by Dismondy (2008), various creative art supplies such as paper, crayons, markers, colored pencils, stickers, glue, and scissors.

Description of the Activity:

1. Read aloud with the child client the book *Spaghetti in a Hot Dog Bun: Having the Courage to Be Who You Are* by Maria Dismondy. As you are reading the book, take time to highlight the illustrations and discuss how Lucy may be feeling as the story progresses.

2. Discuss with the child client the various problems that Lucy faces and how she feels in each situation that she experiences in the story.
3. Explore with child ways in which they identify with Lucy or any of the other characters in the story.
4. Provide the child with a piece of paper and have them fold it length wise like a "hot dog bun." Have them unfold the paper and invite them to create on one side of the paper's fold an artistic depiction (such as drawing a picture) of what one of the characters from the story may have felt, and on the other side of the paper's fold invite them to depict some healthy ways that the character could possibly cope with the various situations presented in the story.
5. Process and reflect with the child client ways in which they sometime feel similar to the character in their artistic depictions and how they may be able to apply some of the coping skills represented in their artwork to their own life.

*Adapted from Spaghetti in a hot dog bun (WITS Program Foundation, n.d.), and *Alexander and the Terrible, No Good, Very Bad Day* – book (Thrive Therapy Houston, LLC., n.d.)

Macro-Processing:

No loading:

Present the opportunity for the child to create an artistic depiction of a character from the story.

Front and back loading:

Front: While the book is being read have the child identify the situation(s) or character(s) they connect with the most.
Back: Allow the child to describe the character(s) and situation(s) as they are creating their artwork.

Micro-Processing:

Observations while reading the book aloud: Some children are more aware of the feelings that they experience than others. Also, some may experience discomfort with some of the situations/feelings that are shared in the story.

Comments/questions:
Use verbal and non-verbal cues to address comfort or discomfort as you read the book aloud.

— "What parts of the story do you find most interesting? What are the best/worst thing(s) that happen in the story?"
— "What are some things about you that you consider to be unique or different? Which of those things about you are you most proud of?"
— "How are the situations in the story similar to thing that you have experienced in your own life?"

Observations making art: What to look for...

— "What does the _____ [something in the drawing they are creating] represent?
— "What do you think they [the character in the drawing] are felt when _____ [situation that occurred in the story]?"
— "What can they [the character they are drawing] do when they feel that way?"

Debrief and Transfer:
Potential questions to debrief and transfer:
— In the book, the character Papa states, "Even if we are different from others on the outside we all have a heart with feelings on the inside." What do you think he means when he says this?

- What kinds of feelings do you have on the inside? How might you be able to tell what types of feelings others may be having on the inside?
- What are some ways that you could respond if you heard someone being teased (or if you were being teased) the way that Lucy was teased in the book?

Tips or Lessons Learned for Counselors:

Make sure to provide plenty of time for the child to engage in the art activity while also allowing ample time for them to share and process during the session. Some children may experience difficulties expressing themselves artistically and/or verbally. Fear of being judged for their artistic abilities, certain disabilities, or a lack of interest in the book represent some potential barriers to using this activity. In such cases, it may be helpful to explore with the child their feelings and experiences through other activities or by having additional options/alternatives for the book and a wide range of artistic supplies representing various creative mediums available. The child is then still able to see that there are other books/stories with similar themes and numerous healthy mediums for expressing themselves.

About the Author: Robert Paul Maddox II, PhD, LPC (MO & WY), NCC, is a counselor educator at the University of Wyoming at Casper. His academic credentials include a PhD in Counselor Education and Supervision, an EdS in Counseling Education, and an MA in Community Counseling. Additionally, he is a Licensed Professional Counselor (LPC) and a National Certified Counselor (NCC) with experience as a school counselor and a mental health counselor.

Activity 8.4: In My Heart – Feelings Creative Activity

R. Paul Maddox II

Theme/Goals of Activity	Identification of feelings, communication of feelings, increase self-awareness
Population/Age	6–12
Intrapersonal Skills	Recognizing healthy ways to communicate feelings, self-awareness, managing emotions
Interpersonal Skills	Expressing emotions appropriately and effectively, giving and receiving feedback, awareness of one's own impact on others
Coping/Solution-Focused Skills	Feelings identification, problem-solving
Materials	Book: *In My Heart: A Book of Feelings* (Witek & Roussey, 2014), *Feelings in My Heart* worksheet, writing/coloring instruments (such as crayons, markers, colored pencils), optional: various other creative art supplies such as colored construction paper (consisting of sheets of various different colors), scissors, glue, tape, stickers, glitter, etc. *Note: There are a number of links online of the book being read aloud.

Description of the Activity:

1. Read aloud with the child client the book *In My Heart: A Book of Feelings* by Jo Witek. As you are reading the book, take time to highlight the illustrations and discuss the various feelings expressed in the book as the story progresses.
2. Discuss with the child client the various feelings and how they feel in each situation that is expressed in the story.
3. Explore with child ways in which they identify with the various feelings and situations in the story.
4. Provide the child with the *Feelings in My Heart* worksheet and writing/coloring instruments (e.g. crayons, markers, colored pencils). It is advisable to also provide the child with a wide variety of art supplies that include colored construction paper (consisting of sheets of various different colors), scissors, and glue/tape which they can use to help create/decorate the hearts on the *Feelings in My Heart* worksheet.
5. Invite the child to write a feeling on each square of the *Feelings in My Heart* worksheet and use the various art supplies to create/color/decorate hearts on the *Feelings in My Heart* worksheet that to them represent various situations and corresponding/related feelings that they experience in their own lives.

6. Process and reflect with the child ways in which they experience the emotions in their artistic depictions and how they may be able to appropriately communicate the feelings represented in their artwork to people in their own life.

* Adapted from The Color-Your-Life Technique (O'Connor, 1983) and Color Your Feelings Activity

Macro-Processing:

No loading:

Present the opportunity for the child to create artistic depictions of various feelings they experience.

Front and back loading:

Front: While the book is being read have the child identify the situation(s) or feeling(s) they connect with the most.
    Back: Allow the child to describe the feeling(s) and situation(s) as they are creating their artwork.

Micro-Processing:

Observations while reading the book aloud: Some children are more aware of how thoughts can influence the feelings that they experience than others. Also, some may experience discomfort with some of the situations that Lucy experiences in the story.

Comments/questions: Use verbal and non-verbal cues to address comfort or discomfort as you read the story aloud.
−   "What parts of the book do you find most interesting?"
−   "What are the best/worst thing(s) that happen in the book?"
−   "How are the situations and feelings in the book similar to thing that you have experienced in your own life?"

Observations making art: What to look for...
−   "What does the _____ [something that they are drawing/creating on the *Feelings in My Heart* worksheet] represent?
−   "What are some things you can do when you are experiencing that feeling?"

Debrief and Transfer:

Potential questions to debrief and transfer:
−   What feelings do you have on the inside most often?
−   What feelings do you have right now as you are creating each heart?
−   How might you be able to communicate to others the types of feelings you may be having on the inside?

Tips or Lessons Learned for Counselors:

Make sure to provide plenty of time for the child to engage in the art activity while also allowing ample time for them to share and process during the session. Some children may experience difficulties expressing themselves artistically and/or verbally. Fear of being judged for their artistic abilities, certain disabilities, or a lack of interest in the story represent some potential barriers to using this activity. In such cases, it may helpful to explore with the child their feelings and experiences through other activities or by having additional options/alternatives for the book and a wide range of artistic supplies representing various creative mediums available. The child is then still able to see that there are other books/stories with similar themes and numerous healthy mediums for expressing themselves.

About the Author: Robert Paul Maddox II, PhD, LPC (MO & WY), NCC, is a counselor educator at the University of Wyoming at Casper. His academic credentials include a PhD in Counselor Education and Supervision, an EdS in Counseling Education, and an MA in Community Counseling. Additionally, he is a Licensed Professional Counselor (LPC) and a National Certified Counselor (NCC) with experience as a school counselor and a mental health counselor.

Chapter 9

Board games and video games

Susan Hurley and Monica Phelps-Pineda

Games are a great source of entertainment for children and adolescents and have become a popular medium through which to provide therapy. Games are a part of a child's culture and allow for them to communicate, learn, and develop skills all in a simple state of play (Oren, 2008). Children tend to relate to games in a positive and enjoyable fashion, which helps to build a safe and comfortable atmosphere in which the counseling relationship and therapeutic process will take place. This more relaxed environment helps the child or adolescent find the therapy session less threatening, provide an opportunity for fun, while naturally encouraging the exploration of self-awareness, growth, and problem solving.

Game play in counseling is described as an approach that allows for the incorporation of games into the therapeutic process (Schaefer & Reid, 2001). This description does not specify procedures but rather opens the door for therapists to approach the use of games in any way that will benefit the client (Swank, 2008). Games are quite versatile and are incorporated at the beginning of a therapy session to help a client relax or lower their defenses, just as easily as they are introduced during the middle of a session as a learning tool to increase self-esteem, work on behavioral changes, or gain a better understanding of emotions. Clinicians can integrate traditional games or design games to work on specific clinical issues within individual, family, or group therapy. Lowenstein (1999, 2002) described a three-stage process for using games as part of a therapy session. The therapist creatively introduces the game into the session in order to gain the client's interest. While the game is in process the therapist encourages the client to process issues and concerns that come up while playing. At the end of game play, the therapist continues processing the experience with the client helping them to relate the experience of the game to their personal life.

Counseling children and adolescents with board games

A review of the literature shows support for the use of games in therapy, focusing on their projective value dating as far back as when Loomis (1957) used checkers to engage clients in therapy, resulting in lower levels of resistance to treatment. Games have been valued since the 1970s in the therapeutic process as a means for opening the lines of communication in the counseling session. During the 1970s, several games like the *Ungame* (Founds, 2011) and *Talking, Feeling and Doing Game* (Gardner, 1973) were developed specifically for use in therapy. Incorporating games into the therapeutic process has been shown to build rapport, engage the client (Fried, 1992; Schaefer & Reid, 2001), and promote positive self-esteem and emotional growth (Gotay, 2013). Several theoretical constructs have stressed the importance of using games or board games as a therapeutic alliance, including Social Learning Theory, Cognitive Behavioral Therapy, and Psychoanalytic and Gestalt Therapy. Each of these theories states that successful outcomes greatly depend on the counselor's ability to build rapport and connect to the child's experiences (Halstead et al., 2011; Landreth, 2012).

Swank (2008) suggests that games may be broken into three categories: physical, strategic, and games of chance. Games that use physical activity or skill to challenge the client's use of gross and fine motor skills include tag, basketball, or throwing beanbags for a life-size game of tic-tac-toe and work well with children who are hyperactive or have difficulty with impulse control. These physical games can be structured to help with the development of self-control where following the rules is required or waiting for a turn is important.

Strategy games like checkers or *Sorry* help clients with socialization skills by focusing on evaluating, problem solving, and taking responsibility for the consequences of the choices they make (Hromek & Roffey, 2009; Serok & Blum, 1979). For example, *Sorry* allows the players to better understand how to manage anger when one of their game pieces is sent back to start over when they were so close to winning. Children can learn how to work through thoughts, emotions and develop emotion regulation without any modifications to the game itself. As Reid (2001) indicates, traditional competitive type games help enhance ego functioning, including feelings of competence, self-doubt, impulse control, and self-image.

DOI: 10.4324/9781315213767-10

Games of chance like *Uno, Chutes and Ladders*, or *Candyland* do not allow the client to control the outcome (Sutton-Smith & Roberts, 1971). These types of games tend to work better when introduced at the beginning of a session and are described by Reid (2001) as a good introduction to the use of games in therapy, creating the more relaxed and safe counseling environment. As games of chance [without modification] require little skill to win, one runs the risk of losing the clients interest along with the purpose and benefit of integrating game play. However, all of the examples used here as games of chance are easily modified to include discussions related to self-awareness, identification of feelings, patience, and rule following.

In the past 20 years a number of therapeutic games have been developed to help children, adolescents, and families work through specific life problems, including divorce, sexual abuse, and anger management issues to name just a few. Therapists can purchase a variety of games or modify existing games to incorporate a therapeutic outcome (Matorin & McNamara, 1996). When modifying games or when creating a new game, it is important to identify what therapeutic issues will be addressed while maintaining a diverse target audience. Swank (2008) encourages the incorporation of a variety of learning styles and is developmentally and age-appropriate, as well as culturally sensitive while maintaining a fun and light atmosphere. As an example, Reycraft (2007) modified a game of chance, Candyland, by developing the story of Lord Licorice who has an anger management problem. Along the route of the game board the game players suggest, discuss, and demonstrate healthy ways for Lord Licorice to cope with his anger.

Board games provide an opportunity for structure by requiring players to take turns, follow rules, agree on rules that have been modified, control impulses, and maintain constant interaction with other players (Hromek & Roffey, 2009). The literature suggests that board games can elicit a wealth of information in a very short time span (Schaefer & Reid, 2001; Sutton-Smith & Roberts, 1971). Checkers is a good example that can be used to create a nonthreatening environment in less than 20 minutes (Loomis, 1957). Observing the way that the child/adolescent approaches playing may provide a wealth of diagnostic information regarding the client's interpersonal and intrapersonal skills (Turner et al., 2016). For example, checkers is a strategy type game that consists of one winner and one loser. Children who struggle with the concept of losing tend to feel inadequate as winning was a way to compensate for low self-esteem, thus making them hesitant to play a strategic type game. Through continued conversation however, self-esteem, losing, and taking risks are all topics that can be easily addressed while engaging the child during play.

Games such as *Go Fish, Concentration*, or any game that requires drawing pairs of cards can help the client expand their vocabulary of feeling words. While playing either game the players work to gain pairs of matching cards. The cards will have a feeling word and a picture showing an expression of the word. As the players make matches, they must show how they would express the feeling on the paired cards or relate the feeling to an experience in their lives. Feeling cards are available for purchase or can be easily modified with a regular deck of cards to display emotions. The *Self Esteem Card Game* is an example of a specifically designed solution-focused intervention to help build rapport and engage in meaningful conversations. This game, played in groups, individual and family sessions, encourages the players to reflect on their existing strengths while reinforcing a positive self-concept and sense of self-efficacy.

Jenga is another game that has been successfully modified in numerous ways to support the therapeutic process. The game requires each player in turn to remove a block, without tipping the structure over and placing that block back on the stack. Some of the modifications for use in therapy include adding feelings words to the sides of the blocks to be used as discussion points when selected and removed from the tower. Other variations include having another player decide which block the client must move and processing the thoughts and feelings that go along with having to take direction from another person. *Jenga* has also been modified for feeling/emotion recognition or with "get to know you" questions that must be responded to in order to continue play.

Children of the digital age

Technology, including computers, laptops, tablets, and smartphones, plays a major role and is part of everyday life for many children and adolescents, particularly in the United States. As the youth of the 21st century become more oriented toward technology, therapists are encouraged to consider the pros and cons of video games within the therapeutic setting (Annema et al., 2013). Recent research supports the idea that cognitive, motivational, emotional, and social skills learned through video gaming can be transferable outside of the video game context (Granic et al., 2014). A few therapy-related research studies have studied the use of videos to increase motivation and attention, increase mood and emotions, and treat depression. For example, playing a puzzle video game, like *Angry Birds*, helps the player to relax, decreases anxiety, and improves the child's/adolescent's overall mood (Russoniello et al., 2009), which helps to provide an appealing, comfortable therapeutic environment in which they can connect, communicate, and process (Barak & Grohol, 2011). A fantasy role-playing game titled *Sparx* was developed for use in treating depression using a Cognitive Behavioral Model (Merry et al., 2012). In a controlled study the game has been found to be as effective in treating depression as CBT administered by a counselor (Merry et al., 2012).

A successful example of a game-based therapeutic intervention is *Breathe, Think, Do with Sesame*, a free bilingual resource application easily downloaded to iPhone, iPod touch, iPad, and Androids. This fun game targets both English- and Spanish-speaking children ages four and up, using a friendly monster to simulate real-life situations to teach behavioral and cognitive skills. While children play tapping on bubbles and sliding through scenarios, they are challenged to explore feelings while learning various decision-making, self-control, problem solving, and coping skills. Resources, tips, and strategies are also provided in the parenting section to help parents positively reinforce what is learned throughout the game. Onscreen treatment such as the *Breathe, Think, Do with Sesame* app by Sesame Street reinforces positive behavioral changes allowing for an opportunity to practice these new skills outside of the counseling setting. This nonthreatening approach to psychotherapy is a way for therapists to adapt to the times while staying true to the client's treatment goals of behavior change, self-awareness, healing, etc. (Aymard, 2002).

Interpersonal and intrapersonal skills

Interpersonal skills measure how well the client interacts with others while intrapersonal skills relate to how the client communicates with themselves. Games are an effective tool in treatment to identify and adjust both intrapersonal and interpersonal thinking by identifying low self-worth and building self-confidence (Dufwenberg et al., 2011). Games also help with learning patience when having to wait for a turn or following a rule (Schaefer & Reid, 2001). Communication becomes key when using games in a group setting as the players will have to listen and speak clearly to the other members of the group playing the game (Martinez & Lasser, 2013). *Jenga* is one of those games that lends itself easily to both interpersonal and intrapersonal skills and can be played individually (therapist and client) or in a group setting (Berger & Gehart-Brooks, 2000). A variety of both deep thought and simple surface questions are provided for each turn. A player pulls a block from the stack, reads the question, and responds prior to placing the block back on the stack. From an interpersonal perspective, the skills being learned are listening when other members are responding, communicating responses, and using boundaries in play (i.e., taking turns, following the rules). From an intrapersonal perspective, the client or group members learn to identify, express, and manage both thoughts and emotions.

Coping and solution-focused skills

As described in an earlier chapter, a positive psychological approach assumes that everyone has strengths that can be used to overcome obstacles (Seligman & Csikszentmihalyi, 2000). Whether using checkers to observe how a client approaches interpersonal and intrapersonal skills or *Candyland* to identify healthy ways to cope with emotions, games use a positive psychological orientation that helps the therapist reach the client quickly and increases the rate of response to the therapy process (Swank, 2008). The majority of therapeutic games are created to promote a positive more solution-focused approach. For example, the *Self Esteem Game* is developed as a solution-focused intervention to support rapport building and start a meaningful conversation between the client and the therapist. A solution-focused approach allows the counselor to work with the client in a collaborative relationship to help the client to find exceptions or solutions to issues being brought to counseling. Games provide a good conduit allowing for nonthreatening atmosphere. Fitting with solution-focused techniques, games can be introduced in the beginning of the therapy session to relax the client and encourage a willingness to participate. As the game progresses, the therapist subtly encourages the client to talk about and process issues that arise during play. At the end of the play the therapist helps the client relate the experiences they discussed during the play to their personal everyday life. There are a number of video games with connections to mindfulness, communication, and self-regulation skills (Colder Carras et al., 2018; Hemenover & Bowman, 2018).

Strengths and limitations

Much has been written about the use of therapeutic games and their ability to enhance the treatment process; however, there is a limited amount of scientific research supporting the use of games in treatment. The majority of information reported in the literature regarding the benefits of therapeutic games is provided by clinicians who have developed games and discuss their use in therapy (Ceranoglu, 2010; Swank, 2008). Games have been shown to control urges, provide reality checks, help regulate frustration and anxiety, and provide a better understanding of the relationship between action and outcome (Bow & Quinell, 2000).

Gotay (2013) found that the use of games in counseling adolescents presented fewer demands and expectations, resulting in adolescents being more verbally and emotionally engaged. Purchasing therapeutic games may be cost prohibitive for clinics and private practice; however, using some creativity, existing games can be adapted for therapeutic play. *Pintrest* as well as other creative type websites appears to be a great resource for ideas that can be developed and used in a therapeutic setting. When deciding to modify an existing game or create a new game, make sure to consider the purpose of the game, the audience who will be playing it, and the therapeutic concerns that it will be addressing. Martinez and Lasser (2013) encourage not making a game too complex, as the time commitment for developing or modifying a game varies depending on the complexity of the intended learning experience.

Meaning-making

Encouraging children and adolescents to participate in the counseling process can be a challenge. Nontraditional approaches such as the use of games as part of treatment may help to remove some of the concerns about children and adolescents being open or emotionally vulnerable in a session (Swank, 2008). There is a consensus in the literature that games help to exam, strengthen, and improve ego function (Schaefer & Reid, 2001; Sutton-Smith & Roberts, 1971). Studies suggest that games assist with controlling urges, reality checking, understanding the difference between actions and outcomes, and anxiety. They also appear to help children to develop coping skills, exercise self-discipline, respond to social norms, self-control, and enhance socialization (Bow & Quinell, 2000).

When using games in therapy it is critical to select age-appropriate materials, provide structure to the game as part of the therapy session, and monitor and help the client interpret the outcome. The literature review shows that while there is a consensus regarding the use of games when counseling children and adolescents, there is a lack of empirical evidence and research establishing the efficacy of this approach (Matorin & McNamara, 1996). Aymard (2002) suggests that the psychotherapeutic value of toys and games lies in the therapist's creative ability to adapt it into a successful therapeutic tool. Psychotherapeutic approaches and interventions are forever being developed, refined, and improved. Innovative methods that promote the well-being and treatment of mental health issues in youth should be welcomed and further researched. The mental health field also encourages and supports research and the creation of new video games for children and adolescents, designed to target clear therapeutic treatment goals in an entertaining way (Colder Carras et al., 2018).

References

Annema, J. H., Verstraete, M., Abeele, V. V., Desmet, S., & Geerts, D. (2013). Video games in therapy: A therapist's perspective. *International Journal of Arts and Technology, 6*(1), 106–122.

Aymard, L. L. (2002). "Funny face": Shareware for child counseling and play therapy. *Journal of Technology in Human Services, 20*(1–2), 11–29.

Barak, A., & Grohol, J. M. (2011). Current and future trends in internet-supported mental health interventions. *Journal of Technology in Human Services, 29*(3), 155–196.

Berger, V., & Gehart-Brooks, D. R. (2000). "Feelings jenga:" Facilitating family communication through play. *Journal of Family Psychotherapy, 11*(1), 81–85.

Bow, N. J., & Quinell, F. (2000). Therapeutic use of games with fine motor component. In C. E. Schaefer & S. E. Reid (Eds.), *Game Play: Therapeutic Use of Childhood Game* (2nd ed., pp. 243–256). Wiley.

Ceranoglu, T. A. (2010). Video games in psychotherapy. *Review of General Psychology, 14*(2), 141–146.

Colder Carras, M., Van Rooij, A. J., Spruijt-Metz, D., Kvedar, J., Griffiths, M. D., Carabas, Y., & Labrique, A. (2018). Commercial video games as therapy: A new research agenda to unlock the potential of a global pastime. *Frontiers in Psychiatry, 8*, 300–307.

Dufwenberg, M., Gächter, S., & Hennig-Schmidt, H. (2011). The framing of games and the psychology of play. *Games and Economic Behavior, 73*(2), 459–478.

Founds, K. (2011). The un-game. *Booth, 3*(7), 5.

Fried, S. (1992). Chess: A psychoanalytic tool in the treatment of children. *International Journal of Play Therapy, 1*(1), 43.

Gardner, R. A. (1973). *The talking, feeling, and doing game.* Creative Therapeutics.

Gotay, S. (2013). Enhancing emotional awareness of at-risk youth through game play. *Journal of Creativity in Mental Health, 8*(2), 151–161.

Granic, I., Lobel, A., & Engels, R. C. (2014). The benefits of playing video games. *American Psychologist, 69*(1), 66.

Halstead, R. W., Pehrsson, D. E., & Mullen, J. A. (2011). *Counseling children: A core issues approach.* American Counseling Association.

Hemenover, S. H., & Bowman, N. D. (2018). Video games, emotion, and emotion regulation: Expanding the scope. *Annals of the International Communication Association, 42*(2), 125–143.

Hromek, R., & Roffey, S. (2009). Promoting social and emotional learning with games: "It's fun and we learn things". *Simulation & Gaming, 40*(5), 626–644.

Landreth, G. L. (2012). *Play therapy: The art of the relationship* (3rd ed.). Routledge

Loomis Jr, E. A. (1957). The use of checkers in handling certain resistances in child therapy and child analysis. *Journal of the American Psychoanalytic Association, 5*(1), 130–135.

Lowenstein, L. (1999). *Creative interventions for troubled children & youth*. Champion Press.

Lowenstein, L., & Lowenstein, L. (2002). *More creative interventions for troubled children & youth*. Champion Press.

Martinez, A., & Lasser, J. (2013). Thinking outside the box while playing the game: A creative school-based approach to working with children and adolescents. *Journal of Creativity in Mental Health, 8*(1), 81–91.

Matorin, A. I., & McNamara, J. R. (1996). Using board games in therapy with children. *International Journal of Play Therapy, 5*(2), 3.

Merry, S. N., Stasiak, K., Shepherd, M., Frampton, C., Fleming, T., & Lucassen, M. F. (2012). The effectiveness of SPARX, a computerised self help intervention for adolescents seeking help for depression: Randomised controlled non-inferiority trial. *BMJ, 344*(e2598), 1–16.

Oren, A. (2008). The use of board games in child psychotherapy. *Journal of Child Psychotherapy, 34*(3), 364–383.

Reid, S. E. (2001). The psychology of play and games. In C. E. Schaefer & S. E. Reid (Eds.), *Game Play: Therapeutic use of Childhood Games* (2nd ed., pp. 1–12). Wiley and Sons.

Reycraft, J. (2007). Candy land or angry land. *The Playful Healer, 13*, 7.

Russoniello, C. V., O'Brien, K., & Parks, J. M. (2009). EEG, HRV and psychological correlates while playing Bejeweled II: A randomized controlled study. *Annual Review of Cybertherapy and Telemedicine, 7*(1), 189–192.

Schaefer, C. E., & Reid, S. E. (2001). *Game play: Therapeutic use of childhood games* (2nd ed.) Wiley.

Seligman, M. E. P., & Csikszentmihalyi, M. (2000). Positive psychology: An introduction. *American Psychologist, 55*(1), 5–14.

Serok, S., & Blum, A. (1979). Games: A treatment vehicle for delinquent youths. *Crime & Delinquency, 25*(3), 358–363.

Sutton-Smith, B., & Roberts, J. M. (1971). The cross-cultural and psychological study of games. *International Review of Sport Sociology, 6*(1), 79–87.

Swank, J. M. (2008). The use of games: A therapeutic tool with children and families. *International Journal of Play Therapy, 17*(2), 154.

Turner, W. A., Thomas, B., & Casey, L. M. (2016). Developing games for mental health: A primer. *Professional Psychology: Research and Practice, 47*(3), 242.

Activity 9.1: "You Gotta Be Kidding!"

Monica Phelps-Pineda

Theme/Goals of Activity	The goal of this interactive game is: to promote conversation on thought process, to promote conversation on priority setting, to promote conversation on values, to promote conversation on assertiveness skills, to promote reframing, to assess current ability for self-expression, to assess decision-making skills, to assess communication skills
Population/Age	7–17
Intrapersonal Skills	Identifying thoughts and emotions, confidence, managing emotions, motivation
Interpersonal Skills	Listening, communication, empathy, sensitivity to individual and cultural differences, expressing emotions appropriately and effectively
Coping/Solution-Focused Skills	Problem solving, decision-making, assertiveness
Materials	A board game of "You Gotta Be Kidding!" The Crazy Game of "Would you rather...?"

Description of the Activity:

The object of this board game is to make a choice on a "Would You Rather" card and tell the other players the choice you made and the reason why. This activity has been used in both a group and an individual counseling setting. This game is meant to promote the assessment and discussion of a variety of skills such as but not limited to communication, self-expression, decision-making, assertiveness, etc. The estimated time this game takes to complete is about 30 minutes.

"You Gotta Be Kidding" contains one game board, 100 "Would You Rather" cards, four player pawns, four Choice Tokens, one die, and one Challenge Card Kit (with 15 Challenge Cards, one 90-second sand timer, one Red Chili Pepper toy, one pencil, and a drawing pad).

1. Shuffle the "Would You Rather" Cards and place this deck on the table.
2. Shuffle Challenge Cards and place the deck face down on the table as well.
3. Each player chooses a player pawn and a Choice Token. Place your pawn on the correct colored "Start" space.
4. Play moves in a clockwise direction. The youngest player goes first.
5. Each turn begins with a roll of the die. Roll the die and move your pawn to land on either a Number Space or a Challenge Space. During your turn you are "The Roller."
6. If you roll takes you to a Number Space, pick a "Would You Rather" card. Read out loud the "Would You Rather" question that matches the number you landed on. It is OK to pass the card around for other players to see.
7. Each player should now make their secret choice by placing his or her Choice Token on the table so that "Choice 1" or "Choice 2" faces up.
8. All players should be careful to completely cover their tokens with their palms.
9. Once everyone is finished choosing, they all should keep their tokens covered while you (the roller) uncover your token and explain why you made your specific choice
10. Once you have explained your choice, you now try to guess, one player at a time, if each other player agrees or disagrees with you. Everyone, except you, should still have their Tokens covered. You get to move forward ONE bonus space for each correct answer.
11. If your roll takes you to a Challenge Space do this, pick a Challenge Card and read the entire Challenge Card out loud, before you do anything so that everybody understands. Then do what your card says and try to successfully complete your challenge. If you complete the challenge successfully, move your pawn forward exactly as the Challenge Card says.
12. Each time you successfully complete a challenge, you take your bonus moves. After a challenge, your turn ends whether you succeed or not. You must wait until your next turn to roll again.
13. A player wins the game immediately after he or she crosses the FINISH LINE!

Macro-Processing:

No loading:

Present the opportunity to play the icebreaker "You Gotta Be Kidding!" The Crazy Game of "Would you rather...?" to build rapport and allow clients to make meaning for themselves through the answers they give.

Micro-Processing:

Some children make their choices impulsively, others are more comfortable making their choices after some careful thought processing, and then there are those who have a difficult time choosing anything at all. Addressing these observations and generalizing them can allow for self-awareness development in the client, i.e.:

— "Wow! That was fast! Do you usually make decisions this quickly?"
— "I see you're really thinking through this one! Could you share with me the process you tend to go through (the steps you take) in order to decide on something?
— "I sense that you're having a difficult time choosing between these options. What do you usually do in order to come to a final decision?"

A teachable moment can present itself during the process of the child's decision-making. Lead the client in eliciting insight and promoting self-awareness by asking questions to promote thoughtful decisions such as:

— "What do you like about that choice?"
— "What makes the other choice least appealing to you?"
— "What makes this the best option between the two?"

There are a variety of both surface and deep thought questions provided in the 100 "Would you rather cards." The surface questions are an opportunity for the child to share a lighthearted exchange and connection with the therapist. The deep thought questions are an opportunity to address exactly what is happening in the "here and now" by calling attention to the current dynamic, addressing both verbal and non-verbal communication, i.e., child becomes hesitant and quiet when choosing one of the two options in Deep Thought Example #3. The clinician can observe and call attention the client's sudden withdrawal to allow for self-awareness that something has been triggered and then even enhance the experience in the moment even more by asking what specific memories came to mind that they would choose to erase and why?

Debrief and Transfer:

The client had a difficult time coming to a decision between two choices. They identified the problem (can't come to a conclusion) and was prompted to think out loud and process with clinician (problem solving) in order to come to a decision. Highlight the process of identifying the problem and then generalize it to everyday life decisions such as: "Next time you come to a difficult decision, it's helpful to talk through the advantages and disadvantages of each choice with someone in order to help you evaluate which one might be the best option for you."

Tips or Lessons Learned for Counselors:

Sometimes children can really enjoy answering the surface questions and choose to avoid the deep thought ones. In this case, using good judgment to assess the rapport you have with your client, you can decide to show flexibility by allowing to skip over some of the deep thought questions that may have triggered something they are not ready to share with you OR choose to lightly challenge your client in the moment to allow for the development of trust and growth in your counseling relationship.

> **About the Author:** Monica Phelps-Pineda, MS, NCC, PLPC, is a Counseling Education and Supervision doctoral candidate at the University of Missouri – St. Louis. Her counseling, teaching, research, and clinical supervision experiences are centered on implementing multiculturally responsive practices to work with children, adolescents, and families of minoritized racial and ethnic identities.

Activity 9.2: Lego Tower Replica Challenge

Monica Phelps-Pineda

Theme/Goals of Activity	The goal of this interactive game is: to promote, assess, and improve communication skills, to promote and assess listening skills, to promote self-awareness, to promote critical thinking, to promote conversation on roles and responsibilities, to promote conversation on noticing and accepting varying perceptions, to assess and improve decision-making skills, learn and use conflict resolution skills
Population/Age	*11–17*
Intrapersonal Skills	Showing initiative, motivation, confidence
Interpersonal Skills	Listening, communication, giving and receiving feedback, awareness of own impact on others, expressing emotions appropriately and effectively
Coping/Solution-Focused Skills	Problem solving, assertiveness and caring confrontations, decision-making, conflict resolution, leadership, initiating change
Materials	A box of classic Legos, two cups/jars/tins, a timer, two chairs, two stools, small tables, or flat surfaces on which the activity will be performed

Description of the Activity:

The goal of this activity is for the Builder to complete an exact replica of the original model created by the Director. This activity is played in two rounds of about 30 minutes each. Each round includes three minutes to create an original model, two minutes for directions, ten minutes to replicate the model, 15 minutes of discussion, repeat.

1. Fill each of the two cups with an exact number of identical Legos that vary in size, color, and shape.
2. Place the chairs with the backs to each other (so as to not see what the other player is constructing). In front of them place a workspace flat surface (i.e., a stool, small table, etc.)
3. Hand one cup of Lego's to each of the two players.
4. Round 1: Assign one of the players to be the Builder and the other to be the Director. (In round two the roles will switch so that both players have an opportunity to experience each of the two roles.)
5. Set a timer for three minutes and instruct the Director to build a creative and somewhat complicated model for the Builder to replicate (instruct the Builder to not look or communicate with the Director during this time).

Once the Director has completed his/her creation, instruct the Director and Builder of the rules (give as little direction as possible so as to build self-awareness of their natural communication style):

- *The Director:* "You may not look at the other players work. You may not ask questions. Your task is to simply instruct the Builder on steps for replicating your tower at your own pace."
- *The Builder:* "You may not look at the other players work. You may not ask questions or communicate in any way. Your task is to simply replicate the original model as best you can with the instructions that are given to you by the Director."

After instructions have been read and understood, set a timer for ten minutes. During this ten minutes, the Director is giving instructions for how to replicate the tower and the Builder is using the instructions to build the replica. During this time, take the opportunity to observe non-verbal communication – shifts in mood, behaviors/actions, etc. – and use these observations as part of the discussion in the debrief portion of the activity.

1. Once the time is up, allow for the following discussion questions BEFORE sharing the outcome of their models:

    - What was it like being the communicator (Director)?
    - What was it like being the receiver (Builder)?
    - "How do you think you did?"

2. REVEAL: During the reveal, there usually tends to be strong opinions and heated exchange as to where things went wrong.
3. Discussion: Take this opportunity to model effective communication, elicit insight, and promote self-awareness through some open-ended discussion questions.

Round 2:

For this second round, have the players take apart their Lego models and place the pieces back in the cups. Have them now switch roles (i.e., the player who was once the Director now takes the role as the Builder). Play this next round the same as the first. Take notice of any changes (i.e., communication style, pace, patience, receptiveness, etc.). Follow that with the reveal, the same discussion questions, and address whether or not the execution improved or worsened.

Macro-Processing:

Back loading: I have found it most effective in this activity to have my clients learn by reflecting and discovering meaning once the activity is complete. If too much direction is given prior to the activity, clients tend to not be as transparent about their natural (non-influenced) communication style.

Micro-Processing:

During the activity it is important to take the opportunity to observe the following in the moment and to use these observations as part of the discussion portion of the activity:

— Is there consistency in the descriptions that the Director uses to explain what specific piece is being placed in what specific location?
— Does the Director explain once? Or does he/she repeat?
— Is the Director confident in their explanation or do they back track? (i.e., "oh wait…hold on…no…I meant…")
— Does the Director move at a fast pace? Or does he/she give the other player time to construct?
— Does the Builder follow instruction as the Director gives them?
— Does the Builder fix mistakes along the way once more information is given? Or do they continue to build regardless?
— Does the Builder show frustration through non-verbals and give up? Or does the Builder continue to the end?

During the reveal, the players see that their goal was not met and therefore blame tends to be assigned to one another for a variety of reasons. The following are some examples of open-ended discussion and processing questions that can be expanded upon as teaching moments. This usually takes up the rest of the session as part of reflection and learning:

— What successes did you have as a team?
— What difficulties did you face as a team?
— What was it that made the Director's communication effective?
— What was most difficult for you as a Director?
— What was most difficult for you as a Builder?
— What could be done differently to accomplish the goal more efficiently?
— What could be done differently to improve communication in the future?

Debrief and Transfer:

Prior to this activity, the client and the family member (parents, grandparents, or sibling) participating are usually familiar with the way they tend to communicate with each other. This activity helps them visualize how their individually unique communication styles can either contribute to positive or destructive results. This activity helps bring awareness to the choices in one's non-verbal behavior and language in order to assess their impact on the relationship. Highlight some points learned from this activity that can be applied to their everyday life interactions such as:

- "We all communicate differently: we share, receive, and interpret information in our own way."
- "Gain self-awareness of your own communication style and learn about your partner's as well. Let this influence your approach in order to be most effective when sharing information."
- "Show flexibility by trying something different if what you're doing is not working," etc.

Tips or Lessons Learned for Counselors:

Some clients may get so frustrated during the activity that they decide to forfeit before completion. This is okay. In this case, it is helpful to go right into discussion and allow for both clients to process their emotions in the moment. Allow for an opportunity to start once again.

About the Author: Monica Phelps-Pineda, MS, NCC, PLPC, is a Counseling Education and Supervision doctoral candidate at the University of Missouri – St. Louis. Her counseling, teaching, research, and clinical supervision experiences are centered on implementing multiculturally responsive practices to work with children, adolescents, and families of minoritized racial and ethnic identities.

Activity 9.3: "In My Control"

Monica Phelps-Pineda

Theme/Goals of Activity	The goal of this interactive game is: to assess decision-making skills, to assess current ability for self-expression, to assess impulsivity, to assess social skills, to promote conversation on their thought process, to promote conversation on assertiveness skills, to promote conversation on ones openness to trying new things, to promote critical thinking, to promote reframing, to learn and use conflict resolution skills
Population/Age	6–15
Intrapersonal Skills	Identifying thoughts and emotions, motivation, managing emotions, mindfulness
Interpersonal Skills	Empathy, communication, boundaries, expressing emotions appropriately and effectively
Coping/Solution-Focused Skills	Problem solving, decision-making, assertiveness
Materials	Construction paper, scissors, poster board paper, markers, tape, a stop watch/timer, a coin

Description of the Activity:

The client is given a poster board on which to outline with markers "In My Control" and "Out of My Control." The poster board is then hung at eye level on the wall. Therapist prepares beforehand several pieces of construction paper with examples of situations that could be categorized as either "in my control" or "out of my control" to be matched in the game (leave several pieces of construction paper blank for the second portion of the game).

- "Out of my control" examples will include things such as other peoples actions, other peoples words, other peoples behavior, other peoples ideas, other peoples feelings, other peoples mistakes.
- "In my control" examples will include things such as my words, my actions, my ideas, my effort, my behavior, my mistakes, etc.

After discussing the importance of acknowledging "what is beyond the scope of our control," there was practice and application, which is what this game was created for. The therapist will instruct the client to "call a side" of a coin prior to each turn to decide who will go next.

Several of the construction cards with the previously mentioned examples are placed in a stack. The therapist and client will take turns depending on the flip of the coin to draw a card from the deck and sticking them to the poster board under one of the two categories, "in my control" or "out of my control," with a 15-second time limit. After being encouraged to process and decide out loud where the example belongs, the player must explain what makes it fit in that specific category and then match an "out of my control" example with a positive "in my control" solution card.

- "Out of my control" example: "Susie's brother continues to make fun of her in front of his friends." Susie cannot control her brother's words or his actions although they are hurtful.
- "In my control" examples: "I can talk walk away" Or "I can explain how those words make me feel" OR "I can ask them to please stop." Susie can only control her words, behaviors, and actions in response to her brother with these examples.

After some practice, the board is cleared and the game becomes more personal. The client is given two stacks of construction cards (red and green in this example). The client is given the red stack of construction cards and some time to think about life situations that they recognize are out of their control. After filling in the cards they are encouraged to take a deep breath, read the card out loud, and say, "…and this is not in my control. I can't control others behaviors but I can control my response to them." This in itself allows for a therapeutic moment as they are given permission to let go of the anger or hurt they are experiencing due to the lack of control they have over someone or a situation.

Once they have placed each of the "out of my control" cards on the poster board, the therapist then encourages the client to think about previous responses they would have had to these "out of my control" situations and evaluate together if their response was the most appropriate one. Most of the time the client will respond that they probably could have done something different, which leads you to the next step. The therapist then allows the client to brain-storm and think "what control do I have in this situation?" and what can be a positive "go to" response that I can start practicing? These "in my control" situations are then written on the green construction cards and also placed on the poster board under the "in my control" section to be reviewed together.

Macro-Processing:

Front and back loading: I have found it most effective to give little instruction prior to this activity on how they can gain meaning while allowing for time at the end for reflection and recognition of the teachable moments once the activity is complete.

Micro-Processing:

During the activity it is important to observe the following and use these observations as part of the discussion portion of the activity:

- Does the client hesitate identifying between the two categories, or were they impulsive, or were they confident?
- How does the client react to being challenged with the idea of not having control in a given situation?
- Were there any situation cards they couldn't decide on for what category to place them in?
- When writing their personal "in my control" and "out of my control" cards observe the comfortability, hesitancy, or resistance to share an experience.
- Was the activity mostly a collaborative effort being flexible and open to new ideas?

Debrief and Transfer:

Prior to this activity, the client has made clear their communication style, their problem-solving skills level, and their openness to try new things. This activity helps bring awareness to the client the control one has in any given situation and what to do about it. This game allows for an opportunity to call attention to dysfunctional communication, lack of control over others, opportunities for positive choices, and whether they wish to change these negative behavior patterns and refine their communication methods.

Tips or Lessons Learned for Counselors:

Some clients may not be willing to share personal situations to place under the categories. If so, stick with the practice cards.

About the Author: Monica Phelps-Pineda, MS, NCC, PLPC, is a Counseling Education and Supervision doctoral candidate at the University of Missouri – St. Louis. Her counseling, teaching, research, and clinical supervision experiences are centered on implementing multiculturally responsive practices to work with children, adolescents, and families of minoritized racial and ethnic identities.

Activity 9.4: TOTIKA

Lay-nah Blue Morris-Howe

Theme/Goals of Activity	Self-esteem, self-confidence building
Population/Age	8+
Intrapersonal Skills	Ability to personally reflect on experiences and personal attributes
Interpersonal Skills	Ability to communicate with another player, interact respectfully, not demean other players or their responses
Coping/Solution-Focused Skills	Personal introspection into strengths, acknowledgment of feelings, ideas for personal improvement of life situations
Materials	TOTIKA ™ Game

Description of the Activity:

TOTIKA is a game that involved stacking blocks of various colors. The game comes with a set of cards that correspond to the block colors. As players pull blocks from the stack, the objective is to not knock over the whole tower of stacked blocks. Also, as players pull blocks from the stack they answer a question from the cards. These self-esteem cards have questions to help learn about the person answering the question. Use of this game is meant to help build rapport with a client who may be uncomfortable or resistant.

Macro-Processing:

No loading:

Read the game instructions to the client(s)/player(s).

Front and back loading:

Front: This game gives us the opportunity to explore questions that make us think about our strengths and accomplishments, because sometimes it's hard for us to remember or think of all the things that we are good at or that we can do!

Back: How did it feel for you to be able to answer those questions while we played the game? What was it like to hear yourself identify those strengths/areas of pride/things you like about yourself/etc.?

Micro-Processing:

Observations:

- I noticed that you hesitated to answer the question about naming things you liked about yourself. That seemed challenging for you.
- You smiled when other client/player in the game answered that question on the card. It seemed to make you happy for them that they could share that experience.

– I saw both of you nod your head in agreement about that question. That seemed like a tough one for both of you! (connection)

Debrief and Transfer:

Clients/players had challenges at times answering some questions when more than just the counselor was present for the game. In this situation, the counselor can normalize by saying

– "Sometimes it can feel strange or uncomfortable to talk about ourselves in front of other people. I wonder if anyone else feels like this?"

Another way to normalize and invite players to share is for the counselor to join in the game from the beginning, allowing for the process of modeling sharing about oneself. Then, when difficult questions arise from the cards, the counselor can name that for themselves, and still share, to demonstrate courage in sharing. Joining the players by making connection can also help normalize fear of sharing or discomfort in sharing when the game is played in a group setting.

– For example, stating "Client/player A, you seemed a bit hesitant to share your answer to the question about how it feels when someone gives you a compliment, but you were able to do it and then I noticed that client/player B also agreed with you about your answer! That seems like a really normal feeling to have about that. Next time someone gives you a compliment, maybe we can all think about how it makes us feel and what we think about that.

Tips or Lessons Learned for Counselors:

When this game is played in a group setting, it may be beneficial to add a "pass rule" for safety and comfort. Allowing youth to set their own level of comfort when answering the questions on the cards will teach them personal agency in the game and that they have control over what they share. Being considerate of the group dynamics is important in establishing the game rules. Talking the group about being respectful of each client/player's responses is crucial to the game's success. This game is also extremely beneficial and appropriate for sibling pairs/groups.

About the Author: Dr. Lay-nah Blue Morris-Howe is an Assistant Professor at the University of Wyoming. She is also a licensed professional counselor with 15 years of experience who works with youth, families, couples, individuals, and groups from a multiculturally informed humanistic approach.

Chapter 10

Expressive and creative arts

Keith Davis and Melia A. Snyder

Expressive and creative arts

Expressive Arts Therapy is a distinct discipline of integrated and intermodal arts practice that fosters human growth, development, and healing (Atkins at al., 2003). Expressive artists may use imagery, storytelling, dance, music, drama, poetry, movement, dreamwork, clay work, and visual arts, for example, together or separately to support clients in reconnecting with their internal resources. Through expressive arts, clients are supported in reclaiming their innate capacity as human beings for creative expression (Atkins, 2014). Rooted in existential, humanistic, postmodern, and phenomenological traditions, Expressive Arts Therapy is supported by the literature to promote meaning-making, manageability, positive coping, and understanding of life's challenges (Snyder, 2014). Additionally, Expressive Arts Therapy has been used with diverse populations and in diverse settings to promote positive mental health (Atkins, 2014; Atkins et al., 2003; Knill et al., 2005; Malchiodi, 2013; McNiff, 2009; Rogers, 1993) and substance abuse outcomes (Brooke, 2009).

Expressive arts in counseling can be used with specific training from organizations such as the International Expressive Arts Therapy Association (IEATA; 2017), which provides specific training and credentialing in Expressive Arts Therapy as an adjunct to graduate-level therapy training. Expressive arts and creativity can also be used without formal training as a supplement to evidence-based practice for mental health and school counseling professionals. Organizations such as the Association for Creativity in Counseling (ACC; n.d.) provide a collective space for creative counselors to share ideas and inspiration without the formal training and credentialing process provided through IEATA.

When engaging in creativity, children and adolescents utilize divergent thinking which fosters positive coping strategies, emotional regulation, and resilience (Gladding, 2021). Divergent thinking entails incorporating flexibility and generating new and different ideas outside of the norm (Malikiosi-Loizos, 1997). Through expressive arts, adolescents often describe feeling a sense of empowerment, an increased sense of agency and control, and a sense of relief or catharsis at having expressed in a language beyond words what is most true for them (Degges-White & Davis, 2017; Lahad, 2000). Expressive arts can be a culturally sensitive, developmentally appropriate way of working with adolescents to promote identity formation, transform trauma, center the attention, and provide prosocial expression.

Counseling children and adolescents with expressive and creative arts

Natalie Rogers, daughter of Carl Rogers, developed Expressive Arts Therapy by integrating creative mediums into the core counseling skills developed by her father (Rogers, 1993). Expressive Arts Therapy was developed as a humanistic and creative supplement to person-centered therapy using arts mediums to facilitate a helping relationship (Kim, 2010). Therapists may use different mediums, or multiple mediums to facilitate client expression. Use of expressive arts as a medium combines auditory, visual, and kinesthetic modalities, thus honoring various learning styles and modes of expression within the safety of the therapeutic relationship (Lahad, 2000). Expressive arts engage clients in low skill-high sensitivity art making and values the process of art making itself (Degges-White & Davis, 2017). The aesthetic quality of the product is less important than the expressive process for the client. What is true is not always pretty. Within the field of expressive arts, the therapist acts as a witness to the process and product and offers a therapeutic response to the client. This type of response departs from an evaluative appraisal of the art product but rather offers rich, descriptive language and arts-based response based on what moved or touched you as the witness. Thus, the relationship becomes a container for dialoguing through the arts.

The use of empirically based creative and expressive arts therapies with children and adolescents has since seen a significant increase in the counseling literature over the last 15 years (Degges-White & Davis, 2017;

DOI: 10.4324/9781315213767-11

Rogers, 1993). Much of the research has focused on the development of self-expression, relational, and social skills, with the transfer of those skills to environments outside the counseling context. Integrating creativity and expressive arts into therapy work as a technique differs from the practice of Art Therapy which has specific training, ethical standards, and credentialing (American Art Therapy Association, 2017). The use of creative and expressive arts activities in counseling is a versatile compliment to most counseling modalities and theories.

Expressive techniques offer counselors a creative means to process experiences with clients beyond verbal expression (Bradley et al., 2008). These powerful expressive tools help externalize emotions and consider a new perspective. Creative expression is also an important aspect of cultural identity (Gladding, 2008). Integration of expressive arts is effective across the lifespan with lasting positive impacts to mental health after terminating the therapy process. Rogers (2021) promotes Expressive Arts Therapy as a useful tool integrated with common evidence-based practice in counseling, including Cognitive Behavioral Therapy (CBT), Dialectical Behavioral Therapy (DBT), Acceptance and Commitment Therapy (ACT), and Motivational Interviewing (MI). Shifting to a more digital world, expressive arts therapists are integrating technology and software designed for creative expression in counseling work (Evans, 2012).

Interpersonal and intrapersonal skills

Combining these two Positive Psychology foundations, intrapersonal and interpersonal skills, results from the fact that research in creative and expressive arts with children and adolescents often integrates both simultaneously. Intrapersonal skill development is manifested by positively increasing the level of self-awareness, self-expression, cognitive skill development, emotional regulation, confidence, and instillation of hope in children and adolescents through creative and expressive arts. Since a primary developmental task of children and adolescents is social and relational skills, it follows that once they have begun increasing their intrapersonal skill functioning, they can begin applying such skills to their interpersonal relationships with others. The combining of these two Positive Psychology functions simultaneously within a given creative and expressive arts modality is common practice according to the following research, presented here as research citing intrapersonal skill development and then the integration of both intrapersonal and interpersonal skill development.

Creative and expressive arts have been used successfully with children and adolescents experiencing health and disability challenges. Using dramatic invention and skit performances, children diagnosed with cystic fibrosis were able to develop a sense of empowerment in discovering their own voices in deepening understanding of their medical condition (Basso et al., 2008). Skudrzyk et al. (2009) successfully employed visual and performing arts in a group of adolescent boys of varying levels of special needs in helping them to improve their cognitive and social skills. Also working with adolescent boys, Davis (2012) described strategies for building counseling rapport with them through drumming. Davis (2010) also demonstrated the use of drumming and music-making in helping elementary-aged children process feelings of trauma related to a natural disaster. In processing grief through the loss of loved ones, Slyter (2012) used music, visual arts, bibliotherapy, drama, and cinematherapy in helping adolescents with developmentally appropriate responses to death and dying. In working with mood disorders and their symptomatology, drama and art making were used to treat selective mutism (i.e., anxiety disorder) in a child (Fernandez et al., 2014), and photography (i.e., phototherapy) was used in treating an adolescent female experiencing depression and suicidal ideation (Ginicola et al., 2012).

Leggett (2009) provided evidence of how a child's verbal and non-verbal expression of thoughts, feelings, and behaviors was facilitated through the creative integration of solution-focused counseling with children's literature and visual arts techniques. Using drumming groups, Davis (2012) described improvement in the expression of anger and aggression of elementary-aged boys who were referred to counseling for such behavioral concerns. The use of drama and playwriting demonstrated effectiveness in improving self-expression and social skills for at-risk adolescents (Bernstein et al., 2014; Lenz et al., 2010); while additional creative and expressive arts modalities such as movement, music, literature, visual art, and journaling have equally contributed to improved social, relational, and self-expression skills among adolescents (Utley & Garza, 2011; Veach & Gladding, 2007). Finally, expressive activities were also employed in humanistic-focused play groups to help in the social transition of children to preadolescence (Bratton et al., 2009).

Coping and solution-focused skills

Counseling with children and adolescents often takes place in their school environment, as well as at summer camps, hospitals, and community counseling settings. Ideally, these are positive and safe environments that allow for the creation of a trusting counseling relationship so that children and adolescents can work on intrapersonal and interpersonal skills, and a perfect opportunity to practice and transfer such skill development to a larger socio-cultural context (e.g., family, neighborhood, and school).

For example, Ziff et al. (2012) describe their creation of a school-based creative group counseling program for elementary school-aged children aimed at building social skills, developing problem-solving abilities, and expressing feelings through art making. Gibbons (2010) used literature and art making in an elementary school classroom as part of an eight-week creative arts program focused on conflict resolution skills for children living in urban areas plagued by violence. Buskirk-Cohen (2015) documented the effectiveness of a creative arts summer camp for children with social, emotional, and learning difficulties. Using a combination of creative modalities such as movement therapy, yoga, art making, and music, Buskirk-Cohen noted significant improvement in children's behaviors and relationships. In a group context, mindfulness and expressive arts are a useful intervention to help address stress for adolescents in school counseling settings (Lindsey et al., 2018). Finally, creative and expressive arts have been successfully used in helping children and adolescents cope with their own and their family's substance-abuse behaviors. More specifically, Oklan and Henderson (2014) documented how songwriting, recording, and music production reduced psychiatric symptoms and enhanced coping of inhalant use for adolescents; while a group for African American children of families with drug addictions improved their coping, emotional regulation, and self-confidence through culturally sensitive activities such as African dance, mask-making, and storytelling (Goicoechea et al., 2014).

Strengths and limitations

Children and adolescents are naturally creative and expressive in their thoughts and emotions. From a developmental perspective, children especially, but many adolescents as well, do not always have the words to express what they are thinking and feeling, let alone how they are trying to make meaning in their lived experiences. Through creative expression, whether it is music, movement, drama, writing, poetry, visual arts, storytelling, or any other medium, children and adolescents are given an opportunity to put voice to their thoughts and emotions. The idea is that as human beings, there is an innate capacity for creative expression of individual and collective experience in artistic form (Atkins et al., 2003). Within this innate capacity for creative expression, and combined with natural curiosity, creative and Expressive Arts Therapy and interventions are a logical choice for use with children and adolescents. Finally, given the interactive nature and process-oriented focus of creative and Expressive Arts Therapy, group work lends itself especially well to this particular approach, especially for those counselors working in schools.

The primary limitation in employing creative and expressive arts with children and adolescents is in facilitator training, understanding, and preparation. Creativity in counseling and Expressive Arts Therapy is not simply a technique-driven approach to working with clients in a therapeutic setting. Expressive Arts Therapy, in particular, is an emerging field grounded in theories and philosophical approaches just as diverse as those of the counseling profession. There is degree and certificate programs, both within the United States and internationally, where those interested in Expressive Arts Therapy can receive advanced training and education. The International Expressive Arts Therapy Association (IEATA) also provides guidelines for training, a code of ethics, information regarding credentialing as a Registered Expressive Arts Therapist (REAT) or Registered Expressive Arts Consultant/Educator (REACE), and information on professional development. Equally, the reference section at the end of this chapter can help those interested in understanding more the theories and philosophical approaches in the creative and expressive arts therapies.

Further limitations to using creativity and Expressive Arts Therapy with children and adolescents are time and materials. Creative and Expressive Arts Therapy has the potential to evoke strong emotions. Thus, it is important for the facilitator to allow adequate time for processing such emotions in a safe space. Equally, many modalities of creative and expressive arts use materials such as paint, paintbrushes, clay, paper, chalk, pens, pencils, musical instruments, and a variety of other art-making mediums. In a time of budget cuts, facilitators of creative and expressive arts with children and adolescents need themselves to be creative in resource management.

Meaning-making

With children being innately curious and creative, especially since they function in a less linear and more holistic way, engaging them in creativity and the expressive arts comes quite naturally. Equally, adolescents respond well to opportunities to express themselves emotionally through the arts. Deciding how to use creative and expressive arts with children and adolescents, and what specific modalities to consider, is largely a function of (1) developmental level, (2) what the specific issues are, and (3) whether or not it's a group or individual. As described in this chapter and other chapters throughout this book, some activities require more cognitive complexity in direction and processing. Children are typically concrete operational processors while adolescents are more formal operational processors (Piaget, 1963), which influences the activity and/or modality chosen by the facilitator. Relatedly, the complexity of the presented issue determines the level of meaning creation and processing that can be obtained through the employment of creative and expressive arts therapies. The bottom line is that the facilitator needs to use professional and clinical judgment to determine which specific creative and/or Expressive Arts Therapy modality is warranted based on the developmental level of the group and/or individual and the ability to process it.

References

American Art Therapy Association (2017). *About art therapy.* https://arttherapy.org/about-art-therapy/

Association for Creativity in Counseling (n.d.). *About the association for creativity in counseling.* https://www.creativecounselor.org/about-acc

Atkins, S. (2014). *Presence and process in expressive arts work: At the edge of wonder.* Jessica Kingsley Publishers.

Atkins, S., Adams, M., McKinney, C., McKinney, H., Rose, L., Wentworth, J., & Woodworth, J. (2003). *Expressive arts therapy: Creative process in art and life.* Parkway Publishers, Inc.

Basso, R., Laurier, W., & Pelech, W. (2008). Creative arts in a children's cystic fibrosis continuing care program: A Canadian case study. *The International Journal of Learning, 15*(5), 219–224.

Bernstein, R. E., Ablow, J. C., Maloney, K. C., & Nigg, J. T. (2014). Piloting playwrite: Feasibility and efficacy of a playwriting intervention for at-risk adolescents. *Journal of Creativity in Mental Health, 9,* 446–467.

Bradley, L. J., Whiting, P., Hendricks, B., Parr, G., & Jones Jr, E. G. (2008). The use of expressive techniques in counseling. *Journal of Creativity in Mental Health, 3*(1), 44–59.

Bratton, S. C., Ceballos, P. L., & Ferebee, K. W. (2009). Integration of structured expressive activities within a humanistic group play therapy format for preadolescents. *The Journal for Specialists in Group Work, 34*(3), 251–275.

Brooke, S. L. (Ed.). (2009). *The use of the creative therapies with chemical dependency issues.* Springfield, IL: Charles C Thomas Publisher.

Buskirk-Cohen, A. A. (2015). Effectiveness of a creative arts summer camp: Benefits of a short-term, intensive program on children's social behaviors and relationships. *Journal of Creativity in Mental Health, 10,* 34–45.

Davis, K. M. (2010). Music and the expressive arts with children experiencing trauma. *Journal of Creativity in Mental Health, 5,* 125–133.

Davis, K. M. (2012). Talking to the beat of a different drum: Speaking so he can listen and listening so he can speak. In S. Degges-White & B. Colon (Eds.), *Counseling Boys and Young Men* (pp. 29–40). New York: Springer Publishing.

Degges-White, S., & Davis, N. L. (Eds.). (2017). *Integrating the expressive arts into counseling practice: Theory-based interventions.* Springer Publishing Company.

Evans, S. (2012). Using computer technology in expressive arts therapy practice: A proposal for increased use. *Journal of Creativity in Mental Health, 7*(1), 49–63.

Fernandez, K. T. G., Serrano, K. C. M., & Tongson, M. C. C. (2014). An intervention in treating selective mutism using the expressive therapies continuum framework. *Journal of Creativity in Mental Health, 9,* 19–32.

Gibbons, K. (2010). Circle justice: A creative arts approach to conflict resolution in the classroom. *Art Therapy: Journal of the American Art Therapy Association, 27*(2), 84–89.

Ginicola, M. M., Smith, C., & Trzaska, J. (2012). Using photography in counseling: Images of healing. *The International Journal of the Image, 2*(1), 29–44.

Gladding, S. T. (2008). The impact of creativity in counseling. *Journal of Creativity in Mental Health, 3*(2), 97–104.

Gladding, S. T. (2021). *The creative arts in counseling* (6th ed.). American Counseling Association.

Goicoechea, J., Wagner, K., Yahalom, J., & Medina, T. (2014). Group counseling for at-risk African American youth: A collaboration between therapists and artists. *Journal of Creativity in Mental Health, 9,* 69–82.

International Expressive Arts Therapy Association (2017). *Professional registration: Choose your path.* https://www.ieata.org/reatorreace

Kim, S. (2010). A story of a healing relationship: The person-centered approach in expressive arts therapy. *Journal of Creativity in Mental Health, 5*(1), 93–98.

Knill, P., Levine, E., & Levine, S. K. (2005). *Principles and practice of expressive arts therapy: Toward a therapeutic aesthetics.* Jessica Kingsley Publishers.

Lahad, M. (2000). *Creative supervision: The use of expressive arts in supervision and self supervision.* Jessica Kingsley Publishers.

Leggett, E. S. (2009). A creative application of solution-focused counseling: An integration with children's literature and visual arts. *Journal of Creativity in Mental Health, 4,* 191–200.

Lenz, A. S., Holman, R. L., & Dominguez, D. L. (2010). Encouraging connections: Integrating expressive art and drama into therapeutic social skills training with adolescents. *Journal of Creativity in Mental Health, 5,* 142–157.

Lindsey, L., Robertson, P., & Lindsey, B. (2018). Expressive arts and mindfulness: Aiding adolescents in understanding and managing their stress. *Journal of Creativity in Mental Health, 13*(3), 288–297.

Malchiodi, C. A. (Ed.). (2013). *Expressive therapies*. Guilford Publications.

Malikiosi-Loizos, M. (1997). Creative thinking: A cognitive process in counseling. *Psychology: the Journal of the Hellenic Psychological Society, 4*(2), 129–136.

McNiff, S. (2009). *Integrating the arts in therapy: History, theory, and practice*. Charles C. Thomas Publisher.

Oklan, A. M., & Henderson, S. J. (2014). Treating inhalant abuse in adolescence: A recorded music expressive arts intervention. *Psychomusicology: Music, Mind, and Brain, 24*(3), 231–237.

Piaget, J. (1963). *The origins of intelligence in children*. Norton.

Rogers, N. (1993). *The creative connection: Expressive arts as healing*. Science and Behavior Books.

Rogers, N. (2021). Person-centered expressive arts therapy: A path to wholeness. In J. A. Rubin (Ed.), *Approaches to Art Therapy* (3rd ed., pp. 230–248). Routledge.

Skudrzyk, B., Zera, D. A., McMahon, G., Schmidt, R., Boyne, J., & Spannaus, R. L. (2009). Learning to relate: Interweaving creative approaches in group counseling with adolescents. *Journal of Creativity in Mental Health, 4*, 249–261.

Slyter, M. (2012). Creative counseling interventions for grieving adolescents. *Journal of Creativity in Mental Health, 7*, 17–34.

Snyder, M. A. (2014). *Sense of coherence and daily spiritual experience among pregnant, post-partum, and parenting women in recovery from substance abuse: An expressive arts group therapy intervention* (Doctoral dissertation, The University of North Carolina at Charlotte).

Utley, A., & Garza, Y. (2011). The therapeutic use of journaling with adolescents. *Journal of Creativity of Mental Health, 6*, 29–41.

Veach, L. J., & Gladding, S. T. (2007). Using creative group techniques in high schools. *The Journal for Specialists in Group Work, 32*(1), 71–81.

Ziff, K., Pierce, L., Johanson, S., & King, M. (2012). ArtBreak: A creative group counseling program for children. *Journal of Creativity in Mental Health, 7*, 108–121.

Activity 10.1: Emotions Ensemble

Keith Davis and Sharon Blackwell Jones

Theme/Goals of Activity:	Identify feelings and emotions about concerns and challenges currently experiencing. Compose music to express feelings and emotions
Population/Age	6–18/groups of 4–20
Intrapersonal Skills	Self-awareness, identify emotions and feelings
Interpersonal Skills	Express emotions and feelings
Coping/Solution-Focused Skills	N/A
Materials	A variety of musical instruments and/or noisemakers (e.g., buckets, coffee cans, pencils, and hand-clapping)

Description of the Activity:

The counselor processes with the participants current concerns and challenges that are being faced (e.g., for children, making friends, parental divorce, bullying; for adolescents, peer pressure, relationships, going to college). The counselor then asks the participants to begin identifying the emotions that are associated with the concerns and challenges (e.g., sad, glad, mad, scared, anxious). The counselor writes down the identified emotions on a piece of paper.

The counselor introduces the participants to the instruments and/or noisemakers and invites them to experiment with them until one is chosen. The counselor then randomly assigns the participants to a group (ensemble), forming as many groups as possible. The counselor gives each group one of the emotions identified earlier and only that particular group should know their emotion word.

Each group ensemble is then instructed to find a place to formulate a composition representing the specific emotion word. After the compositions have been created, all groups are reassembled. Each group then has the opportunity to play their composition while the other groups listen. At the end of each composition, the other groups attempt to guess what emotion is being played. This is continued until all groups have performed their emotion compositions. Process questions from the counselor are described below.

*Note: this exercise is an adaptation of Bowman (1987) and Davis (2007).

Macro-Processing:

No loading:

At the beginning, ask participants to identify specific emotions each has felt, followed by asking them what type of music they enjoy.

Front and back loading:

Front: Group members can be asked to identify emotions connected with certain events in their lives, find an instrument or noisemaker that might best represent where each is currently at in her/his challenge or concern, and express feelings about composing music to represent individual emotions (see micro-processing).
Back: Once the music has been composed and shared, questions can include having participants guess which emotion was being played during the group compositions (see micro-processing).

Metaphor:

Music can serve as a metaphor in many ways. In this activity, the choice of instrument is metaphorical (e.g., a large loud drum may represent a large loud emotion such as anger, or a soft sounding rattle may represent feeling timid). A particular composition is often metaphoric for the rhythm, cadence, and intensity of emotions and how that emotion may manifest in self or the observation of others.

Micro-Processing:

Observations: During the activity, the counselor first facilitates questions that help promote participants' self-awareness in identifying emotions and the expression of them. For example:

- "What kinds of things are happening right now that present a challenge for you?" (self-awareness)
- "What emotions (i.e., sad, mad, glad, scared, anxious) can you identify?" (self-awareness, identify emotions and feelings)
- "What makes you choose that particular instrument to demonstrate that particular emotion?" (expression of emotions)

Observations during music composition: During the formulation of the compositions, the counselor visits each group to observe the decision-making process of the composition. Some process questions might include:

- "How many different ways can that emotion be expressed?" (expression of emotions)
- "What do you notice about the group when trying to represent the emotion?" (identify emotions)
- "How are you feeling when playing that composition?" (expression of emotion)

Observations while compositions are presented to the group: As the groups share their compositions with another, the counselor continues to facilitate the process with such questions as:

- "How is everyone feeling after hearing this composition?" (self-awareness and identification of emotions)
- "What emotion do you think this group was trying to demonstrate?" "What makes you think it was (that) emotion?" (expression of emotion)

Debrief and Transfer:

Children and adolescents are emotional beings. To be able to have self-awareness and express emotions in socially acceptable and healthy ways aids in their personal, social, and psychological development. Thus, debriefing and transfer of learning involves helping to affirm for children and adolescent that it's ok to have a range of emotions, to be self-aware of the emotions, and to express them in ways that others can understand. The teachable moment is grounded in having children and adolescents understand their metaphoric "rhythm" and how that rhythm impacts others around them when they choose how to "compose" specific emotions. To value individual differences within this group activity, it is important to emphasize that each individual may choose a different instrument to represent the same emotion. As a result, each individual's "rhythm" may be expressed differently even though it's the same emotion being felt.

Tips or Lessons Learned for Counselors:

The primary tip and lesson here is to help children and adolescents not focus on the "quality" of an emotion composition, but rather the emotion itself. The counselor should be aware to steer the participants away from musical composition judgments and offer aesthetic responses such as "that made me feel…" Equally, having a wide assortment of instruments is not always possible. Collecting a variety of noisemakers can easily be accomplished (buckets, coffee cans, pots, pans, pencils, etc.) by the counselor for little to no cost.

About the Author: Keith M. Davis, PhD, NCC, is a Professor at Radford University. Dr. Davis teaches courses in both school and clinical mental health counseling and has more than 20 years of experience teaching, working as an elementary and high school counselor, a family intervention specialist, and an EAP therapist. Dr. Sharon Blackwell Jones is an Assistant Professor and Faculty member at Radford University for the past 8 years. Over the past 22 years, Dr. Jones has taught graduate courses in diversity, counseling skills, drug and alcohol counseling, and practicum for individual counseling and groups.

Activity 10.2: River Rocks and Cairn

Keith Davis and Malia Snyder

Theme/Goals of Activity	The participants will discover how their life concerns, challenges, and burdens "weigh" them down, aggravate them, and how a cairn can offer symbolic guidance
Population/Age	13–18/groups of 6+
Intrapersonal Skills	Self-awareness
Interpersonal Skills	Express emotions and feelings
Coping/Solution-Focused Skills	N/A
Materials	Access to a river, stream, or creek; with rocks, stones, and pebbles for gathering

Description of the Activity:

The counselor gathers the group next to a river, stream, or creek and asks them to think about a current concern, challenge, or burden they are facing. The counselor then asks participants to spend time near the water and collect a variety of rocks, stones, and pebbles that represent the size of the various concerns, challenges, or burdens they are currently facing. After the collection, participants are asked to carry their rocks, stones, and pebbles with them at all times. The counselor then leads the participants on a short group hike along the river, stream, creek, or nearby trail. To finalize the activity, the participants are asked by the counselor to create a group cairn with the collected rocks, stones, and pebbles.

Macro-Processing:

No loading:

Group members are invited outdoors while walking in nature can use time to build rapport.

Front and back loading:

Front: Group members are asked to identify current concerns and challenges and begin collecting rocks, stones, and pebbles for proportional representations (i.e., big rocks = big concerns, challenges, burdens, etc.) (see micro-processing).

   Back: As members begin to collect their rocks, they can begin to assess the size of each challenge as well as the burden of multiple concerns.

*Front- and back-loading questions can best be represented in the creation of a group cairn. Cairns are an opportunity to incorporate cultural lessons regarding how they were used in certain cultures to represent a beacon of guidance and support on a trail. Thus, front- and back-loading questions can be used to illustrate how participants can use the "cairn" guidance and support of others in overcoming life's concerns, challenges, and burdens (see micro-processing).

Metaphor:

The bigger the stone or burden, and the more stones or burdens a person carries, the more difficult the journey. Unloading the burden is necessary for a journey that is enjoyable.

Micro-Processing:

Observations during rapport building: Involving adolescents in the outdoors offers opportunities for them to experience the wonders of nature and the gifts that are offered through intentional interactions with the natural world. Nature and the outdoors are wonderful examples of the cyclical ebbing and flowing of growth and development. Nature itself is creative and expressive as demonstrated in the change of seasons (e.g., rain, snow, sun, changing leaves, blooming of plants and trees).

- "How often do you get to go outside?" "How does it feel to be outside rather than in the... group room?" (self-awareness)
- "What does the change of seasons mean to you?" "How are changes and creativity reflective of your personal feelings and negotiating life concerns and challenges?" (self-awareness)

Observations while collecting stones: What do you look for and what questions/comments: (include skill of self-awareness and if different skills come up such as self-expression and coping with stress, then include in intra-, interpersonal, or coping/solution-focused at beginning).

- Questions to promote skill development.

Debrief and Transfer:

Counselors working with adolescents in this exercise can metaphorically relate how carrying concerns, challenges, and burdens can impact their personal, social, and psychological development. Adolescents often need support, from adults, and just as importantly from their peers. The creation of a group cairn can demonstrate how relying upon others for support in life's challenges can be beneficial. Life's concerns, challenges, and burdens can either be "heavy" rocks and stones, or a pebble in a shoe that is "small" but can be a constant reminder of how daily lives and energy are impacted by external circumstance.

Tips or Lessons Learned for Counselors:

For the counselor facilitating this activity, it is important to keep in mind the physical ability of adolescents in carrying out the requested exercises. Every effort to be inclusive of all adolescents, regardless of physical ability level, is tantamount in ensuring equal access in supporting their personal, social, and psychological development.

About the Author: Keith M. Davis, PhD, NCC, is a Professor at Radford University. Dr. Davis teaches courses in both school and clinical mental health counseling and has more than 20 years of experience teaching, working as an elementary and high school counselor, a family intervention specialist, and an EAP therapist.

Activity 10.3: Color My Emotions

Jenna Hepp

Theme/Goals of Activity	Creative expression and understanding of emotions
Population/Age	Early to late adolescence
Intrapersonal Skills	Visualization, self-awareness
Interpersonal Skills	Identifying emotions and feelings in the moment, reflection of feelings
Coping/Solution-Focused Skills	Expressive arts, homework, positive coping mechanisms
Materials	Paper, pen, markers, crayons, paint, oils, etc.

Description of the Activity:

This activity is appropriate for many ages, including early to late adolescence and even adults. The main focus is to have clients identify their emotions daily and express them in a creative way. This homework activity helps those struggling with recognizing the events or thoughts that could precipitate those emotions. This activity also helps clients become aware of their own emotions and gives them a chance to practice naming emotions. This activity could be used individually, in a group, or with a family. Challenge the client to paint, draw, color, write, or use any artistic expression that they can document each day before their next session. They will reflect on their day and express artistically the emotions that they had felt that day as well as document somewhere what had happened to bring that specific emotion on. When assigning this as homework, express that it can take as much or as little time as it needs to take each day, but that it is important to be consistent with doing it each day.

Macro-Processing:

No loading

Explain how the homework activity is being assigned to navigate and become more aware of our emotions day-to-day to understand ourselves better as well as name emotions when we feel them.

Front and back loading:

Front: Provide information about how we all feel a range of emotions and something that can help identify why we feel the way we do is to become aware and reflect on what had happened to make us feel that way. Sometimes it is nothing, sometimes it is our guardian getting mad at us for not cleaning our room, etc. (tailor examples to your client, you know them best).

Back: After they report back to session the next week, have them start by reporting how the experience of engaging in the activity was for them, and have them explain each piece (there should be an art expression for each day that they have not seen you but you can make a couple work – it works best the more pieces you have to compare and contrast). Notice the emotions they are showing in session while talking about each different piece and what had happened to precipitate that emotion.

Metaphors:

Metaphors of medium in the art activity could be a potential. Such as a client who often feels angry and uses dark colors on an art project over light ones or vice versa.

Micro-Processing:

Observation: As most of the teachable moments with this activity will come after the homework is completed, notice how the client is feeling about the activity before assigning it.

- Is the client ready to navigate their emotions on their own?
- Do they have the materials and/or the time to engage in this activity
- Is it something that they seem charged or fueled by instead of drained?

Observation: They may not have known how they were feeling that day and feel like they were unable to identify how to feel and how to portray that feeling artistically. That may bring up a conversation on how to recognize specific feelings and may be a helpful gauge of where the client is in recognizing and naming emotions.

Debrief and Transfer:

After assigning homework you may want to check in with the client and ask questions such as:

- Does that seem doable for you?
- How does this task make you feel?
- Is there anything you would like to tailor about this task (empowering them to make it their own)

If client did not complete homework, ask questions such as:

- What do you think held you back from completing this task?
- Is there something we could do differently next time to make it more manageable?

If the client did report, ask questions such as:

- What did you learn about yourself from this activity?
- What was easy about it?
- What was more difficult?
- What was the thought process into choosing the medium that you did for each day?
- Were there more consistencies in feeling or inconsistencies?

Tips or Lessons Learned for Counselors:

It will be most helpful to have examples of what they could create but encourage artistic freedom. Have examples ready for what could precipitate a good day, a bad day, a day where it feels like going through the motions. If the assignment does not get completed, reflect in session on why that is and what can be helpful instead. It may also be helpful to do a practice example in the session that it is being assigned.

About the Author: Jenna Hepp, PPC, MS, NCC, is a doctoral student at the University of Wyoming studying Counselor Education and Supervision. She grew up in Douglas, Wyoming. Her interests include adolescent group therapy, the self-esteem of early to late adolescence and their struggle with mental health, as well as suicide intervention for Wyoming youth.

Activity 10.4: Album of My Life

Jenna Hepp

Theme/Goals of Activity	Creative expression and understanding of emotions
Population/Age	Early to late adolescence
Intrapersonal Skills	Visualization, self-awareness
Interpersonal Skills	Identifying emotions and feelings, reflection
Coping/Solution-Focused Skills	Expressive arts, music
Materials	Paper, pen, markers, crayons, paint, oils, etc.

Description of the Activity:

This activity is appropriate for many ages, including early to late adolescence and even adults. The main focus is to have clients identify songs that they feel best represent their lives and how they feel. This could work individually as well as in a group. After explaining the importance of albums to artists, such as that being a creative outlet on how they have experienced their life. You may even use examples if you feel connected to certain albums. The client will then get a piece of paper that can be folded to the size of an album cover. They may decorate the album cover how they want and then add songs to their album that they feel would best describe their lives. The client can then explain why they chose each song, and how they identify to it, or they could describe how all the songs work together (themes, patterns, sounds), the meaning of the title, and what the cover art means for their own personal album.

Macro-Processing:

No loading

Ask clients if they have ever listened to a song and had a personal attachment to it in some way. This could look like they really identified with the lyrics or the melody made them feel a specific way.

Front and back loading:

Front: Provide information about how music can be a positive coping mechanism and an outlet to experience all sorts of different emotions. Similar to poetry, writing, or even playing music, it can also be therapeutic to just engage in. Explain how an album is different than a single in music. That an album represents a body of work and sometimes represents a longer story that collectively makes sense when you listen to the whole thing.

Back: After they create their own album cover and pick songs that they identify with for their own personal album, have them share with you like they were an artist selling their album what the key points are to take away from listening to it would be. They will explain the cover art album, the title, and the music.

Metaphors:

Metaphors can then be created after recognizing the theme or pattern to the album, such as the sequence of songs or the noticing of the same kind of genre reoccurring.

Micro-Processing:

Observation: The client may have trouble coming up with more than a couple songs; that is okay; have them just come up with as many as they can to again represent the "body of work" to relate their life too. And you can have them brainstorm by asking these questions:

- What kind of songs are your favorites?
- What artists do you find yourself listening to most often?
- Have you listened to a song or album on repeat? What was it about that in particular?
- What do you want people to learn about you after listening to your album?

Observation: It's important to note that music is interpreted by each individual very differently. For example, some can hear the beat while others only listen to the lyrics. The most therapeutic part about this activity is hearing from the client why the album makes sense to them and their own life. Ask questions while they are creating their album such as:

- When do you find yourself using music as an outlet?
- What does music do for you?
- When you feel _____ what do you listen to?

Debrief and Transfer:

This activity could be used in group therapy or individually. Many times clients may like a song so they will put it on their album but do not recognize how it relates to their life, so asking questions to understand how they identify with each song may be helpful. These questions could be used to debrief activity after the album is finished:

- What do you want listeners to understand about you after listening to this album?
- What would you rate your album out of ten?
- What would I know about you now that I did not before?
- How did it feel choosing music to describe yourself?
- If there was a song that you could add that does not exist what would you want that song to be titled?

Tips or Lessons Learned for Counselors:

This activity was used with adolescent males who had difficulty identifying emotions and communicating their feelings. Some client's may identify with this activity much more than others based on their interest level in music. As stated before, music is very subjective, so some clients may choose songs because they really look up to the artist; it is in the questions and debriefing that you will learn much more than just seeing what songs they chose for their album.

About the Author: Jenna Hepp, PPC, MS, NCC, is a doctoral student at the University of Wyoming studying Counselor Education and Supervision. She grew up in Douglas, Wyoming. Her interests include adolescent group therapy, the self-esteem of early to late adolescence and their struggle with mental health, as well as suicide intervention for Wyoming youth.

Chapter 11

Scientific thinking

Ana K. Houseal, Teresa Behrend Fletcher, Tanner Biwer, and Joshua Zettel

Science teaching and learning has benefited from decades of research guiding the latest science education reform efforts. These efforts are based on "A Framework for K-12 Education" (National Research Center [NRC], 2012), which laid out a structure for much needed changes. From this, experts from all over the US and a non-profit non-governmental organization, Achieve, developed the Next Generation Science Standards (NGSS Lead States, 2013). Forty-four states have fully adopted or developed standards based on the NGSS (NSTA.org, 2022), affecting over 78% of the K-12 student population in the US. The shifts in instruction these documents call for seek to make scientific ways of thinking and knowing more accessible, equitable, and connected to other disciplines by providing students with opportunities to learn science by doing science in ways that parallel those of scientists.

This chapter provides some initial background regarding these instructional shifts and means of engaging with science that can be leveraged specifically by school and mental health counselors to connect with child and adolescent clients. The use of scientific thinking skills helps to connect to development experiences, interests, and school science learning. The examples provided in the text and activities at the end of the chapter are designed to capture interest and provide rich connections to both the scientific thinking and the counseling goals in individual and small group settings.

Current science instruction

"Scientists use *patterns* to connect *observations* they make about the world to the models they construct to understand the world" (ital. added, Grotzer, 2021, p. 87). Given shifts in science education teaching standards, many terms counselors would recognize are no longer commonplace in K-12 science curriculum. These might include "the scientific method," experiments, hypothesis writing, and inquiry. This is, in part, because the field of science education, or the study of how people learn science and the best way to instructionally support them, has shifted dramatically. Current science instruction and terminology align with the concept of authentic scientific inquiry, or the way in which scientists engage in making sense of the world and building new knowledge (Crawford, 2014). This is different than "inquiry" instruction, which are comprised of a set of strategies for teaching. These two ideas were heavily conflated in the 1990s and 2000s, creating more confusion. Thus, a more contemporary approach, as outlined in A Framework for K-12 Science Education (NRC, 2012) and the NGSS (NGSS Lead States, 2013), employs the use of scientific practices and Crosscutting Concepts to facilitate sense making of complex, puzzling phenomena and to solve problems using science and engineering ideas which have replaced both "the scientific method" and "inquiry instruction."

A Framework for K-12 Science Education (NRC, 2012) specifies three integrated dimensions for learning science (see Figure 11.1).

The most familiar of the dimensions are the Disciplinary Core Ideas, which include the four content areas: Life Science, Physical Science, Earth and Space Science, and Engineering. Scientific and Engineering Practices consist of eight collaborative practices used to explore and make sense of science ideas. These practices are used to explore, investigate or experiment, and make sense of and explain phenomena using evidence. They include asking question/defining problems and developing and using models. The Crosscutting Concepts are seven big ideas that connect all science disciplines as well as other content areas. They include ideas such as patterns, cause and effect – mechanism and explanation. In addition, the Nature of Science helps us understand the "...enterprise of science as a whole – the wondering, investigating, questioning, data collection, and analyzing" (NGSS Lead States, 2013, Appendix H, p. 96). The Nature of Science's eight themes include science investigations use a variety of method, and scientific knowledge is based on empirical evidence. They are embedded within the three dimensions.

DOI: 10.4324/9781315213767-12

A Model of the Three Dimensions of Science Learning

Adapted from: Houseal, A. (2015). A visual representation of three-dimensional learning. A tool for evaluating curriculum. Science Scope 39 (1): 58-62.

Disciplinary Core Ideas (DCIs)
CONTENT

- Life Sciences
- Physical Sciences
- Earth and Space Sciences
- Engineering, Technology, and Applications of Science

Integration of content and big ideas

Cross Cutting Concepts (CCCs)
BIG IDEAS

1. Patterns
2. Cause & effect
3. Scale, proportion, and quantity
4. Systems & systems models
5. Energy & matter
6. Structure & function
7. Stability & change

Integration of content, process, and big ideas

Integration of content and process

Integration of big ideas and process

Nature of Science
- Scientific Investigations Use a Variety of Methods
- Scientific Knowledge Is Based on Empirical Evidence
- Scientific Knowledge Is Open to Revision in Light of New Evidence
- Scientific Models, Laws, Mechanisms, and Theories Explain Natural Phenomena

Scientific and Engineering Practices (SEPs)
PROCESS

1. Asking questions/Defining problems
2. Developing and using models
3. Planning and carrying out investigations
4. Analyzing and interpreting data
5. Using mathematical and computational thinking
6. Constructing explanations/Designing solutions
7. Engaging in arguments from evidence
8. Obtaining, evaluating and communicating information

Nature of Science, cont.
- Science Is a Way of Knowing
- Scientific Knowledge Assumes an Order and Consistency in Natural Systems
- Science Is a Human Endeavor
- Science Addresses Questions About the Natural and Material

National Research Council. (2012). *A Framework for K-12 Science Education: Practices, Crosscutting Concepts, and Core Ideas.* The National Academies Press. https://doi.org/10.17226/13165.
National Academies of Sciences, Engineering, and Medicine. (2013). *Next Generation Science Standards: For States, By States.* The National Academies Press. https://doi.org/10.17226/18290.

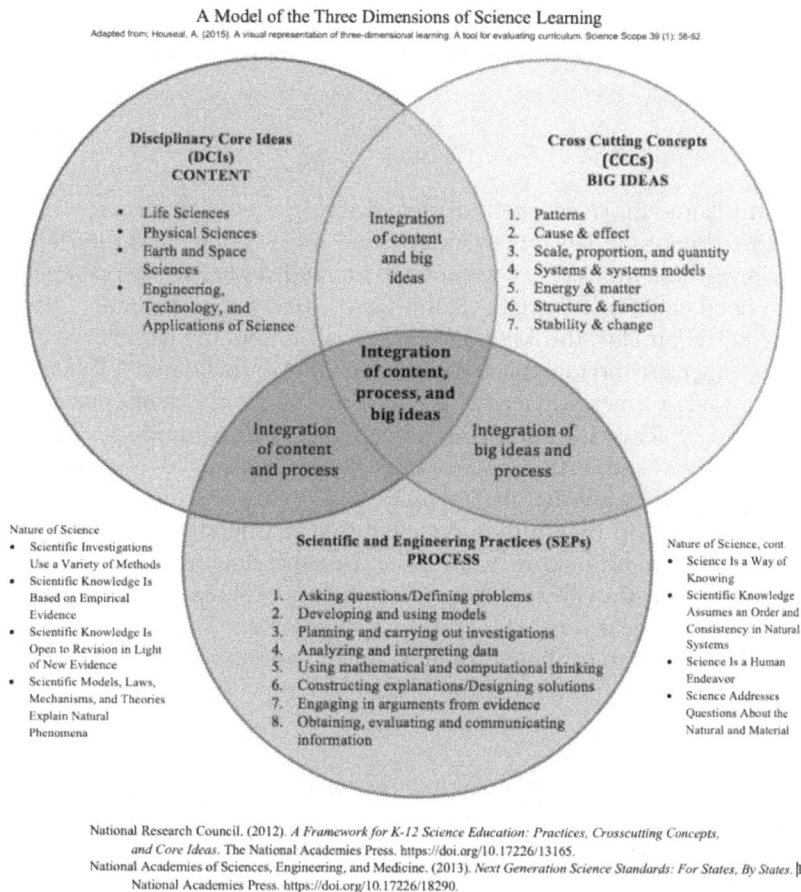

Figure 11.1 Three-dimensional science learning with Nature of Science themes (Houseal, 2015).

Throughout K-12 science education, these dimensions and Nature of Science themes are integrated and used in various combinations to make sense of interesting phenomena or solve problems. We define a phenomenon in this context to be a specific, observable, contextual event or problem that requires science or engineering ideas to make sense of and explain (Inouye et al., 2020).

In response to this shift to three-dimensional teaching as outlined in the NGSS, the terminology has changed. The word "experiment" has been replaced by "demonstration" or "investigation," depending on the context and use of the science-related phenomenon or activity. This is purposeful. An "experiment" in science is something very specific. It involves all of the following – proposing an explanation and then identifying variables that are set up in a way to collect, analyze, and interpret data that either supports or refutes that explanation. This type of explanation is a hypothesis, often mislabeled in school science as an "educated guess." True experiments are rarely conducted in school science, for good reasons. Students are building their science ideas about the way the world works, and instruction is designed to provide them with experiences that include demonstrations and investigations to explore how these ideas connect to what youth already know and generate new knowledge. None of the science-related activities in this chapter fit into the definition of an experiment, so that term will not be used.

Likewise, the difference between a demonstration and an investigation has to do with *who* is doing the activity. Demonstrations are conducted by the adult in charge or a single person showing a group of others something interesting. Investigations are set up so that all participants can explore what is happening directly. In education, these terms might be labeled as demonstrations being teacher-centered and investigations as learner-centered. Both are useful and appropriate and depend on many factors, such as setting, goals, safety, and time and material constraints.

Scientific thinking ideas

Scientific thinking can support the development of coping skills in counseling settings. Examples of scientific thinking ideas with potential connections to the counseling process include a Nature of Science principle (scientific knowledge is open to revision in light of new evidence – NGSS Appendix H), one Scientific and Engineering Practice (constructing explanations), and two Crosscutting Concepts (patterns and cause and effect – mechanism and explanation). These ideas are grounded in fast and slow thinking, which represent the complex human decision-making process.

Fast and slow thinking

Humans have evolved to think and make decisions using parallel processes that each serve us in different ways – fast and slow thinking. Fast thinking allows us to make rapid observations and interferences. Fast thinking is especially useful in situations where quick decisions need to be made either to avert danger or because decisions are routine enough not to need deliberate thought (Kahneman, 2011; Schwartz et al., 2017). For example, many decisions made when driving require fast thinking. Driving requires noticing patterns and applying prior experiences to respond quickly to expected and unexpected events at a rate of speed much faster than might be required while walking or running. At other times, we need to use slow thinking – the deliberate, conscious effort to notice and then actively question our typically instantaneous perceptions and assumptions (Kahneman, 2011).

Perhaps a quick observation and connection to prior experiences leads us to an assumption or incorrect inference, which might be challenged when another person picks up a "lit candle," blows it out, takes a bite, crunches it loudly, and swallows (see Activity 11.1). Fast thinking might guide an inference that a teacher or counselor simply has a lit candle, but it would lead to an incorrect inference. Instead, slowing down to rethink observations and verify claims allows an expansion of thoughts, and openness to new explanations in light of new evidence. In the case of the "candle," the new evidence is "crunchy, edible wax!" Slow thinking leveraged in the scientific practice of constructing explanations helps us to get beyond simple linear cause-and-effect explanations (NRC, 2012).

Nature of Science

Nature of Science consists of a way of knowing, including the understanding that scientific knowledge is tentative yet durable, empirically based, theory-laden, produced by humans, and is socially and culturally embedded. Thus, science has particular characteristics, including values, language, practices, and assumptions regarding how knowledge is developed (Abd-El-Khalick et al., 1998).

Early in the pandemic (beginning in the spring of 2020), scientists did not know how SARS-CoV-2 (the official name of the virus that causes the disease Covid-19) spread. Lacking evidence because the virus was completely new (novel), they based their claims on evidence from prior viruses, many of which spread via virus transmission through high touch surfaces. When people contacted those surfaces and then touched their faces, this provided a way for the virus to get into their mouths. Thus, surface cleanliness was posed as one way to keep people safe. As new evidence emerged about SARS-CoV-2, scientists learned the virus was more readily spread via airborne particles. The claims about how to keep safe changed, causing the Centers for Disease Control's guidelines to focus on the use of cloth masks by the general population to reduce the spread of these particles between people. During the Alpha and Delta phases of the pandemic, this was helpful, but then came Omicron – a new variant that changed the game. This variant seemed to elude the protection of cloth masks, and this evidence led to new claims and recommendations for different types of masks. Other COVID-19 variants and more evidence will continue to shift the claims and recommendations throughout the pandemic, as this is the way scientific knowledge is built.

Constructing explanations

Constructing explanations in science requires slow thinking. Scientists use constructing explanations to build knowledge by developing an account to answer questions about how or why a phenomenon is happening or how a problem can be solved. Investigators might be trying to answer questions such as: (a) What is going on here? (b) Why do I think it is happening? (c) What (science or engineering) ideas and evidence can I use to explain the phenomenon or solve the problem? (d) What connections can I make in my explanation?

Constructing explanations goes beyond defining terms or concepts, describing a process, or providing evidence without explaining how or why (Schwartz et al., 2017). When children and adolescents learn how to engage in this practice, they can move beyond the idea that science is a series of facts to be memorized. Instead, they begin to work through the logic of ideas necessary to construct explanations. Often times, scientific explanations are based on claims that are backed up with empirical evidence. This connects to the Nature of Science theme (NGSS, Appendix H; NGSS Lead States, 2013), *scientific knowledge is open to revision in light of new evidence*. In other words, a set of claims that make up an explanation may be revised if new evidence supports a new claim. This requires flexible thinking and can be transferred to explore ideas outside of science as well. There are several ways in which these scientific thinking ideas can be leveraged in counseling settings.

Patterns

In a universe that is always moving toward disorder, or entropy, human brains are wired to seek out patterns. Sometimes these patterns are obvious and easy to find, such as the way petals are arranged on flowers, the rhythm of waves rolling into a shoreline. Other times, our brains find patterns that are not really there. For instance, since our survival is dependent on it, the pattern of the arrangement of features on the human face is one of the first ones we learn. It is important to recognize our caregivers when we are pre-verbal and very helpless. This also means we easily find patterns in other objects that resemble faces, such as a random arrangement of rocks and sticks along a trail, or the headlights, logo, and grill on certain cars. Our *fast thinking* skills find these patterns and tell us to pay attention long enough to notice them. Our *slow thinking* skills help us to realize that these are not actually faces. In exploring biases and prejudice, our brain has a tendency to make assumptions or automatically categorize types of people based on race, ethnicity, or other characteristics. It takes intentional reflection using slow thinking to grow awareness of biases.

Cause and effect

Many children naturally ask questions and explore the natural and designed world. These queries set them up for developing life skills through a scientific lens. There are many phenomena that spark curiosity. Making observations, the basis of building all scientific knowledge, can be leveraged in many ways – both within the scientific disciplines and in other areas including social emotional learning. Children bring experiences and ideas about cause and effect to the table at a very young age. They will always look for a cause; if there is no obvious one, children may revert to magical thinking or develop their own reasons for phenomena. A primary example is the explanations children develop (e.g., the stork) for how babies are born. When lacking the biological knowledge of this phenomenon, children use magical thinking to develop personal theories about the origin of babies.

Therefore, cause and effect is familiar and can be used even in situations where the science content may be too complex to explain. For example, some children may have observed the effects of dropping a piece of candy (Mentos) into a diet soda and the subsequent eruption. The reaction caused by the interaction of mixing the candy and soda might be used to explain divorce, as each parent is good individually, but when combined, they create a mess that impacts everyone. Just as in the demonstration, the candy partially dissolves, and the soda becomes flat. Similar metaphors can be used to understand bullying or friendships.

Counseling children and adolescents supported by scientific thinking

Scientific thinking ideas connect well with behavioral approaches used to work with children and adolescents. Science investigations and demonstrations in the counseling environment can be used to harness scientific thinking ideas and link this counseling space to school science. Concepts of scientific thinking can help with explaining the brain's process in mental illness, but also illustrate counseling concepts such as Cognitive Behavioral Therapy (CBT).

Psychoeducation

Beyond interventions and investigations, science-related activities can be useful in psychoeducation. For adolescents who struggle with delayed gratification (Kumar & Pareek, 2018; Wulfert et al., 2002), understanding the nature of anti-depressants can be challenging. Using concepts from neuroscience in developmentally accessible ways can help adolescents and their parents understand the chemical imbalance of depression and how selective serotonin reuptake inhibitors (SSRIs) and monoamine oxidase inhibitors (MAOIs) work differently to address issues in the transmission of neurotransmitters that regulate mood (Ramachandraih et al., 2011). Using an image such as octopus tentacles or demonstrating by holding up both hands held a few inches apart with fingers separated, counselors can explain how neurotransmitters move along a chain of neurons and pass in a synapse from the dendrites of one neuron to the next (see Figure 11.2).

When serotonin or dopamine, the neurotransmitters that play a role in increasing positive feelings and attitudes, regulating mood swings, and decreasing anxiety in the brain, jumps the gap between the neurons,

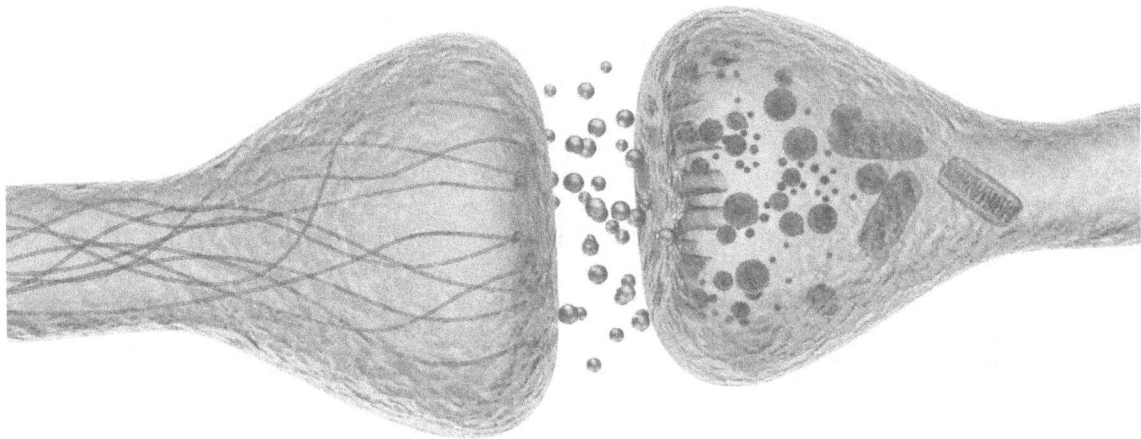

Figure 11.2 Neurons and synapse.

sometimes problems arise. In one case, the first neuron may be wired to keep too much (reuptake), so when the neurotransmitters reach the end of the chain, there are not enough of them. This can cause the brain to be inefficient at regulating mood and anxiety. However, the receiving dendrites may have malfunctioning "suction cups or vacuums" (receptors) and be unable to move the chemicals along the chain. Unfortunately, there is no diagnostic test to tell exactly which type of problem is causing the lack of neurotransmitters. Thus, by noting patterns in behavior, mood, and anxiety regulation while trying various pharmaceuticals, the prescribing physician must determine if the problem is with a greedy dendrite or a faulty vacuum. In other words, using scientific thinking can help determine if the depression is caused by an issue on the "sending" or "receiving" end of the neural chain.

Interpersonal and intrapersonal skills

Counseling children and adolescents supported by scientific thinking through engaging in demonstrations and investigations provides a tangible way to represent abstract experiences. The scientific practice of *constructing explanations*, Crosscutting Concepts of recognizing *patterns* and *cause and effect – mechanism and explanation* along with the Nature of Science theme of *scientific knowledge is open to revision in light of new evidence* provide a framework for clients to develop and intentionally implement intrapersonal and interpersonal skills. For example, when children are struggling to understand emotional regulation and aggression, a counselor could incorporate a demonstration that requires slow thinking to observe the patterns in the limited stretching nature of polymer strands in balloons through a "balloon skewers" demonstration.

This demonstration presents different size balloons that can be used to represent different individuals and their stressors. The insertion of a single skewer through the balloon could exemplify a stressor or "button pushing" done to that individual. When clients are asked to observe this balloon demonstration, they will note that the smaller balloons have more room for stretching and can endure more skewers than the larger balloons. Through metaphor, a child or adolescent would be guided to connect these balloons with differing levels of emotional regulation and the effects different interactions may have for different people. People with larger balloons may "pop" more easily from stressors than those with smaller balloons. This metaphor and the use of slow thinking to help to construct explanations about what may be happening could also be used to explain intrapersonal dynamics as children with a positive support system. This support system may provide a safe space to let out some of the air in their balloon so that they can tolerate more stressors and be able to stretch farther.

A baking soda-vinegar reaction or the process of using yeast, water, and sugar to make bread dough are two of many examples that rely on a catalyst to create an effect. You may recall from high school chemistry that a catalyst is "a substance that enables a chemical reaction to proceed at a usually faster rate or under different conditions (as at a lower temperature) than otherwise possible" (Merriam-Webster, 2022). *Cause and effect – mechanism and explanation* can be used to think about how these reactions happen and help to exemplify how behaviors can manifest different outcomes in daily life. By framing assertive behaviors as a metaphorical catalyst in their lives, children or adolescents who struggle being assertive may see opportunities to advocate for their needs in different environments.

Just as in the reactions explored, various catalysts cause different results. When children use fast thinking and engage in physical aggression to resolve conflict, a counselor can challenge clients to use slow thinking to change how they perceive a situation (intrapersonal) and then use words to express thoughts and feelings (interpersonal) without inflicting physical harm on others. This process of engaging in aggression or losing control can be simulated by a volcano where emotions under the surface exist and eventually end in an eruption with too much pressure. However, unlike a volcano, these underlying feelings can be explored to prevent the eruption where damage (physical and emotional) can be prevented.

Coping and solution-focused skills

Scientific thinking connects well with CBT in that these scientific ideas reinforce the exploration of how thoughts and feelings drive actions (see Figure 11.3).

With the use of scientific thinking, counselors can teach and reinforce positive coping skills to navigate thoughts and feelings. For example, scientific thinking nicely illustrates the CBT process. External or internal stimuli, or triggers, instigate fast thinking in the brain, which pulls from familiar reactions or previous experience to guide decision-making. In this way, the effects of the triggers lead the brain to jump quickly to a cause, which may or may not be accurate. By examining thoughts, behaviors, and emotions with slow thinking, clients can construct explanations based on observations and create new patterns of reaction to triggers. In CBT, clients examine automatic thoughts that can feed anxiety or maladaptive coping. As clients use slow thinking, they can be guided to see new patterns or evidence, and then these can be used to change their thinking and battle automatic thoughts.

The use of a demonstration called "Color-Changing Milk" also incorporates scientific thinking. The client applies drops of food coloring to a shallow dish of milk. The colors are used to represent different types of communications or interactions. When a drop of dish soap is added, the colors mix with each other forming a burst of colors. By observing the effects and the changes in the mixture of metaphorical "interactions or communication," the client could be prompted to reflect on how they are triggered by others around them. Using concepts of slow thinking and cause and effect, the client can start to identify how interactions and environments impact them and how they can use coping skills to navigate challenging situations. Through these strategic discussions during and after this investigation, the client could also explore skills such as problem-solving, decision-making, and the ability to seek social support.

Strengths and limitations

Children and adolescence do not always have the verbal resources to explain their thoughts and emotional responses. Using scientific thinking as metaphor, clients and counselors may have concrete examples or concepts to discuss as opposed to complex emotional processes. Many concepts of scientific thinking apply to skills developed in child and adolescent therapy work. These skills can be used to encourage children and adolescence to put their lived experiences into a visual display and reflect afterword. Finally, as this is a strong interactive approach to experiential learning, it connects to the scientific thinking skills embedded within K-8 education. For children

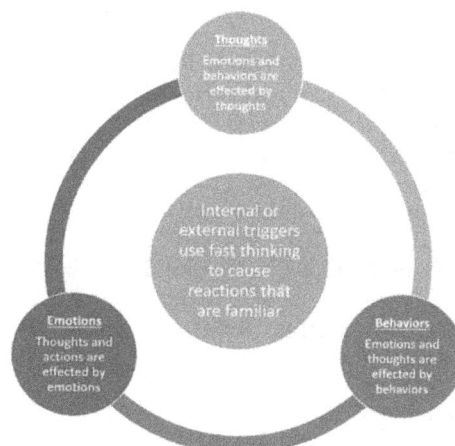

Figure 11.3 Applying fast and slow thinking to CBT.

and adolescents who are excited by science, bringing scientific thinking into the counseling settings can be very engaging. Further, scientific thinking concepts are a great connection for comprehensive school counseling programs to tie social emotional learning into other school science initiatives. For school-based counselors, consulting with science teachers for developmentally appropriate materials to use scientific thinking could be helpful in preparing to use this tool.

As for limitations, implementing demonstrations and investigations as a way of connecting science with counseling, there is a possibility that materials, space, time, and safety may limit the number and type of experience that can be provided in a given counseling setting. Further, science education standards and curricula have changed drastically over recent years, and so clinicians may need some additional information and mentorship in understanding modern concepts in science classrooms. Since terms such as "experiment" and "scientific method" are no longer used, it is critical that clinicians understand both the therapeutic process and the scientific process taking place when using science activities. In addition, these activities may not always work as planned. Practicing more complex demonstrations and investigations ahead of time and thinking through the scientific thinking ideas and researching the underlying science concepts will be critical. This will allow one to improvise and still help their clients make the connections should the experience go awry.

Meaning-making

Children are imaginative and curious; thus, using scientific demonstrations and investigations can create engaging opportunities to explore, understand, and reflect on their experiences. For the counselor, it will be important for them to determining the complexity of the specific issue and type of scientific thinking connections they want to make. They will need to decide which type of experience is acceptable for the developmental level and type of group or individual and how the scientific thinking ideas can be used to create connection to and deepen the meaning of the experiences. The ideas in this chapter depend heavily on the use of metaphor. In order to build strong metaphors, counselors need to take time to truly understand both the scientific thinking elements and dig deeply into understanding the science ideas underlying the content connections that may be made. This may involve supplementary research or consulting with other professionals.

Using the ideas of fast and slow thinking, the science and engineering practice of constructing explanations, the Crosscutting Concepts of (observing) patterns and (determining) cause and effect – mechanism and explanation, and the Nature of Science theme, scientific knowledge is open to revision in light of new evidence described in this chapter as the vehicle to produce the metaphors will provide counselors with a good connection. In addition, it may be helpful for community counselors to build a "toolbox" of demonstrations and investigations that they use often and truly understand. Using scientific thinking allows the metaphors to be shifted as needed, as metaphors are often interchangeable, especially as counselors gain confidence and knowledge about scientific thinking ideas.

References

Abd-El-Khalick, F., Bell, R. L., & Lederman, N. G. (1998). The nature of science and instructional practice: Making the unnatural natural. *Science Education, 82*(4), 417–436.

"Catalyst" (2022, March). *Merriam-webster.com Dictionary*. Merriam-Webster. https://www.merriam-webster.com/dictionary/catalyst

Crawford, B. A. (2014). From inquiry to scientific practices in the science classroom. In N. G. Lederman & S. K. Abell (Eds.), *Handbook of Research on Science Education Volume II*, (pp. 515–541). Routledge. ISBN 0–8058–4713–8.

Grotzer, T., Gonzalez, E., & Schibuk, E. (2021). Cause and effect: Mechanism and explanation. In J. Nordine & O. Lee (Eds.), *Crosscutting Concepts: Strengthening Science and Engineering Learning*. (pp. 89–113). NSTA. ISBN 978-1-68140-728-9.

Houseal, A. K. (2012). *Student experience 05: The candle*. University of Wyoming. Educational resource. https://doi.org/10.15786/13700128.v3

Houseal, A. K. (2015). A visual representation of three-dimensional learning: A tool for evaluating curriculum. *Science Scope, 39*(1), 58–62.

Inouye, M. C., Houseal, A. K., & Gunshenan, C. I. (2020). Beyond the hook: What is a phenomenon and how is it used?. *The Science Teacher, 87*(9), 60–63.

Kahneman, D. (2011). *Thinking, fast and slow*. Farrar, Straus and Giroux. ISBN: 978037427563-1.

Khan Academy (n.d.). *The synapse*. https://www.khanacademy.org/science/biology/human-biology/neuron-nervous-system/a/the-synapse

Kumar, S., & Pareek, K. (2018). Role of ability to delay gratification and regulate emotions in adolescents' psychological well-being. *Indian Journal of Positive Psychology*, 9(2), 215–218.

National Research Council (2012). *A framework for K-12 science education: Practices, crosscutting concepts, and core ideas*. The National Academies Press. https://doi.org/10.17226/13165

NGSS Lead States (2013). *Next generation science standards: For states, by states*. National Academies Press. https://doi.org/10.17226/18290.

NSTA.org. (2022, March). *K–12 science standards adoption*. https://ngss.nsta.org/about.aspx

Schwarz, C., Passmore, C., & Reiser, B. (2017). *Helping students make sense of the world through next generation science and engineering practices*. National Science Teaching Association. ISBN: 9781938946042

Ramachandraih, C. T., Subramanyam, N., Bar, K. J., Baker, G., & Yeragani, V. K. (2011). Antidepressants: From MAOIs to SSRIs and more. *Indian Journal of Psychiatry*, *53*(2), 180.

Wulfert, E., Block, J. A., Santa Ana, E., Rodriguez, M. L., & Colsman, M. (2002). Delay of gratification: Impulsive choices and problem behaviors in early and late adolescence. *Journal of Personality*, *70*(4), 533–552.

Activity 11.1: The "Candle"

Ana K. Houseal

Theme/Goals of Activity	Observing and developing explanations; changing claims (or one's mind) based on new evidence
Population/Age	5–18
Intrapersonal Skills	Recognizing and challenging assumptions, slow thinking
Interpersonal Skills	Openness to ideas from others
Coping/Solution-Focused Skills	Critical thinking, using evidence to reach conclusions
Materials	Large uncooked potato or turnip, salt or lemon water and a seal-able container, paper towels to dry off the potato, almond slivers (slightly burnt on one end to simulate a burnt wick), matches/lighters, a taper candle holder (the silver-plated adds a nice touch!), and a real white or off-white colored candle placed in the candle holder 48–72 hours prior to the demonstration, in a prominent location in the setting if possible

Description of the Activity:

Sometimes objects turn out to be something other than what we think we are observing. Learning to make careful observations provides the basis for students to engage in further observations of objects that are both familiar and unfamiliar. In this lesson, students make observations while the facilitator manipulates an object that appears to be a candle. This leads to the exploration of the differences between observations and inferences.

Prep work: The potato needs to be "carved" into a taper candle shape using a knife and peeler. It takes some practice! After it is carved, it will be important to store it in salt or lemon water until you need to use it. (It is a good idea to make an extra one, in case one of them gets too many dark spots.)

The almond slivers should be burned ahead of time and stored in a baggie with the paper towels. Cut a slit at the top of the potato with a knife so the almond sliver slides in easily. The paper towels are used to wipe water off the "candle" during set-up, away from the students' view. Make sure the "candle" fits in the candle holder. Practice lighting the almond sliver to see how it burns. Practice eating the "candle." Practice will ensure the demonstration looks realistic and runs smoothly.

Activity: Instruct client to number a piece of paper from one to three, leaving space to write. With lights a little dim and no one looking very closely, set out the "candle" in the holder and ask the client to write three to five observations about the two objects you have placed in front of them. Be sure to NOT call it a candle. If the client asks, "Do you mean the candle?" reply that you want them to make observations about the object(s) in front of them. (The "candle" is one object, the holder is the second. Sometimes this needs to be clarified. Do so by pointing to them but continue to call them "objects.") Clients should be discouraged from getting up to see the "candle" better.

After a few moments, ask the client to write (at #2) three to five more observations as you "do something" to one of the objects. Now, light the almond sliver. It will burn for about 30–45 seconds, so have them to write their observations quickly.

Make sure everyone is watching for the final step. Hold up the holder, blow out the "candle," and then immediately take a bite out of it. The almond sliver will be hot! To prevent a burnt tongue, make sure there is plenty of saliva in your mouth before biting into the "candle." For additional drama, walk around the room chewing on it, acting as though it is really tasty. There is always great excitement at this part. Try not to burst out laughing! Have client write down three to five more observations at #3, after they calm down.

*Adapted from Houseal, 2012

Macro-Processing:

Front and back loading:

Front: Ask students about their first set of observations. Any students who have described the objects with specific names like candle and candle holder have made *fast thinking* inferences; those who have choose words like "cylindrical," "off-white," or "about X inches tall" have made *slow thinking* observations. It is important that students are not chastised for using *fast thinking*/making inferences. The key is that they will be able to identify the differences between inferences and observations (*slow thinking*).

Micro-Processing:

Observation: Ask clients about their first set of observations. Any clients who have described the objects with specific names like candle and candle holder have made *fast thinking* inferences; those who have choose words like "cylindrical," "off-white," or "about X inches tall" have made *slow thinking* observations. It is important that clients are not chastised for using *fast thinking*/making inferences. The key is that they will be able to identify the differences between inferences and observations (*slow thinking*).

Observation: What happened when I ate it? What were some new observations you made? Were you able to change your thinking about what it was based on your observations? What do you think the "candle" or object was made of? Now that you had some new evidence and you used *slow thinking* to realize you may have made some inferences initially, you can revise your thinking like scientists do and make a new claim.

Debrief and Transfer:

This activity could be used in group therapy or in a classroom setting.
While debriefing, counselors can lead discussion with these questions:

–   What do you think was my purpose in going through this activity? Have you experienced things in life when something was not what it seemed?
–   What observations would you make about what happened?
–   What evidence changed your thinking about the object you thought was a candle? How is this related to how you think about constructing explanations in life?

Tips or Lessons Learned for Counselors:

Scientific Explanation: Observation is a critical tool used in scientific inquiry. However, as humans, we are programmed to quickly turn our observations into inferences (fast thinking). This particular adaptation is very useful in everyday life. For example, seeing a yellow stoplight leads to the inference that it will soon turn red. One does not have to wait and observe the change to infer that it will happen. We also infer that the cars coming to stop signs will stop and we can proceed safely through a crosswalk. Making inference can get in the way of making slow-thinking objective observations. This activity can be used to demonstrate how we can be "fooled" by our inference-making (fast thinking) abilities. Further, it demonstrates that new information can be used to change our minds and explanations regarding what we observe.

About the Author: Ana K. Houseal, PhD, is an associate professor of science education in the Science and Mathematics Teaching Center at the University of Wyoming. At this point in her career, she focuses on researching and empowering formal and non-formal educators to facilitate exceptional science learning in a variety of settings.

Activity 11.2: Emotional Diffusion

Rachel Ratliff

Theme/Goals of Activity	Understand emotional regulation
Population/Age	8+
Intrapersonal Skills	Identifying thoughts and emotions, managing emotions, mindfulness, confidence
Interpersonal Skills	Communication, empathy, awareness of own impact on others, expressing emotions appropriately and effectively
Coping/Solution-Focused Skills	Problem-solving, conflict resolution, or initiating change
Materials	Two transparent glasses, hot water, cold water, two different colors of food coloring, paper, writing utensils (can be colored)

Description of the Activity:

Diffusion is a movement of particles from the area of high concentration to an area of low concentration. It usually occurs in liquids and gases. Let's get some complex-sounding terminology out of the way. When talking about diffusion, we often hear something about the concentration gradient (or electrical gradient if looking at electrons). Gradient just means a change in the quantity of a variable over some distance. In the case of concentration gradient, a variable that changes is the concentration of a substance. So, we can define the concentration gradient as space over which the concentration of our substance changes.

For example, think of the situation when we spray the air freshener in the room. There is one spot where the concentration of our substance is very high (where we sprayed it initially) and in the rest of the room it is very low (nothing initially). Slowly concentration gradient is diffusing – our freshener is moving through the air. When the concentration gradient is diffused, we reach equilibrium – the state at which a substance is equally distributed throughout a space.

Instructions for demonstration or investigation*

Take two transparent glasses and fill them with the water. In one glass, pour the cold water and in the other hot water. As we mentioned, near-boiling water for hot and regular temperature water from the pipe will be good to demonstrate the diffusion.

Drop a few drops of food coloring in each cup. Three to four drops are enough and you should not put too much food color. If you put too much, the concentration of food color will be too large and it will defuse too fast in both glasses.

Watch closely how the color spreads. You will notice how color diffuses faster in hot water. It will take longer to diffuse if there is more water, less food color and if the water is cooler.

*Depends on whether or not clients are watching or engaging with their own materials. Adapted from Stem Little Explorers

Macro-processing:

No loading:

Discuss diffusion and engage in the demonstration, ask participants how this might also apply to various emotions that we feel.

Front and back loading:

Front: Relate emotions with the colors that will be used in the demonstration. Discuss how some feelings may feel cold and some may feel hot. Discuss how participants react when feeling a variety of emotions.
Back: Discuss how the demonstration is similar to feelings, relating new learning back to comments made before the demonstration. Discuss what it can mean for some feelings to get so big that we feel that we can't control them and what participants do when that happens. Explore a variety of ways that participants can handle emotions in ways that is not destructive to themselves.

Micro-processing:

Before demonstration:

- What variety of feelings do we have?
- How are some different ways that we handle our emotions?
- Can our feelings have an effect on others?

During demonstration:

- What do we notice is happening to the dye in the hot water? In the cold water?
- How is this similar to what happens when we are experiencing intense feelings?

After the demonstration:

− What are some ways that we can handle intense emotions?

Debrief and Transfer:

Participants can have the opportunity to use what is learned in the demonstration to more fully understand how their emotions can feel inside their bodies and affect others around them. Having an opportunity to explore their feelings while using the language and example of the demonstration can be easier for some participants. In follow-up sessions, participants can explore ways that they were able to regulate their emotions between sessions.

Tips or Lessons Learned for Counselors:

Hot and cold water − The larger the difference in temperature in two glasses, the larger the difference in diffusion will be observed. You can heat the water to near-boiling or boiling state and use it as hot water. Use regular tap water as "cold water." That will provide enough difference to observe the effects of temperature on diffusion.

Food coloring – Regular food coloring or some other colors like tempera (poster paint) will do the trick. Color is required to observe the diffusion in our solvent (water). To make it more fun, you can use two different colors. Like red for hot and blue for cold.

About the Author: Rachel Ratliff has a Master of Science degree in Counseling from the University of Wyoming and is a doctoral student in Counselor Education and Supervision. She is currently provisionally licensed by the State of Wyoming Mental Health Board.

Activity 11.3: Web of Life/Interconnectedness

Ana K. Houseal

Theme/Goals of Activity	Discuss concepts of diversity and inclusion.
Population/Age	5–14
Intrapersonal Skills	Identifying supports, identifying needs
Interpersonal Skills	Developing relationships with new people
Coping/Solution-Focused Skills	Seeking help
Materials	A sizeable ball of string, yarn, or twine. The string will likely cross the length of the room many times; thus, the more participants in the activity, the more yarn/twine needed

Description of the Activity:

Background: Food chains and webs are often taught concepts in life science classes − starting at a very early age and extending into complicated versions in high school and beyond. Food chains model the movement of energy along a simple chain of organisms. For example, the sun provides energy for photosynthetic plants, which in turn provide energy for animals that eat the plants, which are consumed by animals that eat animals. In a food web, there is additional complexity in the model as it may include multiple food chains with overlapping components. For example, hawks, owls, and wolves may all consume similar rodents who consume similar (though various) plants. These models can be used and studies at many levels (micro to macro) and using various lenses (e.g., cause and effect, energy transfer, stability, and change in ecosystems). These same ideas are presented in this exercise for counseling and can be framed in many ways, depending on the group and its needs.

In this version, a facilitator/counselor poses a discussion question or questions. A simple chain can be produced by having the facilitator pose a question and toss the ball of string to one person, who responds to the question. They pass this ball along to one or two others, who respond to them. This would represent a single discussion chain. The string is re-gathered between "chains" and could be good for practicing appropriate responses.

For a discussion "web," the same ball of string is passed to each person who speaks. After a participant speaks, they hold on to part of the string and pass or toss the ball to the next speaker. In this way, each of the chains is connected. By the discussion's end, the string will form another web among the participants showing who spoke and how the conversation connected them to each other.

A way to demonstrate the connectedness: have the facilitator drop their string (or ask a participant to). This shows how the web falls apart when the web is not supported by everyone. Examining the web could also help the participants understand the amount of participation and discuss how to help those who do not participate as well as those who may dominate conversations.

Participants may need to be reminded to hold on to their string tightly.

* Adapted from The Program on Intergroup Relations, University of Michigan (2003).

Macro-Processing:

The goals of this activity can shift depending on how the instructor chooses to implement it.

1. In situations where the facilitator finds they are having to drive discussion, the activity can be used as a way for them to step back and let students initiate the passing of the ball of string.
2. If used during a discussion, in which the facilitator wants more equitable input, the activity can be used to make participants more aware of how much they are speaking in comparison to their peers. Facilitators can use this as a way to encourage students to step up (speak more if they are not frequent participants) or step back (speak less if they are frequent participants).
3. At the discussion's conclusion, the web will help participants to visualize their and their peers' contributions to the exploration of the topic at hand. The web can symbolize the complex understanding of the topic as arrived at through the sharing and discussion of everyone's perspectives. It could also be used to show how the conversation and building of ideas is dependent on everyone in the web.

Micro-Processing:

Observations:

– This activity can be used as a way to affirm participants (the person who catches the string they should acknowledge some way that the thrower's participation aided the conversation) or collective reflection, in which each person shares one take-away from the group.
– Prepare students for what role you will play in this activity; let them know if you will only ask the starting question, or if they should pass the ball to you when you speak.

Debrief and Transfer:

There are many opportunities to create metaphors in this exercise. Explore who represents supports in the client's life and who holds the string for them. Clinicians can process trauma by talking about times that other people have "dropped the string." Further the connections can represent specific topics or people, such as creating their family constellation or exploring who supports adolescents in sobriety.

Tips or Lessons Learned for Counselors:

1. This activity will only work in groups in which the diameter of the circle will fit all of participants in the room you are in.
2. This activity requires that participants be able to hold the yarn/twine and throw it. Participants who have disabilities that affect their ability to participate in this activity could be paired with partners or

alternatively map the conversation by drawing lines between participants as they speak, showing the same web that the use of string would.

About the Author: Ana K. Houseal, PhD, is an associate professor of science education in the Science and Mathematics Teaching Center at the University of Wyoming. At this point in her career, she focuses on researching and empowering formal and non-formal educators to facilitate exceptional science learning in a variety of settings.

Activity 11.4: Mentos and Diet Soda

Amanda C. DeDiego

Theme/Goals of Activity	Explore concepts of friendship and peer relationships; connect social-emotional learning to STEM
Population/Age	6–12
Intrapersonal Skills	Self-awareness, considering connections with peers
Interpersonal Skills	Understand own triggers
Coping/Solution-Focused Skills	Identifying peers that are triggers or relationships that may not be healthy
Materials	Skittles, Mentos, two-liter plastic bottle of diet soda, and outside space

Description of the Activity:

The counselor discusses with the client that not all people connect in healthy ways. Some people connect in healthy ways that include supporting and communicating effectively with each other. Some people connect in unhealthy ways that result in anger, arguments, or even bullying.

To demonstrate this concept, you will need a two-liter, room temperature bottle of diet soda (any brand will work), some skittles, and some Mentos. Have the client first put a few skittles in the bottle of soda. This will create a minor reaction of some fizzing in the bottle but no major reaction. Then have the client put five to six Mentos in the bottle, dropping them in all at the same time. This will create a major reaction with the soda fizzing up and out of the bottle. It's a good idea to try this yourself ahead of time. Making a paper tube out of a 4×6 index card to hold the Mentos in before dropping them in the soda will help to make sure they all go in and to the bottom at the same time.

Macro-Processing:

Front loading: This activity works best with some front loading. Talking about relationships and types of healthy and unhealthy connections with peers helps to frame this activity well.
Back loading: In processing this activity, have the client consider peers in their class or people in their family that represent healthy relationships and not so healthy relationships.
Metaphor: Skittles and Mentos represent different types of people/personalities, the diet soda represents the client. This can also work with the client represented as the candy.

Micro-Processing:

Observations during demonstration: Ask the client what kinds of reactions happened after dropping the skittles and then the Mentos into the diet soda.

- What happened when we dropped the skittles in the bottle?
- What happened when we dropped the Mentos in the bottle?
- Both of these are candy, what do you think is different to create such a great reaction?

Cause and effect – mechanism and explanation:

Comments: The Mentos elicits a reaction in the diet soda due to porosity of the candy's surface and the density of the candy. The rough surface (not visible to the eye) causes a physical reaction in which the carbon dioxide attaches to this new surface area and releases. There is not enough room in the bottle for the release of the gases and it forces its way out of the bottle. The resulting "explosion" is impressive.

*Explanation adapted from Scientific American

Debrief and Transfer:

Debrief after the demonstration:

Discuss how the demonstration relates to the client's relationships to others in school or at home.

- Who are the skittles (that create minimal conflict) and who are the Mentos (who create disruptive amounts of conflict) in your life?
- Does the client interact with others as a skittle or a Mentos?
- What does it look like when they interact with a Mentos personality type?

Transfer to Life:

Consider how to recognize when others are triggering, or when the client may be triggering to others. This can be connected to social-emotional learning, demonstrating empathy or emotional regulation.

- How do you react when you meet someone who is a Mentos to your diet soda?
- What coping skills can you use to manage your reactions to others?

Tips or Lessons Learned for Counselors:

This is a great activity for individuals or groups. This can also be used in a group that is volatile to explore how the dynamics is not supportive of the group process. Be sure to complete this activity outside or in a space that is protected. The reaction of the Mentos and diet soda will be messy! The bigger the soda bottle and the more Mentos, the bigger the reaction.

About the Author: Amanda C. DeDiego, PhD, NCC, is an Associate Professor of Counseling. Her research in counselor development includes counseling pedagogy and creative interventions useful in coursework and supervision.

Chapter 12

Group activities

Amanda C. DeDiego

Children do not grow up in a vacuum; they must learn to function in social contexts and in society developing in environments of potential criticism, comment, and judgment, particularly in the age of social media (O'Keeffe & Clarke-Pearson, 2011). Children and adolescents can learn from interactions with their peers, sometimes finding this influence more meaningful than with caregivers or adults, which can lead to both positive and negative influence on decision-making and behavior (Prinstein & Dodge, 2008; Ziff et al., 2012). Children and adolescents can benefit from group counseling experiences in schools and community settings, as clients can connect with peers over developmental difficulties and find emotional support through the group process (Shechtman, 2007). For adolescents, having activities incorporated into groups can externalize the conversation and allow group members to be less resistant (Lindsey et al., 2018). Similarly, talk therapy with an adult counselor may not feel safe, but interacting with peers in an experiential group counseling setting may offer more opportunities for growth (Jacobs et al., 2012).

Incorporating experiential activities in groups can provide counselors with a creative means of engaging children and adolescents in the group experience (Gladding, 2019, 2021). Innovative counselors can incorporate a variety of activities into groups, including rope courses, art, music, and sports (Gladding, 2021; Johnson, 2014; Lopez & Burt, 2013; Skudrzyk et al., 2009). Group activities can use many props and have a variety of goals or foci. However, activities are not as effective when used randomly and should also compliment the stage of the group (DeDiego et al., 2017). The curriculum should be implemented intentionally to achieve a specific goal by sequencing or planning a series of activities focused on an outcome or goal for the group (Schoel et al., 1988). According to Schoel et al. (1988), activities should begin with icebreakers, designed to be fun and help build rapport among the group members. Then group facilitators can introduce activities focused on building trust and encouraging members to take small risks and shift into the stretch zone. Having built some trust, a group leader can then help facilitate empathy among group members by focusing on activities centered on group communication (Ashby et al., 2008). Moving from an intrapersonal to interpersonal focus, after trust and communication exist within a group, the facilitator can focus on activities to build skills useful beyond the group (Schoel et al., 1988). These activities may include coping, decision-making, and problem-solving. Further, the activities may incorporate more emphasis on personal responsibility within the group, community, or larger society.

Counseling children and adolescents with group activities

Children as young as 4 years old can participate in groups; however, reasonable expectations about the ability of children to verbalize complex emotions are important (Jacobs et al., 2012). Groups can use a variety of theoretical approaches to address different issues (Gladding, 2019; Yalom & Leszcz, 2005). Group leaders must consider group stages and how groups build cohesion and therapeutic factors in the natural group process (Gladding, 2019; Tuckman & Jensen, 1977; Yalom & Leszcz, 2005). Activities in groups with children can offer a medium for processing, which is often more developmentally appropriate than talk therapy. Thus, groups with children should focus more on activity and less on verbal processing (Ziff et al., 2012). Examples of useful topics for groups with adolescents include self-worth, drugs and alcohol, college readiness, sexuality, and grief. It is especially important for counselors conducting groups with adolescents to give group members space to share their stories, remembering that the client is the expert in their own experience (Jacobs et al., 2012). Research has shown group counseling can be an effective tool for counselors to address behavioral and emotional issues with adolescents (Shechtman & Sarig, 2016).

In creating a counseling group, it is important to screen potential members to ensure all members are appropriate for the group (Yalom & Leszcz, 2005). Creating a safe space with members who are motivated and connected to the group goal can help create a dynamic experience. Once the group members are selected and the group

DOI: 10.4324/9781315213767-13

sessions begin, the group leader must facilitate the group to support the development of therapeutic factors and facilitate the exchange of feedback within the group (Shechtman, 2007; Yalom & Leszcz, 2005). Having clarity of focus and practicing intentionality with activities can allow for deeper exploration, considering the developmental level of the group members during the group experience. Activities with symbolism or metaphor, which allow process to align with the focus of the group, can be a powerful experience (Skudrzyk et al., 2009). Activities when thoughtfully used with intentionality help build cohesion and develop therapeutic factors as a group progresses. Counselors incorporating experiential activities in groups should choose activities based on the stage of the group and group goals (Jacobs et al., 2012; Robak et al., 2013). For example, a counselor with a group in the forming stage may choose icebreaker activities to encourage bonding and sharing within the group. A counselor with a group in the storming stage may present a puzzle activity to encourage group members to talk through conflict. A counselor with a group in the adjourning stage may have group members create collages or give symbolic gifts to each other to symbolize the group experience and process the closing of the group.

Interpersonal and intrapersonal skills

Counselors use different types of groups in counseling settings to facilitate therapeutic intrapersonal processes and interpersonal growth (Thomas & Pender, 2008; Yalom & Leszcz, 2005). Participation in a group experience can be a transformational experience inspiring growth and self-awareness for each member (Torosyan, 2008). Examples include groups focused on strategies for managing anxiety, bullying prevention, or learning about grief. Within a group, group members learn through interactions with others, known as interpersonal learning, and about themselves as individuals, known as intrapersonal learning (Ashby et al., 2008). As children and adolescents develop, they learn and develop identity through interactions with others (Erikson, 1982). Interpersonal learning allows for externalizing of individual issues and provides the opportunity for clients to grow through interactions with other group members (Yalom & Leszcz, 2005). As group counseling allows children to access a peer group, counseling groups offer interpersonal learning to develop social skills and self-worth (Mishna & Muskat, 2004). When children and adolescents experience emotional or behavioral issues, they may feel isolated from other peer groups. Participating in a group experience allows clients to connect with peers who also struggle with such issues.

For example, an activity called "Molten Lava" includes group members standing together, stranded in an ocean of molten lava. The only way to travel to a designate safe area, which is several yards away, is by using a magical object to grant immunity to the molten lava. This magical object can only be used for a one-way trip for each member and cannot be thrown between the two locations. Group members must problem-solve a way to save all the members of their group using the magical object. As group members work together, they learn communication, collaboration, and consideration of others. Group members could take the object and save themselves, but the only way to successfully complete the activity is to ensure all members of the group traverse the lava safely. Group members also create connection in working together to solve a problem, and in this scenario the group members share a single goal regardless of other differences they may have. These intrapersonal skills can be highlighted in the processing after the conclusion of the activity.

Yalom and Leszcz (2005) describe the group counseling experience as a social microcosm in that eventually group member interactions within a group will begin to mimic their interactions with others in society. As such, interpersonal skills developed in a group through activities are transferrable to situations occurring in real life outside the group. Within a group, children and adolescents, supported by the group facilitator, can reenact life situations within the supported environment of the group (Shechtman, 2007). Debriefing, or processing discussions after an experiential activity, is critical for interpersonal skill development (Schoel et al., 1988). For example, a group can create a sand tray together. Even though the group is completing the activity together, in contributing to the creation of the sand tray, each individual is processing their own experience while contributing to the sand tray. Self-awareness, self-worth, and empathy may be developed, and revealed through processing the sand tray.

Interpersonal and intrapersonal growth are not mutually exclusive. In a group activity, a client can both connect with group members and grow as an individual (Malott & Paone, 2013). For example, in a problem-solving activity, a group member can gain both communication skills and empathy for others. In an icebreaker, a child can gain communication skills as well as a sense of belonging.

Coping and solution-focused skills

Developing coping skills, like other social and emotional skills, is often learned through observing and interacting with peers and role models (Mishara & Ystgaard, 2006; Thomas & Pender, 2008). In a group setting, the group facilitator models coping skills, but children also observe how other members of the group react to challenges during group activities. Having a safe place to try new things, and potentially fail, as well as a facilitator to help process coping through an activity, is a useful resource for the development of coping skills and resilience. Group facilitators should adapt activities based on the goals of the group and the demographics of the group (Paone et al., 2008). Life changes beyond everyday stressors, for example, the death of a loved one, can present challenges to coping, which would result in a need for counseling (Koralek, 2008).

When facing trauma or adversity, children and adolescents can develop a mindset to overcome challenges and problem solve, known as resilience (Goldstein et al., 2013). Youth with resilience also demonstrate strong coping skills (Smith et al., 2013). Facilitating the development of resilience in children can include a strength-based approach to processing group activities. Resilient youth demonstrate coping skills including problem-solving, effective interpersonal skills, the ability to ask for help, the ability to connect with others, and a realistic locus of control (Goldstein et al., 2013). For example, children in a group focused on grief would find validation in peers struggling with similar grief issues. Additionally, they would look to group members and the facilitator to learn about how to cope with grief. Activities provide structure for processing grief and can foster the development of coping skills what children or adolescents could developmentally achieve through talk therapy. A group leader may use an activity where the children create memory books about their loved one, and then through creating memory books they can learn how to remember positive memories to comfort them in times of grief. Similarly, adolescents may write letters to their loved one and share them in the group. External processing and hearing others group members' letters can address guilt often associated with grief. In both examples, the focus of the activities is building coping skills and addressing grief. Activities provide an experiential opportunity to practice coping skills and observe coping modeled by the group facilitator and group members.

Strengths and limitations

Like any counseling approach, group counseling as an approach to work with children and adolescents has strengths and limitations. Research supports group counseling as an effective and useful approach to work with children and adolescents (Shechtman, 2007). Clients also gain validation in realizing they are not alone is struggling with certain issues. Especially with adolescents, connecting and processing with peers may also help clients to be less resistant than they may be with individual counseling with an adult counselor (Harel et al., 2011). Incorporating experiential activities can provide an engaging and dynamic experience for child and adolescent clients participating in counseling groups (Skudrzyk, 2009). Beyond processing the topic of the group, group members gain valuable social skills as they progress through the stages of a group (Ivey et al., 2001).

One limitation of group counseling for children and adolescents is that the group leader must focus on multiple clients, meaning each client may not always get the attention needed (Macnair-Semands, 1988). For clients needing more support, counselors may choose treatment that includes a combination of individual and group counseling. An additional limitation of any group is a lack of guarantee of confidentiality (American Counseling Association, 2014). While the counselor may respect the privacy of clients, there is no guarantee that group members will not discuss topics shared in the group in outside settings. Thus, during informed consent, it is important to inform both clients and caregivers that confidentiality cannot be guaranteed in groups. A potential limitation is the possibility of harm to the client through negative interactions between members. While screening of clients should minimize this risk, it is always the responsibility of the group facilitator to observe group interactions and protect clients from harm (American Counseling Association, 2014). Finally, especially with children and adolescents, group members may differ in developmental skills. Group members who are more advanced or behind other group members developmentally may be frustrated and struggle to connect with other members of the group. Screening for developmental ability of group members and considering adaptations of activities can help accommodate such differences. With careful planning and group processing skills, group counseling represents a dynamic and engaging experience for clients and an opportunity for creative counselors to incorporate experiential activities.

Meaning-making

Positives outcomes for group experiences are dependent upon the dynamics within a group (Robak et al., 2013). In groups, meaning making is largely facilitated through processing. Schoel et al. (1988) discuss structuring processing to reflect the content of the group, as well as connecting the group process to life outside of the group. They suggest processing to include what happened among the group members during the activity, what life lessons were gained during the activity, and how the activity connects to goals beyond the group experience.

Group members develop meaning through a combination of their own experiences and shared knowledge gained through interactions with other group members (Southerland et al., 2005). For example, a group facilitator may ask group members at the end of an experience to share challenges and feelings they faced in completing the activity. Once one member shares their experience, the facilitator may then turn to the group and ask if any other group members had similar experiences. This connecting of members' experiences is known as linking (Gladding, 2019). To further this connection, a group facilitator may ask, "Tell me about a time you faced a challenge outside of the group." This encourages group members to connect the group experiences to challenges in real life. Thus, in both individual sharing and validation through hearing the experiences of peers, group members can make meaning out of group activities.

While group facilitators should encourage feedback and challenge in a group, it is also important to protect group members. For example, cultural identity, gender, and societal factors play out in group interactions, and so group leaders must always practice cultural awareness (Bemak & Chung, 2015). Group leaders can model appropriate dialogue and respect for diversity in the group. Facilitators also carry the responsibility of intervening if group members "gang up" on a single group member. This practice, known as scapegoating, involves group members blaming one group member, or singling out one group member's behavior instead of sharing blame (Gladding, 2019. The group facilitator can combat this practice by creating a space for the scapegoat to share, helping connect the scapegoat to her peers through common experiences (Malekoff, 1994).

References

American Counseling Association (2014). *ACA code of ethics.* Author.

Ashby, J. S., Kottman, T., & DeGraaf, D. (2008). *Active interventions for kids and teens: Adding adventure and fun to counseling.* American Counseling Association.

Bemak, F., & Chung, C. Y. R. (2015). Critical issues in international group counseling. *The Journal for Specialists in Group Work, 40*(1), 6–21.

DeDiego, A. C., Wheat, L. S., & Fletcher, T. B. (2017). Overcoming obstacles: Exploring the use of adventure based counseling in youth grief camps. *Journal of Creativity in Mental Health, 12*(2), 230–241.

Erikson, E. H. (1982). *The life cycle completed: A review.* W. W. Norton & Company.

Gladding, S. T. (2019). *Groups: A counseling specialty* (8th ed.). Pearson.

Gladding, S. T. (2021). *The creative arts in counseling* (6th ed.). American Counseling Association.

Goldstein, S., Brooks, R., & DeVries, M. (2013). Translating resilience theory for application with children and adolescents by parents, teachers, and mental health professionals. In S. Prince-Embury & D. H. Saklofske (Eds.), *Resilience in Children, Adolescents, and Adults: Translating Research into Practice* (pp. 73–90). Springer.

Harel, Y., Shechtman, Z., & Cutrona, C. (2011). Individual and group process variables that affect social support in counseling groups. *Group Dynamics: Theory, Research, and Practice, 15*(4), 297–310.

Ivey, A. E., Pederson, P. B., & Ivey, M. B. (2001). *Intentional group counseling: A microskills approach.* Brooks/Cole.

Jacobs, E. E., Masson, R. L., Harvill, R. L., & Schimmel, C. J. (2012). *Group counseling: Strategies and skills* (7th ed.). Brooks/Cole.

Johnson, A. H. (2014). Counseling outside the lines: Creative arts intervention for children and adolescents, individual, small group and classroom applications. *Social Work Groups, 37*(3), 265–266.

Koralek, D. (2008). Helping children, families, and early childhood educators build coping skills. *YC Young Children, 63*(5), 10.

Lindsey, L., Robertson, P., & Lindsey, B. (2018). Expressive arts and mindfulness: Aiding adolescents in understanding and managing their stress. *Journal of Creativity in Mental Health, 13*(3), 288–297.

Lopez, A., & Burt, I. (2013). Counseling groups: A creative strategy increasing children of incarcerated parents' sociorelational interactions. *Journal of Creativity in Mental Health, 8*(4), 395–415.

Macnair-Semands, R. R. (1998). Encompassing the complexity of group work. *The Journal for Specialists in Group Work, 23*(2), 208–214.

Malekoff, A. (1994). A guideline for group work with adolescents. *Social Work with Groups, 17*(1–2), 5–19.

Malott, K. M., & Paone, T. R. (2013). Mexican-origin adolescents' exploration of a group experience. *Journal of Creativity in Mental Health, 8*(3), 204–218.

Mishara, B. L., & Ystgaard, M. (2006). Effectiveness of a mental health promotion program to improve coping skills in young children: Zippy's friends. *Early Childhood Research Quarterly, 21,* 110–123.

Mishna, F., & Muskat, B. (2004). "I'm not the only one!" Group therapy with older children and adolescents who have learning disabilities. *International Journal of Group Psychotherapy, 54*(4), 455–476.

O'Keeffe, G. S., & Clarke-Pearson, K. (2011). The impact of social media on children, adolescents, and families. *Pediatrics, 127*(4), 800–804.

Paone, T. R., & Malott, K. M., & Maldonado, J. M. (2008). Exploring group activity therapy with ethnically diverse adolescents. *Journal of Creativity in Mental Health, 3*(3), 285–302.

Prinstein, M. J., & Dodge, K. A. (Eds.). (2008). *Understanding peer influence in children and adolescents*. Guilford Press.

Robak, R. W., Kangos, K. A., Chiffriller, S. H., & Griffin, P. W. (2013). The working alliance in group counseling: An exploratory study. *Psychological Reports: Relationships & Communications, 113*(2), 591–604.

Schoel, J., Prouty, D., & Radcliffe, P. (1988). *Islands of healing: A guide to adventure based counseling*. Project Adventure, Inc.

Shechtman, Z. (2007). *Group counseling and psychotherapy with children and adolescents: Theory, research, and practice*. Lawrence Erlbaum Associates.

Shechtman, Z., & Sarig, O. (2016). The effect of client progress feedback on child/adolescent's group-counseling outcomes. *The Journal for Specialists in Group Work, 41*(4), 334–349.

Skudrzyk, B., Zera, D. A., McMahon, G., Schmidt, R., Boyne, J., & Spannaus, R. L. (2009). Learning to relate: Interweaving creative approaches in group counseling with adolescents. *Journal of Creativity in Mental Health, 4*(3), 249–261.

Smith, B. W., Epstein, E. M., Ortiz, J. A., Christopher, P. J., & Tooley, E. M. (2013). The foundations of resilience: What are the critical resources for bouncing back from stress. In S. Prince-Embury & D. H. Saklofske (Eds.), *Resilience in Children, Adolescents, and Adults: Translating Research into Practice* (pp. 167–188). Springer.

Southerland, S., Kittleson, J., Settlage, J., & Lanier, K. (2005). Individual and group meaning-making in an urban third grade classroom: Red fog, cold cans, and seeping vapor. *Journal of Research in Science Teaching, 42*(9), 1032–1061.

Thomas, R. V., & Pender, D. A. (2008). Association for specialists in group work: Best practice guidelines 2007 revisions. *The Journal for Specialists in Group Work, 33*(2), 111–117.

Torosyan, R. (2008). Self-reflections on group dynamics. *Journal of Creativity in Mental Health, 3*(1), 78–92.

Tuckman, B. W., & Jensen, M. A. C. (1977). Stages of small-group development revisited. *Group & Organization Studies, 2*(4), 419–427.

Yalom, I. D., & Leszcz, M. (2005). *The theory and practice of group psychotherapy* (5th ed.). Basic Books.

Ziff, K., Pierce, L., Johanson, S., & King, M. (2012). Artbreak: A creative group counseling program for children. *Journal of Creativity in Mental Health, 7*(1), 107–121.

Activity 12.1: Future Me Interview

Jenna Hepp

Theme/Goals of Activity	Finding hope and recognition of present strengths for the future
Population/Age	Group: early to late adolescence
Intrapersonal Skills	Self-awareness, visualization, group compassion
Interpersonal Skills	Ability to communicate about one's goals, dreams, and desires
Coping/Solution-Focused Skills	Strengths-based identification
Materials	None. However, pen and paper may be helpful to write down questions and answers to remember

Description of the Activity:

This activity is appropriate for many ages, including early to late adolescence. The focus is to get client's thinking about their strengths, interests, passions, the future, and desires. As well as having their pair try to visualize and listen with compassion to their partner's share. Group members are paired into two and one will ask "interview-like" strength-based questions to their pair as if it was 5 years from now or "x" amount of years. After some time, the interviewer will become the interviewee. This works best if you have a pair perform the interview in front of the rest of the group, and then when both partners go, invite another pair in order for all members to get to hear the rest of the group members answers and understand their peers better. While interviewees answer, they must answer in the present tense and the audience may "buzz" when they do not speak in the present tense. For example, they would answer "I am a librarian" instead of "I want to be a librarian."

Macro-Processing:

No loading

At the beginning of the activity introduce this as a way to get ourselves to think about what we love to do, what our strengths are, and what we want life to look like in the future to help assist us in what we could do in the present – which is why they will answer in the present tense.

Front and back loading:

Front: Be thoughtful in how the group members are paired together to ask each other questions. The interviewer will ask questions (a template of universal questions would be most helpful) such as "What are your relationships like?" and the interviewee will answer "I have a lot of supportive friendships as well as a partner." If they speak in "dream-like" terms such as "I want to have supportive friendships," the audience (other group members) may buzz, so the interviewee must reword their answer.
Back: After each interviewee has answered, the audience may ask if there was curiosity behind a question, as well as other questions.
Metaphors: Metaphors can then be created from what is learned about the individual after they answer.

Micro-Processing:

Observation: The clients may experience and show a variety of emotions while sharing their desires when answering the interviewer. The clinician may observe and state those observations to bring that into the client's awareness.

Observation: Clients will get notably more passionate with specific questions, reflecting on the hope and the strengths that you see in them as a client may be extremely beneficial.

Comments/Questions: (include skill identified)

- "I wonder where that passion began for you?"
- "I see you light up when you talk about _____."
- "It appeared that you became less motivated when talking about future relationships versus occupation."

Debrief and Transfer:

This activity could be used in group therapy or in the classroom.
While debriefing with the group questions that could be asked are:

– Were any of you surprised by a peer response?
– Did any of you notice strengths in each other that someone did not mention in their answers?
– Was it difficult to think about the future?
– What was easy about this activity?
– What was more difficult about it?
– Do you have any follow-up questions for each other?

Tips or Lessons Learned for Counselors:

This activity has been used in groups with conflict to cultivate empathy toward one another. Most often the clients have been excited to answer interview questions; it may be helpful to have a written out template of how many questions are asked and the exact questions to answer so all members are asked the same thing. Group members often get more curious about each other after answering and are engaged when they have to look for present-tense wording. Some members may not have any thoughts about the future or think that they are not good at anything and that is when you can use the group to brainstorm strengths with them.

About the Author: Jenna Hepp, PPC, MS, NCC, is a doctoral student at the University of Wyoming studying Counselor Education and Supervision. She grew up in Douglas, Wyoming. Her interests include adolescent group therapy, the self-esteem of early to late adolescence, and their struggle with mental health, as well as suicide intervention for Wyoming youth.

Activity 12.2: A Portrait Come to Life

Jenna Hepp

Theme/Goals of Activity	Identifying positive past memories in order to recognize what brings peace or joy to life to incorporate that in the present
Population/Age	Group: early to late adolescence
Intrapersonal Skills	Self-awareness, group compassion, and empathetic building
Interpersonal Skills	Expressing empathy, identifying feelings
Coping/Solution-Focused Skills	Creating a creative outlet for both positive and negative emotions; drama therapy
Materials	None

Description of the Activity:

This activity is appropriate for many ages, including early to late adolescence. The main focus is having clients identify memories in their lives that bring them joy, as well as be an observer and listener to their peers. The group members will individually think of a time/memory that brought them a lot of joy, happiness, peace, or any positive feeling. In a group of three or more, the individual will set up the people as props in this memory. Then the individual will yell out the words "action" and that memory will come to life.

For example, a positive memory could be the first time they had gone to the beach. They would set up people in the scene as props and/or people. One person may be lying on the ground portraying the water (when they come to life, they would make waves), one could represent the sand, and another person could be the individual at the beach. When the individual says "action," the actors will then come to life and represent to the best of their ability what the memory represents. If it is a more advanced group, you could also have the audience guess what the memory is or what the scene is trying to convey – the groups would just speak in silence or leave the room and come back before acting.

Macro-Processing:

No loading:

At the beginning of the activity, have the group brainstorm positive words to associate with happy, peaceful, and joy. Then have them reflect on times when they felt that they most identified to that feeling.

Front and back loading:

Front: Group members will then be asked to think of one memory in particular that made them feel the most (fill in positive emotion word). Then explain that as a group they will make the memory come to life. They will get to choose people to play a role in the picture of the memory and then make it come to life. It may be helpful to show an example at first, such as the beach example.

   Back: After creating their scene and watching it "come to life" the individual will reflect on the accuracy or describe the importance of the scene to them. How it felt to watch it instead of remembering it, and brainstorm ways to cultivate that same positive feeling for them in the future.

   Metaphors: This activity in itself uses a metaphor approach of symbols coming to life. As the clinician you may draw attention to those that appear to stand out. For example, the person playing the part of the "waves" on the beach may move at a rapid pace but in the real memory the waves were moving slower, representing the positive memory being placed because of the peace and slowness of the waves.

Micro-Processing:

Observation: The client is their own expert at their experiences; however, the props (actors) may act differently than the individual remembers the scene being in their mind. They will be quick (usually) to discuss that, if not infer about the difference between watching it and how they remember it.

   Ask questions like:

—   How did it feel to watch the memory played back?
—   How do you think it represented the actual memory?
—   If you could change anything what would you have changed?
—   What was it about this scene that made you feel _____?
—   How could you feel that same feeling in a new way?

You may have the scene replay after learning more about the memory if it feels appropriate.

Observation: The actors/symbols may also have had a unique experience playing the part of someone else's memory and/or may relate to the memory or be unaware how they are supposed to act because they don't understand how someone could feel that way about something they don't.

   Ask the actors questions like:

—   How did it feel to play someone else's memory?
—   What was difficult about it?
—   Why was your first instinct to play it the way you did? (cultivates other's awareness on what the symbol meant to them specifically)

Debrief and Transfer:

After all individuals have gone center back together as a group and debrief together on how the activity was for them; based on their answers, you could tailor how it looks in the future.
—   How was that activity for everyone?
—   What was it like to watch everyone's favorite memories?
—   What did you learn from each other?
—   What did you learn about yourself?

Tips or Lessons Learned for Counselors:

This activity was used with groups that had difficulty identifying emotions and understanding where their emotions come from. There may be members who cannot identify a good memory; you may have them act out a negative one if the member is ready for it, or they can make up a portrait that is not a memory but one they would like to create in the future. The same debriefing questions can be asked. If it seems the group has a great grasp and motivation for this activity you can change the emotion. Instead of positive memories it could be a time they were scared, a conflict, a negative emotion, etc. The debriefing time and questions may need to be tailored based on the heaviness of the group.

About the Author: Jenna Hepp, PPC, MS, NCC, is a doctoral student at the University of Wyoming studying Counselor Education and Supervision. She grew up in Douglas, Wyoming. Her interests include adolescent group therapy, the self-esteem of early to late adolescence, and their struggle with mental health, as well as suicide intervention for Wyoming youth.

Activity 12.3: Finding Your Strengths: Four Animal Personality Test Activity

Sangmin Park

Theme/Goals of Activity	This group activity helps children and adolescents to gain self-awareness. Students will discover the qualities and characteristics of their own personality style or type. They will gain an understanding of other personality styles. Students will be able to understand how their perspective affects relationships and how they communicate with others. Students will be able to understand why others may have a different perspective and utilize this understanding to improve relationships
Population/Age	10–19
Intrapersonal Skills	Self-esteem and self-awareness
Interpersonal Skills	Initiating better communication and understanding between people in various places
Coping/Solution-Focused Skills	Understanding conflicts and appreciating differences
Materials	Large enough room for small group discussion, four tables and posted signs (or colored dots stickers) for each personality type – lion, otter, golden retriever, and beaver, Four Animal Personality Test – handout or presentation slides, poster paper, and colored markers

Description of the Activity:

Begin with asking students to consider the following questions:

— How well do you know yourself?
— How well do you know your classmates?

Distribute the Four Animal Personality Test without presenting descriptions of each animal.

— "Each of us has a different and unique personality; however, there are some common traits that we share. The Animal Personality Test is an attempt to identify various personalities with colors. Each animal is associated with certain personality traits or behaviors. Everyone has some degree of each animal, but one is predominant. The following quiz will identify your animal type. Follow the directions carefully and transfer your scores to the score sheet. If you have two animals with the same score, you can pick one animal that more accurately describes you."

Administer Animal Personality Test and score to determine each student's type. Have students place their animal sign or colored sticker so others can see what type they are. (ten minutes)

Explain each different personality type using power point, pictures, video, or examples. Explain that individuals are a spectrum of personalities and there are times they will use each animal type, but they basically operate in one animal type. (five minutes)

Divide students into animal groups. Provide each group with large sheets of paper and markers to match their animal type. Have them work as a group, brainstorm, and write:

– Things they like to do or things they like
– Things they don't like or what drives them crazy

Have them report to the group and hang the paper in the room. (30 minutes)

After the group work, introduce the reframing exercise by asking students what would happen if we didn't have any lions, otters, golden retrievers, and beavers. Discuss how the world would be different if one of the groups was missing. Discuss how we need every animal type to enhance and widen our perspectives. Have each group use reframing worksheets to change negative statements to positive statements and report to class. Some sample negative statements for each animal are:

– **Lion:** arrogant, heartless, don't care about people, or ruthless
– **Otter:** irresponsible, wishy-washy, not serious about serious matters, or disobeying rules
– **Golden Retriever:** over-emotional, mushy, hopelessly naïve, or a pushover
– **Beaver:** rigid, controlling, stubborn, or uncreative

Assign lion and otter to reframe each other and golden retriever and beaver to reframe each other. Discuss how each animal builds self-esteem. (15 minutes)

Macro-Processing:

Front and back loading:

Front: Highlight the below points to students when distributing Animal Personality Test:

– Animal is a metaphor.
– Each person is a blend of the four animals.
– There are no bad or good animals.
– There are many variations within each animal.

Back: Discuss how the descriptions of each animal relate to their personality and communication styles. Open discussion about an ideal business/school/activity that utilizes the strengths of each personality.

Micro-Processing:

Administering Animal Personality Test: While completing the test, provide an instruction of NOT analyzing each word in the worksheet, but just getting a general sense of words.

Debriefing test results: The following discussion prompts can help students process the test results.

– Do you agree with the results? Why or why not?
– Discuss what you learn about your primary animal from the assessment.
– What strengths, joys, and value of your primary animal resonate the most?
– What stressors resonate the most?
– Develop a picture, list, story, or song that will help others understand your animal personality.

Group presentation and discussion: During the small group presentation and discussion, you may notice differences between groups. Assist students engage in the activity and enhance their self-awareness. Below final discussion questions can be used for conclusion and recap.

- What is your biggest lesson learned from today?
- How did it feel to work in a group of people with similar personalities to you?
- What was the best/most meaningful part of today's activity?

Debrief and Transfer:

Animal personality activity is focused upon the unique characteristics of individuals and those that are common among groups. This activity can help students with their relationships by understanding themselves and how they interact with others. Once students learn their animal and that of their classmates, they will have a better understanding of why they and others behave in certain ways. With an increased understanding of themselves and others, conflicts will decrease.

Tips or Lessons Learned for Counselors:

It is possible that students may not be familiar with particular words used in the Animal Personality Test. Pictures may be used to make the personality assessments for diverse learners.

This exercise may feel especially vulnerable to students with invisible identities that they may not want to disclose to the class. Disclosure in verbal or written form should be voluntary and discussion questions should be broad enough that students can opt to not talk about more vulnerable aspects of their identities while still leaving space for them to share if they wish.

About the Author: Dr. Sangmin Park is an Assistant Professor at California State University, Sacramento in Counselor Education in the Career Counseling Specialization. Her career counseling work focused on career decision-making and career identity development for Asian American college students, minority faculty members' professional development, and cross-cultural supervision relationships in counseling.

To complete this survey, think about how you naturally react when you're at home with your fiancé or spouse. Read through all four boxes (the L, O, G, and B boxes) and count every word and phrase in each box that describes who you are as a person (Table 12.1). After you've gone through each box counting every word and phrase that describes you, do what it says at the bottom of each box and "double the number counted."

Table 12.1 Animal Personality Test

L	G
[Box_End]Takes charge	Loyal
Determined	Nondemanding
Assertive	Even keel
Firm	Avoids conflict
Enterprising	Enjoys routine
Competitive	Dislikes change
Enjoys challenges	Deep relationships
Bold	Adaptable
Purposeful	Sympathetic
Decision maker	Thoughtful
Leader	Nurturing
Goal-driven	Patient
Self-reliant	Tolerant
Adventurous	Good listener
"Let's do it now!"	**"Let's keep things the way they are."**
Double the number counted _____	Double the number counted _____
O	**B**
Takes risks	Deliberate
Visionary	Controlled
Motivator	Reserved
Energetic	Predictable
Very verbal	Practical
Promoter	Orderly

Avoids details	Factual
Fun-loving	Discerning
Likes variety	Detailed
Enjoys change	Analytical
Creative	Inquisitive
Group-oriented	Precise
Mixes easily	Persistent
Optimistic	Scheduled
"Trust me! It'll work out!"	**"How was it done in the past?"**
Double the number counted _____	Double the number counted _____

Activity 12.4: Values Auction for Career Development

Rachael C. Marshall

Theme/Goals of Activity	This group activity using career values aids children and adolescents to explore their career values (*traits*): gain awareness of their values in relation to work – *intrapersonal skill development*, evaluate values and work environments – *career development*, negotiate and compete for specific values and assign their own value – *interpersonal skill development*
Population/Age	12–19
Intrapersonal Skills	Self-worth, showing initiative, and finding meaning in values
Interpersonal Skills	Cooperativeness with others and awareness of own impact on others as they compete in the auction to buy specific values
Coping/Solution-Focused Skills	Decision-making and career decision-making skills
Materials	Fake money – each participant gets $100 (you can change the values based on your discretion), a list of values (handout and larger format so you can announce), pictures of the values so when they win the bid they can share them, and the skills of talking like an auctioneer – it really sets the tone

Description of the Activity:

Allow time to discuss example of where you get these values. Handout the values list and ask them to rank (try for 16 values). Example values in visual. Then introduce the Values Auction (Basic Directions):

- "You have $100 to bid on your values
- Minimum bid is $10 and you must increase by at least $10 to bid up
- Raise your hand if you bidding"

While they know all of the values each child will rank them differently. Show each values and give time to bid. This is the time for using your auctioneer voice. Start the bidding off with the first value – let the highest bid go once….twice… and sold. Hand the picture of the value to the winner. Then move to the next value.

Macro-Processing:

No loading:

Present the opportunity to go outside to collect materials for an art project.

Front and back loading:

Front: Begin with a discussion of values.

- "What is a value?" (brief discussion)
- A principle, standard, or quality considered important and desirable to you

- Work values are a subset of values that pertain to your (desired) career
- Where do you get your values? Family? Friends? Culture? Experience?

Back: After all the values are sold, discuss the highest and lowest bids. Explore the experience of those that did not win a bid.

Micro-Processing:

Observations during values discussion and ranking (front-loading discussion): (self-awareness)
- Where did the highest values you ranked come from?
- How do your values relate to your career interests?
- Are the highest values the ones you would spend the most money on?

Observations during auction: During the bidding process, it can be fun the comment. For example, if a child spends all their money on one value (now they cannot bid anymore). (problem-solving)
- A popular one is "Complete self-confidence and a positive outlook on life" – "congratulations you win the bid you are very confident and broke." It is a fun activity to get a bit cheeky.

Observations after bidding: This is a good time to discuss how the money they "spent" on these values is actually time. Generally, we pay for creating space for values in our life by dedicating time to it. Ask all participants to explore which values they would make time for and how. This is a great activity to lead into SMART goals. (decision-making)
- If you were to dedicate time to this value how would you do it?
- SMART goals – specific, measurable, attainable, relevant, time-bound

Debrief and Transfer:

For this group activity, it can cause lots of competition. Negotiating between what other want and what you want. Finding other with similar values and helping each other create goals can help with communication skills.

Tips or Lessons Learned for Counselors:

Always consider that children may get upset when they lose a bidding and value. It is a great time to explore feelings related to loss and good sportsmanship. Bring those with similar values together to explore goals is a great way to share the values and increase communication. Competition can be a lot of fun, and not every child enjoys competition so the discussion of goals could reach them more easily than the actual bidding.

Taking time to explore how money is a metaphor for time is very helpful to helping those who felt unable or too cautious to bid feel included. They made a decision about their time and money and how they wanted to spend it; now discuss what decision they can make with values impacting their goals.

This can be a very loud activity, be sure to either be in a space where you can get loud or let other know that you will have a louder activity today.

About the Author: Dr. Rachael C. Marshall is an Assistant Professor and Fieldwork Coordinator at California State University, Sacramento in Counselor Education in the Career Counseling Specialization. Her career counseling work focused on trauma, grief, and advocacy with first-generation college students, immigrants, international students, and LGBTQ+ clients.

Chapter 13

Extracurricular activities

Felix Yu and Amanda C. DeDiego

Counselors have the ability to positively impact children and their families both inside and outside the counseling session. Mental health professionals may find incorporating outside resources useful to strengthen work within sessions to acquire and practice skills. Parents, caregivers, teachers, coaches, and/or family members typically spend more time and have the most influence on youth development. Through deep understanding of the client and their families, counselors can collaborate to identify skills that need to be developed to cultivate interests and engage in activities intentionally for positive development. Resources may be dependent on accessibility, proximity, and transportation as well as affordability and time commitment. Self-exploration and the development of competence (intrapersonal) and engaging with peers outside of their comfort zones (interpersonal) are worthwhile in learning prosocial behavior.

For example, a child struggling with self-esteem may benefit from karate or martial arts activities to gain a sense of empowerment (intrapersonal), interact with peers at the same skill level (interpersonal), and utilize time in the dojo to relieve stress (coping/solution-focused). These resources can be continually sought out because of the efficacy in helping children and families deal with mental health issues, problematic behavior, and delayed social skill development (Beals-Erickson & Roberts, 2016). What makes experiential activities and programs so impactful is the endless potential – skills can be developed regardless of the setting. Extracurricular activities including clubs, sports, and other programming employ the concept of Positive Youth Development, which is a strength-based approach to child development (Lerner et al., 2002). The foundations of Positive Youth Development within most youth-serving programs draw upon one or more of the five Cs: competence, confidence, connection, character, and caring/compassion (Lerner et al., 2002).

Counseling children and adolescents supported by extracurricular activities

When an environment is created where the strengths of the child align with the positive forces around them, their development is well supported (DuBois & Rhodes, 2006; Lerner, 2004; Rhodes & Lowe, 2009). The use of community-based interventions as part of a child's system of support to develop a host of interpersonal, intrapersonal, and coping skills has been widely researched. Children and adolescents commonly engage with extracurricular programs, including community engagement programs (e.g., Boy Scouts, Girl Scouts, 4H Club) and sports programs.

Community engagement programs

Examples of established community engagement programs with research support are Boys and Girls Clubs of America, which predominately serves minority and underserved youth, and Youth Men's Christian Association (YMCA). Boys and Girls Clubs of America provides after-school programming focused on supporting academic success and decreasing juvenile delinquency (Anderson-Butcher et al., 2003; Pierre et al., 1997). One of the oldest international community programs is the YMCA, originally formed in London, England, in 1844, which has been a mainstay within American society with over 2700 YMCAs across the country. Like Boys and Girls Clubs of America, the YMCA serves diverse and low-income youth to foster leadership and community involvement through various programming (O'Donnell et al., 2006).

Further examples of community engagement programs include the Boy Scouts of America and the Girl Scouts of America. The Boy Scouts of America, founded in 1908 by Sir Robert Baden-Powell as a Positive Youth Development program, focuses primarily on youth character and leadership development (Urban et al., 2020). The Girl Scouts of America, founded in 1912 by Juliette Gordon Lowe, sought to create empowered spaces for girls to be fostered to reach their full potential and grow into engaged citizens regardless of race, ethnicity, disability,

DOI: 10.4324/9781315213767-14

or socioeconomic status (Christiansen, 2017). These organizations offer comprehensive programs, as they serve multiple age groups over numerous years and provide an array of activities that teach participants a wide variety of skills (Mekinda & Hirsch, 2014). The environment created by these programs enhances life skills, with impacts lasting long after involvement with the program (Lerner et al., 2015). Further, community engagement programs create opportunities for children and adolescents to have consistent exposure to positive adult role models which creates a broader network of social supports (Schwartz et al., 2012).

Sports programs

Approximately 45 million youth participate in organized sports every year. Sport is widely accepted as an entity with the ability to break down race, creed, religion, culture, gender, and economic status (Perkins & Noam, 2007; Zarrett et al., 2009). However, it is important to not assume that being around a sporting environment automatically develops the character of adolescents. Experiences in a sport setting can largely depend on environment, including coaching style and team dynamics (Jones et al., 2020). When sport coaching and focus include mental health and developmental considerations, sports can offer a positive venue for skill development. Beyond physical and mental skills, sports can create opportunities for connection and inclusion. For example, a wheelchair sports club called "The Cheetahs" facilitated wheelchair sports teams that included children with and without disabilities (Carter et al., 2014). This experience created opportunities for connection and inclusion for the children with disabilities while fostering empathy and perspective for the children without disabilities.

Children and adolescents may engage in sport as an activity in itself, or in programs designed to combine sports with Positive Youth Development. These programs have grown substantially in the last few decades and research has shown that they have been successful in enhancing interpersonal, intrapersonal, and coping skills. For example, Waldron (2009) investigated interpersonal communication, problem-solving, health maintenance, and identity development within a sport-specific program called Girls on the Run. The Girls on the Run program focuses on physical, personal, and social skill development for sixth- through eighth-grade girls. Overall, regardless of type of sport, sports-focused programming teaches sport but also seeks to foster life skills transferable beyond the context of sports participation (Hemphill et al., 2019). Children and adolescents may engage with many extracurricular programs; however, there is no evidence that engagement in many different sports or community engagement programs is more beneficial than meaningful engagement in only one or two activities (Champine et al., 2016).

Interpersonal and intrapersonal skills

Hirsch et al. (2011) extensively explored first-hand accounts from participants in community engagement programs to highlight the types of interpersonal relationships between mentor and mentee that were present at these organizations. One factor particular that Hirsch et al. (2011) noted was the use of both collective and individual mentoring. The power of these relationships allowed youth to build trust, develop social skills, and begin to have a more positive outlook on life. Opportunities to participate in mentorship help develop interpersonal and intrapersonal skills. Deutsch (2008) examined Boys and Girls Clubs and identified that they make the most of tri-level mentoring, where the child can be with either an adult or a same-age peer while acting as a mentor to a younger individual mentee at the same time. Their research found that this system promoted youth leadership development and built self-efficacy.

Engagement with activities outside of the school context provides new venues for relationship-building and self-awareness which support success in school (Fredricks, 2011). The largest organization that provides school-based mentoring is the Big Brothers Big Sisters of America program, first created in 1904 (Herrera et al., 2007). "Bigs" partner with "Littles" not just as academic support, but also to enhance their well-being, create strong friendships, and inspire "Littles" to reach their potential. Moreover, when a school-based mentoring program is paired with a support service, like extracurricular activities, there is a significant positive effect on the development of intrapersonal and interpersonal skills compared to those who only receive a school support service (Karcher, 2008).

Martial arts have long been lauded as positive environments for youth. For example, youth engaged with Brazilian Jiu-Jitsu (BJJ) gained self-regulation and pro-social habits with decreased aggressive behavior over time (Mickelsson, 2020). Further, the life skills such as self-discipline and respect reduce externalizing behavior and help decrease the prevalence of behavioral issues for children and adolescents (Harwood et al., 2017). The positive impact of sport or community engagement programming lasts after involvement. A study of a community engagement program showed continued improvement in interpersonal skills even a year after youth were no longer enrolled in the program (Deane et al., 2017). The Learning in Fitness and Education Sports Camp (LiFE) seeks to develop interpersonal skills through a variety of activities ranging from sport to education (Anderson-Butcher, 2014), and it also supports marginalized youth from communities in Columbus, Ohio. LiFE places great emphasis on having a specific structure in their curriculum throughout the duration of the camp to teach skills such as self-control, effort, teamwork, and social responsibility.

Coping and solution-focused skills

Outside of the counseling room, children are exposed to a variety of environments that have the potential to teach them a host of life skills that complement the work counselors do within sessions. A sport-based program that has demonstrated positive benefits in learning coping skills is the Sports United to Promote Education and Recreation Program (SUPER). One of the main components of this program is that it bridges the gap between marginalized youth and access to extracurricular activities. Youth sports and community engagement programming seek to address these needs in a positive environment. The SUPER program utilizes sport to educate and teach children not only physical skills but mental skills that can be transferred to life. For example, SUPER addresses goal setting to improve problem-solving and team development is used to enhance interpersonal skills (Waldron, 2009).

Underserved youth are less likely to participate in out-of-school activities, struggle with nutrition and health, and have higher rates of family volatility (Bradley & Corwyn, 2004; Holt et al., 2008). In working through challenges in sports, youth gain resilience and coping skills for adversity which are useful in settings outside of sport. The Hockey Is For Everyone (HIFE) program is another initiative that helps the marginalized youth learn goal setting, manage emotions, and seek help from others during conflict. Papacharisis et al. (2005) found supporting evidence to suggest that individuals who participated in sports programming reported greater insight into life skills, problem-solving ability, and positive thinking. These studies highlight the many similarities between sport and life where skills can be taught and transferred between the two entities.

Strengths and limitations

There are multiple programs that can benefit children and adolescents' interpersonal, intrapersonal, and coping skill development. Through the widespread nature of these programs, they provide children a chance to develop skills in a way that can be unique and appealing to them. There are a variety of sports and community engagement programs, so children can find an option that connects with their interests and developmental needs. Sports programs encourage growth not just developmentally but with physical activity and so sports involvement potentially addresses the needs of youth in multiple realms (Hemphill et al., 2019; Papacharisis, 2005). Children and adolescents can engage in individual sports or team sports with the potential for positive influence from coaching and mentorship in either setting. Further, sports can be offered as part of school or within community-based settings.

Community engagement programs offer a host of venues for children and adolescents to find connections and space to foster their interests. Seeking programming options through local schools, churches, community centers, and public libraries can represent a variety of options for youth clubs and programs. The structure of programs like Girls Scouts, Boy Scouts, Boys and Girls Clubs, and others is helpful for students who lack stable and safe home environments. The mentorship offered in programs like Big Brothers and Big Sisters also creates opportunities for positive attachment for youth who lack healthy caregiver attachments (Herrera et al., 2007). The impact of involvement with sports and mentorship last long after their time engaged with the activity. Extracurricular activities provide structure, supervision, and opportunity for love, belonging, and connectedness. These programs can also assist in preventing boredom, which often precedes engaging in problematic behaviors.

However, despite studies clearly showing positive influence in terms of youth interpersonal, intrapersonal, and coping skill development, there needs to be a greater consideration for the population of children that are not represented in these programs. Factors such as socioeconomic status, geographic location, parental support, and transportation all contribute to inequity in access to youth sports and activities (Dowling et al., 2012; Sabo, 2009). Some sports require purchasing expensive equipment or require transportation to practice locations or games that conflict with caregiver's work schedules. Further, low-income schools may not have as many options for extracurricular activities due to staffing or facilities. In recommended engagement with community programming or sports, counselors must consider availability and access to such options for youth and their families.

In order for these programs and activities to be successful, kids need to find them overall enjoyable and feel supported and valued. When youth engage in activities through caregiver pressure, the activity is no longer enjoyable or engaging. Further, especially with sports, when focus becomes more on performance than personal growth opportunities, engaging in the activity may no longer therapeutic.

Meaning-making

There are a host of ways meaning can be drawn from sports and extracurricular activities in the therapy process. Through use of metaphor, counselors can connect a win or loss in sports to resilience in personal challenges. Empathy and consideration for teammates represent transferable skills that are useful in other relationships. Further, the positive influence of mentorship from a coach or peer-mentor builds a positive sense of self-worth that can be explored and applied to therapy goals. As youth develop a sense of self, they seek independence and opportunities to explore their own interests and passions (Erikson, 1982). Children and adolescents can explore interests in activities within and outside of school to explore their own beliefs, values, and strengths.

The family can also be encouraged to explore and take part in activities rather than focusing on just the development of the child. Many organizations work with parents and families to promote healthy development and positive parenting, and actively seek parent volunteers to assist with activities. This can help caregivers to reinforce meaning at home beyond just the positive environment of the activity. Spending time together as a family also promotes interpersonal skills such as listening and communicating as well as problem-solving as a group. For youth in community engagement programs, acting as a peer-mentor to others and advancing through "ranks" (e.g., Boys Scouts, Girl Scouts) builds self-worth and offers a long-term meaningful connection to a community. Counselors can draw meaningful connections to therapy goals by building on transferable skills gained through involvement in extracurricular activities and sports. As such, asking about engagement in extracurricular activities is an important piece of an intake interview to understand how goals can be supported by activities outside of the therapy room.

References

Anderson-Butcher, D., Newsome, W. S., & Ferrari, T. M. (2003). Participation in boys and girls clubs and relationships to youth outcomes. *Journal of Community Psychology, 31*(1), 39–55.

Anderson-Butcher, D., Riley, A., Amorose, A., Iachini, A., & Wade-Mdivanian, R. (2014). Maximizing youth experiences in community sport settings: The design and impact of the life sports camp. *Journal of Sport Management, 28*(2), 236–249.

Beals-Erickson, S. E., & Roberts, M. C. (2016). Youth development program participation and changes in help-seeking intentions. *Journal of Child and Family Studies, 25*(5), 1634–1645.

Bradley, R. H., & Corwyn, R. F. (2004). Family process investments that matter for child well-being. In A. Kalil & T. DeLeire (Eds.), *Family Investments in Children's Potential: Resources and Parenting Behaviors That Promote Success* (pp. 1–32). Psychology Press.

Carter, B., Grey, J., McWilliams, E., Clair, Z., Blake, K., & Byatt, R. (2014). 'Just kids playing sport (in a chair)': Experiences of children, families and stakeholders attending a wheelchair sports club. *Disability & Society, 29*(6), 938–952.

Champine, R. B., Wang, J., Ferris, K. A., Hershberg, R. M., Erickson, K., Johnson, B. R., & Lerner, R. M. (2016). Exploring the out-of-school time program ecology of boy scouts. *Research in Human Development, 13*(2), 97–110.

Christiansen, B. (2017). *Girl scouts: A celebration of 100 trailblazing years.* Abrams.

Deane, K. L., Harré, N., Moore, J., & Courtney, M. G. (2017). The impact of the Project K youth development program on self-efficacy: A randomized controlled trial. *Journal of Youth and Adolescence, 46*(3), 516–537.

Deutsch, N. L. (2008). *Pride in the projects: Teens building identities in urban contexts* (Vol. 5). NYU Press.

Dowling, F., Fitzgerald, H., & Flintoff, A. (Eds.). (2012). *Equity and difference in physical education, youth sport and health: A narrative approach.* Routledge.

Erikson, E. H. (1982). *The life cycle completed: A review.* W. W. Norton & Company.

Fredricks, J. A. (2011). Engagement in school and out-of-school contexts: A multidimensional view of engagement. *Theory Into Practice, 50*(4), 327–335.

Harwood, A., Lavidor, M., & Rassovsky, Y. (2017). Reducing aggression with martial arts: A meta-analysis of child and youth studies. *Aggression and Violent Behavior, 34*, 96–101.

Hemphill, M. A., Gordon, B., & Wright, P. M. (2019). Sports as a passport to success: Life skill integration in a positive youth development program. *Physical Education and Sport Pedagogy, 24*(4), 390–401.

Herrera, C., Grossman, J. B., Kauh, T. J., Feldman, A. F., & McMaken, J. (2007). *Making a difference in schools: The big brothers big sisters school-based mentoring impact study.* Public/Private Ventures.

Hirsch, B. J., Deutsch, N. L., & DuBois, D. L. (2011). *After-school centers and youth development: Case studies of success and failure.* Cambridge University Press.

Holt, N. L., Tink, L. N., Mandigo, J. L., & Fox, K. R. (2008). Do youth learn life skills through their involvement in high school sport? A case study. *Canadian Journal of Education, 31*(2), 281–304.

Jones, G. J., Edwards, M. B., Bocarro, J. N., Svensson, P. G., & Misener, K. (2020). A community capacity building approach to sport-based youth development. *Sport Management Review, 23*(4), 563–575.

Karcher, M. J. (2008). The study of mentoring in the learning environment (SMILE): A randomized evaluation of the effectiveness of school-based mentoring. *Prevention Science, 9*(2), 99.

Lerner, R. M. (2004). *Liberty: Thriving and civic engagement among America's youth*. Sage.

Lerner, R. M. (2015). Promoting positive human development and social justice: Integrating theory, research and application in contemporary developmental science. *International Journal of Psychology, 50*(3), 165–173.

Lerner, R. M., Brentano, C., Dowling, E. M., & Anderson, P. M. (2002). Positive youth development: Thriving as the basis of personhood and civil society. *New Directions for Youth Development, 2002*(95), 11–34.

Lerner, R. M., Lerner, J. V., Bowers, E. P., & Geldhof, G. J. (2015). Positive youth development and relational-developmental-systems. In W. F. Overton, P. C. M. Molenaar, & R. M. Lerner (Eds.), *Handbook of Child Psychology and Developmental Science: Theory and Method* (pp. 607–651). John Wiley & Sons, Inc.

Mekinda, M. A., & Hirsch, B. J. (2014). After-school programs. In D. L. DuBois & M. J. Karcher (Eds.), *Handbook of Youth Mentoring* (2nd ed., pp. 221–232). Sage.

Mickelsson, T. B. (2020). Modern unexplored martial arts–what can mixed martial arts and Brazilian Jiu-Jitsu do for youth development? *European Journal of Sport Science, 20*(3), 386–393.

O'Donnell, J., & Coe-Regan, J. A. R. (2006). Promoting youth development and community involvement with technology: The long beach YMCA CORAL youth institute. *Journal of Technology in Human Services, 24*(2–3), 55–82.

Papacharisis, V., Goudas, M., Danish, S. J., & Theodorakis, Y. (2005). The effectiveness of teaching a life skills program in a sport context. *Journal of Applied Sport Psychology, 17*(3), 247–254.

Perkins, D. F., & Noam, G. G. (2007). Characteristics of sports-based youth development programs. *New Directions for Youth Development, 2007*(115), 75–84.

Pierre, T. L. S., Mark, M. M., Kaltreider, D. L., & Aikin, K. J. (1997). Involving parents of high-risk youth in drug prevention: A three-year longitudinal study in boys & girls clubs. *The Journal of Early Adolescence, 17*(1), 21–50.

Rhodes, J. E., & DuBois, D. L. (2006). Understanding and facilitating the youth mentoring movement. *Social Policy Report, 20*(3), 1–20.

Rhodes, J. E., & Lowe, S. R. (2009). Mentoring in adolescence. In R. M. Lerner & L. Steinberg (Eds.), *Handbook of Adolescent Psychology: Contextual Influences on Adolescent Development* (pp. 152–190). John Wiley & Sons, Inc.

Sabo, D. (2009). The gender gap in youth sports: Too many urban girls are being left behind. *Journal of Physical Education, Recreation & Dance, 80*(8), 35–40.

Schwartz, S. E., Lowe, S. R., & Rhodes, J. E. (2012). Mentoring relationships and adolescent self-esteem. *The Prevention Researcher, 19*(2), 17–20.

Urban, J. B., Linver, M. R., Moroney, D., Nichols, T., Hargraves, M., Roberts, E. D., Quinn, J., Brown, M., Gama, L., Doubledee, R., & Cox, M. (2020). Developing and testing a theory of change for boy scouts of America. *Applied Developmental Science, 26*(3), 443–459.

Waldron, J. J. (2009). Development of life skills and involvement in the girls on track program. *Women in Sport and Physical Activity Journal, 18*(2), 60–73.

Zarrett, N., Fay, K., Li, Y., Carrano, J., Phelps, E., & Lerner, R. M. (2009). More than child's play: Variable-and pattern-centered approaches for examining effects of sports participation on youth development. *Developmental Psychology, 45*(2), 368.

Activity 13.1: Singles and Doubles Tennis

Ffion Davies

Theme/Goals of Activity	Connecting counseling with sport, pulling transferable lessons from sport to real-life skills
Population/Age	6–18
Intrapersonal Skills	Builds confidence and self-worth
Interpersonal Skills	Listening, giving, and receiving feedback
Coping/Solution-Focused Skills	Problem-solving, assertiveness and caring confrontations, decision-making, conflict resolution, leadership, or initiating change
Materials	Tennis balls, tennis racquets, tennis court, cones, or materials that could be used as a target

Description of the Activity:

A basic knowledge of tennis is required for prompts and to set up activity. Also, some basic tennis skills could be required for more advanced students.

Tennis is a traditionally individual sport but there is a growing amount of popularity with doubles or team tennis. Tennis can be utilized to discuss accomplishments, let out frustrations, and build patience and self-worth.

Individual:

Counselors could utilize many elements of tennis when working with their clients.

– *Basic individual*:

Counselors with limited exposure to tennis could work on dropping the ball in front of the client so the client can hit the ball. The counselor can set up cones or targets for the client to aim at.

– *Advanced Team/Doubles*:

Counselors could work on cross-court rallies or specific plays if the client and counselors understand how to play tennis. Counselors should challenge the client if they have tennis skills/knowledge.

Team or doubles:

Doubles or team tennis can be utilized to work with children, adolescents, and their parents.

– *Basic Team/Doubles*:

Counselors could invite the child/client and their parent to take turns dropping the balls and working together to hit the targets/cones.

– Advanced Team/Doubles:

Counselors could invite the child/client and their parent to work together to build rallies or play points.

Macro-Processing:

Front and back loading:

Front: While the client is playing tennis or hitting the ball, express that sometimes it takes patience to hit the target. Or how can they relate tennis to other aspects of life such as school or relationships with family and friends?

Back: Allow the child to describe their experience on the court or while playing. Give the child space to express their intentions or what they are trying to achieve in the activity.

Metaphors:

Metaphors can be utilized all throughout tennis. Building a rally up (five shots, ten shots, 15 shots, etc.,) is like building a relationship. Hitting the target is like getting a good score on a test.

Micro-Processing:

Observations while playing tennis:

Basic: some children/adolescents will be more comfortable playing tennis or sport so both verbal and non-verbal cues can be used during this time.

- "Do you like playing tennis? What do you like/dislike it? Are there other parts of your life that you feel like this?"
- "You are working very hard to figure out how to hit that target or get that ball over the net."
- "How does it feel to hit that target?"

Advanced:

- "How does it feel to build on your last record?"
- "Was there an activity that gave you a certain reaction? What about that activity made you feel that way?"

Debrief and Transfer:

The client had difficulty hitting a target or getting the ball over the net. Child labeled the problem (not hitting the ball over the net) and asked the counselor if they could give some guidance or find a better solution (problem-solving). Share overview of the process of identifying the issue, and the solution.

- "You had an issue, you identified that issue, you expressed concerns about the issue, and then you found a solution."

This activity can be transferred to other problems/solutions areas. Follow-up could include issues at school/home, communication, or lack thereof, and any solutions that were created. Positive reinforcement could be utilized here as well as opportunities to practice the solutions or try other solutions.

Tips or Lessons Learned for Counselors:

Inclement weather can be a barrier if the only tennis court accessible is an outdoor tennis court. This can be avoided if there is access to an indoor tennis court or an indoor space where a tennis court (or mini tennis court) can be set up. Counselors can also draw connection to tennis without actively being on the court through metaphors and tracking what happens during practice and competitions.

About the Author: Ffion Davies, MS, NCC, is a doctoral student at the University of Wyoming. She specializes in clinical mental health counseling with experience working with juvenile offenders. She competed as a student athlete in Division I collegiate tennis.

Activity 13.2: Journaling for Athletics Teams

Babbs Weissman

Theme/Goals of Activity	Promoting mental wellness, self-care, and self-confidence, building interpersonal skills, and allowing space for group process of gym/academic/existential issues
Population/Age	12+
Intrapersonal Skills	Self-confidence, resilience, self-compassion, mindfulness, emotion management
Interpersonal Skills	Teamwork, motivation, leadership, empathy
Coping/Solution-Focused Skills	Focusing forward (i.e., letting go of poor performance at a competition so the next event can be successful), accountability, self-awareness
Materials	Journal

Description of the Activity:

Journaling from a prompt, followed by space for sharing of what was written and feedback.

This activity evolved while supporting a gymnastics team. During the first phase of the pandemic, the goal of journaling was to focus on the positive things going on in these individuals' lives both in and out of the gym (installation of hope). The journal prompt during that time was to write a rose (something good that had happened in the past week) and a rosebud (something(s) they were looking forward to). More recently, prompts have to do with goal creation, facing fears by writing them down, mind-body connection (i.e., how our bodies show anxiety), the brain and the body (how the brain can inhibit the body from doing what it knows how to do when not properly anchored), etc.

The athletes are given the opportunity to share what they wrote about if they feel compelled. Individuals are asked for consent to provide feedback prior to it being offered. The use of metaphors is common between the athletes when providing thoughts/feedback to each other (Universality). The coach occasionally gets involved in the sharing and/or conversation, using paraphrasing for clarity if the idea is unclear or if miscommunications occur, as well as to reinforce commonalities.

Macro-Processing:

No loading

"Please get out your journals out and let's do some free-writing – write about whatever comes to mind."

Front loading: "Please get your journals and write your rose – something good that happened – from this past week and your rosebud – what you are looking forward to. We are focusing our journaling on things that make us happy this week to remind our brains how to focus on the positive things happening in our lives."

Back loading: Before: "Please get your journals and write your rose – something good that happened – from this past week and your rosebud – what you are looking forward to.

After members have been given the opportunity to share*: Reflection Prompt Option*: "Were you able to focus on only the positives? If not, what came up for you?" *Teachable Moment:* Discussion of why the exercise is important, for example, to train the brain to identify positive moments in challenging times, to write experiences down as a form of self-expression and catharsis, to share experiences to feel support and community, etc.

Micro-Processing:

Observations: Most of the time each person chose to share, so it was important to determine if those who chose not to simply didn't want to or if they may have wanted to but needed support to feel comfortable doing so. If the body language of the individual choosing not to share appeared more open, ask them if they would like to share. If the body language appears more closed, try to have a non-verbal interaction with them through eye contact. The nature of competitive gymnastics revolves around non-verbal interactions between athletes and coaches, so this is a common interplay.

As the group leader, if an individual voiced having a difficult time with something going on in their life, I would ask the group if anyone who might be able to relate would like to share their experience.

Debrief and Transfer:

There were occasions to translate an experience that was shared with the group to their lives outside the group and the gym. Fears and blocks occurring in the gym were also happening at home and/or school but in varied ways. For example, when a high-level athlete first tries a new skill, the fun of doing something new drives the experience. Once the novelty dissipates, the reality of wanting and needing to perfect the skill sets in, which is regularly accompanied by feelings of failure and self-doubt. Before they know it, the athlete's brain is so busy that their body is no longer able to perform the skill at all. Similar to this is when an individual prepares diligently for a test at school but when it comes time to take the test, the mind goes blank. Helping these folks to "*connect the dots*," or connecting similar behaviors in all settings, promotes self-awareness.

Tips or Lessons Learned for Counselors:

My group took place after a five-hour weekend practice, so I always encouraged the group members to do whatever they needed to do in order to feel comfortable, i.e., putting on comfy clothes, grabbing blankets, and bringing food. Having creature comforts enabled the group members to leave the physical practice behind and transition to the mental/emotional work.

Providing structure in terms of guidelines was important in building a therapeutic, safe environment. Each group began with a brief sharing of the agenda for expectation management, a reminder that respect was shown by listening to each person as they spoke, not interrupting each other, and using "I" statements as often as possible.

About the Author: Babbs Weissman has a master's in Psychology and is a Development Program Optional Teams Coach and Mental Curriculum Director at Axis Gymnastics & Sports Academy in Jackson, Wyoming. She has a passion for supporting high-level competitive athletes and promoting mental health awareness in the community. Babbs is a believer in lifelong learning and growth, allowing her actions to speak for themselves by consistently working to model the behavior she encourages those around her to strive for.

Activity 13.3: Tabletop Role Play Games

Heidi Umberger

Theme/Goals of Activity	Social skills, critical thinking, problem-solving
Population/Age	12+
Intrapersonal Skills	Self-esteem, self-confidence, self-motivation, being able to take initiative, self-starter, overcome boredom, patience to name a few
Interpersonal Skills	Teamwork, motivation, leadership, flexibility, and active listening
Coping/Solution-Focused Skills	Combating isolation and loneliness, learning conflict-resolution and problem-solving skills by working with others to resolve problems, healthy escapism/distraction (helping to keep from ruminating on issues), self-care, communication: healthy boundary setting, talking to others, working with others, critical thinking, and problem-solving
Materials	Character sheet, pencil, D20 dice set, player's handbook facilitator will need their story/scenarios as well as some guidelines

Description of the Activity:

The facilitator will get the gameplay started by introducing a scenario to the players. The players ask questions to reveal more about that scenario. Once the players have learned what they can, they will discuss among themselves that they can do, and then declare what their characters will do. When players want their character to attempt certain tasks, they will roll a die to determine how that attempt plays out.

The facilitator's job is to challenge the players and continue the story, presenting them with challenges and problems that the players must work together to solve or overcome. Sometimes the players will be successful and other times they will fail.

This type of activity allows players to get the chance to be creative and collaborate with others to solve different problems. Working with others helps players to increase social skills and work as a team. These social skills assist players both within and outside the gameplay. Players develop relationships with one another, which makes each campaign unique from another.

Facilitators help players to create a character that they will control during gameplay. This is the ideal time for facilitators to explain any nuances and mechanics of the gameplay to the players. Players will need to roll dice for certain character qualities and write the results on their character sheets. They will be able to choose other traits of the characters and will write them down on their sheets as well. Players will also create a backstory for their character that will be part of their character sheets.

Within gameplay facilitators will present the players with the "story" and players will make decisions together for their characters to determine what will happen next. Scenarios will often present a challenge or problem that must be solved, or a decision that will determine what will happen next. These outcomes are also determined by a D20 dice system. Which dice to roll for what and when is determined by the character sheet or the facilitators.

Macro-Processing:

Front and back loading:

Front: Frame metaphors relating treatment goals to DND gameplay.
Back: Reinforce how group dynamics played out during the game, and how challenges and victories could connect with life experience.

Micro-Processing:

Observations in the beginning: Within the beginning phase where players create their characters, facilitators will see that some players will take to the creation of their character with ease, while others are less comfortable and will need more reassurance and assistance. Depending on the age of the players, this may be a time that the facilitators can have other players assist or will have to be more hands on. Asking questions about interests, likes, dislikes, and who would they like to be.

Observations during introduction: During the introduction, players will get to know each other, and some will be more outgoing than others. Facilitators should encourage all players to have a turn and share.

Observations during gameplay: As the gameplay continues facilitators will most likely have players who are shy and struggle with taking initiative, while other players take the lead often. Facilitators should allow for opportunities for those who are natural leaders to be so, but also encourage them to help those who don't often take the lead to have the opportunity to help make decisions for the group.

Debrief and Transfer:

Having a check in question at the beginning of the group can help each player get into their character role play, and help give insight into them, their character, or both. These checks in questions should ask about the player and their character. Contrasting their differences or highlighting their similarities.

Having the more outspoken players let those who do not tend to be the first with an idea allows others to apply their critical thinking skills and it helps those outspoken players work better with others and build patience.

Through game play their will be teachable moments where players will work on communication, problem-solving, social skills, relationships, teamwork, etc. These moments will give facilitators the opportunity to ask about how those things can be translated into the player's everyday lives.

Tips or Lessons Learned for Counselors:

There are times when players will take the gameplay in an unexpected direction. Facilitators will need to be flexible and roll with the outcome, as well as use those times as teachable moments for the players and ask about the process that resulted in the surprise. I currently use tabletop roleplaying to help clients with combating isolation and loneliness, learning conflict resolution and problem-solving skills by working with others to resolve problems, utilizing healthy escapism self-care, communication, healthy boundary setting, talking and working with others, critical thinking, and problem-solving. It is also a sober living activity.

About the Author: Heidi Umberger MA, LPC, is a professional counselor in Casper, Wyoming. She currently works with adult men in residential treatment for substance use disorders at a community-based, dual diagnosis treatment center.

Activity 13.4: Religious Involvement and Spiritual Communities

Andrew Southerland

Theme/Goals of Activity	Extracurricular activities
Population/Age	4–18
Intrapersonal Skills	Managing emotions, mindfulness, optimism, self-worth, finding meaning
Interpersonal Skills	Listening, communication, empathy, boundaries, cooperativeness with others, awareness of own impact on others, sensitivity to individual and cultural differences and expressing emotions appropriately and effectively
Coping/Solution-Focused Skills	Caring confrontations, decision-making, conflict resolution, leadership, or initiating change
Materials	N/A

Description of the Activity:

Children and adolescent clients might be involved in local religious and spiritual communities, which can offer counselors a unique opportunity. Clients who attend regular religious gathering, such as church, mass, or synagogues, might be able to relate their experiences in those settings to topics discussed in counseling. Using a strengths-based approach, clinicians can address a wide range of themes that may be present within these experiences, such as communication skill development, emotional regulation, community and social support, empathy and compassion, transcendent meaning, integrity, and self-reflection. Overall, the intention of this activity is to promote self-awareness by drawing connection between skill development and the client's involvement in their religious and spiritual communities.

Macro-Processing:

No loading

Clinicians should spend time attuning to the various activities that their clients engage in throughout the week. Throughout the conversation, clinicians might notice that a client mentions their involvement in a religious or spiritual community. The clinicians should then provide a therapeutic opportunity for the client to further discuss their involvement in these settings, including associated experiences and relationships.

Front and back loading:

Front: Encourage the client to discuss their experiences and involvement in these communities. Then, invite the client to share how their experiences and involvement might relate the specific skills they are working on in therapy.

Back: At the conclusion of this activity, spend time processing and discussing possible next steps for how the client might either use their skills in these communities or draw upon themes from these settings in areas outside these communities.

Micro-Processing:

Observations: During this conversation, clinicians should be attuned to different themes that relate to the skills being focused on in therapy. For example, if the focus of therapy is on developing social skills and reducing social anxiety, it would be beneficial to notice how connected the client feels in these settings. Additionally, if working on emotional regulation, it could be worth noticing how spiritual activities, such as prayer or meditation, might be used as a way to ground oneself and reflect. By naming these observations during the session, clinicians can begin to help clients build self-awareness of how these communities can aid in developing skills outside of these settings.

Debrief and Transfer:

As you conclude discussing the client's involvement in religious and spiritual communities, it would be helpful to spend time discussing how the client can either apply skills that are focused on in therapy in these settings or how their experiences in these communities can aid work being done in therapy. For example, a client might be able to relate a topic or skill discussed in therapy to a less from their Sunday school class. These types of connections can help deepen the meaning of the therapeutic process or at least act as an additionally reminder during the week.

Tips or Lessons Learned for Counselors:

As a counselor, it is crucial to be aware of your own values and biases toward religious and spiritual communities. At times, our own values and beliefs can negatively impact the effectiveness of these types of discussion, as well as the therapeutic relationship as a whole. Therefore, spend time reflecting on you own values regarding religious and spiritual beliefs and communities. It is also worth noting that while being aware of your values is imperative when working with clients from different faith traditions, you should also be mindful when working with clients who might share similar beliefs to your own, as these close similarities might make it easier to make assumptions.

About the Author: Andrew Southerland, PhD, LPC, NCC, is a counselor educator and community mental health counseling based in Laramie, Wyoming. Andrew has over 5 years of clinical experience supporting clients across the life-span and has effective utilized Expressive and Reflective Scheduling with children, adolescents, and college students.

Chapter 14

Animal-assisted activities and interventions

Leslie A. Stewart

Animal-Assisted Interventions are relational approaches within the realm of experiential interventions, promoting connection and deeper understanding with oneself and others through intentionally applied here-and-now experiences designed to bring awareness to our internal experiences as well as to ourselves in relation to others (Chandler, 2017). Animal-Assisted Interventions is an umbrella term for multiple therapeutic, educational, and recreational activities such as Animal-Assisted Activities (AAA), Animal-Assisted Therapy (AAT), and Animal-Assisted Education (AAE). While great variability is found among Animal-Assisted Interventions depending on the professional identity of the human practitioner and the needs of the client(s) involved, all Animal-Assisted Intervention modalities are goal oriented and intentional, designed to improve client functioning, and delivered by a practitioner with specialized expertise and training within his/her scope of practice (Animal Assisted Interventions International, 2013). Currently, many mental health practitioners, medical care providers, and the general public are enthusiastic and curious about the role of Animal-Assisted Interventions in human wellness, but overall, much confusion and misunderstanding occurs about the approach.

A plethora of terms exist within the field of Animal-Assisted Interventions, which can make defining and understanding the specific applications of this experiential modality difficult for new and experienced Animal-Assisted Intervention practitioners alike. Although evidence exists that animals have been assisting human healers for centuries (Fine, 2015), the formal professionalization of the approach is relatively new in comparison to other interventions in healthcare and human services. Thus, terminology and taxonomy relevant to Animal-Assisted Interventions are still in development and will likely continue to evolve.

Animal-Assisted Interventions involve specially trained and evaluated animals; however, the goals of the interaction may vary widely based on the role of the provider (volunteer, paraprofessional, professional, etc.) as well as the professional identity of the provider (professional counselor, occupational therapist, etc.; Table 14.1).

While animals help people in a variety of ways, laws, public access, and training/evaluation are very different for each category of helper animals. Gaining accurate and thorough understanding of relevant local, state, and federal laws, personal and professional liability, and appropriate documentation are crucial for differentiating

Table 14.1 Industry-preferred terms for Animal-Assisted Interventions

Term	Definition/Goals	Providers
Animal-Assisted Activities (AAA)	Informal opportunities for motivational, educational, and/or recreational benefits to enhance quality of life delivered by an appropriately trained and evaluated volunteer-animal team	Volunteers and/or paraprofessionals
Animal-Assisted Interventions (AAI)	Goal oriented, planned, structured, and documented therapeutic interventions directed by health and human service providers as part of their profession	Physicians, occupational therapists, physical therapists, certified therapeutic recreation specialists, nurses, social workers, speech therapists, or mental health professionals, in partnership with an animal that meets specific criteria for suitability
Animal-Assisted Interventions in Counseling (AAI-C)	Subspecialty of Animal-Assisted Interventions specific to the discipline of mental health during which an appropriately competent professional counselor incorporates specially trained and evaluated animals as therapeutic agents into the counseling process	Professional counselors, licensed clinical social workers, or counseling psychologists, in partnership with an animal that meets specific criteria for suitability

DOI: 10.4324/9781315213767-15

Table 14.2 Helper animal taxonomies

Term	Species	Role	Training/Evaluation	Access
Service/ assistance animal (Americans with disabilities Act, 1990)	Dogs only	Performance of specific tasks directly related to a person's diagnosed disability	Advanced and intensive disability-specific, individual training and rigorous suitability and temperament evaluations	General public access
Therapy Animal (pet partners, 2022)	Dogs, cats, horses, llamas/alpaca, guinea pigs, rats, rabbits, pot-bellied pigs, and some species of parrots	Engage the public and healthcare or human service clients in therapeutic human-animal interactions and interventions in partnership with a specially trained healthcare or human service provider	Must be trained to reliably perform basic obedience tasks and possess consistent and predictable manners and behavior in public and is formally evaluated through a recognized Therapy Animal organization	Only where invited
Emotional Support Animal (ESA; Americans with disabilities Act, 1990)	Varied	A personal pet, prescribed by a healthcare provider, which provides emotional comfort to a person with a verifiable mental illness	No formal training or evaluation of animal or human handler. ESAs do not perform specific tasks or behaviors to assist the human handler	Housing situations and airline cabins only; no additional public access rights

among helper animals. When implementing Animal-Assisted Interventions in counseling, professional counselors are most often working with what is known as a Therapy Animal (Pet Partners, 2022; Table 14.2).

Terminology and training

Pet Partners (2022) asserts that the term "pet therapy" should be avoided, as it implies a lack of professionalization and formal training/evaluation, which are critical to the safe and ethical application of Animal-Assisted Interventions. Additionally, using accurate terminology regarding the type of human-animal interaction and in reference to the correct classification of helper animals is crucial to professional advocacy and colleague/client/public clarification. For example, it is not uncommon for clients with an Emotional Support Animal to request/demand public access for that animal as a service animal, or for a client to inadvertently refer to his/her "Emotional Support Animal" as a "Therapy Animal." While this may seem a trivial matter of semantics, the implications of using inaccurate terms can impact the client, the provider, the public, the community, and the emergent professionalization of the Animal-Assisted Interventions field. In many states, misrepresenting the type of helper animal in order to gain public access for that animal carries heavy fines, potential jail time, and increased liability for the human who accompanies the misrepresented animal.

When an Emotional Support Animal is misrepresented as a Service or Therapy Animal, the person using the inaccurate term is implying a false level of specific training and evaluation (for both the human and the animal), as Emotional Support Animals do not have any special training or preparation to face the complex demands of public human environments (Americans with Disabilities Act, 1990), nor do the human handlers have any preparation or training to help support the animal in those contexts. Another terminology consideration, which is of particular importance among Animal-Assisted Interventions professionals, is the intentional avoidance of the term "use" when referring to a Therapy Animal partner. A counselor may "use" a sand tray, a mandala, bibliotherapy, etc., because those interventions constitute non-living things. A counselor "worked with/included/partnered with/etc." helper animals to emphasize the respect and relationship with the animal.

There is consensus among leaders in Animal-Assisted Interventions across professional disciplines that avoiding the term "use" in reference to therapy animals or Animal-Assisted Interventions techniques is highly preferred and considered best practices. Very often, especially among new Animal-Assisted Interventions enthusiasts and those unfamiliar with the highly professionalized nature of Animal-Assisted Interventions, animals in Animal-Assisted Interventions are inadvertently objectified and/or unintentionally exploited in both language and in action. Animal advocacy is more than a moral consideration for animal lovers; it is also directly linked to client safety in Animal-Assisted Interventions and the success of Animal-Assisted Interventions, especially considering the relational nature of Animal-Assisted Interventions in counseling.

Selecting a Therapy Animal partner

As per Pet Partners policy, there are currently no breed restrictions for potential therapy animals. The most popular species selected as partners by human Animal-Assisted Intervention providers are dogs and horses (Pet Partners, 2022), although a number of other species may also make excellent co-counselors. In order to work with any species of animal, the provider must have extensive species-specific knowledge about each animal species he/she works with, as well as intimate knowledge of the individual animal's personality, needs, and preferences (Stewart et al., 2016).

When determining whether an individual animal is a suitable fit for Animal-Assisted Interventions-C, providers should be looking for a multitude of traits that tend to be encompassed under three major categories: social affilitiveness, skill and aptitude suitability, and effective preparation and handler support (Pelar, 2022; Pet Partners, 2022; Van Fleet, 2008; Winkle, 2012). Unless counselors already work with trained and/or certified helper animals, counselors will need to seek additional resources and training to integrate Animal-Assisted Interventions in counseling work. Counselors may also seek partners who work with various helper animals to create new and creative counseling opportunities.

Counseling children and adolescents with Animal-Assisted Interventions

When formally integrating Animal-Assisted Interventions in professional counseling context, a professional counselor is implementing what is known as Animal-Assisted Therapy in counseling (Animal-Assisted Interventions-C). Animal-Assisted Interventions-C, a subspecialty of Animal-Assisted Interventions for mental health professionals, is defined as the incorporation of specially trained and evaluated animals as therapeutic agents into the counseling process; thus, professional counselors utilize the human-animal bond in goal-directed interventions as part of the treatment process (Chandler, 2017). When implemented with the appropriate education and training, Animal-Assisted Interventions-C offers several overarching benefits to the counseling process, including: (1) reducing treatment anxiety, (2) facilitating the development of a strong therapeutic rapport, (3) decreasing feelings of detachment from others, and (4) offering expressive, non-verbal avenues for expression and processing (Fine, 2015; Stewart et al., 2013).

Animal-Assisted Interventions-C may be impactful with many client populations because of its unique impact on the therapeutic alliance, which is the top predictor of positive outcomes in counseling, regardless of client population or treatment modality used. Multiple authors (Chandler, 2017; Fine, 2015; Reichert, 1998; Yorke et al., 2008) have found that Animal-Assisted Interventions-C uniquely impact the therapeutic relationship, particularly helping the professional counselor build positive alliances with clients more quickly and with greater perceived genuineness, warmth, and empathy. This means that when practiced competently, Animal-Assisted Interventions-C may be useful with many client populations, but especially with children or adolescents who may be experiencing especially high levels of treatment anxiety or who have had difficulty building positive and trusting working relationships with counselors or other adults in the past, such as children with trauma/abuse histories, social anxiety, generalized anxiety, depression, and/or low self-esteem.

Reichert (1998) further asserted that the Therapy Animal's warm, nonjudgmental nature might facilitate client disclosure during counseling sessions with child survivors of abuse. George (1988) observed that the need for language in therapy decreased when a Therapy Animal is introduced in counseling with child survivors of trauma, as clients might find it easier to express themselves through physical interaction with the animal. Yorke et al. (2008) noted the development of a relationship with a Therapy Animal may offer the unique opportunity for acceptance, nurturance, intimacy, safe touch, and physical affection. Provided that Animal-Assisted Interventions-C interventions are conducted by an appropriately competent handler and suitably evaluated Therapy Animal partner, the potential for counselors to create and invent impactful Animal-Assisted Interventions-C techniques and exercises appropriate to individual client goals is limitless.

Interpersonal and intrapersonal skills

When a provider is appropriately trained in species-specific behavior and familiar with the individual Therapy Animal, the counselor may be able to interpret the animal's responses toward a client to gain and reflect important information. Interpretation will vary depending on the species of animal and individual animal's personality. An example of this kind of intervention is demonstrated through the story of a (now retired) German Shepherd therapy dog named "Sophie May" and her responsiveness to changes in client arousal. This particular animal consistently noticed even subtle changes in client anxiety, stress, or arousal and would observably respond with curiosity and concern toward the client. When subtle shifts in the client's internal tension or arousal occurred, "Sophie May" almost always responded by gently but insistently nudging the client's hand, arm, or feet. As the counselor pointed out the dog's responses, the client developed enhanced self-awareness and emotional regulation over time. In this way, "Sophie May" was able to alert a client to their own subtly shifting intrapersonal experience, which facilitated the client's ability to recognize those shifts in him/herself, eventually without the help of the Therapy Animal.

The potential for Animal-Assisted Interventions-C to positively impact the therapeutic relationship-building process in counseling makes it a unique avenue for clients to build foundational interpersonal skills. As the therapeutic relationship between the counselor and the client often serves as a template or model of healthy interpersonal relationships in the client's life outside of session, interventions that facilitate and enhance that rapport may be particularly meaningful. A primary foundation and key commonality among all Animal-Assisted Interventions-C interventions is the highly developed working relationship between the counselor and the Therapy Animal. This complex and mutually beneficial relationship serves as a powerful modeling intervention that may enhance the process of counseling in ways that would not be possible without the inclusion of the animal (Stewart et al., 2013). Much like the therapeutic relationship between counselor and client, this counselor-Therapy Animal relationship is characterized by mutual trust, accurate empathy, respect, and advocacy (Stewart et al., 2013). This counselor-animal relationship serves as a model of healthy interdependent relationships as well as a concrete and observable way for a counselor to demonstrate his/her own interpersonal skills, trustworthiness, and ability to effectively and empathetically respond to the needs of others. A skilled Animal-Assisted Interventions-C provider is then able to translate the strengths of the counselor-animal relationship into operationalized goals that the client may learn and implement as the client builds his/her own positive relationship with the Therapy Animal. The skills learned by the client in building a positive relationship with the Therapy Animal can then be translated and generalized into helping the client build similar interpersonal skills with other people outside of the counseling process.

Coping and solution-focused skills

A crucial element of ethical and competent Animal-Assisted Interventions-C is consistent attention to Therapy Animal welfare and advocacy before, during, and outside of sessions. Many Animal-Assisted Interventions-C providers educate clients about this crucial role and recruit their help as part of the treatment process. The process of learning how to assess and effectively intervene on behalf of the Therapy Animal's needs can be a powerful experiential learning opportunity for children building coping/solution-focused skills through the "traffic light" metaphor (Pelar, 2022). This traffic light metaphor is developmentally appropriate for a wide range of child and adult development stages and is a favorite of the author for educating clients about animal communication and advocacy. Green indicates that the animal is actively enjoying the situation/interaction and wishes for it to continue. Yellow indicates that the animal is politely tolerating the situation/interaction but wishes for the situation to cease or change. Red indicates that the animal has reached a point at which it cannot continue tolerating the situation and is actively trying to make the situation end. From the perspective of Pelar's (2022) work, this "Red zone" is when animal behavior that is defined by humans as aggressive or inappropriate occurs (i.e., growling, biting, hiding, etc.).

When educating clients about the traffic light metaphor of animal experiences, a particular focus is placed on recognizing and intervening when a dog enters a "yellow zone" experience. For example, if it is recognizable that a dog is no longer actively enjoying an interaction or activity with a client, the client and the counselor then collaborate to either end the situation for the dog OR change something about the situation to make it more enjoyable for the dog. Not only does this promote empathy and an awareness of non-verbal communication in others, this adjustment also serves as a powerful experiential learning metaphor for the client to learn skills to cope with their own unhealthy or unpleasant environments by making changes when possible, or limiting contact or exposure with that situation/environment. Further, it serves as a safeguard for client safety and animal welfare by greatly decreasing the likelihood of the animal acting aggressively or suffering negative health consequences due to stress. This way of conceptualizing interactions with therapy animals (or even the client's household pets) helps clients generalize these ideas and develop relevant skills in their own lives.

Strengths and limitations

As discussed above, Animal-Assisted Interventions-C interventions offer unique opportunities to enhance the counseling process in ways that would not be possible without the inclusion of the Therapy Animal. The intervention's broad applicability, flexibility, and empirically supported positive influence on the counselor-client relationship make it an attractive and valuable option for many counselors. However, unlike many other experiential and expressive modalities, the incorporation of Animal-Assisted Interventions-C involves the inclusion of another sentient being with its own thoughts, feelings, needs, and responses. While it is true that many therapy animals enjoy their role as co-counselors, it is important to consider that the therapy animals involved often do not get to "choose" their careers or give informed consent to their role. As such, there are considerable ethical and competency-related considerations for counselor to address before incorporating Animal-Assisted Interventions-C with clients. If professional counselors are to provide this intervention ethically and effectively, specialized knowledge and training are necessary (Stewart et al., 2016).

According to Stewart and Chang (2013), in addition to upholding all American Counseling Association ethical codes, professional counselors implementing Animal-Assisted Interventions-C must remain especially attuned to certain considerations that are especially relevant to the approach. Working with animals, regardless of temperament or training, carries certain unavoidable risks, so it is important to clearly discuss risks of harm with each client before interactions with the animal begin (Shelton et al., 2011). Such risks may include (but are not limited to): accidental scratches or damage to clothing, unknown/unforeseen allergies, and defensive or even aggressive behavior if the animal feels threatened, stressed, or intimidated. It is recommended that clients engaging in Animal-Assisted Interventions undergo an additional informed consent process before interacting with a Therapy Animal.

While Emotional Support Animals may be an attractive option for some people, there are considerable risks and ethical considerations involved. Because of the lack of animal and handler training and evaluation, the presence of an Emotional Support Animal may pose significant risk for the people and animals. Untrained and unevaluated animals are at an elevated risk for experiencing undue stress in public situations, which is an ethical issue relevant to animal welfare/advocacy and increases the likelihood that the animal may behave unpredictably or aggressively due to fear or stress. Not only is attendance to animal welfare a moral issue, it is directly related to client safety. Because therapy animals cannot verbally communicate their needs, it is the professional counselor's responsibility to recognize, address, and prevent animal stress and fatigue and protect the Therapy Animal from intentional or unintentional exploitation or harm (Stewart & Chang, 2013).

Meaning-making

A core commonality among Animal-Assisted Interventions-C interventions is the use of the here and now to process and interpret the client-animal interaction. In this way, the counselor's role is to relate client-animal relational successes, challenges, and animal feedback to the client's overall goals for treatment. A skilled Animal-Assisted Interventions-C provider can translate these real-time experiences into therapeutically meaningful metaphors, skills, or insights relevant to the individual client's experience, thus enhancing a client's emotional, behavioral, and cognitive self-awareness and regulation. The Therapy Animal's congruent and accepting temperament allows the client access to genuine relational feedback from the animal that is often inaccessible in human relationships.

References

Americans With Disabilities Act of 1990, 42 U.S.C. § 12101 *et seq.* (1990).

Animal Assisted Interventions International (2013). *Animal assisted intervention.* http://www.aai-int.org/aai/animal-assisted-intervention/

Chandler, C. K. (2017). *Animal-assisted therapy in counseling.* Routledge.

Fine, A. H. (2015). Incorporating animal-assisted therapy into psychotherapy: Guidelines and suggestions for therapists. In A. H. Fine (Ed.), *Handbook on Animal-Assisted Therapy: Theoretical Foundations and Guidelines for Practice* (pp. 167–206). Academic Press.

George, M. (1988). Child therapy and animals: A new way for an old relationship. In C. E. Schaefer (Ed.), *Innovative Interventions in Child and Adolescent Therapy* (pp. 400–419). John Wiley & Sons.

Pelar, C. (2022). *Parenting secrets for a safe and happy home.* https://www.livingwithkidsanddogs.com/

Pet Partners (2022). *Learn.* https://petpartners.org/learn/

Reichert, E. (1998). Individual counseling for sexually abused children: A role for animals and storytelling. *Child and Adolescent Social Work Journal, 15*(3), 177–185.

Shelton, L., Leeman, M., & O'Hara, C. (2011). *Introduction to animal assisted therapy in counseling: A paper based on a program presented at the 2011 American Counseling Association conference.* VISTAS 2011: American Counseling Association.

Stewart, L., & Chang, C. (2013). *Animal assisted therapy in counseling.* ACA: Practice Briefs.

Stewart, L., Chang, C., & Rice, R. (2013). Emergent theory and model of practice in animal-assisted therapy in counseling. *Journal of Creativity in Mental Health, 8*(4), 329–348.

Stewart, L. A., Chang, C. Y., Parker, L. K., & Grubbs, N. (2016). *Animal-assisted therapy in counseling competencies.* American Counseling Association, Animal-Assisted Therapy in Mental Health Interest Network.VanFleet, R. (2008). *Play therapy with kids & canines: Benefits for children's developmental and psychosocial health.* Professional Resource Press.

Winkle, M., & Jackson, L. (2012). Animal kindness: Best practices for the animal-assisted therapy practitioner. *OT Practice, 17*(6), 10–14.

Yorke, J., Adams, C., & Coady, N. (2008). Therapeutic value of equine-human bonding in recovery from trauma. *Anthrozoos, 21*(1), 17–30.

Activity 14.1: Herd Observation

Mattni Reo Becker

Theme/Goals of Activity	Awareness
Population/Age	All-inclusive
Intrapersonal Skills	Vision, strategic thinking
Interpersonal Skills	Non-verbal cues and body language
Coping/Solution-Focused Skills	The client sees themselves in one of the horses in the herd. The client can then notice how their horse relates with the other horses in the herd and decipher how that relates to their life. The client can have a real-time visual of how they interact with the world and why it may or may not always work well
Materials	At least three horses and a large, enclosed pen

Description of the Activity:

There will be several horses loose in the arena. The client is told to enter the arena and spend a few minutes observing how the horses interact with one another. If the horses approach the client, it is okay. When the client feels ready, they can begin to approach the horses and immerse themselves into the herd. The client's goal is to choose a horse out of the herd that they feel shares similar traits with them and is a good representation of self. Once the client figures out which horse they relate to most, the clinician can challenge the client to give names to the other horses in the arena as individuals in the client's life. The clinician can facilitate a conversation with the client about why they relate to the horse they chose and why they decided the other horses represented alternative individuals in the client's life.

Macro-Processing:

No loading:

Present the opportunity for the client to enter the arena to observe the herd of horses that are turned loose in the area.

Front and back loading:

Front: While the client is walking into the arena, mention that their goal will be to decide which horse they see themselves in the most.

Back: Allow the client time and space to observe the herd of horses from afar before asking them to co-mingle with the herd.

Metaphor:

One of the horses will represent the client and the rest of the herd will represent other individuals in the client's life.

Micro-Processing:

Observations while client watches the herd: It is important to point out a few behavioral characteristics the horses display to encourage the client to begin seeing characteristics they can relate to

- "Did you see how that horse pinned his ears at the other horse and made it move?" (awareness)
- "Did you see how that horse led all the other horses around the arena?" (non-verbal cues from the horses)

Debrief and Transfer:

Example of transfer: The client arrives at the arena. The horses will have already been put into the arena before the client's arrival. The therapist will explain the goal of the session to the client. The client's goal is to decipher which horse they feel represents themselves the most. The client will be asked to step into the arena and observe how the horses interact with one another for a few minutes. During this time, the therapist can point out behavioral cues between the horses to help the client understand the hierarchy of the herd; however, this step is not always necessary. It can be helpful to stay quiet and let the client draw their own conclusions on how the horses are getting along and explain their ideas later in the session. The therapist will let the client know they are able to approach the horses and begin co-mingling with them whenever the client feels ready. It is important to allow the client to choose the timeframe because they may feel intimidated or unsure of how to approach the horses. In this case, do not worry because the horses always do the work and will end up approaching the client on their own. It is important for the therapist to allow space for the client and horses to explore one another and this requires silence. Once the client has been directly interacting with the horses for a few minutes, remind the client of their goal to find a horse they feel most represents their own character. Then, let the client know once they have chosen a horse to come back out of the arena and meet with you. When the client is ready to discuss things, ask the client which horse they chose and have the client explain how they came to that choice. The horse the client chooses will tell the therapist a lot if they know the horses in the herd well. The client may have chosen the horse that is commonly the bully, the horse that stands off in the background, the outgoing horse, or a disabled horse. The client doesn't have to tell the therapist where they are in themselves because the horse they chose will tell the therapist a lot of what they need to know. This makes this exercise a great opening activity with equine therapy. Once the client shares the reasoning behind the horse they chose, the therapist can take it a step further and ask the client if they saw anyone else in their life through the horses. This discussion can be helpful for further understanding of the client's relationships. For example, the client could say the big horse that was chasing all the other horses around reminded them of their brother because he is always causing chaos at home.

Tips or Lessons Learned for Counselors:

Some options for customization of the activity:

- Allow the client to groom the horse they chose to represent themselves while finishing the discussion.
- Allow the client to go back and spend additional time with the horses to see if any other horses remind them of people they have relationships with in their day-to-day lives.
- Remember to allow silence; the horses do the majority of the work in the activity and filling the silence can be damaging to the quality of the session.
- Know the horses you are working with inside and out so the client's choice of horse can help bring understanding to the counselor without them having to ask a lot of questions.

About the Author: Mattni Reo Becker was born and raised in Wyoming and on her family's farm in Eastern Montana. She has always had a huge passion for horses and experienced first-hand how much healing horses can provide mentally and physically. She wanted to share that healing with people through Equine-Assisted Psychotherapy, so she started her own program as a counseling master's student.

Activity 14.2: Agricultural Education-Based Youth Development Organizations

Andrew Southerland

Theme/Goals of Activity	Extracurricular activities and Animal-Assisted Activities
Population/Age	5–18 (Children and Adolescents)
Intrapersonal Skills	Managing Emotions, Mindfulness, Patience, Responsibility, Self-Worth, Finding Meaning
Interpersonal Skills	Listening, Communication, Empathy, Boundaries, Cooperativeness with Others, Awareness of Own Impact on Others, and Work Ethic
Coping/Solution-Focused Skills	Caring Confrontations, Decision-Making, Conflict Resolution, Leadership, or Initiating Change
Materials	N/A

Description of the Activity:

Many children and adolescents across the United States are involved in after-school programs designed to promote youth development and agricultural education. For example, in particularly rural and agricultural communities, students are often encouraged to participate in organizations such as Future Farmers of America (FFA) and 4-H. The purpose of this clinical activity is to build a connection between skills developed through student involvement in these organizations and work focused on in therapy. Skills that can be related to therapeutic areas of emphasis include, but are not limited to, responsibility, work ethics, communication skills, emotional regulation, patience, leadership, and decision-making.

Macro-Processing:

No loading:

Clinicians are encouraged to remain attentive to their clients' involvement in extracurricular activities. While not limited to rural or agricultural communities, clinicians should be aware of clients' potential involvement in organization such as FFA and 4-H.

Front and back loading:

Front: Encourage clients to discuss their experiences in agricultural education-based youth development organizations. For example, clinicians can provide space for clients to discuss different responsibilities or current lessons they are focusing on in their involvement in FFA and 4-H.

  Back: During this discussion, spend time inviting clients to discuss how the skills they have developed in these organizations might relate to their clinical work and to other areas of their lives. For example, many students involved in these organizations are required to raise and care for livestock in preparation for competitions, which can create an opportunity for clients to share their development of personal responsibility, worth ethic, and patience.

Micro-Processing:

Observations: During this conversation, clinicians should be attuned to different themes that relate to the skills being focused on in therapy. For example, a client might share their frustration with having to complete chores every day or discuss how they developed a close bond with the animals they have cared for. In these instances, clinicians can recognize skills of self-disciple and the development of empathy. By naming these skills, clinicians can help build self-awareness within their clients, which can assist in the translation of these skills to other areas of life.

Debrief and Transfer:

Following this discussion, clinicians should be intentional in inviting clients to discuss how they might translate the skills learned in FFA or 4-H to other social settings. For example, clinicians could notice how a client was able to be patient in raising livestock, yet get quickly frustrated in school when the day does not feel fast enough. By naming these contrasting circumstances, clinicians can give clients an opportunity to explore how they might be able to translate their skillsets.

Tips or Lessons Learned for Counselors:

As a clinician, there are a few considerations that might be worth noting when working with clients who are involved in these types of organization. First, it is important to use a culturally informed approach to supporting these clients. Clinicians may have personal values that do not align with some of the tenets of these organizations, such as the treatment of animals or the favoring of certain character traits over others. Furthermore, some clients may be involved in these organizations as a result of family expectations and pressure. Therefore, clinicians should be mindful of the impact that family dynamics may have on their extracurricular involvement. Furthermore, clients in these communities may not be involved in these organizations but might still be required to complete chores on a family farm or ranch, which can also offer an opportunity to discuss the development of various relatable skills.

About the Author: Andrew Southerland is a counselor educator and community mental health counseling based in Laramie, Wyoming. Andrew has experience working with children and adolescents who have been involved in various agriculture education-based youth development programs.

Activity 14.3: Exploring Boundaries with Animal-Assisted Therapy

Kimberly Emery

Theme/Goals of Activity	Assist client in exploring their own boundaries setting, teaching and understanding the concept of boundaries, assist clients in practicing the setting of their own boundaries and honoring the boundaries of others
Population/Age	5–16
Intrapersonal Skills	Boundaries, resilience, identifying emotions, self-worth
Interpersonal Skills	Empathy, openness to feedback, giving and receiving feedback, assertiveness, sensitivity to differences, awareness of own impact on others, expressing emotions appropriately and effectively
Coping/Solution-Focused Skills	Assertiveness, decision-making, initiating change, cultivating safety, addressing trauma
Materials	Variety of dog toys, grooming tools, book of tricks to teach the dog, agility obstacles, dog treats, clicker, dog bed

Description of the Activity:

The clinician will introduce the client to the animal assistant and review ways to safely engage with the animal assistant. They will remind the client that in that setting there is no use of negative reinforcement, force, or violence against the animal assistant. They will review the importance of giving the animal assistant autonomy during session, highlighting how the animal assistant is treated with respect and dignity. They will explain that the animal assistant has the same rights as the client and the therapist and will set their own boundaries throughout session by opting in and out of activity and through other behaviors. The clinician will define boundaries if needed and review known boundaries that the animal assistant may have (does not like when their toes or touched or tail, loves to play fetch but does not like tug of war games, etc.). They will remind the client that they are encouraged to set boundaries with the animal assistant, using examples like what behaviors the client will accept from the animal assistant, what proximity feels safe for them when working with the animal assistant, etc. They will then allow the client to pick an activity (teaching a trick, grooming, playing a game, etc.) and assist the client in identifying how the animal assistant is setting boundaries.

Examples including if the animal assistant is showing interest, exhibiting signs of discomfort or uncertainty, if the animal assistant is somehow redirecting clinician or client. The clinician will assist client in processing the animal assistant's boundaries, exploring how it feels for the client to receive those messages and if they may relate to client's own experiences of boundary setting. They may also bring up the animal assistant's history of having boundaries crossed, exploring safety, and learning to assert themselves if pertinent. They will encourage the client to explore and process how they are setting boundaries with the animal assistant (whether they are letting the assistant lick them or sit too close to them, if there are games they do not like to play or rewards they are not comfortable giving, etc.). The clinician and the client may discuss the experience of setting and receiving boundaries with the animal assistant and connect them to real-life events client has been through or is currently experiencing.

Macro-Processing:

Front and back loading:

Front: Informing the client of the purpose of the activity and giving client adequate information to safely and comfortably engage with the animal assistant. "Today we are going to work with [Animal Assistant] in a way that allows both of you to establish the boundaries that feel safe and comfortable for your relationship."

Back: Exploring the client's experience during the activities and what they have learned about themselves and their relationships. "What was it like for you to navigate the setting of boundaries with [Animal Assistant]? What do you think it was like for them to set boundaries with you, or receive your boundaries? What are you feeling about your relationship with [Animal Assistant] after this session?"

The clinician may explore with the client how experiences with the animal assistant may mirror or contrast other relationships. The client can compare and contrast experience with the animal assistant with other people in client's life (family, friends, abuser, partner, etc.).

Micro-Processing:

Observations: Observe the client's response to initial setting of boundaries and check in about client's understanding along with any initial resistance or concerns the client may express (awareness of own impact on others, sensitivity to differences, cultivating safety).

- Monitor and respond to any discomfort observed in the client or animal assistant throughout their time together, pausing to allow the client to connect to what they are experiencing and ensuring the safety and comfort of the animal assistant (assertiveness, decision-making, initiating change).
- The clinician will assist the client in being mindful of their own reactions, difficulties setting boundaries, and help the client to process at the moment when the animal assistant sets a boundary (openness to feedback, giving and receiving feedback, sensitivity to differences, awareness of own impact on others, identifying emotions).
- Observe and process successes in setting boundaries or appropriately responding to boundaries set by the animal assistant (self-worth, initiating changes, resilience, and cultivating safety).
- Debriefing successes in setting and receiving boundaries may include exploring what was happening for the client in those moments that allowed them to be successful, and how they may replicate that experience in other relationships. What do they need to continue repeating that pattern outside of session (resilience, cultivating safety, assertiveness, and self-worth)?

Examples include:

- "What concerns do you have about setting your own boundaries with [Animal Assistant]?"
- "How might [Animal Assistant] let you know that he is setting a boundary?"
- When the animal assistant sets a boundary or redirects client, "What are you experiencing right now? How are you feeling about the boundary {Animal Assistant} is setting? How are you experiencing this boundary? What do you think [Animal assistant] is asking of you right now? What do you need from [Animal Assistant] in this moment? How might you let them know?"
- Throughout the session observe and assist the client in identifying their own emotions and needs, along with the animal assistant's emotions and needs (identifying emotions, empathy, expressing emotions appropriately, and healthy self-preservation).

Debrief and Transfer:

Teachable moments include identifying and processing client's moments of success setting or responding to boundaries, difficulties setting or accepting a boundary, and assisting client in identifying patterns in how they set or experience boundaries (boundaries, resilience, self-worth, assertiveness, awareness of own impact on others, decision-making, initiating change).

- The clinician should review the client's experience at the end of the session, and explore with the client how they may translate what they experienced in the session to the relationships they have outside of the session.
- If the client experienced difficulties accepting a boundary, what do they believe to be the barrier in appropriately responding to the boundary (awareness of own impact on others, openness to feedback)? How will they continue working on responding to boundaries set by others outside of session (initiating change, decision-making)? What internal beliefs and feelings may be inhibiting their ability to respond to the boundary that was set (identifying emotions)?
- If the client had difficulties setting their own boundaries with the animal assistant, what do they believe to be the barrier in setting boundary (identifying emotions, sensitivity to differences, expressing emotions appropriately and effectively)? How may they continue exploring that barrier outside of session (initiating change)? What internal beliefs and feelings may contribute to difficulty setting that boundary (identifying emotions)?
- Debriefing successes in setting and receiving boundaries may include exploring what was happening for the client in those moments that allowed them to be successful, and how they may replicate that experience in other relationships. What do they need to continue repeating that pattern outside of session (resilience, cultivating safety, assertiveness, and self-worth)?

Tips or Lessons Learned for Counselors:

The client and the animal assistant may have a session that involves limited boundary setting. In that case, the clinician can explore the sense of safety in the relationship and allow the client to process the felt sense of what it's like to have safe relationships. The client or animal assistant may have moments where they need to take space, and the clinician should have space available for the client or animal assistant to find safety. For the animal assistant this may be their crate or bed, where they can go to opt out of the session. If the animal assistant needs to opt out of the session to take care of themselves, that offers an opportunity to process the experience with the client. If the animal assistant exhibits any signs of distress, their emotional and physical safety is to be prioritized.

It is important to process these experiences with the client, assist the client in cultivating empathy for the animal assistant, and potentially process how the client may related to the animal assistant's experience. The client can explore what it is like to respond to the animal assistant's needs, and may examine personal relationships and how others either respond to or ignore/invalidate client's needs.

If the client is having a difficult time honoring the animal assistant's boundaries, the animal assistant should be given a safe space to spend the session while the difficulties are processed with the client. Attention should be given to what the client is experiencing in their body, how they are interpreting the animal assistant's behaviors, and what they are telling themselves about the situation.

About the Author: Kimberly Emery, LMFT, LAC, CCTS, is an animal-assisted therapist and trauma specialist. She is a full operating sex offender management board provider, with extensive experience treating both adolescent survivors of trauma and perpetrators of sexual assault.

Activity 14.4: Mindfulness with Animal Assistants

Kimberly Emery

Theme/Goals of Activity	Teaching mindfulness
Population/Age	5–16
Intrapersonal Skills	Identifying thoughts and emotions, mindfulness, managing emotions
Interpersonal Skills	Listening, empathy
Coping/Solution-Focused Skills	Grounding skills
Materials	Variety of dog toys, grooming tools, book of tricks to teach the dog, agility obstacles, dog treats, clicker, dog bed

Description of the Activity:

The clinician will introduce the client to the animal assistant and review ways to safely engage with the animal assistant. They will remind the client that in this setting there is no use of negative reinforcement, force, or violence against the animal assistant. They will review the importance of giving the animal assistant autonomy during session, highlighting how the animal assistant is treated with respect and dignity. They will offer education on mindfulness and uses for mindfulness, and then introduce the activity.

The clinician will instruct the client to take a couple deep breaths, and focus on being present to the animal assistant. They will instruct the client to identify five things they observe about the animal assistant, such as physical characteristics or how the dog is behaving. They will invite the client to first take note of what they are currently feeling in their body. They will then invite the client to interact with the animal assistant, and note four things they physically feel when interacting with the animal assistant (texture of their fur, the animal's heartbeat, how any toys they are using feel in their hands, etc.). As the client is being present to the animal assist, encourage them to notice three things they hear, like the animal's licking, breathing, or squeaking of toys. Ask the client to then notice two things they smell. Then encourage the client to notice how they are feeling in their body, and process what it was like to spend the past few minutes mindfully.

Macro-Processing:

Front and back loading:

Front: The clinician will offer education about mindfulness, including what it is, how it can be used proactively or reactively, and the benefits of mindfulness practices. They will review safety measures for interacting with an animal assistant and explain the activity.

Back: The clinician will invite the client to reflect on the activity afterward and explore ways mindfulness can be integrated into the client's coping and wellness habits.

Micro-Processing:

Observations: The clinician may reflect after the activity is finished on any observance they have of the client's experience, including shifts in mood or physiological changes. They will encourage the client to reflect on any changes they noticed in mood or body during the exercise.

- "What did you notice in your mind or body as you started the exercise? What are you noticing now?" (mindfulness, identifying emotions, managing emotions, grounding skills)
- "What was different about how you interacted with [Animal Assistant] when you sat/engaged with him mindfully?" (listening, empathy)

Debrief and Transfer:

Ask the client about any barriers to mindfulness or difficulties they may have experienced during the activity, and process any discomfort that may have arisen. Explore potential barriers to mindfulness that the client may experience outside of session (identifying thoughts and emotions, mindfulness, managing emotions, listening, empathy, coping skills). Assist the client in exploring ways to integrate mindfulness into daily activities, or explore with clients the ways they may use mindfulness as a coping strategy during stressful situations (coping skills).

Tips or Lessons Learned for Counselors:

Some clients with trauma histories may struggle with being present to their own body, or may report discomfort sitting in a mindful space. It may be appropriate to engage the animal assistant's story or experiences if they are relatable to the client's history, and the animal assistant can serve as an example of mindfulness. The animal assistant may also be used as a model of mindfulness to the client.

This is a great activity for when the animal assistant is in a calm mood, as the client can pet the assistant, feel its heartbeat, or notice more of the animal's physical body if the client is lying down or sitting with the animal assistant. If the animal assistant is playing more actively with toys, the clinician may need to assist the client in finding some ways to be mindful in observing the animal, like paying attention to the animal's gait or noticing the way the animal's eyes light up when the client or clinician tosses it the ball.

About the Author: Kimberly Emery, LMFT, LAC, CCTS, is an animal-assisted therapist and trauma specialist. She is a full operating sex offender management board provider, with extensive experience treating both adolescent survivors of trauma and perpetrators of sexual assault.

Chapter 15

Adventure Based Counseling

Amanda C. DeDiego

Adventure Based Counseling is an integrative therapeutic concept adapted from the philosophy of experiential education (Gass, 1993; Marx, 1988). This modality of therapy can be applied in almost any setting or situation as a multidimensional intervention combining experiential learning, outdoor education, group counseling, and intrapersonal exploration (Fletcher & Hinkle, 2002; Schoel et al., 1988). Adventure Based Counseling provides a therapeutic practice through which participants learn by doing (Gass, 1993) and then process the events in a way that promotes positive change. Adventure Based Counseling as a modality of counseling has been incorporated in counseling work with individuals, groups, and families integrating a variety of counseling theories (Schoel et al., 1988). Introducing an appropriate level of real or perceived risk through Adventure Based Counseling provides trained counselors an effective form of experiential learning to help supplement the goals of counseling (Fletcher & Hinkle, 2002).

Activities in which real risk is inherent, such as backcountry travel, rock climbing, rappelling, mountaineering, challenge ropes courses, caving or spelunking, flat water and white-water rafting, on-road and off-road bicycling, cross-country skiing, hot air ballooning, rafting, snowshoeing, orienteering, wilderness camping, sailing, scuba diving, sky diving, and hang gliding, also include considerations of the skills required to safely guide the activity (DeAngelis, 2013; Ewert, 1989; Fletcher & Hinkle, 2002; Priest & Gass, 2005). While there are some limitations accompanying the use of Adventure Based Counseling, when used effectively, this positive intervention can have a lasting impact in a variety of settings and for a broad range of populations, from middle schools and adolescents to elite sports teams and families (Liermann & Norton, 2016; Tucker et al., 2016).

Counseling children and adolescents with Adventure Based Counseling

The key to using Adventure Based Counseling with any client population, but especially children and adolescent clients, is creativity. Depending on ability, developmental level, and resources available, practitioners can use a variety of mediums and activities to apply the Adventure Based Counseling model. Practitioners must consider developmental level, emotional tolerance of stress and risk, as well as physical ability when incorporating Adventure Based Counseling in counseling (DeDiego et al., 2017; Fletcher & Hinkle, 2002).

The Adventure Based Counseling model is based on the concept of perceived risk being a catalyst for personal growth. Lev Vygotsky (1978) explored the idea of challenge, risk, and growth in education with the Zone of Proximal Development (see Figure 15.1).

Clients have skills and activities that are comfortable for them, known as the Zone of Achieved Development or the "Comfort Zone." These are typically things a client does not perceive as a risk or challenging to their current skill level. Counselors teach new skills or introduce perceived risk through Adventure Based Counseling work, and push clients "outside of the comfort zone" into the Zone of Proximal Development or the "Growth Zone." In this space, with appropriate supports, a client can develop new skills, challenge their perspective, and learn about themselves through navigating risk and challenge. If perceived risk for clients pushes them too far from the "Comfort Zone," or they are in the "Growth Zone" for too long, then clients may reach a state of overwhelm which is represented by the "Danger Zone." In this space, clients are too overwhelmed to gain interpersonal growth from the experience. Counselors must determine a client's level of comfort and trauma history, as trauma triggers can quickly push a client into the "Danger Zone." Explaining the idea that clients will be challenged in order to grow is an important part of the informed consent process in Adventure Based Counseling (Gass, 1993). Counselors must observe clients and determine when a client is reaching the state of overwhelm and adjust before a client reaches the "Danger Zone."

Practitioners must also "think outside the therapy room" to consider creative ways to incorporate new environments and tools available to them. Adventure Based Counseling might involve water sports such as kayaking, canoeing, or sailing (Scarf et al., 2016). Other activities showing effectiveness for positive change could

DOI: 10.4324/9781315213767-16

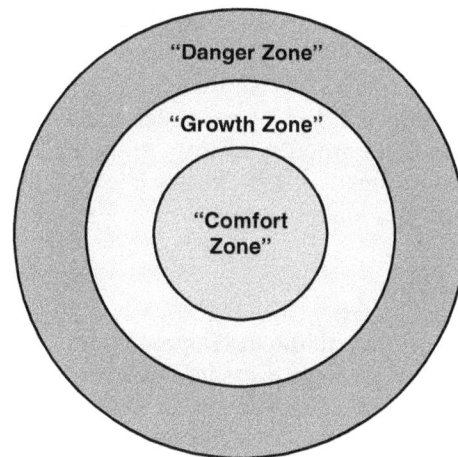

Figure 15.1 Zone of proximal development.

entail a more wilderness type setting such as rock climbing, hiking, camping, backpacking, and mountaineering (Caulkins et al., 2006; Deane et al., 2017; Dolgin, 2014). Ropes challenge courses have been successful in working with sports teams and individuals (Fletcher & Meyer, 2009; Wolf & Mehl, 2011). Regardless of medium used, Adventure Based Counseling activities such as these include a measure of real and perceived risk (Fletcher & Hinkle, 2002). In using Adventure Based Counseling activities, counselors need both soft and hard skills. Soft skills are facilitation and processing skills typically included in the basic counseling such as reflective listening, verbal and non-verbal communication, reframing, and leadership skills and reflective skills taught in counselor training. Hard skills are any skills needed for the activity, such as rock climbing, belaying, use of sports equipment, and any skills needed to ensure client safety during the Adventure Based Counseling experience.

Adventure Based Counseling is a versatile experiential tool for the creative counselor. For more information on adventure-based programming, the Association for Experiential Education and Project Adventure provide models and ideas for activities that can be used with a variety of supplies and resources. The Association for Experiential Education lists wilderness and adventure programs bearing accreditation and oversight for high standards ensuring best practices. Among these programs listed are more popular ones such as Project Adventure and Outward Bound, which have therapeutic manuals with activity ideas and guides for sequencing.

Interpersonal and intrapersonal skills

Counselors can facilitate the development of interpersonal and intrapersonal skills through Adventure Based Counseling activities and the transfer of skills to real life through processing and debriefing. Adventure Based Counseling, especially in groups, provides an opportunity for individuals to engage in social interactions and practice developing intrapersonal skills such as communication, conflict resolution, giving and receiving feedback, and learning how to work with a team (Liermann & Norton, 2016; Tucker et al., 2016). Similar to intrapersonal skill development, interpersonal skills are developed in contexts with perceived risk requiring the client to overcome obstacles. With a little creativity, counselors using Adventure Based Counseling activities can facilitate the development of a variety of skills. For example, Lubans et al. (2012) used Adventure Based Counseling to develop intrapersonal skills of self-worth, self-concept, and self-control by navigating challenging activities. Another example is a counselor creating adversity through Adventure Based Counseling activities to foster self-efficacy and resilience (Deane et al., 2017; Neill & Dias, 2001; Scarf et al., 2016).

Skill transfer becomes apparent during *debriefing* when the participant of an adventure-based program is able to connect the adversity of the environment to the adversity they are currently facing in life. For example, Scarf et al. (2016) created a ten-day sailing adventure to show how a sailing environment can increase resilience in adolescents. Clients were assigned duties critical to "staying afloat" such as pulling ropes, standing watch, and cleaning into the late hours of the night only to wake up at 6 am and repeat the difficult task of maintaining and sailing a ship the following day. Fighting off seasickness and growing accustomed to not showering, the clients were able to pull together and create a sense of duty and belonging that improved resilience lasting months after the adventure itself. Some adventure activities have an inherent element of risk to them.

It is important to take into consideration all clients' levels of ability, whether they are physical, cognitive, social, or emotional in nature. An important element of Adventure Based Counseling is the concept of challenge by choice (Schoel et al., 1988). Challenge by choice provides each individual with the chance to take charge of their own varying levels of ability and push themselves to their own personal limits. Expert knowledge from the leader of the activity and peers, paired with support and encouragement, can help clients explore and surpass perceived limits. Ultimately it is up to the individual to practice assertive communication if an activity is beyond their capability; however, to encourage the development of self-efficacy it is vital to the process to allow an individual to explore pushing interpersonal and intrapersonal boundaries.

Coping and solution-focused skills

Adventure Based Counseling is also applicable in the development and use of coping and solution-focused skills. Especially for youth, Adventure Based Counseling presents opportunities to cope with adversity and potential conflict (Lee, 2009). Often, skill development occurs through metaphors (Gass, 1995) which connect the skills used in the Adventure Based Counseling experience to the coping skills required to overcome stressors in life. Experiential ways of learning can provide a context for problem-solving and coping skills. Clients experience adversity during Adventure Based Counseling experiences. Counselors may feel temptation to "save" the client from the adversity inherent in adventure challenges. However, in allowing the client to struggle in a supported therapeutic environment, adversity in Adventure Based Counseling can foster development of resilience and coping skills (Ewert & Yoshino, 2011). Metaphors used in adventure experiences can also represent opportunities to develop coping skills for trauma too difficult to confront and reconcile directly, helping the client to develop transferrable coping skills (Kelly, 2006).

In the perceived risk and challenge associated with Adventure Based Counseling activities, the client shares responsibility for the direction and outcome of the experience. In this experience of personal responsibility, it the opportunity to use problem-solving skills (Glass & Myers, 2001). The reliance on interpersonal skills and social connection in adventure activities create an environment in which individuals must address interpersonal dynamics and generate problem-solving strategies to effectively identify stressors and develop solutions (Fletcher & Hinkle, 2002). In framing experiences to transfer to life outside of counseling, Adventure Based Counseling can employ a solution-focused approach. Adventure Based Counseling can be either proactive or reactive, designing experiences to learn how to navigate challenges or choices presented in life outside of counseling (Nassar-McMillan & Cashwell, 1997).

Strengths and limitations

The unpredictability and perceived risk of Adventure Based Counseling represents strength as a form of therapy. Having flexibility to shift focus as the clients derive meaning from experience is critical. A skilled counselor may better meet the needs of a group by balancing structured and unstructured experience through processing choices (Lang, 2016; Tucker et al., 2016). An activity may shift from a pre-determined goal, such as developing leadership skills, and then require more immediate attention to a different focus more closely connected to the client experience beyond the counseling environment. As the activity progresses, focus and purpose can be adjusted to better meet the clients where they are, and provide them some control over the process (Tucker et al., 2016). Experiential learning activities can enhance the content of therapeutic programs and help create more of a working knowledge of the skills taught to clients (Rohnke, 1984). Adventure Based Counseling is also a versatile tool that can be paired with almost any theoretical model of counseling practice (Schoel et al., 1988).

A limitation of using Adventure Based Counseling is the potential lack of training in hard skills. In order for counselors to be intentional in their delivery of Adventure Based Counseling, it is vital to have proper training. Priest and Gass (2005) suggest that some skills important to the process include both practical application and organizational skills. Within these skills are the technical and safety skills of the activity they are leading, for example how to belay when rock climbing. Environmental and trip-planning skills for the area the activity is held in are also important. Lastly, risk assessment and management skills to maintain legal and ethical practice in the outdoor environment are vital. Proper training and oversight by an accredited experiential education entity help alleviate stressors caused by improper training and practice (Association for Experiential Education, n.d.; Marchand & Russell, 2013; Norton et al., 2014; Outdoor Behavioral Healthcare Industry Council, 2014; Sacksteder, 2012). Further, partnering with a co-facilitator who possesses the hard skills necessary, like a rock-climbing instructor, to oversee safety can be a solution to the lack of training.

Another limitation could be a lack of resources. Counselors are often location-bound and may not have financial resources or client willingness to travel in order to go hiking, rafting, or other outdoor activities. Facilitators may have limited funding for supplies in their treatment environment and, for example, may not have access to or capability to maintain a ropes course even if they have outdoor space to work. As such, counselors using the Adventure Based Counseling model must consider ways to get creative! Adventure Based Counseling can be facilitated without a ropes course, sophisticated supplies, or a vast mountain range. Some unconventional thinking, permission from the client to try new things, and effective processing can provide a meaningful Adventure Based Counseling experience.

Meaning-making

Processing activities is critical in the Adventure Based Counseling model. Processing and meaning-making are the difference between therapeutic interventions and playing games. In processing, counselors have options in how they would like to potentially frame an activity around a specific issue, or allow the client to direct the meaning-making. Within the Adventure Based Counseling model, processing is referred to as loading, or choices intentionally made by practitioners to facilitate processing (Schoel et al., 1988; Swank, 2013). Counselors can choose to allow the client to organically derive meaning through facilitating processing without direction from the counselor, known as no loading. Alternately, a counselor may choose to frame an Adventure Based Counseling activity around trauma, anxiety, relationships, or other issues. In this case they may connect the activity with the identified issues from the beginning or use frontloading. The counselor may also choose to make this connection after completing the activity using backloading. In being creative and reacting the moment, a counselor can use a combination of frontloading and backloading to create a meaningful experience for a client. When using Adventure Based activities, a counselor may use only one activity, like taking a client on a hike. If the therapeutic environment allows, a counselor may also use multiple Adventure Based Counseling activities connected through processing. The process of thoughtfully and intentionally connecting activities is sequencing. By creating and connecting the metaphor of an adventure-based activity to real life (Gass, 1995), counselors can reinforce client development of intrapersonal and interpersonal skill, as well as coping and solution-focused skills (Fletcher & Hinkle, 2002).

Processing Adventure Based Counseling activities to connect to life outside of the counseling environment is critical to therapeutic process. Debriefing is the use of processing the overall Adventure Based experience to transfer interpersonal and intrapersonal growth from the Adventure Based Counseling experience to real life. Schoel et al. (1988) recommend that counselors debrief by exploring (a) what happened during the experience, (b) how clients plan to use insight gained during the experience, and (c) what goals the client has moving forward.

References

Association for Experiential Education (n.d.). *Accreditation for adventure education programs.* http://www.aee.org/accreditation-for-adventure-education-programs

Caulkins, M. C., White, D. D., & Russell, K. D. (2006). The role of physical exercise in wilderness therapy for troubled adolescent women. *Journal of Experiential Education, 29,* 18–37.

Deane, K. L., Harre, N., Moore, J., & Courtney, M. G. R. (2017). The impact of the Project K youth development program on self-efficacy: A randomized controlled trial. *Journal of Youth and Adolescence, 46,* 516–537.

DeAngelis, T. (2013). Therapy gone wild. *American Psychological Association September Monitor, 44*(8), 48.

DeDiego, A. C., Wheat, L. S., & Fletcher, T. B. (2017). Overcoming obstacles: Exploring the use of adventure based counseling in youth grief camps. *Journal of Creativity in Mental Health, 12*(2), 230–241.

Dolgin, R. (2014). Into the wild: A group wilderness intervention to build coping strategies in high school youth through collaboration and shared experience. *Journal of Creativity in Mental Health, 9,* 83–98.

Ewert, A. W. (1989). *Outdoor adventure pursuits: Foundations, models and theories.* Publishing Horizons.

Ewert, A., & Yoshino, A. (2011). The influence of short-term adventure-based experiences on levels of resilience. *Journal of Adventure Education and Outdoor Learning, 11*(1), 35–50.

Fletcher, T. B., & Hinkle, J. S. (2002). Adventure based counseling: An innovation in counseling. *Journal of Counseling & Development, 80,* 277–285.

Fletcher, T. B., & Meyer, B. B. (2009). Cohesion and trauma: An Examination of a collegiate women's volleyball team. *Journal of Humanistic Counseling, Education, and Development, 48,* 173–194.

Gass, M. A. (1993). *Adventure therapy: Therapeutic applications of adventure programming.* Kendall/Hunt.

Gass, M. A. (1995). *Book of metaphors: Volume II.* Kendall/Hunt.

Glass, J. S., & Myers, J. E. (2001). Combining the old and the new to help adolescents: Individual psychology and adventure based counseling. *Journal of Mental Health Counseling, 23*(2), 101–114.

Kelly, V. A. (2006). Women of courage: A personal account of a wilderness-based experiential group for survivors of abuse. *The Journal for Specialists in Group Work, 31*(2), 99–111.

Lang, N. C. (2016). Nondeliberative forms of practice in social work: Artful, actional, analogic. *Social Work with Groups, 39*(2/3), 97–117.

Lee, F. W. L. (2009). Adventure-based counselling (ABC) approach: Working with young people in a world of conflicts. *International Journal of Child Health and Human Development, 2*(4), 403–408.

Liermann, K., & Norton, C. L. (2016). Enhancing family communication: Examining the impact of a therapeutic wilderness program for struggling teens and parents. *Contemporary Family Therapy, 38*, 14–22.

Lubans, D. R., Plotnikoff, R. C., & Lubans, N. J. (2012). A systematic review of the impact of physical activity programmes on social and emotional well-being in at-risk youth. *Child and Adolescent Mental Health, 17*(1), 2–13.

Marchand, G., & Russell, K. C. (2013). Examining the role of expectations and perceived job demand stressors for field instructors in outdoor behavioral healthcare. *Residential Treatment for Children & Youth, 30*, 55–71.

Marx, J. D. (1988). An outdoor adventure counseling program for adolescents. *Social Work, 33*, 517–520.

Nassar-McMillan, S. C., & Cashwell, C. S. (1997). Building self-esteem of children and adolescents through adventure-based counseling. *Journal of Humanistic Education and Development, 36*, 59–67.

Neill, J. T., & Dias, K. L. (2001). Adventure education and resilience: The double-edged sword. *Journal of Adventure Education and Outdoor Learning, 1*, 35–42.

Norton, C. L., Tucker, A., Russell, K. C., Bettmann, J. E., Gass, M. A., Gillis, H. L., & Behrens, E. (2014). Adventure therapy with youth. *Journal of Experiential Education, 37*(1), 46–59.

Outdoor Behavioral Healthcare Industry Council (2014). *About: Best practices.* http://www.obhcouncil.com/about/best-practices/

Priest, S., & Gass, M. A. (2005). *Effective leadership in adventure programming* (2nd ed.). Human Kinetics.

Rohnke, R. (1984). *Silver bullets: A guide to initiative problems, adventure games, stunts, and trust activities.* Project Adventure, Inc.

Sacksteder, K. (2012). Development of best practices for at. In A. Pryor, C. Carpenter, C. L. Norton, & J. Kirchner (Eds.), *Emerging Insights: Proceedings of the 5th International AT Conference 2009* (pp. 92–103). European Science and Art Publishing.

Scarf, D., Moradi, S., McGaw, K., Hewitt, J., Hayhurst, J. G., Boyes, M., Ruffman, T., & Hunter, J. A. (2016). Somewhere I belong: Long-term increases in adolescents' resilience are predicted by perceived belonging to the in-group. *British Journal of Social Psychology, 55*, 588–599.

Schoel, J., Prouty, D., & Radcliffe, P. (1988). *Islands of healing: A guide to adventure based counseling.* Project Adventure

Swank, J. (2013). Obstacles of grief: The experiences of children processing grief on the ropes course. *Journal of Creativity in Mental Health, 8*, 235–248.

Tucker, A. R., Norton, C. L., Itin, C. Hobson, J., & Alvarez, M. A. (2016). Adventure therapy: Nondeliberative group work in action. *Social Work with Groups, 39*(2–3), 194–207.

Vygotsky, L. S. (1978). Socio-cultural theory. *Mind in Society, 6*, 52–58.

Wolf, M., & Mehl, K. (2011). Experiential learning in psychotherapy: Ropes course exposures as an adjunct to inpatient treatment. *Clinical Psychology and Psychotherapy, 18*, 60–74.

Activity 15.1: The Follower and the Guide

Monica Phelps-Pineda

Theme/Goals of Activity	The goal of this interactive game is to promote conversation on trust/mistrust, to promote conversation on safety, to promote conversation on assertiveness skills, to assess decision-making skills, to assess communication skills
Population/Age	7–17; pairs
Intrapersonal Skills	Mindfulness, showing initiative, motivation, confidence
Interpersonal Skills	Listening, communication, empathy, boundaries, giving and receiving feedback, cooperativeness with others
Coping/Solution-Focused Skills	Problem-solving, assertiveness, decision-making, leadership, initiating change
Materials	A large open area (both indoor or outdoor works), one blindfold (i.e., bandana or scarf), one plastic egg (or a few real ones), one spoon, one timer, several pre-printed cut outs of what would be considered "safe zones" (i.e., I used 25 cut-outs of clouds), several pre-printed cut-outs of what would be considered "obstacles" (i.e., I used 25 cut-outs of cartoon volcanoes, bombs, mud pits, fallen bridge, tree, tornado, etc.)

Description of the Activity:

The object of this game is to have the "Guide" lead the "Followers" from the start to the finish line blind folded, without dropping the egg, and without hitting obstacles (Figure 15.2). This game is meant to promote conversation on trust/mistrust, safety, assertiveness skills, decision-making skills, communication skills, etc.

This activity is played in two rounds of about 20 minutes each:

- Three minutes to create an obstacle course
- Two minutes for directions
- Five minutes to replicate the model
- Ten minutes of discussion

Round 1: Assign one of the players to be the "Follower" and the other to be the "Guide" (In round two the roles will switch so that both players have an opportunity to experience each of the two roles.) Set a timer for three minutes. During that time the Facilitator must create an obstacle course for which the "Guide" must lead the "Follower." Once the Facilitator has completed the course that consists of multiple "safe zone" stepping stones and obstacles throughout, instruct both the Follower and the Guide of the rules (give as little direction as possible so as to build self-awareness of their natural communication style and tendency to trust one another):

- The penalty for hitting an obstacle or dropping the egg at any point in the game causes the "Follower" player to restart the course from the start line.
- Counting up how many "safe zones" the player reaches (you must step on each of the safe zones for them to count) before being disqualified due to the timer going off determines the points you get for that round (i.e., you stepped on 12 safe zones. This gives you 12 points).
- **The Guide:** "You may not ask questions. You may not touch the other player. Your task is to simply instruct the Follower (with your words) on which steps to take in order to get to the finish line without dropping the egg and without running into the obstacles."
- **The Follower:** "You may not ask questions or communicate in any way. Your task is to simply be lead through this obstacle by following the instructions that are given to you by your Guide in order to get to the finish line without dropping the egg and without running into the obstacles."

After instructions have been read and understood, set both players at the START line. Have the Follower place a blindfold over their own eyes and hand them the spoon with the egg. Now set a timer for ten minutes and allow for the Guide to begin instructing the Follower on how to get through the obstacle course. During this time, take the opportunity to observe non-verbal communication – shifts in mood, behaviors/actions, etc. – and use these observations as part of discussion in the debrief portion of the activity. Once the time is up and the round has ended, allow for the following discussion questions BEFORE sharing the outcome of their models:

- What was it like being the communicator (Guide)?
- What was it like being the receiver (Follower)?
- "How do you think you did?"

Reveal: During the reveal, there usually tends to be strong opinions and heated exchanges as to where things went wrong.

Discussion: Take this opportunity to model effective communication, elicit insight, and promote self-awareness through some open-ended discussion questions.

For this second round, have the players switch roles (i.e., the player who was once the Guide now takes on the role of the Follower, puts on the blindfold, and holds the egg in the spoon).

Macro-Processing:

Front and back loading:

Back: I have found it most effective in this activity to have my clients learn by reflecting and discovering meaning once the activity is complete. If too much direction is given prior to engaging in the activity, clients can tend to not be as transparent about their natural (non-influenced) communication style and tendency to trust/mistrust.

Micro-Processing:

During the activity it is important to take the opportunity to observe the following in the moment and to use these observations as part of the discussion portion of the activity:

- Is there consistency in the descriptions/directions that the Guide uses to lead the Follower through the course?
- Does the Guide explain directions once? Or do they repeat?
- Is the Guide confident in their directions or do they back track? (i.e., "oh wait…hold on…no…I meant…)
- Does the Guide move at a fast pace? Or do they give the other player time to think and respond?
- Does the Follower follow instruction as the Guide gives them? Or is there hesitancy?
- Does the Follower show frustration through non-verbals and give up? Or does the Follower continue to the end?

During the reveal, the players see that their goal was not met and therefore blame tends to be assigned to one another for a variety of reasons. The following are some examples of open-ended trust and communication discussion and processing questions that can be expanded upon as teaching moments. This usually takes up the last 15 minutes of each round as part of reflection and learning:

*Trust:

- What is trust? What does it mean to you?
- When is it good/bad to trust someone?
- How much did you trust your partner (out of ten) at the beginning of this game?
- How much did you trust your partner (out of ten) at the end of this game?

- How was trusting your partner imperative in this activity?
- How difficult was it to not peak?
- What did your partner do to help you feel safe and secure?
- What could your partner have done to help make you feel more safe/secure?
- When have you experienced trust with your partner outside of this activity? How was that important?

*Communication:

- What successes did you have as a team?
- What difficulties did you face as a team?
- What was it that made the Guide's communication effective?
- What was most difficult for you as a Guide?
- What was most difficult for you as the Follower player?
- Which did you like being better (the Guide or the Follower?) and why?
- What could be done differently to accomplish the goal more efficiently?
- What could be done differently to improve communication in the future?

Debrief and Transfer:

Prior to this activity, the client and the family members (parents, grandparents, or sibling) participating are usually familiar with the way they tend to communicate with each other. This activity helps them visualize how both their individually unique communication styles and their trust/mistrust for each other can either contribute to positive or destructive results. This activity helps bring awareness to the choices in one's non-verbal behavior and language in order to assess its impact on the relationship. Now there is an opportunity to call attention to repetitive dysfunctional communication and discuss whether they wish to change these patterns and refine their communication methods. Highlight some points learned from this activity that can be applied to their everyday life interactions such as:

- "We all communicate differently: we share, receive, and interpret information in our own way."
- "Gain self-awareness of your own communication style and learn about your partners as well. Let this influence your approach in order to be most effective when sharing information."
- "Show flexibility by trying something different if what you're doing is not working," etc.
- "There will always be obstacles in relationships. How will you choose to handle them? We must learn to guide each other through these life obstacles and trust that we will each do our part when an opportunity presents itself."

Tips or Lessons Learned for Counselors:

Some clients may object to being blindfolded. If that's the case, then have them close their eyes and abide the honor code. Some clients may have experienced trauma with some of the obstacles in this game. If that's the case, then simply replace them with "Xs."

About the Author: Monica Phelps-Pineda, MS, NCC, PLPC, is a Counseling Education and Supervision doctoral candidate at the University of Missouri – St. Louis. Her counseling, teaching, research, and clinical supervision experiences are centered on implementing multiculturally responsive practices to work with children, adolescents, and families of minoritized racial and ethnic identities.

Figure 15.2 Example of "obstacles."

Activity 15.2: Metaphoric Mountains

Teresa B. Fletcher

Theme/Goals of Activity	Navigating adversity, building resilience
Population/Age	12+
Intrapersonal Skills	Self-awareness, resilience, coping skills
Interpersonal Skills	Vocalizing struggle, processing trauma
Coping/Solution-Focused Skills	Problem-solving, setting smaller more manageable goals
Materials	Mountain or large hills, hiking trail, ski and/or snowshoe equipment if using during winter

Description of the Activity:

A challenging hike with obstacles or terrain that presents a substantial challenge is needed to serve as a metaphor for life. When individuals approach challenges, they often view them as insurmountable and give up. This presents an opportunity to get clients outside and change the venue for the counseling process. This activity can be incorporated into camp settings or arranged as an adjunct to other treatment settings.

The counselor can take the client to the mountains. In the summer, the counselor can take the client on a strenuous hike. The physicality of the hike will be relative to the client. In the winter, the counselor can take the client cross-country skiing or snowshoeing. As the client struggles or becomes out of breath, the counselor can seize these moments to talk with the client about challenges and how they have coped with adversity. In the moments when the hike is not challenges, the counselor can discuss how the client experiences life when things are smooth. At the summit or the end of the hike, the client has opportunities for meditation or processing of overcoming obstacles.

Macro-Processing:

No loading

The counselor can take the client on a hike/ski/snowshoe excursion with little to no loading in connection to treatment.

Front and back loading:

Front: The counselor can prepare the client for the outdoor experience. They may work on trauma and the counselor may make early connections to the hike which may be the culmination of the counseling experience.

Back: Take moments at the summit or end of the outdoor experience to process in a peaceful outdoor space. Process with the client what the experience of the hike was like for them. Explore when they struggled and what skills/strengths they used to continue when the hike was challenging.

Micro-Processing:

Observations:

The counselor will need to observe the client as you accompany them on the hike. The counselor can note when they are out of breath or struggling with the process of the hike. In these moments, the counselor can ask about other struggles:

- I see you are getting tired and out of breath. What experiences in your life represent moments when you are tired and out of breath in this phase of life?
- Reinforce skills the client is using (e.g., taking a minute to catch their breath, focusing on one step at a time, sustaining their energy with water and/or snacks).
- Reflect client emotions when reaching the end of the hike.

Debrief and Transfer:

There are many opportunities to connect the hiking experience to life through metaphor. The mountain may serve as a metaphor for challenges or trauma. The process of moving up the mountain can represent different life experiences. Clients will need to use skills to traverse the hike; these may connect to skills used in other areas. Clients will also get frustrated or have other emotions during the hike. These can connect to their process of dealing with trauma or adversity in life. At the end of the hike, it is important to connect the process of finishing the hike to overcoming challenges in life.

Tips or Lessons Learned for Counselors:

It is important to screen for physical issues with your client and assess the tolerance for exercise. Some clients may be physically active and need a more challenging hike. Some clients are not as physically active and so a walk on a greenway trail with hills would be sufficient. Further, the counselor would need to traverse the hike in advance to make sure they can manage the physical elements of the hike as well as making sure they can navigate for the client without getting lost.

About the Author: Teresa Fletcher, PhD, LCPC, ACS, is a Counselor Educator and Professor in the Counseling/Sport & Human Performance program at Adler University in Chicago, IL.

Activity 15.3: Hula Hoops and Personal Space

Aaron Temple

Theme/Goals of Activity	Teach young children the concept of personal space
Population/Age	5–10
Intrapersonal Skills	Self-awareness
Interpersonal Skills	A hula hoop is used as a visual representation of their personal space and allows for students to interact with their peers while maintaining appropriate space
Coping/Solution-Focused Skills	Concepts of sharing and asking for permission can easily be integrated into the activity. For example, a child would ask permission to use a toy rather than taking it out of their hand
Materials	Hula hoops

Description of the Activity:

A hula hoop is used as a visual representation of their personal space and allows for students to interact with their peers while maintaining appropriate space. This activity begins with a short discussion of personal space and then progresses into a game that allows students to interact with each other while respecting their personal space.

- Show the students the hula hoop and explain that the hula hoop is to visually represent their personal space.
- Pass a hula hoop out to each student.
- Ask the students to spread out and stand inside their hula hoop.

While students are in their hula hoop ask them to try and reach their classmates while staying inside their hoop.

If working in large outdoor space or gymnasium the students will run around the play area trying without entering each other's space. The play area will need to set up in advance. For example, if you are playing in a gymnasium the area may be the large square around the floor. Additionally, you will act as a referee while the game is being played.

Explain the rules:

- You must always carry your hula hoop around your waist
- You must stay in the boundaries of the play area
- You cannot enter someone's personal space
- If entering another's space, you will step out of the play area until the round is finished
- When the referee says "freeze" you must stop where you are at
- Listen to the directions for each round of play

To incorporate asking for permission and consent:

- Ask students to get into partners
- Once with their partners explain that they can invite the other person into their hula hoop to stand with them
- If they are comfortable, they can ask you to shake their hand and give them a high-five, a hug, etc.
- Explain that at times someone may become uncomfortable if someone is too close in their space. When this happens, they can ask someone to step out of their space.
- Have students practice respectfully asking them to step out of their space. For example, students can ask: "can you please step back?" or to keep a common language for the activity and provide a vocabulary for the group or class "can you please step out of my hula hoop?"

The number of rounds you play is dependent on the time frame you have but leave enough time to debrief at the end.

Macro-Processing:

Front and back loading:

Front: Introduce the concept of personal space or "bubble." Provide a demonstration of appropriate personal space. Approximately an arm's length away but discuss how everyone is unique and they may like personal space.

Back: Provide a demonstration of inappropriate personal space. Depending on the age of the group the students can offer suggestions for inappropriate personal space (e.g., grabbing a toy out of their hand, hugging another student without asking, rough play).

Micro-Processing:

Comments/questions:

- "Can you easily enter your neighbors' personal space?"
- "Can anybody enter your personal space without leaving their hula hoop?"

Debrief and Transfer:

Provide any observations you had during the game. Possible questions to ask:

- "Was it difficult to stay in your space while running in the area?"
- "How did it feel to invite someone into your space?"
- "How did it feel to ask someone to leave your space?"

Review the concepts discussed and reiterate that it is their space and body; it is alright to respectfully ask someone to step out of their space.

Tips or Lessons Learned for Counselors:

For each round you can decide how you want the students move through the area of play. Possible options are:

- Have a race across the field.
- Have students run at random around the field trying to avoid each other.
- Have students line up and run in a circle, attempting to stay out of each other's space.
- These are merely suggestions, and a variety of games could be played. The goals is to have the students become aware of their own space and recognize the space of others.
- Throughout any of these different rounds you can periodically say "freeze" to stop the play. This can be used as a safety measure if the students are beginning to bump into each other or it looks like a student may fall.

About the Author: Aaron Temple is a school counselor with Natrona County School District in Casper Wyoming.

Activity 15.4: Step Up to the Line

James Rujimora

Theme/Goals of Activity	This activity is designed for participants to learn about themselves and others, learn about diversity in communities, find common connections
Population/Age	10+
Intrapersonal Skills	Managing emotions, finding meaning
Interpersonal Skills	Empathy, boundaries, awareness of impact on others
Coping/Solution-Focused Skills	Decision-making, appropriate self-disclosure
Materials	Rope or duct tape

Description of the Activity:

This activity requires participants to reflect on their own lived experiences. When prompted, participants have an opportunity to step forward, or remain in their spot, according to selected statements. Statements can vary depending on the age group, gender, social class, and group setting.

Prompt:
In this activity we'll have the opportunity to learn about each other from our similarities to our differences. We will address some of these differences, and bring to the surface other differences that we might not visibly see. It might be weird, awkward, and strange. I will read one statement, if you agree with the statement, step up to the line. We will reset and read the next statement. This activity is silent.

Expectations:
Respect – whatever is shared should stay confidential and stay in this room. Everyone is different and that is okay.

Challenge by choice – you may wish to participate, or you may wish to not participate. With that being said, you will have to make a choice to step up to the line based on your understanding of the statement.

Prompt:
And finally, there are no right or wrong answers. There is no pressure to answer anything you do not wish to share with the group. If you understand the expectations and agree to participate, step up to the line.

Macro-Processing:

No loading:

Clinician will prompt participants to stand in a row (i.e., shoulder to shoulder), and step up to a line – designated by a long rope, duct tape, or line in the sand.

Front and back loading:
Front: After explaining instructions, share that this activity is designed to manage emotions and find meaning in the voiced statements. Participants will then reflect on their participation afterward.

Back: Use processing questions to discuss feelings of belonging or isolation depending on how many peers stepped up to the line.

Micro-Processing:

Observations during activity: Some participants may find the selected statements thought-provoking or emotionally triggering.

- "How does an individual respond to other individuals when they find out information about themselves or others?"
- "What lessons can we draw from someone disclosing information we did not previously know about them?"

Observations post activity:

- "Was anyone curious to know more about a person after they stepped forward?"
- "How did you decide to step forward to remain in your spot?"
- "When you looked around to see who stepped forward, how did this impact your relationship with them, if at all?"

Processing questions:

- Thumbs up, middle, or down on how they liked it
- What kind of feelings did you have as you participated?
- What does this activity have to do with being a role model?
- What did you learn that could help our week at camp be more welcoming?
- What do you think the purpose of this activity was?
- **What can we learn about others as we meet and make friendships?**
  - Don't judge a book by its cover; so let's get to know each other
- **How did it feel when lots of people were on your side? How did it feel when very few people were on your side?**
  - Everyone has a story and it may not be obvious by just looking at them
- **Did anyone feel better when you were on the line together?**

We are not alone; together we are better. We really do have much more in common than we realize.

Debrief and Transfer:

The following are a list of potential questions for debriefing:

- What kind of feelings did you have as you participated?
- What can we learn about others as we meet new people?
- How did it feel when people were on your side? How did it feel when few, if any people, were on your side?
- Did anyone feel better when you were on the line together?

Takeaways

- Everyone has a story and it may not be obvious by just looking at them
- We cannot be too quick to judge; so let's get to know each other
- We are not alone; together we are better. We really do have much more in common than we realize

Sometimes it can be scary to meet new people, but we can spread kindness and love to everyone no matter their situation.

Tips or Lessons Learned for Counselors:

Inclement weather, disability, or lack of interest in going outside can be barriers to using this activity. In this case, switching formats (i.e., pen and paper, raising hands) may be helpful.

About the Author: James Rujimora is a first-year doctoral student at the University of Central Florida in Counselor Education and Supervision. He is also a registered intern in mental health counseling and marriage and family therapy. When James is not in class or working with clients, he is a frequent volunteer at Camp Boggy Creek, a camp for children with serious illnesses.

Step Up to the Line Activity

Step up to the line if:

- If you are from [state]
- If you are from, or have lived in another state
- It is your first time at camp
- It is your first time in the oldest [cabin/group]
- It is your second time at camp
- If you have been to camp three or more times
- If you are an only child
- If you are the youngest in your family
- If you are the oldest in your family
- If you have a brother or sister
- If you live with both of your parents
- If you are/were homeschooled
- If you prefer coke to Pepsi
- If you prefer vanilla to chocolate
- If you prefer hot dogs to hamburgers
- If you prefer the beach or the mountains
- If you prefer daytime over nighttime
- If you have had surgery
- If you have broken a bone
- If you know someone who has died
- If you have felt alone, unwelcomed, afraid before
- If you have cried at least once in the last month
- If you have been bullied or have seen someone be bullied
- If you know what a role model is
- If you have been a leader in some way
- If you will miss camp after you leave
- If you are excited about this week
- If you are nervous about camp
- If you are willing to understand, support, and celebrate each other

Final reflections

Implications and future directions

Amanda C. DeDiego

I am not afraid of storms, for I am learning how to sail my ship.

(Louisa May Alcott)

Carl Rogers (1958) asserts that the most powerful means of facilitating self-realization and personal growth for a client is to establish a therapeutic relationship built on warmth and respect. Long-term and meaningful growth may be facilitated by engaging in experiential activities; however, research notes that trust, understanding, autonomy, and validation are critical to success in the therapeutic process (Rogers, 1962). This book seeks to offer counselors with opportunities and ideas to engage clients with activities to facilitate the experiential learning process. However, experiential activities can never take the place of core counseling skills and establishing strong rapport.

In counseling children and adolescents, counselors should consider the context of each client and can employ creativity in the counseling process to create spaces for expression and growth inclusive of all client identities. Societal and global context impacts the developmental process for children and adolescents. In navigating shifts in generational values, an industry shift to digital service delivery via telehealth, and the impact of a global pandemic, counselors have a complex landscape to navigate in support of youth moving into the future.

Generational differences

Members of "Generation Z" (born from 1993 to 2005) and "Generation Alpha" (born from 2013 to current day) are characterized by technology, social media, and gamification (Tootell et al., 2014; Turner, 2015; Table 16.1).

Adolescents and emerging adults of Generation Z have never existed in a world without the internet. In navigating the developmental process, "Gen Z" has the advantage and challenge of constant connection to the world. This represents opportunities to connect with peers all over the world with common interests and identities, but it also represents a lack of privacy in the developmental process. Social media offers curated representations of lifestyles, body types, and status that can negatively impact adolescents (Sabik et al., 2020). Social media can also represent a positive influence on youth in support of educational goals and public health awareness initiatives (Greenhow, 2011). Transferable life skills will be important for this generation as the older Gen Z cohort transitions into the work force (Schroth, 2019).

Generation Alpha is the most recent cohort of youth. "Gen Alpha" is represented by children who are growing up in a digital age saturated by exposure to constant information and influence (Tootell et al., 2014). Technology has become a common part of education, connection, and play for children. These digital natives thrive in learning environments using experiential learning tools (Bennett et al., 2008). Gamification, or gameful learning, is an example of experiential learning employed in recent years as a tool to motivate children and adolescents in the active learning process (Cohen, 2011; Putz et al., 2020). Gamification entails using game design in any context

Table 16.1 Generational divide

Generation	Years Born	Current Approximate Age Range
Generation Alpha	2013–current	0–9 years old
Generation Z	1997–2012	10–25 years old
Millennials	1981–1996	26–41 years old
Generation X	1965–1980	42–57 years old
Baby "Boomers"	1946–1964	58–76 years old

DOI: 10.4324/9781315213767-17

to provide extrinsic motivation and encourage intrinsic motivation toward goals or behavior change (Hamari & Keronen, 2017).

In approaching counseling with children of Gen Alpha and adolescents of Gen Z, it is important for counselors to consider the context in which these youth are navigating the developmental process. For current youth, technology, digital literacy, and social media shape part of their generational culture. To overlook or dismiss the digital orientation of children and adolescents represents the exclusion of an aspect of cultural identity in the counseling process.

Telehealth

Telehealth has been an evolving application of technology to expand access to healthcare (Stamm, 1998). With the onset of the COVID-19 pandemic, telehealth usage increased dramatically (Molfenter et al., 2021). With telehealth services becoming more commonplace, clinicians are learning to adapt their practice to online service delivery. Telehealth has evolved rapidly from early implementation of telephone appointments to connect with parents and children (Lingley-Pottie & McGrath, 2008). However, even with wider availability of HIPAA-compliant video conferencing software, telehealth can still perpetuate inequity in communities. Providers cannot assume that families have access to adequate devices or internet to connect with providers from home. Further, home is not always a safe and private space for children and adolescents to be open with clinicians.

In work with children, providers encounter challenges in shifting to online services. For example, in New York trends showed a decrease in mental health services provided to children during early 2020 with increases in services and a swift return to in-person services once such options became available later in the year (Hoffnung et al., 2021). However, there are opportunities to engage with children and adolescents through virtual mental health and school counseling. Working to provide efficacious virtual counseling options for children is essential for equitable and ethical practice (American School Counseling Association, 2017).

Impact of a global pandemic

In the spring of 2020, the global impact of the COVID-19 pandemic became a reality internationally. This dramatic shift to daily life, including concepts of "masking," quarantine, and "shut downs," will leave a lasting impact on the developmental process of children and adolescents (Gurwitch et al., 2020; Table 16.2).

While school closures were necessary for public safety, many children and adolescents find critical sources of support in schools. Beyond social disruption in the shift to home learning, many children are struggling with grief and loss following the death of a loved one due to COVID-19. Play and creativity are natural forms of expression for children, especially when processing challenging experiences such as loss, especially with so much disruption to support systems (Dougy Center, 2020). With lack of such mental health supports, children may experience disruption in the development process, especially if schools do not have plans in place to support student transitions back to the school environment (Phelps & Sperry, 2020). As the pandemic continues, long-term research exploring the developmental impacts of a global pandemic for children is critical to inform future counseling supports as impacts will be present across the lifespan (Wade et al., 2020).

Table 16.2 The last "normal" school year for kids

Grade Level in Current School Year (2021–2022)	Grade Level in Last Typical School Year (2018–2019)
Twelfth grade	Ninth grade
Eleventh grade	Eighth grade
Tenth grade	Seventh grade
Ninth grade	Sixth grade
Eighth grade	Fifth grade
Seventh grade	Fourth grade
Sixth grade	Third grade
Fifth grade	Second grade
Fourth grade	First grade
Third grade	Kindergarten
Second grade	Pre-school
First grade	Pre-school
Kindergarten	N/A

Advocacy considerations

Looking forward, counselors have an ethical responsibility to pursue social justice and implement socially responsible practice (ACA, 2014). In working through the Cycle of Liberation (Harro, 2018), the coalescing and creating change phases involve passion and involvement on a variety of societal levels. However, part of socially responsible practice includes a thoughtful approach to advocacy. Frameworks help guide counselors in creating actionable steps to fulfill this responsibility. The Multicultural and Social Justice Counseling Competencies (MSJCC; Ratts et al., 2016) guide counselors in considering how privilege and marginalization influence the relationship and dynamics with a client. Further, the ACA Advocacy Competency Domains offer a framework for considering how to enact advocacy efforts while empowering clients and communities (Toporek et al., 2010). For school counselors, the ASCA National Model highlights the advocacy role within a school setting on behalf of students (Trusty & Brown, 2005). Enacting the models and guidelines for advocacy efforts that are appropriate for each practice setting helps in conducting socially responsible practice at various systemic levels.

Conclusion

The developmental process is complex and unique to each individual. The most critical means of supporting clients in developing interpersonal skills is for the counselor to model them in the therapeutic relationship (Rogers, 1957). Experiential activities are a catalyst to facilitate the counseling process but are not a means of replacing genuine investment in the growth of a client (Duffey et al., 2009). Youth navigate a complex developmental process including considerations of growth in psychosocial, moral, cultural, spiritual, intellectual, and other aspects of identity (see Appendix A). These developmental processes are impacted by systemic factors resulting in privilege and oppression impacting the individual (Bronfenbrenner, 1994). In using experiential activities, counselors should practice intentionality, carefully considering the needs, cultural identity, and treatment goals of each client before implementing the use of creative activities (see Appendix C). For more information about activities listed in this text, please contact the authors of each activity (see Appendix B).

References

American Counseling Association (2014). *ACA code of ethics.* Author.

American School Counseling Association (2017). *The school counselor and virtual school counseling.* https://school-counselor.org/Standards-Positions/Position-Statements/ASCA-Position-Statements/The-School-Counselor-and-Virtual-School-Counseling

Bennett, S., Maton, K., & Kervin, L. (2008). The 'digital natives' debate: A critical review of the evidence. *British Journal of Educational Technology, 39*(5), 775–786.

Bronfenbrenner, U. (1994). Ecological models of human development. *Readings on the Development of Children, 2*(1), 37–43.

Cohen, A. M. (2011). The gamification of education. *The Futurist, 45*(5), 16.

Dougy Center (2020). *Supporting children & teens when someone dies of Covid-19.* https://www.dougy.org/assets/uploads/Supporting-Children-and-Teens-When-Someone-Dies-of-COVID-19.pdf

Duffey, T., Haberstroh, S., & Trepal, H. (2009). A grounded theory of relational competencies and creativity in counseling: Beginning the dialogue. *Journal of Creativity in Mental Health, 4*(2), 89–112.

Greenhow, C. (2011). Youth, learning, and social media. *Journal of Educational Computing Research, 45*(2), 139–146.

Gurwitch, R. H., Salem, H., Nelson, M. M., & Comer, J. S. (2020). Leveraging parent–child interaction therapy and telehealth capacities to address the unique needs of young children during the COVID-19 public health crisis. *Psychological Trauma: Theory, Research, Practice, and Policy, 12*(S1), S82–S84.

Hamari, J., & Keronen, L. (2017). Why do people play games? A meta-analysis. *International Journal of Information Management, 37*(3), 125–141.

Harro, B. (2018). The cycle of socialization. In M. Adams, W. J. Blumenfeld, D. C. J. Catalano, K. DeJong, H. W. Hackman, L. E. Hopkins, B. J. Love, M. L. Peters, D. Shlasko, & X. Z'uniga (Eds.), *Readings for Diversity and Social Justice* (4th ed., pp. 27–34). Routledge.

Hoffnung, G., Feigenbaum, E., Schechter, A., Guttman, D., Zemon, V., & Schechter, I. (2021). Children and telehealth in mental healthcare: What we have learned from COVID-19 and 40,000+ sessions. *Psychiatric Research and Clinical Practice, 3*(3), 106–114.

Lingley-Pottie, P., & McGrath, P. J. (2008). Telehealth: A child and family-friendly approach to mental health-care reform. *Journal of Telemedicine and Telecare, 14*(5), 225–226.

Molfenter, T., Heitkamp, T., Murphy, A. A., Tapscott, S., Behlman, S., & Cody, O. J. (2021). Use of telehealth in mental health (MH) services during and after COVID-19. *Community Mental Health Journal, 57*(7), 1244–1251.

Phelps, C., & Sperry, L. L. (2020). Children and the COVID-19 pandemic. *Psychological Trauma: Theory, Research, Practice, and Policy, 12*(S1), S73–S75.

Putz, L. M., Hofbauer, F., & Treiblmaier, H. (2020). Can gamification help to improve education? Findings from a longitudinal study. *Computers in Human Behavior, 110*, 106392.

Ratts, M. J., Singh, A. A., Butler, S. K., Nassar-McMillan, S., & McCullough, J. R. (2016). Multicultural and social justice counseling competencies: Practical applications in counseling. *Counseling Today.* https://ct.counseling.org/2016/01/multicultural-and-social-justice-counseling-competencies-practical-applications-in-counseling/

Rogers, C. R. (1957). The necessary and sufficient conditions of therapeutic personality change. *Journal of Consulting Psychology, 21*(2), 95.

Rogers, C. R. (1958). The characteristics of a helping relationship. *Personnel and Guidance Journal, 37*(1), 6–16.

Rogers, C. R. (1962). The interpersonal relationship: The core of guidance. *Harvard Educational Review, 32*(4), 416–429.

Sabik, N. J., Falat, J., & Magagnos, J. (2020). When self-worth depends on social media feedback: Associations with psychological well-being. *Sex Roles, 82*(7), 411–421.

Schroth, H. (2019). Are you ready for Gen Z in the workplace? *California Management Review, 61*(3), 5–18.

Stamm, B. H. (1998). Clinical applications of telehealth in mental health care. *Professional Psychology: Research and Practice, 29*(6), 536–542.

Tootell, H., Freeman, M., & Freeman, A. (2014, January). Generation alpha at the intersection of technology, play and motivation. In *2014 47th Hawaii International Conference on System Sciences* (pp. 82–90). The Institute of Electrical and Electronics Engineers Inc.

Toporek, R. L., Lewis, J. A., & Ratts, M. J. (2010). The ACA advocacy competencies: An overview. In M. J. Ratts, R. L. Toporek, & J. A. Lewis (Eds.), *ACA Advocacy Competencies: A Social Justice Framework for Counselors* (pp. 11–20). American Counseling Association.

Trusty, J., & Brown, D. (2005). Advocacy competencies for professional school counselors. *Professional School Counseling, 8*(3), 259–265.

Turner, A. (2015). Generation Z: Technology and social interest. *The Journal of Individual Psychology, 71*(2), 103–113.

Wade, M., Prime, H., & Browne, D. T. (2020). Why we need longitudinal mental health research with children and youth during (and after) the COVID-19 pandemic. *Psychiatry Research, 290*, 113143.

Table of developmental and influential theories

Attachment Theory

John Bowlby and Mary Ainsworth

Overview: Children have an innate need to form attachments that extend beyond food and nourishment to safety, security, and nurturing

---

Secure Attachment	A safe and dependable bond with caregiver(s).
Ambivalent-Insecure Attachment	Resulting from poor or limited caregiver presence, these children learn they cannot depend on their caregiver(s) presence when they need them. Children may passively reject them or demonstrate aggression toward their caregiver(s).
Avoidant-Insecure Attachment	Children may not reject attention from caregiver(s), however have learned they cannot depend on it, so they do not seek it out. They may avoid caregiver(s) and have no preference of caregiver(s) over strangers.
Disorganized-Insecure Attachment	Children may demonstrate a combination of responses based on inconsistent caregiver behavior without a clear attachment pattern and include both feeling comfort and fear in their presence.

Ainsworth, M. S. (1992). John Bowlby (1907-1990): Obituary. *American Psychologist*, 47(5), 668–668. https://doi.org/10.1037/0003-066X.47.5.668.
Bowlby, J. (1969). *Attachment: Attachment and loss.* Basic Books.
Cherry, K. (2019, July). What is attachment theory? The importance of early emotional bonds. Verywell Mind. https://www.verywellmind.com/what-is-attachment-theory-2795337.

Moral Development Model

Lawrence Kohlberg

Overview: Kohlberg suggests that people move through stages in a fixed order and that moral understanding is connected to cognitive development. He believed not all people reach the highest level of moral development.

Level 1: *Preconventional Morality*	*Most common in children. Those in this stage judge the morality of an action based on the consequences.*
- **Stage 1:** Obedience and Punishment Orientation	Good and bad behavior being directly related to if there is a punishment or not.
- **Stage 2:** Individualism and Exchange	"What's in it for me" like behaviors. This stage reflects an interest in the needs of others only if something is done in return.
Level 2: Conventional Morality	Typical in adolescents and adults. Those in this stage judge the morality of actions by comparing them to what society says and expects.
- **Stage 3:** Good Interpersonal Relationships	Individuals try to be "good" to live up to societal expectations. They are receptive to approval/disapproval in accordance with what society says. There is a desire to maintain rules authorities but only under stereotypical societal roles.
- **Stage 4:** Maintaining Social Order	It is important to obey laws and social constructs in order to function in society. This is beyond stage three, as society now must learn to transcend individual needs.

Level 3: Postconventional Morality	An individual perspective is viewed before society.
- **Stage 5:** Social Contract and Individual Rights	The world is now viewed as holding different opinions, rights, and values. The individual views rules and laws as tools that are flexible for improving human reason.
- **Stage 6:** Universal Principles	The final stage is based on universal ethical principles and abstract reasoning. Those at this stage have developed their own set of moral guidelines.

Kohlberg, L. (1964). Development of moral character and moral ideology. *Review of Child Development Research, 1,* 383–431.
Kohlberg, L. (1975). The cognitive-developmental approach to moral education. *The Phi Delta Kappan, 56*(10), 670–677.
Kohlberg, L., & Hersh, R. H. (1977). Moral development: A review of the theory. *Theory into Practice, 16*(2), 53–59.
Kohlberg, L., & Mayer, R. (1972). Development as the aim of education. *Harvard Educational Review, 42*(4), 449–496.

Sexual Orientation Identity Formation Model

Vivian Cass

Overview: This model is based the lifelong process of the exploration of one's sexual orientation.

Stage 1: *Identity Confusion*	*Incongruence within self-conflict between perception of self as heterosexual and realization of gay or lesbian thoughts and feelings.*
Stage 2: Identity Comparison	This stage includes the beginning process of acceptance of possibly having a predominantly gay or lesbian orientation.
Stage 3: Identity Tolerance	Identity tolerance stage is where the person begins to admit their sexual identity which helps to decrease identity confusion and allows them to explore their own needs.
Stage 4: Identity Acceptance	In this stage, individuals begin to explore people who are a part of their same sexual identity culture or those who are accepting to.
Stage 5: Identity Pride	In this state, individuals often start to become advocates and avoid strategies to hide their sexual orientation. If heterosexual friends' reactions are negative, the person has a tendency to stay in this stage.
Stage 6: Identity Synthesis	The final stage includes feelings of pride but also the recognition that the chasm of gay and straight is not as definite as previously understood. Individuals also start to combine their personal and public views of self.

Cass, V. (1996). Sexual orientation identity formation: A western phenomenon. In R. P. Cabaj & T. S. Stein (Eds.), *Textbook of Homosexuality and Mental Health* (pp. 227–251). American Psychiatric Association.

Model of Acculturation

John W. Berry

Overview: This model of acculturation categorizes the individual adaptation strategies in retention or rejection of one's native culture, as well as the adoption or rejection of the host culture.

Assimilation	Assimilation is where someone from a different culture adopts the cultural norm of the place that they have moved to.
Separation	Separation is when someone rejects the host culture while preserving their culture of origin.
Integration	Individuals are able to adopt the cultural norms or host culture while maintaining their culture of origin.
Marginalization	This occurs when individuals reject both the culture of origin and the host culture.

Berry, J. W. (1992). Acculturation and adaptation in a new society. *International Migration, 30,* 69–69.
Berry, J. W. (2003). *Conceptual approaches to acculturation.* American Psychological Association.
Berry, J. W. (2006). Acculturation: A conceptual overview. In M. H. Bornstein & L. R. Cote (Eds.), *Acculturation and Parent-Child Relationships: Measurement and Development* (pp. 13–30). Lawrence Erlbaum Associates Publishers.

Racial and Cultural Identity Development Model

Donald R. Atkinson, George Morten, and Derald Wing Sue

Overview: Stages of Racial and Cultural Development

Stage 1: Conformity	Individuals have a positive attitude toward dominant cultural values and may hold negative views toward their own race or other racial/ethnic groups.
Stage 2: Dissonance	One begins to develop one's own sense of cultural heritage, recognizes differences, and starts to challenge oneself on conflicting messages.
Stage 3: Resistance and Immersion	In this stage, one begins to hold a positive attitude toward his/her own race and cultural heritage. Individuals may start to reject dominant values of culture and grow to appreciate others from racially and culturally diverse groups.
Stage 4: Introspection	One recognizes that one's own racial/cultural group or other diverse groups may be good or bad. One starts to focus on personal identity while respecting cultural groups.
Stage 5: Synergistic Articulation and Awareness	One maintains pride in racial identity and develops a secure sense or racial/cultural identity. One recognizes racism as a societal affliction which all can be victimized.

Atkinson, D. R., Morten, G., & Sue, D. W. (1979). *Counseling American minorities: A cross-cultural perspective.* Brown & Benchmark.

Atkinson, D. R., Morten, G., & Sue, D. W. (1989). A minority identity development model. *Counseling American Minorities,* 35–52.

ADDRESSING Model of Intersectionality

Pamela Hays

Overview: A model to conceptualize multiple identities and how these can intersect to create both unique and shared experiences

A. Age and Generational Influences	More Power: Adults Less Power: Children, adolescents, older adults
D. Developmental Disability	More Power: Temporarily able-bodied Less Power: Individuals with disabilities
D. Disability Acquired Later in Life	More Power: Temporarily able-bodied Less Power: Individuals with disabilities (dementia, stroke, etc.)
R. Religion and Spiritual Orientation	More Power: Christian (in United States) Less Power: non-Christian (in United States)
E. Ethnicity/Race Identity	More Power: White or Caucasian Less Power: People of Color
S. Socioeconomic Status	More Power: Owning and middle class (access to higher education) Less Power: Low-wage earners because of occupation, education, income, or rural habitat
S. Sexuality	More Power: Heterosexuals Less Power: Lesbian, gay, bisexual
I. Indigenous Heritage	More Power: Non- native Less Power: Native
N. National Origin and Language	More Power: U.S. Born (English as first language) Less Power: Immigrants, refugees, and international students (English as second language)
G. Gender	More Power: Male (binary, cisgender) Less Power: Female, non-binary, transgender, intersex

Hays, P. A. (2016). *Addressing cultural complexities in practice: A framework for clinicians and counselors* (3rd ed.). American Psychological Association.

Ally Identity Development Model

Keith E. Edwards

Overview: A model intended to help inform allies to develop a sense of what it means to be an ally

Aspiring Ally for Self-Interest	Motivation comes from protection, protecting those that they care about from being hurt. They may not view themselves as an "ally" but a good friend. They may be unlikely to confront acts of oppression when those they care about are oppressed. They could also potentially join in the oppressive behavior because it does not directly harm them.
Aspiring Ally for Altruism	Awareness of privilege starts to develop. They may seek to engage in ally behavior to deal with personal feelings of guilt. The guilt may be helpful in recognition of oppression but cannot be the only motivator. They may become defensive when confronted with their own oppressive behaviors.
Ally for Social Justice	They begin to become allies to issues (racism, classism, etc.) rather than individuals. They work with those from the oppressed group in collaboration to end the system of oppression. Allies for social justice also recognize that members of dominant groups are also harmed by the system of oppression.

Edwards, K. E. (2006). Aspiring social justice ally identity development: A conceptual model. *NASPA Journal, 43*(4), 39–60.

Spiritual Identity Development Model

James W. Fowler

Overview: Developmental model on the stages of faith

Stage 1: Intuitive-Projective Faith	(3–7) Children are able to speak and work with symbols and express thoughts. They don't formalize a religious belief at this stage but are exposed via encounters with stories, the influence of others, and intuitive feelings about moral right and wrong.
Stage 2: Mythical-Literal Faith	(7–12) Children start to have a belief in justice and fairness when it comes to religious matters. An example would be, doing good will end in a good result and vice versa. They start to think of an image of God. Religious metaphors start to take a literal meaning, which results in misunderstandings.
Stage 3: Synthetic-Conventional Faith	(12–Adult) At this stage those start to be characterized by their religious institution, belief system, or spiritual identity. If a conflict arises regarding one's faith it is often ignored at this stage because it represents too much of a threat to one's faith identity.
Stage 4: Individuative-Reflective Faith	(Mid-20s–Late 30s) This stage can be characterized by angst and struggle. Individuals begin to take personal responsibility for beliefs. There is a greater sense of open-mindedness which can introduce potential conflicts regarding different beliefs.
Stage 5: Conjunctive Faith	(Mid-Life Crisis) One at this stage begins to acknowledge the paradoxes and mystery of their values. This may lead the person to move on or change from the conventional religious beliefs that have been inherited previously. A resolution of conflicts in this stage happens when a person is able to merge conceptions that previously seemed to be in opposition with each other without feeling that their own belief systems are being jeopardized.
Stage 6: Universalizing Faith	(Later Adulthood) This stage is very rare for individuals to achieve. However, individuals at this stage are able to relate to others without condescension and regard all beings as worthy of compassion and deep understanding.

Fowler, J. W. (1991). Stages in faith consciousness. *New Directions for Child and Adolescent Development, 1991*(52), 27–45.
Fowler, J. W. (2001). *Weaving the new creation: Stages of faith and the public church.* Wipf and Stock Publishers.
Fowler, J. W., & Dell, M. L. (2006). Stages of faith from infancy through adolescence: Reflections on three decades of faith development theory. *The Handbook of Spiritual Development in Childhood and Adolescence,* 34–45.

Multiple Intelligence Theory

Howard Gardner

Overview: Child development through the lens of complex systems and the environment

---

Microsystem	The microsystem represents the first level of the theory. This would be the people and things that have direct contact with the child. This includes parents, siblings, teachers, friends at school, etc. These relationships are essential for the fostering of the child's development. If these relationships are positive this will have a positive effect on the child, whereas a negative experience will have a negative effect.
Mesosystem	The mesosystem includes the interactions between those inside the microsystem (parents and teachers) but does not include the child directly. If those in the microsystem do not have a positive relationship, it can indirectly negatively affect the child.
Exosystem	Exosystems can include the workplace of the parents, the neighbors, media, etc. This system does not include the child directly but can still be affected by them – such as the parents struggling with their workplace.
Macrosystem	The macrosystem represents how the cultural elements affect a child's development. This includes wealth, socioeconomic static, race/ethnicity, etc. This does not refer to a specific environment but rather represents an already established society in which the child is developing.
Chronosystem	The chronosystem represents the final level of this theory, which represents all of the environmental changes that occur in one's lifetime. This includes historical events and major life transitions.

Bronfenbrenner, U. (1992). *Ecological systems theory.* Jessica Kingsley Publishers.
Bronfenbrenner, U. (1994). Ecological models of human development. *Readings on the Development of Children, 2*(1), 37–43.

Ecological Systems Model

Urie Bronfenbrenner

Overview: Gardner proposes that people are not born with all of the intelligence that they will ever have, and that there are multiple types of intelligence.

Linguistic Intelligence	"word smart" These people have the ability to analyze and create products, orally or written, such as books, speeches, and plays.
Intra-personal Intelligence	"self smart" These people understand themselves and have an ability to recognize their own moods, motivations, and intentions. An example of someone with this type of intelligence would be Aristotle.
Interpersonal Intelligence	"people smart" These people have an ability to understand and recognize other people's intentions, moods, and desires.
Logical-Mathematical Intelligence	"number smart" These people have an ability to develop and create equations and proofs. They make calculations and solve abstract problems.
Musical Intelligence	"music smart" These people have the ability to recognize and create musical pitch, tone, and rhythm. They excel in the performance, composition, and appreciation of music.
Bodily-Kinesthetic Intelligence	"body smart" These people have the ability to use one's own body to create or perform skills and solve problems. An example would be Michael Jordan or Tom Brady.
Naturalist Intelligence	"nature smart" The most recent intelligence addition to this theory. These people are more in tune with nature and interested in the exploration of the environment and like to learn about other species, and are aware of subtle changes to their environments.
Spatial Intelligence	"picture smart" These people are often good at visualizing things, good with directions, and also work well with videos and pictures.

Gardner, H. (1993). *Multiple intelligences: The theory in practice.* Basic books.
Gardner, H., & Hatch, T. (1989). Educational implications of the theory of multiple intelligences. *Educational Researcher, 18*(8), 4–10.

Table of activities and author contact information

Chapter 5: Strengths and Skills		
5.1: The Bucket	*Teresa B. Fletcher*	*tfletcher@adler.edu*
5.2: Strength Bubbles	Keith Davis	kdavis188@radford.edu
5.3: Cultural Identity Exploration	Lay-nah Blue Morris-Howe	Laynah@uwyo.edu
5.4: Lost in the RIASEC Island	Rachael C. Marshall	Rachael.marshall@csus.edu
Chapter 6: Stress and Trauma		
6.1: Letter Writing and Cultivating Voice	Tina L. Nirk	tmansfie@uwyo.edu
6.2: The Real Me	Rachel Ratliff	rratliff@uwyo.edu
6.3: The Unfair Game	Tanya Brown	tbrown62@uwyo.edu
6.4: Coloring Your Feeling	Gissel Molina	gisselmolina1997@gmail.com
Chapter 7: Treating DSM-V Diagnoses		
7.1: Externalizing the Disorder	Amanda C. DeDiego	acdediego@gmail.com
7.2: Expressive and Reflective Scheduling	Andrew Southerland	asouther@uwyo.edu
7.3: "Inside Out"	Patrice Parkinson	pparkin1@uwyo.edu
7.4: Melter Beads	Jennifer Bays	jbays@uwyo.edu
Chapter 8: Parables, Storytelling, Literature, and Books		
8.1: Alexander and the Terrible, Horrible, No Good, Very Bad Day	R. Paul Maddox II	rmaddox1@uwyo.edu
8.2: Spaghetti in a Hot Dog Bun	R. Paul Maddox II	rmaddox1@uwyo.edu
8.3: Graphic Novels and Songs	R. Paul Maddox II	rmaddox1@uwyo.edu
8.4: In My Heart – Feelings Creative Activity	R. Paul Maddox II	rmaddox1@uwyo.edu
Chapter 9: Board Games and Video Games		
9.1: "You Gotta Be Kidding"	Monica Phelps	monica.phelps63@gmail.com
9.2: Lego Tower Replica Challenge	Monica Phelps	monica.phelps63@gmail.com
9.3: "In My Control"	Monica Phelps	monica.phelps63@gmail.com
9.4: TOTIKA	Lay-nah Blue Morris-Howe	laynah@uwyo.edu
Chapter 10: Expressive and Creative Arts		
10.1: "Emotions Ensemble"	Keith Davis; Sharon Blackwell Jones	kdavis188@radford.edu ; sjones48@radford.edu
10.2: River Rock and Cairn	Keith Davis; Malia Snyder	kdavis188@radford.edu
10.3: Color My Emotions	Jenna Hepp	jhepp3@uwyo.edu
10.4: Album of My Life	Jenna Hepp	jhepp3@uwyo.edu
Chapter 11: Science Demonstrations and Investigations		
11.1: "The Candle"	Ana Houseal	ahouseal@uwyo.edu
11.2: Emotional Diffusion	Rachel Ratliff	rratliff@uwyo.edu
11.3: Web of Life	Ana Houseal	ahouseal@uwyo.edu
11.4: Mentos and Diet Soda	Amanda C. DeDiego	acdediego@gmail.com

(Continued)

Chapter 12: Group Activities

12.1: Future Me Interview	Jenna Hepp	jhepp3@uwyo.edu
12.2: A Portrait Come to Life	Jenna Hepp	jhepp3@uwyo.edu
12.3: Finding Your Strengths: Four Animal Personality Test Activity	Sangmin Park	sangmin.park@csus.edu
12.4: Values Auction for Career Development	Rachael C. Marshall	Rachael.marshall@csus.edu

Chapter 13: Extracurricular Activities

13.1: Singles and Doubles Tennis	Ffion Davies	ffioneluned@gmail.com
13.2: Journaling for Athletics Teams	Babbs Weissman	babbsweissman@gmail.com
13.3: Tabletop Role Play Games	Heidi Umberger	humberger@cwcc.us
13.4: Religious Involvement and Spiritual Communities	Andrew Southerland	asouther@uwyo.edu

Chapter 14: Animal-Assisted Activities and Interventions

14.1: Herd Observation	Mattni Reo Becker	mattnib@hcbh.org
14.2: Agricultural Education-Based Youth Development Organizations	Andrew Southerland	asouther@uwyo.edu
14.3: Exploring Boundaries with Animal-Assisted Therapy	Kimberly Emery	KLenggie@uwyo.edu
14.4: Mindfulness with Animal Assistants	Kimberly Emery	KLenggie@uwyo.edu

Chapter 15: Adventure-Based Counseling

15.1: The Follower and the Guide	Monica Phelps	monicap@umsl.edu
15.2: Metaphoric Mountains	Teresa B. Fletcher	tfletcher@adler.edu
15.3: Hula Hoops and Personal Space	Aaron Temple	aarondtemple@gmail.com
15.4: Step Up to the Line	James Rujimora	jrujimora@knights.ucf.edu

Table of activities and skills

Theme/Goals of Activity	Corresponding Activities
Anger Management	5.1; 6.3; 7.4; 10.2
Boundaries	9.3; 14.2; 14.3; 15.3
Conflict Resolution	9.3; 13.1
Communication Skills	8.4; 9.1; 9.2; 12.3; 11.3; 13.3; 15.1
Emotional Expression	6.4; 7.1; 7.2; 7.3; 10.1; 10.2; 10.3; 10.4; 11.2; 12.2; 13.4; 14.2
Diversity and Inclusion	5.3; 9.4; 15.4
Grief and Loss	6.1; 6.4
Healthy Relationships	11.4; 12.3
Identify Emotions	8.1; 8.3; 8.4; 10.1; 10.3; 12.2; 14.3
Identify Strengths	5.2; 9.4; 11.3; 11.4; 13.1; 13.3; 15.2
Mindfulness	7.4; 11.1; 11.3; 13.2; 14.4; 15.1
Self-Awareness	8.1; 8.2; 8.3; 8.4; 9.2;11.1; 11.4; 12.3; 14.1
Self-Esteem	6.2; 9.4; 13.2; 13.3
Values and Interests	5.4; 9.1; 11.1; 11.4; 12.4

Client Population/Age	Corresponding Activities
5–10 years old	5.1; 6.1; 6.2; 6.3; 6.4; 7.1; 7.2; 7.3; 7.4; 8.1; 8.3; 8.4; 9.1; 9.3; 9.4; 10.1; 11.1; 11.2; 11.3; 13.1; 13.4; 14.1; 14.3; 14.4; 15.1; 15.3
10–15 years old	5.2; 5.3; 5.4; 6.1; 6.2; 6.3; 7.2; 7.4; 8.2; 8.4; 9.1; 9.2; 9.3; 9.4; 10.1; 10.2;10.3; 10.4; 11.1; 11.2; 11.3; 12.1; 12.2; 12.3; 12.4; 13.1; 13.2; 13.3;13.4; 14.1; 14.2; 14.3; 14.4; 15.1; 15.2; 15.4
15+ years old	5.2; 5.3; 5.4; 6.1; 6.2; 7.2; 8.2; 9.1; 9.2; 9.4; 10.1; 10.2; 10.3; 10.4; 11.1; 11.2;12.1; 12.2; 12.3; 12.4; 13.1; 13.2; 13.3; 13.4; 14.1; 14.2 15.1; 15.2; 15.4

Intrapersonal Skills	Corresponding Activities
Confidence	5.2; 6.2; 7.4; 9.2; 9.4; 10.1;11.2; 12.4; 13.1; 13.2; 13.3; 15.1
Emotional Regulation	5.1; 6.3; 6.4; 7.2; 8.1; 8.2; 8.3; 8.4; 9.1; 9.3; 10.1; 11.2; 11.3; 13.2; 13.4; 14.2; 14.3; 14.4; 15.4
Finding Meaning	5.3; 5.4; 6.1; 6.2; 9.4; 10.4; 11.1; 11.3; 12.2; 13.4; 14.2; 15.4
Identify Strengths	5.2; 5.3; 9.4; 11.2; 11.3;12.4; 15.1
Motivation	7.2; 9.2; 9.3; 12.1; 13.3; 15.1
Mindfulness	7.2; 7.4; 11.1; 11.2; 11.3; 13.2; 13.4; 14.2; 14.4; 15.1
Optimism	7.2; 8.1; 8.2; 8.3; 12.1; 13.4
Resilience	6.1; 7.1; 13.1; 13.2; 14.3; 15.2
Self-Awareness	5.1; 5.3; 7.1; 7.3; 8.4; 9.4; 10.1; 10.2; 10.3; 10.4; 11.1; 11.2; 11.4 12.1; 12.2; 12.3; 12.4; 14.1; 15.2; 15.3; 15.4
Visualization	7.1; 10.3; 11.3; 12.1; 14.1; 15.3

Interpersonal Skills	Corresponding Activities
Communication	5.1; 5.3; 6.3; 7.1; 7.2; 7.3; 9.1; 9.2; 9.4; 11.2; 11.3; 12.1; 12.3; 13.3; 13.4; 14.2; 15.1; 15.3
Connection	5.3; 9.4; 10.1; 10.4; 11.3; 11.4; 13.1; 14.1; 14.4
Empathy	6.2; 9.1; 9.3; 9.4; 11.2; 12.1; 12.2; 13.2; 13.4; 14.2; 14.3; 14.4; 15.1; 15.4
Expressing Emotions	5.1; 6.1; 6.3; 6.4; 7.2; 8.1; 8.2; 8.3; 8.4; 9.1; 9.2; 10.1; 10.2; 10.3; 10.4; 11.2; 12.2; 13.1; 14.3; 15.2
Giving and Accepting Feedback	6.2; 8.1; 8.2; 8.3; 8.4; 11.1; 13.1; 14.3; 15.1; 15.3
Teamwork	5.4; 12.4; 13.2; 13.3; 14.2
Trust	5.3; 7.3; 9.4; 15.3; 15.4

Coping/Solution-Focused Skills	Corresponding Activities
Assertiveness	9.1; 9.2; 14.3; 15.1; 15.3
Conflict Resolution	6.3; 11.2;12.3; 13.3; 13.4; 14.2
Decision Making	5.4; 7.2; 9.3; 11.1; 12.4; 13.4; 14.2; 14.3; 15.4
Emotion-Focused	7.3; 7.4; 10.3; 12.2
Grounding	14.4
Identifying Feelings	6.1; 6.2; 6.4; 7.1; 8.1; 8.2; 8.3; 8.4; 10.2; 11.4; 14.1; 15.3
Identifying Strengths	5.2; 9.4; 12.1; 13.2
Initiating Change	11.1; 11.2; 14.2; 14.3; 15.1
Leadership	6.3; 13.2; 13.3; 14.2; 15.1
Meaning Making	5.3; 7.3; 10.1; 10.4; 11.3; 12.1; 12.2; 14.1; 15.4
Problem Solving	5.1; 7.2; 8.4; 9.1; 9.2; 9.3; 11.1; 11.2; 11.3; 13.3; 15.1; 15.2

Index

For Product Safety Concerns and Information please contact our EU
representative GPSR@taylorandfrancis.com
Taylor & Francis Verlag GmbH, Kaufingerstraße 24, 80331 München, Germany